Baroque Bodies

BAROQUE BODIES

Psychoanalysis and the Culture of French Absolutism

MITCHELL GREENBERG

Cornell University Press

ITHACA AND LONDON

THIS BOOK HAS BEEN PUBLISHED WITH THE AID OF A GRANT FROM
THE HULL MEMORIAL PUBLICATION FUND OF CORNELL UNIVERSITY

First published 2001 by Cornell University Press

Printed in the United States of America

Library of Congress Cataloging-in-Publication Data

Greenberg, Mitchell, 1946–
Baroque bodies : psychoanalysis and the culture of French absolutism / Mitchell Greenberg.
p. cm.
Includes bibliographical references and index.
ISBN 0-8014-3807-1 (acid-free paper)
1. French literature—17th century—History and criticism. 2. Baroque literature—History and criticism. 3. Psychoanalysis and literature—France—History—17th century. 4. Despotism—France—History—17th century. I. Title.
PQ245 .G738 2001
840.9'11—dc21
00-010722

Cornell University Press strives to use environmentally responsible suppliers and materials to the fullest extent possible in the publishing of its books. Such materials include vegetable-based, low-VOC inks and acid-free papers that are recycled, totally chlorine-free, or partly composed of nonwood fibers. Books that bear the logo of the FSC (Forest Stewardship Council) use paper taken from forests that have been inspected and certified as meeting the highest standards for environmental and social responsibility. For further information, visit our website at www.cornellpress.cornell.edu.

Cloth printing 10 9 8 7 6 5 4 3 2 1

Pour Marie-Claire et pour Julia
encore, toujours

Psychoanalysis, both at its beginnings with its work on hysteria, and in its more recent developments, has always stressed the importance of an imaginary anatomy or body, a body, where, most notably, everything that exists on the inside is the object of extravagant fantasies that are without any correlation to scientific discoveries. And we know that it is not enough to be a physician and to have gained a certain knowledge of scientific anatomy to efface these imaginary anatomies.

Jean Laplanche, *Problématiques*

Contents

Acknowledgments

Several chapters in this book have appeared in earlier versions: chapter 1, "Molière's Body Politic," appeared in a shortened French version, "Molière, Corpus Politicum," in *Le labyrinthe de Versailles*, ed. Martine Debaisieux (Rodopi, 1998). A portion of chapter 3 was published in *Repossessions: Psychoanalysis and the Phantasms of Early Modern Culture*, ed. Timothy Murray and Alan Smith (Minneapolis, 1998). Finally, early versions of chapter 5, "Racine's Oedipus," appeared in *L'Esprit Créateur* (summer 1998) and in *Diacritics* (fall 1998).

A Note on Translations

Owing to considerations of length, it was impracticable to offer both the original French version of all the passages quoted in the text and their English translation. After discussion with the publisher, I chose the following compromise: seventeenth-century texts analyzed in the body of the book appear in French; all other texts are given in English translation. Whenever I use a published English translation of a specific work, I first cite bibliographical information on the text in its language of origin followed by the English references. The pages listed refer to the English translation. All other translations from the French, Spanish or Italian that are not thus referenced are my own, and the page references are to the original edition.

Baroque Bodies

Introduction

> Any effort to "explain" a historical phenomenon, even though one may hope to understand some factors by which it was conditioned and with which it was interrelated, remains a hopeless task because there are too many layers of life effective at the same time and actively concatenated as to permit any straightforward explanation.
>
> Ernst Kantorowicz, *The King's Two Bodies*

> We must recognize the possibility for a group to live collectively unconscious fears, to invent solutions for these threats, and to admit that this collective experience cannot be radically distinguished from individual experience.
>
> Eugène Enriquez, *De la horde à l'état*

"Absolutism" is a word more resonant in its abstraction than most, and perhaps more empty too. It nevertheless appears capable of generating a proliferation of both conscious and unconscious associations by which and through which our culture constantly reinvents itself. Scholars are continually seeking to reevaluate Absolutism in order to reach some consensus as to its meaning, its reality.[1] For the majority of contemporary historians,

[1] In the vast literature dedicated to seventeenth-century Absolutism, one could consult among the more recent works: *Absolutism in Seventeenth-Century Europe*, ed. John Miller (New York: St. Martin's Press, 1992); William Beik, *Absolutism and Society in Seventeenth-Century France* (Cambridge: Cambridge University Press, 1985); Richard Bonney *The Limits of Absolutism in "Ancien Régime" France* (Brookfield, VT: Variorum, 1995); *L'état baroque 1610–1652: Regards sur la pensée politique de la France du premier XVIIe* siècle, ed. Henry Méchoulan (Paris: Vrin, 1985); *L'état classique: Regards sur la pensée politique de la France dans le second XVIIe* siècle, ed. Joel Cornette and Henry Méchoulan (Paris: Vrin, 1996); Nannerl Keohane *Philosophy and the State in France* (Princeton: Princeton University Press, 1980); Michael Kimmel *Absolutism and Its Discontents: State and Society in Seventeenth-Century France and England* (New Brunswick: Transaction Books, 1988); Roland Mousnier *La monarchie absolue en Europe du Ve siècle à nos jours* (Paris: P.U.F., 1982); Robert Murchembled *Le temps des supplices: De l'obéissance sous les rois absolus XVe-XVIIe siècles* (Paris: A. Colin, 1992). The inability to reach any consensual view of "Absolutism" is summed up by Bonney: "There is little agreement among historians on the nature of absolutism. It is variously depicted as a conservative political philosophy and a form of political system; it is also used as a synonym for the entire "ancien régime." Some historians adhere to the view that an absolute

Absolutism was never an actually achieved political system. Rather, most tend to view it as an asymptotic ideological trajectory where changes in economy, politics, and religion constantly present different, sometimes congruent, but more often decidedly contradictory demands on the bureaucrats attempting to centralize royal policy in the emerging nation-states of seventeenth-century Europe. Although evolving over a period of more than two hundred years, Absolutism remains for historians more a process than a condition. The reality of Absolutism is as elusive as it is evocative. Detached from any univocal historical anchoring, the word drifts into the realm of myth, where fantasy and reality commingle.

Paradoxically, the very elusiveness that is Absolutism's defining characteristic produces an abundance of interpretative possibilities. Surely, for any study of the enormously rich period of artistic, literary, and political creativity that marked the French seventeenth century, Absolutism as soon as it is pronounced, elicits a vertiginous spiral of images, images of beauty and cruelty that are as much the product of fiction as of history.[2] It is as if Absolutism, always associated with a politics of spectacle, necessarily survives in the vivid theatricality of the images it evokes. Could we not say that more than other equally "theoretical" terms, such as monarchy or democracy, Absolutism's images always return spectacularly to a certain materiality for their grounding, a materiality largely invested in the body? The display of the body, either the rent body of Absolutism's victims, or the glorious body of its charismatic leader(s), seems to exist on the stage upon which the absolutist fantasy is most effectively enacted. Always making a spectacle of the body, Absolutism creates this body as a tantalizing enigma, the focus of a fascinating and deadly scenario of seduction where beauty and cruelty, desire and death, seem not only inseparable, but inevitable.

What are some of the most strikingly dramatic images associated with Absolutism? What scenes are immediately evoked at the mention of the word in the context of the seventeenth century? Let me suggest just a few fleeting associations to the word, associations that, I insist, are not historical but representative of a hybrid accretion across the centuries of history and fiction, of generalizations and myth: the plangent scene of the execution of de Thou and Cinq Mars, the headsman's ax falling in that sacrificial beheading (one of several) that mark the crown's attempt to dismember a rebellious nobility; the sight of the maligned courtier (Fouquet) or the rejected

king in some meaningful sense enjoyed absolute power, others are equally convinced that absolutism might as well be described as a system of limited monarchy" (I:114).

[2] In his analysis of groups, Freud discussed how, precisely, "thinking in images" was one of the most salient characteristics of group psychology: "A group is extraordinarily credulous and open to influence. . . . It thinks in images which call one another up by association . . . and whose agreement with reality is never checked by any reasonable agency" (*Group Psychology and the Analysis of the Ego*, the Standard Edition of the Complete Psychological Works of Sigmund Freud [London: Hogarth Press 1953-74], 18 [1962]: 70), henceforth Standard Edition.

lover (La Vallière) pining away in lonely captivity, exiled far from the court to desolate prisons (Pignerol, le château d'If), and to even more forlorn convents. Their sudden fall from royal grace has cast them into a social limbo—living, yet dead to the world that gave meaning to their lives. Then there are those more immediately sexualized scenarios of the life of the court and its stage, where power and seduction intermingle in dangerous, scandalous intrigues (la Montespan, *Dom Juan*, *Phèdre*). Other images surface of perilous, fateful cabals in mysterious seraglios which although cast in the distant, exotic Orient (*Bajazet*, *Zayde*) nevertheless effectively contaminate our present with the titillating images of mute eunuchs, cloistered women, and transgressive desires all situated under the omniscient but invisible gaze of the oriental despot. In the closed world of Absolutism, amorous fantasy can never be extricated from political conspiracies, and their mutual contamination issues in lethal scenarios corrupting the entire body politic: witness the rumored black masses celebrated in subterranean cellars, where only the dim glow of candles reveals the half-hidden presence of the naked bodies of renegade priests and aristocratic women who in their desperate desire to retain the favor of the king and thus their power at court resort, at least in the legend of the *affaire des poisons*, to sorcery, infanticide, and sexual perversions.[3] To these we must add piteous images conjured up by the *dragonnades*, of forced conversions and exile, of the imperious invasion and violation of individual conscience where, to enforce the absolutist law of "one nation, one king, one faith," families are torn asunder by the arrogance of religious intolerance.[4]

Finally, and most spectacularly, at that point where theology and *raison d'état* are joined, emerges the last, the dominant image of the absolute, the image that contains and grounds all of the others as their origin and their end, the sovereign figure of the monarch. Like all images (and I will return to this in a moment) this last image is inherently ambivalent. The image of the monarch appears as both a benevolent paterfamilias who looks after his people, who is, in the words of Louis XIV, "un véritable père de famille qui fait la provision de sa maison, et partage avec équité les aliments à ses enfants,[5] and, at the same time, a bloodstained tyrant who, revoking the Edict of Nantes and promulgating the Code noir, legislates and thus legitimates with aloof impunity the horrors of the Protestant and African diasporas and the institution of slavery in the New World, who burdens the state with endless military campaigns and equally ruinous building projects that re-

[3] For a useful account of this scabrous affair see, Arlette Lebigre, *L'affaire des poisons* (Brussels: Éditions Complexe, 1989).

[4] I have obviously been enumerating the more theatrical images associated with "absolutism." Obviously the more prosaic, more quotidian images associated with the day-to-day bureaucracy of running a complex government have a less spectacular hold over our historical imagination.

[5] Louis XIV *Mémoires*, ed. Jean Longnon (Paris: Tallandier, 1978), 111.

duce France, in the resonant title of Pierre Jurieu's treatise, to a whimpering, exhausted wreck of a nation.[6]

The image of the king's body, a representational fantasy of enormous power and fascination, haunts our vision of the Grand Siècle. It is the perfect rhetorical conundrum in which all our other images and fantasies of Absolutism become embodied. This body, which is never one, symbolizes the pure conundrum of politics as representation, and spectacle as power. In this one body, in the fiction of the body, Absolutism, a term of abstract, almost platonic idealism, becomes fixed in an image that would ground it, at the same time that that image defies any possible anchoring. The image/fantasy of the king's body is constructed by a long tradition in which history, theology, and jurisprudence, and I would add sexual phantasm, all contribute their own tentacular legacies. These legacies rather than securing the image are constantly at work destabilizing it, sending it reeling through the constant and interconnected generation of new and more powerful fantasies.

We know from the classic study of Kantorowicz and the work of his more contemporary disciples that the king's body is not one, but (at least) two.[7] A long tradition of the "king's two bodies," traced by Kantorowicz, was developed by legal experts in both England and France, and helps explain the particularly intense tie that bound the king (both a physical and metaphysical principle) to his people/kingdom (also a doubled physical/metaphysical concept). The symbol of the body existed simultaneously as a double entity—on the one hand the fallible, physical body of the reigning monarch, on the other the intangible, never dying royal body, in which both the authority and the dignity of the state and crown resided in perpetuity. In a sense, as Kantorowicz demonstrates, the concept of the double body of the king transferred over into the realm of temporal politics the theological concept of the double nature of Christ (divine and human). The concept of the "corpus mysticum," first associated with the Church and then more particularly with the Eucharist, provided the thematic and at times the iconographic details that were, mutatis mutandis, shifted by jurists from the theological to the political domain. Thus as the theological became subsumed into the political realm, the supposedly "mystic" relation that existed be-

[6] Pierre Jurieu, *Soupirs de la France esclave* (1691, re-edition Paris: EDHIS, 1976).

[7] The image of the king's body to which I return in more detail has, of course, been the subject of much analysis in the past two decades. The fundamental study of the significance of the royal body is Ernst Kantorowicz, *The King's Two Bodies: A Study in Medieval Political Theology* (Princeton: Princeton University Press, 1957). This study is the point of departure for Louis Marin, *Le portrait du roi* (Paris: Minuit, 1981), trans. Martha Houle, *Portrait of the King*, (Minneapolis: Universtiy of Minnesota Press, 1988), and *La parole mangée et autres essais théologico-politiques* (Paris: Méridiens Klincksieck, 1986, trans. Mette Hjort, *Food for Thought* (Baltimore: The Johns Hopkins University Press, 1989); and Jean Marie Apostolidès, *Le roi machine* (Paris: Minuit, 1981); and Abby Zanger, *Scenes from the Marriage of Louis XIV: Nuptial Fictions and the Making of Absolutist Power* (Stanford: Stanford University Press, 1997).

tween the king and his realm gained ideological grounding and was reinforced in the sublation in this image of politics-as-theology.[8] In a sense the spectacular production of the royal body in the person/persona of Louis XIV can be seen as the apogee of this long, complex theologico/political image. It was perhaps Louis's particular genius to realize the enormous role that spectacle played in a theoretical elaboration of Absolutism. Having perceived that the essence of political power resided in the images and imaginary of majesty, he proceeded to project these images into the world in a way that had never been seen before. He seems to have understood the enormous power inherent in the manipulation of representations and to have grasped what every actor has perceived: his force comes from his ability to orchestrate reality around spectacular scenarios.[9]

It is not in the intentions or scope of this book to rehearse the many and contradictory historical, political, and theological theories of Absolutism as they intersect the cultural life of seventeenth-century France. I wish at this point only to underline the difficulty we find when we attempt to fix this important, if unstable, term. That Absolutism was not absolute will not surprise the students of the period. What is perhaps less fathomable is the continued seduction of the concept defining an outmoded, political structure that itself was a fantasy and that nevertheless endures and informs our desire for the *Grand Siècle*. Are we not seduced by our own fantasies, and do we not therefore have to explore the fascination of this seduction?[10] Do we not dream, when we fantasize life at Versailles at the apogee of the Sun King's reign, of being in his presence, of being honored by a glance, or of being signaled out to perform one of those many small tasks that were the reward of selected courtiers who were allowed to approach this "divine" body, to touch it and thereby to share in its sacred essence? Did they not wish to display to the world that they too were exceptional, that they too shared in the hallowed aura of the absolute?[11] And is not part of our fascination with this image of the absolute that we too can participate in it, we

[8] See Kantorowicz, *The King's Two Bodies*, 193–232. Kantorowicz's work on the "corpus mysticum" is indebted to the pioneering book by Henri de Lubac, *Corpus mysticum: L'eucharistie et l'église au moyen âge* (Paris: Aubier, 1949).

[9] See Georges Balandier, *Pouvoirs sur scène* (Paris: Balland, 1980), 16, where he states that the force of all charismatic political leaders comes from their ability to "to control the real through the imaginary register." Cf. also Apostolidès, *Le roi machine*, and Marin, *Portrait of the King* and *Food for Thought*.

[10] The role of "seduction" as constitutive not only of our reading of the Grand Siècle but of human relations in general is underlined by Eugène Enriquez (*De la horde à l'état: Essai de psychanalyse du lien social* [Paris: Gallimard, 1986], 143):"Thus seduction and the desire to be seduced are co-terminous, the attempt to dominate and the desire to be subjected are two sides of the same interhuman reality. Seduction, as Laplanche and Pontalis write, is a 'structural given' inherent in all human relations."

[11] Norbert Elias in *The Court Society*, trans. Edmund Jephcott, (New York: Pantheon Books, 1983) offers a now-classic sociological interpretation of the interconnected role of sovereign and courtier, a complex balletic structure that kept both the king and his "servants" in wary codependency.

too can transcend our quotidian existence and, for a moment, partake of the divine? When we fantasize the splendid century, very few of us, very few of the historians who have written the master narrative of that period, elaborate fantasies whose identificatory strategies would (consciously at least) have them working in the kitchens of Versailles, or laboring in the fields of a great noble estate as share-cropping peasants.[12] Rather, the fantasy that seems to possess those who write about the reign of Louis XIV, the "ur-model" of the absolute monarch, is a fantasy, finally of love, but love staged on the grandiose stage that was Versailles, love caught in the dreamlike scenario and phantasmatic settings of "Les plaisirs de l'île enchantée," in the dangerous web of Racinian tragedy, in the comic plots of Molière, or in the splendid melancholia of the *Princesse de Clèves*. We continue to be seduced by whatever forces of cruelty and splendor coalesce in the reflected image of the Sun/King. Even, now, at the very end of the twentieth century, a century that should, perhaps more than any other, have taught us to be wary of charismatic leaders, we persist in being fascinated by the idea of an absolute master, provided, of course, we can, in turn, seduce him, keep his love fixed on us. Should we lose that love we would be plunged, like so many failed courtiers, into an abyss of nonexistence, separated forever from the object of our passion, a passion that gives meaning and pleasure to our existence.

It is interesting to speculate on the power of the image of the king's body, which remains, for all intents and purposes, only ever a "virtual" body, that is, it is only a potential body, a body modeled on the desires of the subjects it holds in its thrall. Finally, this "body" endures as a body of desire, a desired body, a body that is never adequate to the desire it inspires, and because of that inadequacy tantalizes as a constantly receding, illuding representation. Louis Marin has masterfully demonstrated how the king as an embodied exemplum of a metaphysics of power exists solely as a "representation."[13] It was Louis XIV's uncanny ability to discover the force of this representation and to produce himself as a spectacle of universal longing. Marin quotes Pascal to describe the fascination of the king, who beguiles precisely because he appears to offer, in/as an absolute body, the satisfaction of "those things that men's cupidity desires."[14] The double body of the king, underneath the accretion of history and pomp, of theology and jurispru-

[12] Several recent historians have attempted to break with this tradition and to focus on the "twenty million" subjects who inhabited the France of Louis XIV. See, for instance, Boris Porchnev, *Les soulèvements populaires en France au XVIIe siècle* (Paris: Flammarion, 1972); and Pierre Goubert, *La vie quotidienne des paysans français au XVIIe siècle* (Paris: Hachette, 1982), *Le siècle de Louis XIV* (Paris: Éditions de Fallois, 1996), and *Louis XIV et vingt millions de français,* (Paris: Fayard, 1966).

[13] "The King is only truly king, that is, monarch, in images. They are his "real presence" (*Portrait of the King*, 8). See also his analysis of Félibien's discussion of the royal portrait in the chapter "The King's Portrait," 206–14.

[14] Quoted in Marin, *Portrait of the King*, 234.

dence, holds out to the concupiscent eyes for whom it is produced the mystery, the utopian mirage of a body of sensual plenitude.

Although theorized as double the king's body as representation is protean. It is capable of kaleidoscopic metamorphoses—the king appears as a "corps glorieux," swathed in all the regalia of sovereignty, depicted in hundreds of portraits of both high and popular art, disseminated throughout his realm.[15] But Louis also transforms himself into, becomes one with, the Sun as easily as he slips into those heroic figures of the Greco-Latin pantheon (Apollo, Hercules, Mars, Augustus), or veils himself in the more abstract garb of Christian allegories—Charity, Abundance, Fortitude, and so on. The double body of the king is not just two but multiple, or rather we might say that every individual representation is multiply overdetermined. These are polysemic representations that exist simultaneously on several overlapping levels, political, social and sexual. Finally we cannot forget the inherently melancholic link that underpins all these various representations and attaches them to the imperious drive of the absolute which, as Marin reminds us, binds the representation of absolute power to the static, frozen presence of Death. Behind the image of king, behind his double body that does not die, lies the medusan fascination revealing the last, the intimate tie between eros—Louis as sexual plenitude—and the death drive.[16]

What I suggest here is that whatever the phenomenon that we now call Absolutism (a term that comes into common parlance only at the end of the eighteenth century) may have been, it can be seized most profoundly in its phantasmatic aspects. In these aspects the political is never separable from the sexual and the sexual attaches itself to a large panoply of ideologically invested signifiers of gender differences and social empowerment. It is these aspects that continue to fascinate us despite the hundreds of years of political, economic, and technological revolutions that would seem to have forever sundered us from this vanished world.

How are we to understand the fascination of the word, the myth, the idea of the absolute that becomes fixed in the phantasm of one spectacular body—the body of Louis XIV? In what ways does this image incarnate not necessarily the reality but perhaps the truth of a complex sociopolitical system?[17] To this first question a necessary corollary must be added: In what

[15] Roger Chartier talks of the cheap, almanac images of the king that were to be found across France in even the most humble households: " The representations of the sovereign figured in a number of print pieces that common folk encountered in their daily lives. It is quite possible that these banal and familiar images did more to cement widespread belief in the legitimate and inviolable authority of the ruler than the grandiose decorative schemes restricted to a small number of viewers" *(The Cultural Origins of the French Revolution*, trans. Lydia Cochrane [Durham: Duke University Press, 1991], 133).

[16] " We should never lose sight of the fact that the desire for absolute power is but one of many kinds of death drives" (Marin, *Food for Thought*, 208).

[17] In "Function and Field of Speech and Language," in *Écrits : A Selection*, trans. Alan Sheridan (London: Tavistock, 1977), Jacques Lacan talks about "rememoration" (that is, the nar-

ways is the image of the absolute, as it comes to be confused with the body of the king, inextricably tied to an ambivalence that may be masked but that reappears in counterdiscourses, in images tied to, but nevertheless disruptive of the dominant image/fantasy? How and where does the other side of fascination and seduction surface as aggressive rejection, even murderous hate?

I propose, and this of course will be the task of the chapters making up this book, that since we are confronted most radically by a system, a world-view, that despite its extremely complex social, economic, political and sexual interweave, nevertheless seems ultimately to rest on one transcendental fantasy/image—the father/king—as the preeminent avatar of the absolute, that we concentrate briefly, before entering into more detailed analyses, on the different facets of this image in an attempt to reach a closer understanding of its powerful seduction.

In her study of the political philosophy of Absolutism, Keohane underlines the almost visceral and seemingly paradoxical tie that joined the king to his subjects:

> It would be hard to exaggerate the importance of the concept of the French King as the representative of the common interest, the source and embodiment of the good of all. There was a sense of security when the monarch was personally in charge of things, a trust in the benevolence of his will, which can only be explained by the belief that he apprehended and spoke for the good of the entire society in a way no other human being could approach.[18]

Keohane points to the intense emotional bond that existed underneath, or alongside, the more logical political ties that bound rulers and subjects in early modern France. This tie idealizes the ruler as it perhaps infantilizes the subject. As is perfectly consonant with the patriarchal, paternalistic rhetoric that played so large a role in the imaginary construction of the image of the monarch, the political tie that Keohane and many others before her describe is essentially of a "passional" rather than a "rational" nature.[19] While this, of course, can be claimed for any political system from the most primitive to

---

rative by which the analysand re-creates his or her past) and distinguishes between truth (*vérité*) and reality (*réalité*) "in psychoanalytic anamnesis, it is not a question of reality, but of truth, because the effect of full speech is to reorder past contingencies by conferring on them the sense of necessities to come, such as they are constituted by the little freedom through which the subject makes them present" (48).

[18] Keohane, *Philosophy and the State in France*, 59. Mousnier (*La monarchie absolue en Europe*, 155) echoes the same idea: "Louis XIV answered the prayers of the French during the Frondes that the king should rule in his own right."

[19] I have discussed in some detail the patriarchal component, essential for understanding the political and phantasmatical role of the monarch. See Mitchell Greenberg, *Subjectivity and Subjugation in Seventeenth-Century Drama and Prose: The Family Romance of French Classicism* (Cambridge: Cambridge University Press, 1992), and *Canonical States, Canonical Stages: Oedipus, Othering and Seventeenth-Century Drama* (Minneapolis: University of Minnesota Press, 1994).

the most complex, it nevertheless resonates with particular seductive force in the spectacular Absolutism of Louis XIV.

As a discourse that embodies the ambivalent intermesh of the abstract and the concrete, of the physical and the metaphysical, in a fantasy/image of the royal body, an object of adoration (a heady mixture of sacred, sexual, and political identification), Absolutism would seem to inhabit that sphere whose most illuminating analysis is to be sought in that other discourse of power and desire, psychoanalytic theory. From its founding moments psychoanalysis was engaged in understanding how the psyche was inscribed in the body at the same time that the body constantly seems to invade the psyche, in dreams, symptoms, and fantasies. Psychoanalysis has often been dismissed by some theorists as "apolitical" either because clinical theory is thought to be too overtly subjective to be effectively applied to large sociohistorical problems, or because Freud's more abstract musings on the constitution of human societies (*Totem and Taboo, Group Psychology and the Analysis of the Ego, Moses and Monotheism)* have been criticized by political theorists as uninformed fictions.[20] Despite these dismissals, it appears more and more obvious that materialist sociopolitical theories cannot adequately account for precisely the irrational element in the social contract, an irrational that continues to bedevil precisely those theories that would see the passional as an aberration rather than as a constituent part of the human, that is, political, pact. Some of Freud's followers, particularly in recent French contexts, have attempted to account for precisely the "imaginary" (in the sense of unconscious) aspect of ideology that Louis Althusser underscored more than thirty years ago in his own dialogue with psychoanalytical (Lacanian) theory and practice.

In his famous, if contested, definition of ideology Althusser emphasized precisely that the unconscious remains the essence of and yet the rarely examined aspect of the ties binding people together in polity. "Ideology," for Althusser, is "a representation of the imaginary relation between individuals and their actual conditions of existence."[21] and precisely this "imaginary relation," it appears to me, can be best elucidated by psychoanalysis, as a theory of those unconscious, conflicted libidinal forces that, as Freud hypothesized, have their origin in the family history of the subject and that continue to operate in the larger political arena in which this same subject and his/her family are inscribed.[22] Furthermore, as it has been applied by Freud

[20] See, for example Gérard Pommier, *Freud Apolitique?* (Paris: Flammarion, 1998): "Thus we will not be surprised to learn that all Freud's work on this question is still considered today to be either a collection of naive musings or, for the more reverent, as a series of scientific myths without any practical application"(10).

[21] "Ideology is a representation of the imaginary relation individuals have to their real conditions of existence" Louis Althusser, *Positions* (Paris: Éditions Sociales, 1970), 101.

[22] Freud, *Group Psychology*, Standard Edition, 18:70, "the social instinct may not be a primitive one thus insusceptible of dissection, . . . it may be possible to discover the beginnings of its development in a narrower circle, such as that of the family."

and his followers to politics, anthropology, and art, psychoanalysis affords us a particularly fertile theory for understanding not only the seductive power of the images and imaginary of Absolutism represented by and in the person/persona of Louis XIV but also, through a complex analysis of identificatory mechanisms, our own complicitous role in that seduction.

Let us not forget that the country Louis XIV inherited, even after the considerable consolidation achieved under the successive governments of Henri IV, Richelieu, and Mazarin, was still, in the words of one scholar of the period, a "mosaic" of a nation, a patchwork of different principalities, duchies, royal demesnes, urban corporations, with overlapping, contradictory, and often hostilely opposed hereditary rights, customs, and systems of taxation.[23] Hence in the most obvious of senses France was not one, but many. It was a country whose frontiers were still being defined. From the beginning of the century onward a policy of the French crown was to close itself off at its natural border—the Pyrenees to the south, the Rhine to the east, the Atlantic to the west. The northern and northeastern regions where no natural borders existed were a source of constant anxiety—remaining permeable, indistinct, and therefore threatening. It was a strange heterogeneous mixture of "francophone" culture, Spanish political domination, and Teutonic influences.[24] As such an indistinct no-man's-land it was perhaps the most acutely threatened and threatening area on the French map—an open space of passage that could not be properly closed off. We will see how this anxiety of borders is reflected in the analogous anxieties related to bodily orifices in the literary fantasies of the period.

At the same time there existed an inherent contradiction in the absolutist imperative "one law, one king, one faith" which was invoked to impose on the nation an identificatory unity of closure. While the eradication of internal difference was a matter of royal policy, economic and colonialist policies of that same state, unknowingly, opened France up to an invasion of difference: missionaries, colonialists, merchants went forth into the world in unprecedented numbers, intermingled with indigenous populations, and brought back to France, in narratives, artifacts, and peoples, the beginnings of a much more powerful hybridity than the one these policies were attempting to eradicate.

Inside France the diversity of traditions, laws, and, of course, languages was also resistant to centralizing changes imposed from the court in Paris. The constant uprisings throughout the first half of the century under Richelieu and Mazarin, which culminate in the *Frondes* of the mid seventeenth century so traumatizing to the young king, bear witness enough to the enor-

[23] "The France of Louis XIV was essentially a 'mosaic' of a kingdom" (Cornette, "La tente de Darius," in *L'état classique*, 31).

[24] The relation between the anxieties of the body politic and the physical body will be a subject of ongoing discussion throughout this book. Cf. in particular chap. 1, "Molière's Body Politic."

mous and unfinished tasks that confronted Louis XIV when he decided to take matters into his own hands. In his *Mémoires* Louis recalls with anxious rhetoric the turmoil he faced:

> Mais il faut se représenter l'état des choses: des agitations terribles par tout le royaume avant et après ma majorité; une guerre étrangère, où ces troubles domestiques avaient fait perdre à la France mille et mille avantages; un prince de mon sang et d'un très grand nom à la tête des ennemis; beaucoup de cabales dans l'Etat, . . . dans ma cour, très peu de fidélité sans intérêt, et par là mes sujets en apparence les plus soumis, autant à charge et autant à redouter pour moi que les plus rebelles.[25]

The ongoing turmoil of French history as well as the complex political reality of the administration of the kingdom create the image of a rent, disruptive, and noncontinuous body politic. The image of France as a torn, beaten body was most poignantly rendered at the beginning of the seventeenth century, by the Huguenot poet, Agrippa d'Aubigné in his description of the disastrous effects of the civil wars of religion:

> O France désolée! Ô terre sanguinaire,
> Non pas terre, mais cendre! Ô mère, si c'est mère
> Que trahir ses enfans aux douceurs de son sein
> Et quand on les meurtrit les serrer de sa main?
> Tu leur donnes la vie, et dessous ta mammelle
> S'esmeut des obstinez la sanglante querelle;
> Sur ton pis blanchissant ta race se débat,
> Là le fruit de ton flanc faict le champ du combat.[26]

It cannot escape our notice that d'Aubigné's pathetic metaphor for the nation, is a female one; France is equated by the poet first to a mother, and then the maternal image is described as an unnaturally sanguinary locus. The destruction of French society during the religious wars is sexualized by d'Aubigné as an aberrant, I am tempted to say, psychotic breakdown of the maternal body.

Beneath the premonitions of social chaos betrayed by such a image, we can, however, dectect an ambivalent message, both a fear and a desire. The fear was, of course, of total societal anarchy, that surfaced most notably in the enchafed rhetoric of the conservative Catholic *ligue* during the Wars of Religion but also survived in the writings of political theorist from Bodin to Bossuet. This fear was not without its tantalizing aspects, we only have to look at "baroque" paintings and sculptures, or read the rapturous play of metaphors in the poetry and drama of the time, to see the way this spiraling

[25] Louis XIV, *Mémoires*, 33.

[26] Agrippa d'Aubigné, "Misères," *Les tragiques*, vv. 89–92, in *Oeuvres*, ed. Henri Weber (Paris: Gallimard, 1969).

out of control exercises its own powerful attraction. But this baroque erotics of *éclatement* also elicits and appeals to its very opposite: a desire for a cessation of the anarchy, for the imposition of order upon chaos, for a leader, who, subsuming disparity in his own body, the shining "body royal," imposes unity on difference and who can, reasserting paternal authority, heal the breach in the body politic and protect France from the homicidal mother.[27] Beneath the horror and fascination with dispersion lurks an appeal to a stable unity; the monarch/father, who in his own person and persona is made to incarnate the contradictory hopes and desires of his people—the desire of and appeal to the absolute.[28]

From political theorists writing during the harrowing civil turbulence of the sixteenth century emerged a fortified theory of monarchy, deeply rooted in biblical patriarchy. Although the metaphor of the king as father had a long lineage in political theories from Aristotle onward, it received a particularly resonant reinforcement in Europe at the end of the sixteenth and beginning of the seventeenth centuries.[29] Could I propose as a first hypothesis that the fantasy of the "king's two bodies" functions first and perhaps foremost in the paternal metaphor, as a talisman warding off the fear of disintegration, the fear—if we wish to make a theoretical leap into a collective un-

[27] See Enriquez (*De la horde à l'état*) who, elaborating on Freud (particularly on Freud's discussion of the role of the primal father in *Totem and Taboo*), writes (144): "Freud does not deny that individuals can live alongside each other, he simply believes that they cannot exist as a group, as a 'people' without reference to a 'unique'[subject]; the 'people' is thus formed by individuals who are joined together by libidinal force, and this libido cannot traverse the social sphere unless it emanates from an individual who can conjure it up, or, like the father of the primal horde, reject it."

[28] See, for example, Eric Hobsbawm, "The Crisis of the Seventeenth Century," in *Crisis in Europe 1560–1650*, ed. Trevor Aston (London: Routledge and Kegan Paul, 1965), 12: "Only in one respect did the seventeenth century as a whole overcome rather than experience difficulties. . . . Most of Europe found an efficient and stable form of government in absolutism on the French model." Enriquez offers the following psychoanalytically inspired explanation of the appeal of the charismatic leader (*De la horde à l'état*, 334): "[At the same time it is indispensable that this party have as its head] a leader demonstrating at once enough charisma and ability to incarnate and to symbolize the State and the Nation in their permanence so that the majority of the people can have the feeling that the social body finds its unity and identity in a physical body whose beauty, grace, and wealth it can admire. This phenomenon that we will call the 'personalization of power' expresses the people's need to be in the care of an individual who bears witness to their existence not only as a nation but as a chosen people."

[29] Jean Bodin's *Six livres de la république* had a wide European audience. Peter Laslett, in his introduction to another, British treatise on patriarchy and monarchy, Sir Robert Filmer's *Patriarcha* (Oxford: Basil Blackwell, 1949), underscores the rather conventional comparison of the king to the father, and the state to a family (28): "It is obvious . . . that the use of the family analogy created a presumption in favour of monarchy. It is also to be expected that sooner or later the two societies would be merged into one, and that thinkers would be found who could claim that the King *was* the father, and the family *was* the state." Jacques-Bénigne Bossuet later is the theorist of Absolutism who most forcefully continues the metaphor in the seventeenth century. See *Politique tirée des propres paroles de l'écriture sainte*, in *Oeuvres complètes* (Paris: Garnier, 1846), 3:152: "Les hommes qui avoient vu, ainsi qu'il a été dit, une image de royaume dans l'union de plusieurs familles, sous la conduite d'un père commun, et qui avoient trouvé de la douceur dans cette vie, se portèrent aisément à faire des sociétés sous des rois qui leur tinssent lieu de père."

conscious that is slippery to define—of fragmentation, of social disintegration, the fear that can be most intriguingly associated with what on a subjective level we call castration anxiety, the fear of bodily mutilation, of death?[30]

On the first approach, therefore, the shining body royal, the imagined fantasized body of the king would stand as an apotropaic talisman both calling forth and warding off the danger of social disintegration. The king's body here would represent the body of that father who in fantasy appears as effectively and paradoxically "beyond castration." This image is given its most vivid delineation in Freud's myth of the primal horde. There, the father, who keeps all the available females for his own sexual use, effectively castrates his sons' desire, forcing them into a murderous homosociality. The pent-up rage of the brothers erupts in destructive violence. The sons rise up and slay their father and then in a commemorative meal, a meal in which the father's body is consumed and thus assimilated by all the brothers, a sense of community and guilt or community as guilt, is instituted. But with this birth of conscience/guilt, the product of an innate ambivalence of the brothers toward the father, the father returns, symbolically, more powerful then he was in life. The dead father—the father who has gone through death and castration—here emerges as that uncastratable other, the other who cannot be eliminated, cannot be killed because already dead. It is "dead father," who becomes, for Freud and in more recent theory for Lacan, the origin of the Law of renunciation that founds society.[31] At the same time, we cannot but note, that in this scheme of things the Father is here already positioned as the guarantor of a male-dominated society.

Lest Freud's (and Lacan's) insistence that the dead father represents the symbolic, eternal role as arbiter of social law appear too far-fetched, too illusive, we should remember that in a totally different context Kantorowicz offers fascinating iconographic material of the court rituals of the French monarchy in which this dead father is, so to speak, brought to life. He becomes the totemic image to which even in so relatively an advanced and complex society as sixteenth- and seventeenth-century France, people still

[30] I underline here the intense relation that exists in the seventeenth century between symbolic castration and actual bodily mutilation; it is most apparent when we read the travel narratives that were so abundant at the time of those voyagers to the Ottoman and Persian empires, Tavernier, Thevenot, Chardin, Baudier, among others. One way or another they all come back, obsessively, to the image of the eunuch (both "white" and "black") and of the different types of corporal punishment, that is, "slicing of the viscera" that mark these "despotic" regimes and in which, as Enriquez says " We can see how closely tied to each other are symbolic castration and real (physical) castration" (*De la horde à l'état*, 246). See also the analysis of Alain Grosrichard, *Structure du sérail: La fiction du despotisme asiatique dans l'Occident classique* (Paris: Seuil, 1979).

[31] Charles Shepherdson, in *Vital Signs: Nature, Culture, Psychoanalysis* (New York: Routledge, 1999), following Lacan underlines the essential link between the father and death (cf. 145) "As Freud puts it, after his death, the father does not pass away, but returns stronger than ever, for once he is dead, he can no longer be killed."

pay homage. In *The King's Two Bodies* Kantorowicz describes the strangely macabre funerary effigies that were used during the royal obsequies of the sixteenth century. In what cannot but strike us as a vivid mise-en-scène, a veritable acting-out of the Freudian scenario, it became a custom during the late Renaissance upon the death of the king, to garb an effigy of that king, his "person/a" in royal regalia and to have the effigy paraded through the streets as the "king," present during the funeral service. The effigy, the representative of the transcendent body of the king, continued to receive the reverence of the attendant crowd. In a resonantly symbolic chiasmus, the dead king's mortal remains were given the funeral rites of the Church while the effigy of that same king continued to be celebrated, as sovereign, in official state ceremonials:

> At the French funerary rites, another bifocality developed; one ritual of the Church observed by the clergy for the misery of the naked or half-naked man in the coffin . . . and another ritual of the state, celebrating through the effigy the immortal and regal Dignity exposed on the coffin. . . . The triumph of Death and the triumph over Death were shown side by side.[32]

Thus the king/father, as his effigy triumphs over death and continues to preside over the legal administration of the kingdom of which he as "representation" is the embodiment. This embodiment exists beyond time and mortality, revealing that the real king, the real père du peuple, in the last analysis is, as Freud suggested, the father who from beyond the grave continues like the ghostly presence in *Hamlet* to reign with the force and fascination of the undead.[33]

By reigning beyond death, the father necessarily and coterminously legislates the sexuality of his people. When in Freud's myth the brothers have risen up, killed, and devoured the father, he becomes symbolically a part of them all. They now all share in the strength they envied in him. But as we've seen, because of their inherent ambivalence, conscience arises as a sense of guilt. This sense of guilt is marked most especially, according to Freud, by the imposition of the two taboos that found "human society," the taboos against murder and against incest.

The prohibition of incest is simultaneously instituted along with the prohibition against killing. Freud speaks here of the parallel between the murder of the father of the primal horde and the establishment of the law of exogamy in myth and in the (positive) Oedipus complex, which he claims is the universal psychic structure of mankind.[34] Freud thus attempts to draw

[32] Kantorowicz, *The King's Two Bodies*, 425.

[33] Guy Rosolato has written extensively of the importance of the concept of the "dead father" in psychoanalytic theory. See his "Du père" and "Trois générations d'hommes dans le mythe religieux et la généalogie," in *Essais sur le symbolique* (Paris: Gallimard, 1969).

[34] For a discussion of the relation between the myth of the primal horde and the Oedipus complex and their interconnection, see Shepherdson, *Vital Signs*, chap. 5.

an analogy between social myths and individual psychic phenomena in which the one informs and represents the other, establishing a roundelay by which the individual is inscribed symbolically in the social, and the social in turn reappears, in the individual.

The importance of heterosexual marriage, the essential institution for the production and reproduction of society, thus also finds its grounding in the sexualized image of the father/king, as bridegroom who espouses his realm.[35] As we read Kantorowicz we note that at the same time the "royal effigy" replaces the actual dead body of the king at the center of funeral service, the sexualized marriage symbolism of the coronation ceremony also takes on a more dominant role. Starting in 1594 the image of the king and his kingdom joined as "man and wife," in mutual love and "reciprocal conjunction," underlines even more, if need be, the sexual appeal of the sovereign and the reciprocity among the fantasies conjoining sexuality, death, and polity.[36]

The ceremony of the king embracing his realm in marriage institutes, on the one hand as an orthopedic mirror, the heterosexual exogamy necessary for the reproduction of the social edifice; on the other it obscures the other side of the sexual association to the father's body—the homosexual tie that binds the father to the brothers and the brothers to each other. We might speculate that what is thus occulted, because it cannot be allowed into representation, is the force of a homosexual tie that many see as the underlying impetus to social cohesion.[37] In the representation of marriage, that sexu-

[35] See Freud, *Totem and Taboo*, Standard Edition, 13:143, "They revoked their deed by forbidding the killing of the totem, the substitute for their father; and they renounced its fruits by resigning their claim to the women who had now been set free. They thus created out of their filial sense of guilt the two fundamental taboos of totemism, which for that very reason inevitably corresponded to the two repressed wishes of the Oedipus complex. A sense of guilt made its appearance, which in this instance coincided with the remorse felt by the whole group. The dead father became stronger than the living one had been. . . . What had up to then been prevented by his actual existence was thencefoward prohibited by the sons themselves, in accordance with the psychological procedure so familiar to us in psycho-analysis under the name of 'deferred obedience.' "

[36] "Upon the accession of Henry II of France, in 1547, we find, for the first time in a French Coronation Order, the almost juristic rubric before the Bestowal of the Ring, saying that by this ring 'the king solemnly married his realm' *(le roy espousa solemnellement le royaume)*. The rubrics of the Order of 1594 were more explicit. They said that the king, on the day of his consecration, married his kingdom in order to be inseparably bound to his subjects that they may love each other mutually like husband and wife, and that the Bishop of Chartres presented to the king the ring *pour marque de cest reciproque conjonction*" (Kantorowicz, *The King's Two Bodies*, 221–22.)

[37] Recently both Kristeva and Enriquez have underlined the important "homosexual" component in the social tie. Julia Kristeva, in *Sens et non-sens de la révolte: Pouvoirs et limites de la psychanalyse* (Paris: Livre de Poche, 1996), writes (71–72): "But we must admit that Freud remains very reserved in this text about the fate of the femininity of the brothers: how did they resolve that they were also the wives of this father, that is, the subjugated or passive victims of the paternal sexual drive, a fate suggested by the insistance on the homosexual bond established between the brothers who were reconciled around the dead father? . . . Let us at least recognize something that the founder of psychoanalysis had the honesty to express, that is, the homosexual substratum of the sacred covenant." Enriquez (*De la horde à l'état*, 6) states "It is,

ally symbolic ritual for welding the kingdom to its ruler as "man and wife," what goes unsaid is that the kingdom is feminized, to receive the embrace of the king, to corroborate the king as male, and therefore to reaffirm a certain patriarchal phallocracy as the natural (that is, ideologically overdetermined) form of sexuality, the only form of sexuality, the only conjunction of bodies that the State can tolerate. In both the subjective complex and the social myth society can function only by the repression of homosexuality. The father's homosexuality vis-à-vis the brothers and also the brothers' vis-à-vis each other are passed over silently in favor of the proclamation of the institution of heterosexual exogamy. All forms of sexuality outside of the limits of this symbolic marriage (symbolic of the political inscription of the Oedipus complex) are expelled beyond society, beyond religion, and beyond representation. Perhaps, however, beyond is not quite the right term, as they continue to exist, contained in the image of the king's body. That body, as fantasy, continues to function as the means by which death and sexuality are carried along by what precisely is there but cannot be represented.

It is this multiply layered fantasy of the uncastratable father that takes its place as the defender of society against the equally complex fantasy of the violence waiting to be visited on society by the (archaic) mother. Nevertheless this dichotomy, although active on one level in the phantasmatic context of the absolutist double body, is more complexly interwoven on another.

Let us reconsider in juxtaposition two of the most resonant images of the absolute body of Louis XIV, the sun and the famous portrait of the king by Hyacinthe Rigaud. Each image corresponds to the fantasy of the king's "masculine" body, and yet each reflects, as all images do, a multiplicity of associations that also reveal more primitive couplings. First, here is Louis XIV's own description of how and why he chose the emblem of the sun as a symbolic projection of his own phantasmatic (narcissistic) image of himself:

> Ce fut là que je commençais à prendre [cette devise] que j'ai toujours gardée depuis, et que vous voyez en tant de lieux. Je crus que, sans s'arrêter à quelque chose de particulier et de moindre, elle devait représenter en quelque sorte les devoirs d'un prince, et m'exciter éternellement moi-même à les remplir. On choisit pour *corps* le soleil, qui, dans les règles de cet art, est le plus noble de tous, et qui, par la qualité d'unique, par l'éclat qui l'environne, par la lumière qu'il communique aux autres astres qui lui composent comme une espèce de cour, par le partage égal et juste qu'il fait de cette même lumière en tous lieux produisant sans cesse de tous côtés la vie, la joie et l'action, par son mouvement sans relâche, où il paraît néanmoins toujours tranquille, par cette course constante et invariable, dont il ne s'écarte et ne se détourne jamais, est assurément la plus vive et la plus belle image d'un grand monarque.[38]

---

therefore, not heterosexual love, but solely desexualized love, . . . homosexual love . . . repressed or not, that is favorable to collective formations."

[38] Louis XIV, *Mémoires*, 135–36.

The solar image is a complex one. On the one hand it clearly represents in its self-enclosed brilliance a narcissism, that denies any relation to or dependence on objects outside itself.[39] In many cultures, the sun has been conceived as a predominantly male image, as incarnated, for instance, in the Greek god Helios, but associated to other deities, particularly Apollo. Nevertheless, in other societies the sun especially when appearing coupled with the moon has been associated to fertile, female attributes. A powerful symbol of life, and yet, we might say, as that which is everywhere present and yet cannot be seen or gazed upon, the sun has also been a symbol of death.[40] Finally we might further conjecture that associations to the shape, the movement, and the self-containment of the solar image conjure up more resonant, if more ambiguous, allegorical myths, in particular the myth of the androgyne, an image/myth that will continually resurface, in chiaroscuro, during the long seventeenth century. Aristophanes in Plato's account the androgyne myth offers the following description: the primeval man was round, his back and sides forming a circle. . . . He could walk upright as men now do, backwards or forwards as he pleased, and he could also roll over and over at a great pace, turning on his four hands and four feet, eight in all like tumblers going over and over with their legs in the air.[41]

Like the sun, but in more explicitly sexual terms, the androgyne in its figure of perfectly symmetrical circularity would represent the narcissistic self-containment of a non-lacking bisexuality that is both beyond (or before) castration and death. Turning around on itself the androgyne/sun would be self-sufficient, representing a state of plenitude, a nonsexual jouissance, a pleasure not dependent on castration and lack, but rather, like the sun, a self-consuming, self-nourishing totality. Thus, underlying the diversity of these images they would be conjoined on the level of association by a single image that would both conjure up the anxiety of castration/death and deny it.[42] The sun, in other words, functions as Absolutism's most resonant fetish.

[39] The French psychoanalyst André Green offers the following definition of the narcissistic personality: "Portrait of Narcissus, all powerful in his body and in his mind, which becomes embodied in his speech, independent and autonomous when he wishes to be so, but upon whom others depend without his feeling in any way needy of them. Residing among his own, the members of his family, his clan, his race, chosen by the obvious indications of a divinity created in his own likeness. He exists at their head, master of the universe, of time, of death, totally involved in his silent dialogue with the solitary deity who bestows all his blessings upon him—up until the moment of his fall through which he becomes the chosen object of his own sacrifice—an intercessor between God and mortals living in the brilliant isolation of his splendor. This shadow of God traces a figure of the same, of what is unchanging, intangible, immortal, and intemporal" (*Narcississme de vie, narcissime de mort*, [Paris: Minuit, 1983], 55).

[40] The strong link between narcissism and death was first delineated by Freud in *Mourning and Melancholia* (1917), which takes up the problem of narcissism previously discussed in *On Narcissism, An Introduction* (1914); both works are in volume 14 of the Standard Edition.

[41] Plato, *Symposium*, in *The Dialogues of Plato*, trans. Benjamin Jowett 2 vols., (New York: Random House, 1937), 2:317.

[42] For another appreciation of the androgynous aspect of the image of Louis XIV, see M. Francko, "The King Crossed Dressed: Power and Force in Royal Ballets," in *From the Royal to the Republican Body: Incorporating the Political in Seventeenth- and Eighteenth-Century*

Can we not uncover this same ambivalence hidden and revealed in the Rigaud state portrait?[43] The well-known painting(s) by Rigaud portray Louis in his most regal, that is sovereign, persona. While the center of the painting represents the king whose body is presented as a long torque which our gaze follows from the elaborate wig down to those famous high-heeled, bow-tied shoes, the two most salient features are the elderly monarch's head, turned toward the spectator and gazing imperiously out at him/her, a look that in its regal hauteur seems totally impervious to the returned gaze of the world, and his elegantly, silk-clad and turned-out leg. The painting plays with the rest of the royal body and with the spectator in a game of hide and seek: the body there (we imagine), but totally disseminated into and through the accoutrements of royalty. At the same time that it is lost in, it becomes one with the swirling cloaks of ermine and velvet which overflow the body itself and send it (garbed in its regal insignia) out into the borders of the represented space of the painting. There its swirling folds are mirrored in the enormous, overhanging crimson drapery that both hides and reveals the solidly phallic column forming the backdrop of the stage upon which Louis is posed. Marin has talked about the different regalia—the crown, the scepter, the fleur de lys—inscribed in the portrait as so many signposts that point to both the past history of the monarchy now incarnated in the portrait of the monarch and that past's assumption in the present moment of contemplation. He also speaks, and this is the point I find most congenial for my own argument, of the inherently ambiguous mixture in this portrait of the king, of the dominant, masculine imagery that is nevertheless complemented by a certain femininity of the turn of the leg, of the soft velvets and furs, of the portrait as being one more aspect of a certain androgyny that Marin associates with the fetish:

> The king's glorious body makes itself sensuous and feminine by means of the garters and the silky curve of its legs, which are shown to be like those of a dancer in fourth position, the very figure of suspended movement; the king is like a dancer caught in the imminence of another movement in the interspace of a single gesture. Using the example of this royal leg, we should be able to show that the portrait of the king is also the fetish of representation, and that the eroticism and aesthetics, as the sensuous value of taste, are directly related to politics and, more precisely, to the monarch's absolute power, as it is really present in his portrait.[44]

What I should suggest is that the king's body is Absolutism's fetish. By this I mean it is the apotropaic talisman that at one and the same time points

France, ed. Sarah Melzer and Kathryn Norberg (Berkeley: University of California Press, 1998), 64–85.

[43] For a detailed analysis of the painting see Marin, "The Portrait of the King's Glorious Body," in *Food for Thought*, 190–217.

[44] Marin, *Food for Thought*, 206. (Translation has been modified.)

both to this body as a fantasy of masculine perfection, a fantasy in which the king as body appears as the perfect—that is "uncastrated" union of opposites—and, away to another, occulted body, the imaginary, open, that is, castrated female body which is Absolutism's hidden, other body, its secret. In this body difference is subsumed and transcended, chaos—that is, fragmentation, dispersion and death—have been gone through and overcome (thus all the Christological echoes that the image assumes). We can perhaps understand now why the image of the king, by incarnating the fantasy of the absolute, functions as a charismatic icon to which his subjects pay homage. The image of the royal body, which is always a projection of each subject's own fantasy of the absolute thus would serve, as Freud suggests, as a compelling substitute in his subjects for their "ego-ideal."[45] This substitution is a recognition of their own debt, their castration, and at the same time their sublation of that debt in their mutual identification and thus shared love for their totem/fetish. When we remember however that Freud has told us that the "ego-ideal" which the king's body now represents is formed from a residue of primary narcissism, we can perhaps see how, with the recycling of that narcissism, and its projection out into the image/fantasy of an uncastratable object of adoration, we come back full circle to that fantasy's being put into circulation as the sun, the androgyne. Underneath the charisma of the king's body, beneath the conscious fantasy of a unitary being, we can detect perhaps the aggressive conjunction of more primitive images. As we saw in the example taken from d'Aubigné, social fragmentation and chaos were easily portrayed as malevolent maternity. It was partly in response to this sexed image of social anxiety that the Father returns at the end of the sixteenth and beginning of the seventeenth century as a reassuring totality. When we consider the fetishistic component of the image, however, the fact that it conceals and reveals a certain (phantasmatic) femininity along with an apparent masculinity, rather than see it as a "uncontaminated" masculine projection, we realize that the image contains at the same time both the frightening associations to both the affirmation and denial of castration (death). The associations contained in the image of the king's two bodies can, I suggest, be attached to those very primitive fantasies, presexed fantasies, where the archaic, "phallic" mother and the destructive primal father merge.[46] On the manifest level of the fantasy, the image projects the triumph of a certain masculinist desire for unity and order, associated with the entire patriarchal ideology of the absolutist monarchy.

[45] "A primary group . . . is a number of individuals who have put one and the same object in the place of their ego-ideal and have consequently identified themselves with one another in their ego" (*Group Psychology*, 18:116).

[46] For the confusion of the "phallic mother" and the primitive father, see. Guy Rosolato, "L'axe narcissique des dépressions," in *La relation d'inconnu* (Paris: Gallimard, 1978), 9: "The image of the father, of his substitutes, only serves to disguise an unchanging relation with the mother—a phallic, all powerful mother, archaic destroyer; the ideal father, all the while giving the illusion of having detached himself from her, is intimately imbricated in this image."

But it must be remembered that the unspoken secret of the victor is that his victory is purely pyrrhic; the other—female, threatening, destructive—has not been vanquished, but it continues to inhabit and to be carried along by the very image that supposedly most resplendently represents its effacement. In the resonant words of Marin, the secret of the king is that the "absolute monarch is not what he is."[47]

And what he is not—the entire metaphysics of Absolutism that tries to ground itself in the physicality of this body that is a fantasy—will nevertheless go on to colonize the esthetic, ethical, and philosophical corpus of France for over two hundred years. And from France, it will spread, as "Classical" taste and decorum, across Europe. It is fascinating to contemplate the agonistic relation between Classicism, which I here consider the esthetic correlative to Absolutism, and the body. As is well known, the dictates of Classical decorum exile the body from representation.[48] All mention of what is associated with the body, in reality or fantasy (shall we call this discourse, the baroque?), suffers the same fate. But the body does not simply disappear, it inheres in the very discourse that rejects it. It returns, as we know the repressed does, in symptoms, in dreams, in literature. Although it would be a mistake to establish a simple dichotomy opposing an embodied discourse to one from which the body is banished, it would nevertheless be rewarding to inquire first what is at stake in that opposition, and then to place the opposition into its sociocultural sphere. How does the body return in the world of French letters in that period we continue to call absolutist? How do the images, fantasies of the body repressed and/or exultant, work the fabric of absolutist culture? Do these fantasies of the body's return represent an escape from the confinement to which Classical doctrine condemns the body? Or do they, more cynically, simply reinscribe a patriarchal ideology of social and sexual predicates to which the body as it is inscribed in absolutist culture, must also conform?

The following chapters will develop in greater detail the social/sexual stakes that have been only outlined here. The readings offered delve into the ways the ever-renascent fantasy of the body encountered the equally phantasmatic drive of a discourse—political, social, sexual—that strives for hegemony, that strives to attain the absolute that it purportedly represents. Does this confrontation between an esthetics and a rhetoric that are grounded in the fantasy/image of the never-there king's body—a discourse that would paradoxically suppress the body because it is too excessive, too

[47] See Marin's *Portrait of the King*, 232:"Thus the secret of the absolute monarch, the ethical secret, the retreat from the statesman in his portrait, the secret of the all-powerful king, is that he is not so; a hidden thought, never spoken, a thought that is perhaps never thought; . . . the figure, of the fiction, of the figurative, to think that thought—of the impossibility of forgetting that he is not what he is."

[48] For a brilliant analysis of this exiling of the body from representation and of the ideological consequences entailed by such an exile, cf. Francis Barker *The Tremulous Private Body: Essays in Subjection* (London: Methuen, 1984).

fragmented, too motley—and the emergence as symptoms, as fantasies, of an excessive, archaic body, signal spaces of resistance? Are these loci that, while they perhaps do not prevail over the hegemonic thrust of a period's and a nation's dominant discourse, at least create the possibility of thinking, and perhaps more important, of fantasizing a different, more ambivalent inscription of the Classical subject in its representations? To these questions we must now turn, questions that each chapter interrogates differently in the hope of elaborating both a different vision and another fantasy of the seventeenth-century's various bodily incarnations.

1 *Molière's Body Politic*

> To be truthful, the monarch seems to spend a large part of his time on the *chaise percée*. We constantly hear of purges and enemas, of intestinal irritations that sometimes go on for an entire day; of bowel movements repeated up to a dozen times.
>
> François Millepierres,
> *La vie quotidienne des médecins au temps de Molière*

> The body is also directly involved in a political field; power relations have an immediate hold upon it; they invest it, mark it, train it, torture it, force it to carry out tasks, to perform ceremonies, to emit signs. This political investment of the body is bound up in accordance with complex reciprocal relations with its economic use.
>
> Michel Foucault, *Discipline and Punish*

THE COMFORTINGLY MONOCHROMATIC and slightly marmoreal image of the "Grand Siècle" has been a notable victim of the renewed attention literary critics and theoreticians have brought to the study of the Classical age. Gone from recent discussions of seventeenth-century France is that hieratically fixed notion of a structured world in which things and people were believed to be neatly arranged in an ordered and "organic" whole (a vision resonant with the ideological yearnings of certain twentieth-century bourgeois critics). French society of the period is no longer envisioned as a pyramid the apex of which would be fixed at Versailles, seen as the shiny apogee of a Classical moment more ideal than real. In its place, we have been offered a vision of a society in radical transformation. France, like other countries of seventeenth-century Europe situated at the crossroads of epochal changes—changes in epistemology, in economies, in theology and philosophy, in the arts—appears to us now as a rich, often extremely violent nation where political, sexual, and economic differences commingle, divide, are reconfigured.[1]

[1] I am referring in this brief opening paragraph to the idea of a crisis of the seventeenth century, the century seen as period of radical, even revolutionary change that we see expressed in works by historians, philosophers, literary critics. See for the broad general ideas *Crisis in Eu-*

In his many provocative and innovative readings of the origins and ramifications of the "modern" subject, Michel Foucault returns time and again to the seventeenth century. He goes so far as to define this period that retained its fascination for him, whether in his early history of madness, or in his later works on epistemological and sexual revolutions, as one of the two decisive moments of radical change that mark the "modern" period, a moment in which the parameters defining human subjectivity are decisively realigned.[2] At the same time that Foucault marks off the seventeenth century as a period of fundamental realignment of epistemology, he also (and this, of course, is intimately related to epistemology) situates the coming into being, through his mapping of a new confessional policy of morality, of sexuality.[3] This change in sexuality/epistemologies corresponds to the transformation of the concept of "family" that is impelled by the reconfigurations of the socioeconomic sphere that recent demographic historians have also situated during the course of the century. "It seems clear," Jean-Louis Flandrin writes, "that between the sixteenth century and the end of the eighteenth the family radically changed and that a new familial morality had been outlined." [4] For such diverse historians as Flandrin, Lawrance Stone, Peter Laslett, Philippe Ariès, the seventeenth century in Europe marks a moment of essential realignment in the conception of the family which gradually shifts (under the impetus of an emerging precapitalist economy?) from that rather large, inchoate definition of those people who all live and work under the same (extended) roof, be they servants, kinsfolk or other dependents, to the more restricted sense of family as that limited group of blood-relations (parents and children) that the eighteenth century will come to cherish.[5] When we understand the seventeenth century as a period of radical change in both the epistemological and sexual configurations, configurations that are inextricably interwoven with the emerging changes in polity (the imposition of an absolutist conception of the monarchy) and economics (the beginnings of the first precapitalist ventures), we see that the family

rope, 1560–1660, ed. by Trevor Aston (New York Doubleday, 1967); Michel Foucault's *Les mots et les choses: Une archéologie des sciences humaines* (Paris: Gallimard, 1966 trans. *The Order of Things: An Archeology of the Human Sciences* (New York: Pantheon 1971); and *Folie et déraison*: *Histoire de la folie à l'âge classique* (Paris: Gallimard, 1961, trans. Richard Howard, *Madness and Civilization; A History of Insanity in the Age of Reason*, New York: Pantheon, 1965).

[2] "Now, this archaeological inquiry has revealed two great discontinuities in the *episteme* of Western culture: the first inaugurates the Classical age (roughly half-way through the seventeenth century) and the second, at the beginning of the nineteenth century, marks the beginning of the modern age" (*The Order of Things*, xxii).

[3] Cf. *La volonté de savoir: Histoire de la sexualité*, vol. 1 (Paris: Gallimard, 1976), trans. Robert Hurley, *The History of Sexuality*, vol. 1 (New York: Vintage, 1978).

[4] Jean-Louis Flandrin, *Familles, parenté, maison, sexualité dans l'ancienne société* (Paris: Seuil, 1976), 208.

[5] For a more detailed discussion, see Mitchell Greenberg, *Subjectivity and Subjugation in Seventeenth-Century Drama and Prose: The Family Romance of French Classicism*, (Cambridge: Cambridge University Press, 1992), introduction.

is situated as the focal point of these various intermeshings (insofar as the family's main function is to produce new subjects for this network, and thus to reproduce the network).[6] These configurations are not separate but intimately interwoven as the family becomes the center of a seamless roundelay where the economic, social, and political laws governing subjectivity are, by that very subjectivity they subtend, intermeshed with sexuality, in its pleasures and limits. The family thus becomes, in the words of Foucault, "the interchange of sexuality and alliance: it conveys the law and the juridical dimension in the deployment of sexuality; and it conveys the economy of pleasure and the intensity of sensations in the regime of alliance."[7]

In another context I have argued that we must view the theater of the seventeenth century as being essentially the arena in which an inchoate and as yet unbounded ideology of the family is essayed. It strikes me that here the theater's role is proleptically to represent changes in social formations that are still only immanent in society at large.[8] It seems like more than a fortuitous coincidence that the theater should be the privileged form of representation in a society undergoing such fundamental realignment of its most basic structures. Since Aristotle, critics have pointed to the mediating function of theater. The stage mediates between the individual and the collective in an extraordinarily charged moment of dramatic exchange. Anne Ubersfeld, in a Marxist-semiotic perspective, tells us that the theater "appears to be a privileged form of art of capital importance since it demonstrates better than other forms of art how the individual psyche is invested in a collective relation." Furthermore she goes on to say that "every theatrical text is the response to a desire on the part of the audience, and it is in this relation that the articulation of theatrical discourse with history and ideology is most easily made."[9] In a similar vein the French psychoanalyst André Green writes:

> Between the two, at the meeting-point of the individual and society, between the personal resonance of the work's content and its social function, art occupies a transitional position, which qualifies the domain of illusion, which permits an inhibited and displaced *jouissance* obtained by means of objects that both are and are not what they represent.[10]

[6] This "productive" definition of the family is taken from Louis Althusser's well-known essay "L'idéologie et appareils idéologiques de l'état," in *Positions* (Paris: Éditions Sociales, 1970).

[7] Foucault, *The History of Sexuality*, 108.

[8] I have been arguing for this view of the theater/family in my *Corneille, Classicism and the Ruses of Symmetry* (Cambridge, Cambridge University Press, 1986); *Subjectivity and Subjugation*, (Cambridge: Cambridge Un. Press, 1992) and most recently in *Canonical States, Canonical Stages: Oedipus, Othering and Seventeenth Century Drama* (Minneapolis: University of Minnesota Press, 1994).

[9] Anne Ubersfeld, *Lire le théâtre* (Paris: Éditions Sociales, 1978), 15 and 265.

[10] André Green, *Un oeil en trop, le complexe d'Oedipe dans la tragédie* (Paris: Minuit, 1969), trans. Alan Sheridan, *The Tragic Effect: The Oedipus Complex in Tragedy* (Cambridge: Cambridge University Press, 1979), 23.

In his book *The Place of the Stage*, Steven Mullaney, as the title suggests, seductively analyzes the mediating social function of the theater in Elizabethan England. Although he is obviously indebted to Foucault for much of his theoretical vision, Mullaney turns to Raymond Williams's work to argue persuasively for viewing cultural sites (such as the theater) as inclusive (of differences) rather than exclusive.[11] Although Mullaney makes much of the geographical ambivalence of the "place of the stage" in late sixteenth- and early seventeenth-century London, situated in a juridical no-mans-land between the city of London on the one hand and the feudal jurisdictions that prevailed beyond the city's limits on the other, he argues that the theater because of this "neither/nor" relation to law inscribed within itself these diverse and contradictory "jurisdictions."[12] While the French stage of the seventeenth century, unlike the English, was not ex-centric to the sites of power but, on the contrary, situated directly at the seats of power (at Versailles or in the bustle of Paris, at the Hôtel de Bourgogne or the Théâtre du Marais), surely the metaphysical role of the theater as a mediating locus of conflicting and contradictory discourses that Mullaney analyzes is equally valid for France. Although we have too easily a tendency to view the productions of France's great playwrights—Corneille, Racine, Molière—as representing, not unproblematically, but rather monolithically the hegemonic discourse of French Classicism as a reflection of the Absolutism of Richelieu and Louis XIV, we would do well to bear in mind Mullaney's rich redefinition of the role of dominant ideology in dramatic productions:

> Hegemonic culture is (moreover) a historical dynamic, an ongoing, diachronic negotiation between the old and the new. The dominant culture in any given period cannot hope to include or even account for all human aspirations and energies; present culture is continually limited, challenged or modified by culture past and culture yet to come.[13]

How are we to understand this meeting of pleasure and law/economics (*alliance*) in the conflicting representations of seventeenth-century theater? How are we to locate it, how did the seventeenth century locate it, if not by representing this strange configuration—this new configuration, emerging out of and still intimately inextricable from other, older subjective patterns—if not by incorporating this intermeshing network in/on/as the body?

[11] By this I mean that Mullaney and Williams seem to react to the early Foucault where Foucault is more interested in pointing to cultural "ruptures," to (too) clearly defined and separated phenomena, rather than to a later Foucault who, having modified his views, did come to see, especially in transitional periods such as the "baroque," the coexistence of varying and vying discursive possibilities. See Mullaney, *The Place of the Stage: License, Play and Power in Renaissance England* (Chicago: University of Chicago Press, 1988), and cf. for instance, Williams *Problems in Materialism and Culture: Selected Essays* (London: Verso, 1980).

[12] Mullaney, *The Place of the Stage*, cf. esp. the chap. 1, "Toward a Rhetoric of Space in Elizabethan London," 1–25.

[13] *The Place of the Stage*, 130. Here Mullaney is amplifying Williams's distinction between "residual" and "emergent" cultures.

I am speaking of those bodies of the passionate, comic personages that the seventeenth century figures for us (and this is not the least of its radical representations of the human subject) within the dramatic scenarios (the first in European literature) of the family—the family that is born on the stage with all the passion and rage of a deeply conflicted sexuality, and all its comic hilarity too.

But what are we to make of these bodies given to us in representation? Is there a reality there that points to anything other than precisely the configuration and reconfiguration of discursive practices? For, and this is my point here, the body does not exist, is not available to us in some empirical "thereness" but always as a complex nexus of ideological investments. Just as we have seen that for critics, despite their different theoretical perspectives, the theater was perceived as a mediating locus so too, the body is another construct that different critics, especially recent critics of early modern culture, refuse to see as simply a biological given. Although it is the body as cadaver that in an objectifying gaze receives the attention of the seventeenth century anatomist, it is precisely not this "object" that contemporary theoreticians analyze in their discussions. Much recent work, from scholars in varying disciplines, has been brought to bear on the "body" in these cultures, so near, and yet so removed from us. In *The Tremulous Private Body*, for instance, one of the most provocative recent attempts to circumscribe the site and function of the body in early modern culture, Francis Barker argues for seeing the body as "not a hypostasized object, still less a simple biological mechanism of given desires and needs acted on externally by controls and enticements, but a relation in a system of liaisons which are material, discursive, psychic, sexual, but without stop or centre."[14] In their book *The Politics and Poetics of Transgression*, Peter Stallybrass and Allon White, who share many of the same materialist premises of Barker, insist that the "body cannot be thought separately from the social formation, symbolic topography and the constitution of the subject. The body is neither a purely natural given nor is it merely a textual metaphor, it is a privileged operator for the transcoding of these other areas. Thinking the body is thinking social topography and vice versa."[15] In a more new historicist' perspective Gail Kern Paster has written persuasively about seventeenth-century English society's relation to the body. In her *The Body Embarrassed: Drama and the Discipline of Shame in Early Modern England*, she too returns to this complex nexus of intermeshing imperatives that we call the "body": "In the continuous series of negotiations by which the body is inscribed as a social text it also becomes a social 'sub' or 'infra' text, the outward manifestation of an container for desire's inner workings, less visi-

[14] Francis Barker, *The Tremulous Private Body: Essays in Subjection* (London: Methuen, 1984), 12.)

[15] Peter Stallybrass and Allon White, *The Politics and Poetics of Transgression* (Ithaca: Cornell University Press, 1986), 192.

ble than the external habitus but no less subject to social formation and judgments."[16]

In a sense all of these works owe a great debt, on the one hand, to Mikhail Bakhtin's study of Rabelais (to which I shall return in a moment) and, on the other, to the work of anthropologist Mary Douglas. Douglas's influential *Purity and Danger: An Analysis of the Concepts of Pollution and Taboo* provides a structural account of the social symbolization of the body which is congenial to critics who wish precisely to deal with the body as a symbolic system without appealing to the symbolizing processes of psychoanalysis. Douglas's study of the interpretive strategies at work in archaic and primitive societies, where the body is seen as a reflection of the larger world and vice versa, has proved particularly useful as a critical tool, as it seems in a strangely sympathetic fashion to mirror early modern Europe's own interpretive, that is, "analogic" (in Foucault's terms) perception of the world (man being a microcosm that reflects the macrocosm):

> The body is a model which can stand for any bounded system. Its boundaries can represent any boundaries which are threatened or precarious. The body is a complex structure. The functions of its different parts and their relations afford a source of symbols for other complex structures. We cannot possibly interpret rituals concerning excreta, breast milk, saliva and the rest unless we are prepared to see in the body a symbol of society, and to see the powers and dangers credited to social structures reproduced in small on the human body.[17]

From Freud's early studies on hysteria, psychoanalysis has also taught us that the body is a symbolic production. By this is meant of course that there is a complex interweave of the physical and psychic functions in which is produced a "phantasmatic" image in each of us of our own corporeality. Our bodily image reflects as much of how we are inserted in the symbolic, signifying systems of our culture as how that culture is manifested in and as that image.[18] As the French psychoanalyst and critic Guy Rosolato writes, "we cannot approach the subject of the formation of the body image without bearing in mind the complex interaction of libidinal investments, the imaginary narcississtic apprehension of images, and the substitutive and symbolic potential of language which directs identification in general."[19]

[16] Gail Kern Paster, *The Body Embarrassed: Drama and the Discipline of Shame in Early Modern England* (Ithaca: Cornell University Press, 1993), 4.

[17] Mary Douglas, *Purity and Danger: An Analysis of the Concepts of Pollution and Taboo* (London: Routledge and Kegan Paul, 1966), 115.

[18] For a feminist psychoanalytic reading of hysteria, see Monique David-Ménard, *L'hystérique entre Freud et Lacan: Corps et langage en psychanalyse* (Paris: Éditions Universitaires, 1983), trans. Catherine Porter, *Hysteria from Freud to Lacan: Body and Language in Psychoanalysis*, (Ithaca: Cornell University Press, 1989).

[19] Cf. for example these preliminary remarks of Guy Rosolato, in his introductory essay, "Recension du corps," in *Lieux du corps* issue of *Nouvelle Revue de Psychanalyse*, no. 3 (spring 1971): 17. Elaborating even more explicitly on this same idea, François Gantheret, in

The body is inscribed at the interstice of "reality" (social, economic, physiological) and "fantasy" (desire). Furthermore this split between reality and desire is never unilateral, there is no perception of the body—one's own, or others'—that can be separated out from the desiring, phantasmatic structures into which it is inserted, and which it reproduces as its symptoms at the same time, of course, that these "phantasmatic" structures bear the impress of exterior social imperatives.[20]

These different attempts to circumscribe the body in either social-anthropological or psychoanalytical grids, although in many important aspects antithetical in the basic assumptions, can be bridged, it seems to me, by an appeal to the very process of "symbolization" which underpins them all. In a sense Stallybrass and White are provocatively suggestive when they offer the hypothesis: "It might . . . seem plausible to view the discourses of neurosis as the psychic eruption of social practices which have been suppressed."[21] Stallybrass and White of course are referring in their analysis to the evolution of "bourgeois culture" during the nineteenth century. Nevertheless, it seems to me that their remark may be generalized to speak about the symptomatic resistances that the appeal to the body represents in all cultures in crisis, in those fraught historical moments, to return to the conundrum of seventeenth-century France, of history's "becoming."

In the seventeenth century, and particularly on the seventeenth-century stage, questions of the body are inextricably tied to the way(s) the different comic or tragic scenarios insert the body, the body of their contentious protagonist, into the social, sexual, and economic parameters that are waiting to accommodate them. Marriage is the most overdetermined social/sexual apparatus in which and through which the sexed bodies of the seventeenth century are inserted into the familial narratives that Janus-like point both toward the past from whence the subject comes and forward into the future of renewed familial generations. Marriage, by serving as the crossroads in which and by which the past and the future generations meet in the newly consecrated heterosexual couple, serves the oedipal scenario where the difference of generations and of sexes becomes the crucial dilemma that the fractious Classical protagonist must successfully navigate in order to assume his/her proper place in absolutist society.

Where are we to situate Molière, and his cast of characters in the oedipal

---

the same issue, writes, "The body becomes symbolic only when it enters into a relation of meaning with other elements by substituting itself as a symbol for the repressed. There is symbolization only at the intersection of a series of associations and through an anchoring in a signifying system, only when an imaginary series, attaching itself to a biological reality acquires the value of a sign, that is, becomes a part of a system" ("Remarque sur la place et le statut du corps en psychanalyse," 142).

[20] For the important impossible distinction in psychic life between reality and fantasy, cf. Jean Laplanche, *Problématiques*, esp. vol. 2, *Castration, Symbolisations*, and vol. 3 *La Sublimation* (Paris: P.U.F, 1980).

[21] Stallybrass and White, *The Politics and Poetics of Transgression*, 176.

scheme of things? On the one hand we might say that his comedy, which plays out the same scenario over and over again, a scenario in which curmudgeonly *barbons* are continually outwitted and ridiculed by cunning servants and innocent young lovers, besides repeating a culturally inherited scenario, also affirms by this very repetition a social and sexual narrative in which normal love ("nature") successfully parries the invasive threats of perversion. In this overly simplified account of Molière's sexual plots he would clearly seem to proclaim his alignment with and affirmation of a normative oedipal scenario: the triumph of the young (male) over the old (father) for the possession of the coveted sexual (female) prize. On the other hand, a much more ambivalent response might just as well be in order. To begin with, it might be responded that the initial question is flawed, presenting as a universalizing account of sexuality (the oedipal scheme) what for many is a historically circumscribed production of a particular period and culture (late-nineteenth-century Vienna). What can an "oedipal scenario," the product of a developed bourgeois society, its prejudices and peculiarities, have to do with a seventeenth-century playwright and his cast of characters—living and play acting in a world whose subjective parameters are clearly different from, not to say entirely alien to, those of Freud and his patients?

For the time being, rather then situate myself on one side or the other of this dilemma, I shall fence-sit by saying that the question is not as simple as it might first appear and that it admits of no easy answer, neither the apparent transparency of plot, nor the equally simplistic dismissal by those who refuse to look at any early modern social production though the twentieth-century's (supposedly distorting) lenses. When we examine the Molieresque corpus within the complex social networking of seventeenth-century France, we see that what a certain critical shorthand describes as the oedipal problematic does not admit of unidimensional answers. Rather, at the same time that any consideration of the oedipal scenario is necessarily an examination of the sexual (defined in its broadest sense), it is also inseparably linked to the social, political, economic, and religious coordinates that in any culture attend the arrival of the newly born human subject and attend this subject's inscription in his or her culture. These coordinates lay out for the infant an intricately elaborated labyrinth that s/he must negotiate in order to be eventually recognized by that culture as a viable "man" or "woman." That this path is convoluted, full of obstacles, ruts, and dead ends, is readily apparent. One only has to look at those members whom society has branded as its pariahs, those internal outsiders who for reasons that are never quite comprehensible appear (as often as not to themselves and to the others in whose gaze they stand) and are defined as having definitely and inexplicably at one moment or another of their past taken a wrong turn. They remain forever fixed in a position from which there is no return. This point of no return, this position of failed social negotiations, can be ritualistically encoded by the community only with rites of exclusion, either a sacred exclusion (shamanistic), or a ridiculous one (from laughter). In either case the community defends itself from the difference in its midst by taking its revenge on the person who has let it down, who is viewed, if we wish to use a cruel economic metaphor, as having squandered its psychic (mythic, ideological) capital, and who remains, within the psychic (but also very much within the real) economy of that community in the position of dilapidation, representing a waste of economic potential.

For Oedipus in his myth is not only about sexuality. He is, the myth is, also about "sexuality" as community, sexuality connected to yet inextricable from politics, from the economic, social, and mythic interweave that is necessary to constitute any human grouping as a society.[22] Sexuality, therefore, especially reduced to its narrow confines of genitality is not what is at issue here, but rather sexuality in the much larger sense—the scenario of an economy of desire—in which capitalization, exchange, propagation and generation are all inseparable from the particular structures of political power that are at work, in different ways at different times, to produce what any given society names as its own or rejects as its other.

Let us then return to the seventeenth century, using in this case two plays of Molière, to trace the ways a certain dramaturgy figures the transformations of the human subject in the period between the end of the Renaissance and the apogee of the Classical moment. In so doing I hope to be able to circumscribe the emergence of the subject of modernity in its varied convolutions, with the acuity of vision that is permitted, paradoxically, only as this subject, objectified in our attentive gaze, is, so we are told, disappearing forever from our field of vision.

Molière's last play, *Le malade imaginaire*, during the fourth performance of which he suffered his fatal (tubercular?) attack, was written to be staged in celebration of Louis XIV's triumphal return from his Dutch campaign (1672). It was first given on February 10, 1673, that is, if we consult the ecclesiastical calendar, during carnival. At the very end of the comedy, in the concluding lines of Béralde, Argan's brother, there is a direct reference to carnival, and to those liberties that traditionally are permitted during the pre-Lenten festivities. In response to Angélique's timid protest that perhaps the masquerade proposed by Béralde is too cruel a joke to play on Argan, Béralde responds:

> Mais, ma nièce, ce n'est pas tant le jouer que s'accommoder à ses fantaisies. Tout ceci n'est qu'entre nous. Nous y pouvons aussi prendre chacun un per-

[22] Cf. Marie Delcourt, *Oedipe ou la légende du conquérant* (Paris: Faculté de philosophie et lettres, 1944), xxxi: "The story of Oedipus is certainly the most complete of all political myths."

sonnage, et nous donner ainsi la comédie les uns aux autres. Le carnaval autorise cela.[23] (III. xiv; 4:454)

Carnival forms the overarching structure inside of which *Le malade imaginaire* plays out its farcical attack on seventeenth-century medicine in and across the body of the hypochondriac, Argan. These obvious references to carnival and the carnivalesque allow me to fix our attention on two highly invested moments in the history of modern literary/social criticism which will form the outside parameters of my own discussion of Molière, and the subject of political modernity—at the one end of my spectrum I situate Bakhtin, and more precisely, his much commented, highly debated idea of the "carnivalesque," and at the other Freud, or rather a certain twentieth-century "psychoanalytical" vision of the human subject. In between, torn between the one and the other, objects of mediation and change, I shall place Molière, or rather those two characters of Moliere's theater, Harpagon and Argan, the protagonists of *L'avare* and *Le malade imaginaire.*

Bakhtin's rich use of the term "carnivalesque," and the carnivalesque ("grotesque") body to describe what he believed to be a different, premodern subjectivity, exemplified most notably by Rabelais, has proven to be an extremely fertile concept for contemporary criticism. Although the concept is so widely used as to be familiar to most students of the sixteenth and seventeenth centuries I shall highlight just a few aspects of the notion that I find particularly useful for my own discussion. First of all, Bakhtin's description of the carnivalesque body is authorized in his book by its dialectical relation to its supposedly historically later, other—the closed Classical body. In other words the distinction between a carnivalesque and the Classical is one other way of delimiting the difference, the perceived difference in the periods of the Middle Ages and Renaissance from the Classical and modern age. This distinction is, thus, superimposable, it seems to me, on the Foucauldian separation of these two periods—on the one hand the analogic universe of the Renaissance, on the other, and this after the moment of "the great enclosure," the period of Classical representation. I want to stress once again how periods of transition lend themselves to binary powered oppositions, how difficult it is to conceive of the imbrication, the moment of mediation in which the oppositions, not yet separated out, form an inchoate whole.

For Bakhtin, then, here is the grotesque body:

> The grotesque body . . . is a body in the act of becoming. It is never finished, never completed; it is continually built, created, and builds and creates another

[23] All references to Molière are to Molière, *Oeuvres complètes*, 4 vols. (Paris: Flammarion, 1979), *L'avare* (vol. 3), *Le malade imaginaire* (vol. 4). Act and scene numbers are given first in references, followed by volume and page numbers.

> body. Moreover, the body swallows the world and is itself swallowed by the world . . . This is why the essential role belongs to those parts of the grotesque body in which it outgrows its own self, transgressing its own body, in which it conceives a new second body: the bowels and the phallus. These two areas play the leading role in the grotesque image, and it is precisely for this reason that they are predominantly subject to positive exaggeration, to hyperbolization; they can even detach themselves from the body and lead an independent life, for they hide the rest of the body, as something secondary. . . . Next to the bowels and the genital organs is the mouth, through which enters the world to be swallowed up. And next is the anus. All these convexities and orifices have a common characteristic; it is within them that the confines between bodies and between the body and the world are overcome: there is an interchange and an interorientation. This is why the main events in the life of the grotesque body, the acts of the bodily drama, take place in this sphere. Eating, drinking, defecation and other elimination (sweating, blowing of the nose, sneezing), as well as copulation, pregnancy, dismemberment, swallowing up by another body—all these acts are performed on the confines of the body and the outer world, or on the confines of the old and new body. In all these events the beginning and end of life are closely linked and interwoven.[24]

I have quoted this passage extensively because it is important for its description of the grotesque body as a body of organic excess, of openness, of incompletion, in a constantly renewable cycle of life and death. The grotesque is a body that knows no limits, to which limits are death. The social activity that corresponds to the grotesque body is, of course, the carnival which Bakhtin tells us cannot be though of as a function that "distinguishes," or separates out. Once again it is not a (social) organism that creates an exterior and an interior, an in and out: "Carnival is not a spectacle seen by the people: they live in it, and every one participates because it very idea embraces all the people."[25] The utopian, perhaps naively utopian aspect of Bakhtin's description of carnival has been severely criticized by almost all contemporary scholars who have adopted, nevertheless, his delineations of both the grotesque body and the carnival as heuristic devises in their own work.[26]

Although the concept of the grotesque body may be but one way among

[24] Mikhail Bakhtin, *Rabelais and His World*, trans. Helen Iswolsky, (Cambridge Mass.: M.I.T. Press, 1968), 317.

[25] Ibid., 7.

[26] Perhaps the richest use of Bakhtin is by Stallybrass and White. They are careful, however, to distinguish between this optimistic, utopic, and perhaps a-political invocation of carnival and a more nuanced perception. See *The Politics and Poetics of Transgression*, " the politics of carnival cannot be resolved outside of a close historical examination of particular conjunctures: there is not a-priori revolutionary vector to carnival and transgression" (16), and also "the problems raised so far concerning the politics of carnival: its nostalgia; its uncritical populism (carnival often violently abuses and demonizes weaker, not stronger, social groups—women, ethnic and religious minorities, those who 'don't belong'—in a process of displaced abjection); its failure to do away with the official dominant culture, its licensed complicity" (19).

many to describe a different subjective imbrication of the human being in an epistemic formation that has become for us but a nostalgic memory, it does seem to correspond, as an image, to the medical science of the late Middle Ages and the early modern period. Such historians as Thomas Laquer or Caroline Walker-Bynum and literary scholars such as Marie-Hélène Huet and Gail Kern Paster have reminded us not only of the principles of Galenic medicine but of the enormous patriarchal investments such a humoral conception of the human body both obfuscates and reveals.[27] The early modern English and, we can assume, French subject, according to Paster, "grew up with an understanding of his or her body as a semipermeable, irrigated container in which humors moved sluggishly. People imagined that health consisted of a state of internal solubility to be perilously maintained often through a variety of evacuations either self-administered or in consultation with a healer."[28] Obviously, in the masculinized ideology that informed such a conception of the body, the male body was the ideal object of creation, being both more "hot" than the female, and particularly more "closed."[29] The female body because of its effluents was famously described as a "leaky vessel," tautologically dangerous for a society that in the seventeenth century was growing increasingly wary of any "unbounded system."[30]

On the one hand, therefore, we have the open, unfinished, female grotesque body, on the other the Classical closed, male body. And who best represented the shining ideal of bodily and political perfection but the king, the extolled, idolized, and triumphant Louis XIV? *Le malade imaginaire,* let us remember, was written as part of the ceremonies celebrating Louis's triumphal return from the Dutch campaign of 1672. The French had gone off to punish the too-wealthy, too-commercially successful, too-Protestant Dutch Republic. Although the purpose of this particular military action undertaken by the French with Louis at their head was not ostensibly to enlarge their territory, the campaign must obviously be seen as forming an in-

[27] Caroline Walker-Bynum, *Fragmentation and Redemption: Essays on Gender and the Human Body in Medieval Religion* (New York: Zone Books, 1992) particularly chaps. 3, 4, 6; Marie-Hélène Huet, *Monstrous Imagination* (Cambridge Mass.: Harvard University Press, 1994) Thomas Laqueur, *Making Sex: Body and Gender from the Greeks to Freud*, (Cambridge Mass.: Harvard University Press, 1990); Paster, *The Body Embarrassed*

[28] Paster, *The Body Embarrassed*, 8.

[29] Walker-Bynum succinctly sums up the patriarchal ideology of Galenic medical theory: "Ancient biology, especially in its Aristotelian form, made the male body paradigmatic. The male was the form or quiddity of what we are as humans; what was particularly womanly was the unformed-ness, the stuff-ness or physicality, of our humanness. Such a notion identified woman with breaches in boundaries, with lack of shape or definition, with opening and exudings and spillings forth. But this conception also, we should note, put men and women on a continuum. All human beings were form and matter. Women were merely less of what men were more" *(Fragmentation and Redemption*, 109).

[30] Cf. Paster, *The Body Embarrassed*, 25: "Representations of the female body as a leaking vessel display that body as beyond the control of the female subject, and thus as threatening the acquisitive goal of the family and its maintenance of status and power."

tegral part of the policy of territorial aggrandizement of the French state under both Louis XIII and Louis XIV. Rather then simply a disguised form of landgrabbing such as those pre-Classical dynastic marriages, with the ensuing back-and-forth bickering over what territories did and did not become a permanent part of the crown (although, this activity too continues throughout the century, witness the Clèves-Juliers affair), the territorial policy of the French crown in the seventeenth century becomes essentially a consistent and organized attempt to secure natural boundaries (natural in the sense of geography or cultural spheres) for the state. These borders, once secured, were thought to protect the state from the vulnerability of openness. By closing off the frontiers—at the Pyrenees, the Rhine, the Atlantic coast—France became a secured, bounded entity. Once of course this entity was separated out from and defended against external threats, attention could then be directed at securing the internal vulnerabilities of the state. When the outside was kept at bay, the inside could be cleansed of those troublesome others who undermined the state from within: the Huguenots are expulsed (1685), pushed beyond the borders of the realm.

I am suggesting simply that a homology is working throughout the seventeenth century between the geographic integrity of the realm and the ideal of a classical body which Bakhtin defines in the following way: "The new bodily canon . . . presents an entirely finished, completed, strictly limited body, which is shown from the outside as something individual. That which protrudes, bulges, sprouts, or branches off . . . is eliminated, hidden or moderated. All orifices of the body are closed."[31] Mary Douglas, as I mentioned above, has spoken about this analogy between the social body and the physical body in an attempt to equate how the fear of permeable social/political boundaries is reflected by the anxiety associated with bodily orifices, margins: "Any structure of ideas is vulnerable at its margins. We should expect the orifices of the body to symbolize its specially vulnerable points."[32] In a world where precisely not only the political boundaries were in flux but the prevalent (although changing) medical notion of the body was one of contained but infinitely variable fluidity, anxiety about borders, openings, bodily orifices would seem, on still another level, to symbolize a ceaseless back-and-forth dialectic, a struggle between chaos and order, between bodily and social disintegration and societal stability and governance. To instill the conception of an integral body politic in the individual subject, an image must be substantiated which is at once familiar and august, both near and distant. The idea of the state must be made to correspond to the image of the individual body just as the image of the body (of the subject) is made to mediate the distance separating metaphysical ideol-

[31] Bakhtin, *Rabelais and His World*, 320.
[32] Douglas, *Purity and Danger*, 121.

ogy from an anchoring in the physical. The conception of the body fixes the ideological aporia of the state by first identifying with what is recognizably similar in the body of the God/prince and then by denying this equivalence in a metaphysical leap beyond the physical body of the king to his other body—the body royal wherein the state in its transcendental essence resides. The body that mediates between the transcendental concept of the perfect state, and the physical reality of the body in its evanescence becomes fixed upon the shining body Royal, the "corps glorieux" of the king: Louis XIV as he was produced in and as a spectacular embodiment of the ideals toward which the French state moved.[33]

The constant pressure throughout the century to eliminate the extravagant, the obtrusive, the vulgar—the movement that we have come to define as the refining so essential to our contemporary views of French culture this finesse that is the quintessence of abstract sophistication, that marks French Classicism off from the excesses of seventeenth-century English or Spanish culture, so shot through with plebeian elements rather than some simple given of cultural superiority—is the product of a long politicoesthetic struggle to impose order on a threatening chaos.[34] This imposition however was contested and hotly resisted—the Frondes, the peasant rebellions, the Protestant revolts—to name just the most obvious political manifestations. It was a long ongoing struggle, often bloody, in which the first modern totalitarian state attempted with more or less success to impose a homogenous image by subsuming the state in and under the image of the king—finally the image of the Classical male body—on the heterogeneous mixture of French life.

The important point to bear in mind, however, the point Stallybrass and White stress, is the dialectical nature of this change, the way, even as we see in Bakhtin, one form ("the grotesque") exists in an inextricable relation to its other ("the Classical"):

> The classical body splits precisely along the rigid edge which is its defense against heterogeneity: Its closure and purity are quite illusory and it will per-

[33] For a lengthy discussion of the idea of the king, as a representation, as "spectacle," see: Jean-Marie Apostolidès, *Le roi machine*, and the works of Louis Marin, *Portrait of the King* and *Food for Thought*. The by-now classic study of medieval theologico-politics that underlies the above mentioned works is Ernst Kantorowicz, *The King's Two Bodies: A Study in Medieval Political Theology*. (Full references to these works are in introduction, n.7.)

[34] Throughout *The Tremulous Private Body* Barker speaks of the seventeenth century as the period that eliminated the body from discourse. Cf. his comments, for instance, on the "Cartesian body," 99: " The Cartesian body is 'outside' language; it is given to discourse as an object (when it is not in its absent moment exiled altogether) but it is never of language in its essence." In a sense, Barker's argument could be extended to the entire movement of seventeenth-century bienséances as it was imposed upon the rhetorical, theatrical, and artistic practice throughout the century. As many have noted, the French stage becomes disembodied, the characters appearing finally as "talking heads."

> petually rediscover in itself, often with a sense of shock or inner revulsion, the grotesque, the protean and the motley, the neither/nor, the double negation of high and low which was the very precondition for its social identity.[35]

So, although the glorious body royal becomes an icon too sacred to be touched and remaining incorruptible even into advanced old age,[36] the king's surrogate, the father, the king of his family, lends himself to more ambivalence, to the ambivalence of the clash of cultural codes and values, in a way that is more tragic and more comic than the "real" hieratic image of the *père du peuple* ever could.[37]

Borrowing the term "oikodespotès" from Jürgen Habermas who uses it to describe familial-economic organization in Greek society, I suggest that the word fits admirably into our own purposes as a way of introducing the sociosexual dimension of the role of the father in Molière's comedy.[38] It combines the etymological connotations of house and home (and by extension husbandry, household-economy) with the term for controller, ruler. This latter term echoes with the proleptic resonance of despot, tyrant, dictator and in this sense sends us back to the metaphorical conundrum uniting father/king in seventeenth-century culture. The father remains, for seventeenth-century patriarchy, the central figure in familial economy. I think it best to map the economic change, the change that is written on the bodies of these men, and this is, I suggest, interestingly perverse—because, in the Classical period we are discussing, "men" and "bodies" have almost become exclusionary terms. In the emerging redistribution of patriarchal monarchies that mark the introduction of the modern, men who are the arbiters of value and meaning, who are at work in the chancelleries, in the learned societies, in the amphitheaters where more and more readily anatomical dissections and lessons are carried out accentuate the split between the body and the soul, the body and the mind. This metaphysical difference becomes, true to its roots in Aristotelian logic, even more the split between male and female, between masculine and feminine. In this split, women are essentialized as "le sexe" for the men who, although they may "have a sex," certainly refuse any notion that they are "le sexe."[39]

35 Stallybrass and White, *The Politics and Poetics of Transgression*, 113.

36 See, for instance, Marin's discussion of the "body" of Louis XIV in Rigaud's regal portrait, "The Portrait of the King's Glorious Body" (189–217), in *Food for Thought*.

37 For an analysis of the declension, so important for Absolutism, of the slippage the word "father" precipitates from God the father, to the king as "father of his people," to, finally, the father as head of the individual household, see the introduction to Greenberg, *Subjectivity and Subjugation*.

38 Jürgen Habermas, *L'espace public*, French translation, Marc de Launay (Paris: Payot, 1985), 13–17.

39 Barker, talking of this same split, writes: " It is with an identical gesture that the modern structure . . . excludes the body from the proper realm of discourse and simultaneously genders that very structuration. . . . For if the new regime in inaugurating itself deploys a pattern of speech and silence, a semiosis in which the discoursing 'I' is held to be constitutive then it is

"Le sexe" of course, is always the "other," the female other, who in the emergent order of corporate statism, proves all the more necessary for the economic distribution of wealth accumulated and passed down in patrilineal descent. Thus, on the most simple level, the confusion, the heated confusion of "le sexe," sex and money, comes to rest on that roc incontournable of (emergent) bourgeois economies—marriage. It is in terms of marriage that sex and money are inextricably linked to desire and the body politic in Molière's comedy, be it the serious comedy of *L'avare* or the more carnivalesque farce of *Le malade imaginaire,* and they are linked most forcefully though paternal mediation, a mediation that in Molière is always comic because of a flaw in the father that puts him at odds with the system, its values, ideals, and simulacra that he is supposed to embody.

Let us turn our attention to the two father/protagonists of *Le malade imaginaire* and *L'avare* and, rather than view them as separate, exclusive entities (which on the textual level they obviously are), look at them as two sides of the same conflicted coin—the site of political, economic, and sexual agencies that traverse their representation, their beings, their "bodies." On the one side we have a pull toward the carnivalesque, toward the grotesque body, the lower bodily stratum, the body of birthing, of excretion, the open, organic, constantly evolving body, even (if we wish to follow the logic of Bahktin) the maternal body. On the other there is a pull toward the classical, the closed precapitalist body of state corporatism as it reaches its apogee in Louis XIV's France, the body of the father, of the law, the oedipal body of emerging modernity. In other words, it is in and across the body of Harpagon/Argan that Molière traces the emergence—with all its conflicts and tensions, all its halts, insecurities, and regressions—of the *mise-en-place* of the modern. He does this by the ways he incorporates the bodies of the father(s) within the intermeshing flow, through and across these bodies of different but interrelated economies—the economy of excreta (the anal economy), the economy of material exchange (the precapitalist economy of conflict between systems of inheritance and systems of venture capitalism), and the mixed economy of oedipal sexuality (genital and material, i.e., the marriage economy). That these different economies exist together, that one really is not easily isolated from the others, is what makes Molière's plays so

clear that the designated woman is positioned extraneously to the constitutive centre where the male voice speaks: The woman is allotted to the place of the body outside discourse and therefore also outside the pertinent domain of legitimate subjecthood" (*The Tremulous Private Body,* 100). Eugène Enriquez, (*De la horde à l'état: Essai de psychanalyse du lien social* [Paris: Gallimard, 1986], 274) writes:"It is only later when incest has been prohibited that the vision will be born and developed of woman as the archaic devouring mother, or of the woman empowered by a precocious sexuality and thus able to exclude men from her intense pleasure, or having such an overabundant sexuality that men can only be overcome by it. It is the triumph of men that engenders the fear of women. The body of man is thus as much in question as the body of the woman. But man has successfully engineered this forceful 'coup' of having eliminated his body from the comparison."

perversely comic; for in another sense these different economies of plot and character are all subsumed in the economy of laughter which they generate and which, in turn, effects our own system, the audience's system, of bodily economies.

I have already mentioned the carnivalesque framing inside of which *Le malade imaginaire* is inscribed. If we look at *L'avare*, written and performed five years earlier (1668), we find repeatedly stamped in its very center that other, diluted, Bakhtinian category, the "fair." In his attempts at courting Mariane, Harpagon has enlisted the services of Frosine, a go-between. On Harpagon's behalf Frosine has arranged for Mariane pay a visit to Elise, Harpagon's own daughter, and while waiting to dine with the Harpagon family, to accompany her to the fair:[40]

> HARPAGON: C'est que je suis obligé, Frosine, de donner à souper au seigneur Anselme; et je serai bien aise qu'elle soit du régal.
> FROSINE: Vous avez raison. Elle doit, après dîner, rendre visite à votre fille, d'où elle fait son compte d'aller faire un tour à la foire, pour venir ensuite au souper.
> HARPAGON: Hé bien! elles iront ensemble dans mon carrosse, que je leur prêterai. (II,v; 3:346–47)

I point to this apparently inconsequential plot devise because for, as marginal as it seems, it indicates for us another inscription of a public economic locus that in its contrast to the invocation of carnival in the *Malade imaginaire* is revelatory of at least a competing economic sphere coexisting simultaneously in Molière's theatrical universe. While the carnival is used as a metaphor for unlimited spending, for a world that knows no bounds, that knows no hoarding, and while it thus corresponds economically to a (utopian) world of indifference (i.e., wealth in the capitalist sense, of individual, separate possession, is negated in the vast, unregulated carnivalesque disbursing), the fair, as Stallybrass and White tell us, is a much more ambivalent economic locus:

> In so far as it was purely a commercial event it could be envisaged as a practical agency in the progress of capital, an instrument of modernization and a means of connecting up local and communal "markets" to the world market. . . . From the perspective of cultural studies, folklore and social history, the fair has been predominantly thought of in terms of popular revelry and political subversion. From the perspective of economic history . . . fairs have been seen above all as the sites of commercial distribution whose rise and fall depended upon national and international market forces.[41]

[40] Paris had several major fairs, of course. The most important were the Foire St. Germain and the Foire St. Laurent. It is not clear to which of these fairs Molière is referring.

[41] Stallybrass and White, *The Politics and Poetics of Transgression*, 30.

So, in the one case, at least at the very outset, we have a comedy, *Le malade imaginaire*, that with its reference to carnival would seem to be backward looking, economically speaking, while the other *L'avare*, with its reference to the fair, would appear to be pointing toward the (capitalist) future, at least insofar as the realities of seventeenth-century economic life seem to intrude within the confines of the play. This division is, of course, only a heuristic devise: quite clearly what we have is the coexistence in Molière's theater of the transitional moment, the moment that contains both systems, without choosing between them.[42] But let us for the time being continue to view these two plays as representing clearly opposed worldviews, two radically separated views of economics realities. How then are these exterior differences embodied in the comedies?

Argan, the hypochondriacal father of *Le malade imaginaire* is evidently a wealthy bourgeois who, as the introductory scene shows us, is, even in throes of his mania, very close to his *sous*. The play begins with Argan counting his different medications and calculating their cost.

> Trois et deux font cinq, et cinq font dix et dix font vingt. Trois et deux font cinq. "Plus, du vingt-quatrième, un petit clystère insinuatif, préparatif, et rémollient, pour amollir, humecter, et rafraîchir les entrailles de Monsieur." Ce qui me plaît de Monsieur Fleurant, mon apothicaire, c'est que ses parties sont toujours fort civiles: "les entrailles de Monsieur, trente sols." Oui, mais, Monsieur Fleurant, ce n'est pas tout que d'être civil, il faut être aussi raisonnable, et ne pas écorcher les malades. Trente sols un lavement: Je suis votre serviteur, je vous l'ai déjà dit. Vous ne me les avez mis dans les autres parties qu'à vingt sols, et vingt sols en langage d'apothicaire, c'est-à-dire dix sols; les voilà, dix sols. (I.i; 4:388)

Argan is ill, so he believes, and because he is ill with a sickness unto death ("Ah mon Dieu! Ils me laisseront ici mourir"), he desperately tries to restore his health, or at least maintain it in its precarious equilibrium, by fetishistic ministrations to his bowels, ministrations for which he pays dearly. But although from the very beginning the comedy establishes a running equation between the economy of the body and the economy of the marketplace, the laughter of this play is generated by the former rather than the latter. The entire play's comedy turns around the obsessive references Argan makes to his excretory functions. He is continually administering to himself or having others administer to him purges, enemas, and the like. Of all the works in the French canon, including Rabelais's oeuvre no other is so persistently

[42] But is this really so? Why then the qualitative difference of esthetic judgment? Why is *L'avare* a *grande comédie*, while the *Malade* is but a farce. Doesn't this hierarchy already speak, or does it only come later, for the (capitalist) future rather than for the (carnivalesque) past?

scatological, no other as André Glucksmann informs us, so insistently rubs our noses in shit.[43]

For a twentieth-century audience Argan's obsession with his bowels appears much more "symptomatic" than what a contemporary seventeenth-century public would at first notice. In the seventeenth century, during which prevailed, as I mentioned above, a humoral concept of the body, purges, that is the artificially induced elimination of "nefarious" internal "humors," were, as Paster reminds us, a quotidinally familiar treatment. Most of the audience would often have had purges administered to them.[44] The desired effect of these purges was to reestablish a harmonious equilibrium in the body that illness had disturbed. Clearly, however, Argan's attention to his bowel functions, his obsessive interest in maintaining a constant "ebb and flow" of intake and output, goes beyond the socially accepted limits of his time (that is why there is laughter, but not why there is riotous laughter) and places him in the realm of the scatologically outrageous.

If Argan focuses obsessively on his bowels, it is properly because in any society that puts a high price on order, on closure, on a complete, integral structure (any society, in other words, which views the father as embodying a totalizing fantasy of corporate integrity—patriarchy, in sum), the anus is that bodily orifice that first comes up against the social imperatives of renunciation.[45] The control of bodily excretions becomes the locus of a continuing battle between the internal economy of the infant and the external law of his world. It is a battle whose consequences, so Freud tells us, has repercussions on the entire future sociosexual life of the individual. In the *Three Essays on the Theory of Sexuality*, Freud first describes the importance of the "anal zone": "It is to be presumed that the erotogenic significance of this part of the body is very great from the first. We learn with some astonishment from psycho-analysis of the transmutations normally undergone by the sexual excitations arising from this zone and of the frequency with which it retains a considerable amount of susceptibility to genital stimulation throughout life."[46] It is this genital excitability that is, once again according to analytic theory, like all forms of infantile pleasure, so difficult to renounce. Under the pressure of society the anal zone becomes the object of the child's first struggle with the law, the law that says "no":

43 André Glucksmann, *La bêtise* (Paris: Grasset, 1985), 233 "There is no more daring play in the western repertory. *Le Malade Imaginaire* pushes the spectator's nose in shit. Never before, never after, has the theater presented such purtrefaction, floating in an almost nauseating sweatiness."

44 Paster, *The Body Embarrassed*, 113, refers to "the centrality to early modern medical practice of the alimentary purge, administered in the form of emetics, laxatives, and enemas, which was experienced from time to time by nearly everyone from infancy on."

45 Norbert Elias, *The Civilizing Process*, trans. Edmund Jephcott (New York: Urizen Books, 1978), is the classic "sociological" study of the history of the laws of propriety, of manners. Starting with Erasmus, Elias traces the history of bodily policing in Western Europe.

46 Freud, *Three Essays on the Theory of Sexuality*, Standard Edition (above, introduction, n.2), 7:185.

no to his/her pleasure, no to what is quickly defined as dirt, "bad," unacceptable. For Melanie Klein, continuing the theoretical speculations of Karl Abraham, the fixation of the anal stage is marked as "sadistic" in that there seems to predominate an aggressively hostile attitude toward the world—the desire to dominate and destroy the ambient social locus through the manipulation (in the attempts of control) of the anal muscles and the control of the contents of the intestines.[47] The struggle between the child's pleasure and social injunction is an early and deciding factor in the child's relation to his own body, to the psychic image he or she has of his or her own body, and consequently to other peoples' bodies, and to the law:

> Defecation affords the first occasion on which the child must decide between narcissistic and an object-loving attitude. He either parts obediently with his faeces, "sacrifices them" to his love, or else retains them for purposes of autoerotic gratification and later as a means of asserting his own will.[48]

But Argan's fixation on his bowels is only a symptom of his larger problem, hypochondria. What, and this will come as no surprise, underlies Argan's obsessive anal fixation is the fear of/and desire for control. Argan wants order in his world ("Je le dirai à Monsieur Purgon, afin qu'il mette ordre à cela"). From the very beginning, the play underlines the points of intersection between chaos/order, passivity/activity, loss of control/ mastery and the mounting anxiety that is produced when one side of the dichotomy (chaos, passivity, loss of control) seems to Argan to be gaining the upper hand. In the first speech is a growing crescendo of anxiety, marked by the comic buildup of the maniacal economies of Argan, which lead to his anxious outburst—"Il n'y a personne: j'ai beau dire, on me laisse toujours seul. . . . Ils n'entendent point, et ma sonnette ne fait pas assez de bruit. . . . Ils me laisseront ici mourir"—which we can assume is the eruption of the heart of his anxiety and which can be translated as the underlying cry, "I am defenseless, I am vulnerable, I am a helpless (infant) in distress." The anxiety forms the underside, the nonarticulable underside to the public persona Argan, as pater familias, one who is expected to project to the world—"I am strong, I am the father (king), I am one and invincible." Here Argan's angst, which he focalizes on his bowels, represents his desire to create a perfect economy of control, to render his body, in its *Kreaturlichkeit*, unthreatening to his fragile sense of security and integrity. We could see this personal angst (but also this so spectacularly public angst) as expressing—unbeknownst to him, and to Molière—the larger ambient insecurity of boundaries of the emerging nation-states which on the another level the play is purportedly celebrating. It

[47] Melanie Klein, "Some Theoretical Conclusions regarding the emotional life of the infant," in *Developments in Psychoanalysis*, ed. Joan Riviere (London: Hogarth Press, 1952) 198–273.

[48] Freud, "On the Transformation of Instincts with Special Reference to Anal Erotism," Standard Edition, 7:130.

would seem that neither the nation nor the ego is as yet securely buttressed by firm definition. Argan's angst is the anxiety of conflict, the conflict between a pull toward a system into which he (and we may assume the father in general) does not perfectly dovetail but whose lure nevertheless entices him.[49]

In other words, in whatever code we desire to place his symptoms—the humoral code of the seventeenth century, or the analytical code of ours—Argan's initial presentation at the beginning of the play, with the heavily underlined emphasis on the body—the leaky, grotesque body of Galenic theory, or the hypochondriacal anal-sadistic (psychic) body of analysis—places him, as father (that is, as a male subject in a patriarchal culture) at odds with the ambient ideology of masculinity. In both instances Argan is not integral. For the humoral theory, he is split by the constant "quiddity" of his lower bodily stratum which represents a female intrusion into what should be a male subject. His integrity is constantly sundered by the apertures, the flux of excreta, in which he delights, and which constantly call attention to him as an open, effluent body. In Freudian terms Argan would be split between a narcissistic attention to his own body, a sign which Freud considers as a particularly feminine attitude, and a normatively masculine "object-love."[50] At the same time Argan's delectation in his anality would also in a more complex fashion indicate that he is—that the carnivalesque body is—in a schema of Oedipal sexuality in a pregenital stage, a stage that refuses castration and therefore the law of difference, refuses the construction of a "self" that would be defined off from its/an other.[51] So in the first instance what marks Argan as comic, beyond the scatology, beyond the tirades for or against the medical profession, is the copresence in the father, of what seventeenth-century psychology, medicine, theology, and esthetics would suppress—the body, and most particularly, the body coded as feminine and thus passive.

Argan's attention to his excretory functions—although it is, like all psychic phenomena, anchored in the physicality of the body and in ambient bodily practices obviously exceeds these social realities. His own internal

[49] See Douglas, *Purity and Danger*, 124 "Here I am suggesting that when rituals express anxiety about the body's orifices the sociological counterpart of this anxiety is a care to protect the political and cultural unity."

[50] Freud, "On Narcissism: An Introduction," Standard Edition, 14:88: "A comparison of the male and female sexes then show that there are fundamental differences between them in respect of their type of object-choice. . . . Complete object-love of the attachment type is, properly speaking, characteristic of the male. . . . Women, especially if they grow up with good looks, develop a certain self-contentment which compensates them for the social restrictions that are imposed upon them in their choice of object. Strictly speaking, it is only themselves that such women love with an intensity comparable to that of the man's love for them."

[51] For a detailed analysis of this problematic see Julia Kristeva's *Pouvoirs de l'horreur* (Paris: Seuil, 1980), trans. Leon Roudiez, *Powers of Horror: An Essay on Abjection* (New York: Columbia University Press, 1982) esp. the chapters "Something to Be Scared Of" and "From Filth to Defilement."

economy has only a tenuous relation to external reality.[52] It does, on the other hand, have quite a rich and forceful influence on the members of his household. Marriage forms the central conundrum of Molièresque comedy because it is a heavily overinvested locus where social and political economy meets with and is inseparable from personal sexual economy. This extremely enchafed locus produces equally the tragic and comic scenarios of familial/social conflict in seventeenth-century drama. In *Le malade imaginaire* we have two negative types of marriage, the proposed marriage of Angélique to Thomas Diafoirus, and the actual marriage of Argan and Béline. Both, I suggest, correspond to Argan's anal economy in which the passive and aggressive sides of his anality take precedence over any "genital" economy that would supersede it.

Although we might suggest that Argan's hypochondria fixes him in a pregenital relation to sexuality, a relation marked by a desire to control, it interferes with the sexual fulfillment of the other members of his household—particularly his daughter, Angélique. While Argan's anality attempts to control his household economy by an obsessive attention to the free flowing of his intestinal tract, this enforced fluidity leaves his daughter "dammed up" (bouchée):

> il n'est rien de plus fâcheux que la contrainte où l'on me tient, qui bouche tout commerce aux doux empressements de cette mutuelle ardeur que le Ciel nous inspire. (I.iv; 4:393)

Both father and daughter envisage the same type of therapy for this problem (being "blocked" or "backed" up)—marriage. But here, once again, despite his invocation of "nature" ("Cela est plaisant, oui, ce mot de mariage; il n'y a rien de plus drôle pour les jeunes filles: ah! nature, nature!"), the difference between Argan's anal economy and the more "natural" economy of Angélique come into conflict. Angélique desires to marry the young, bright, good-looking fellow who has been courting her (Cléante), while Argan, of course, entirely possessed by his hypochondriacal mania, wishes to use his daughter as part of his economy, wishes to secure through her (through a bartering of her sexuality) a closed circuit where symptoms and on-site medical aid exist in a copresent cycle of need and fulfillment. Argan wants a live-in physician, present *à demeure* to minister to his every demand:

> Ma raison est que, me voyant infirme et malade comme je suis, je veux me faire un gendre et des alliés médecins, afin de m'appuyer de bons secours contre ma maladie, d'avoir dans ma famille les sources des remèdes qui me sont nécessaires, et d'être à même des consultations et des ordonnances. (I.v; 4:395)

[52] Didier Anzieu states in *The Skin Ego*, trans. Chris Turner (New Haven: Yale University Press, 1989), 96, that "every psychical function develops by supporting itself upon a bodily function whose workings it transposes on to the mental plane."

Argan's desire to possess Angélique, to use her as but an extension of his body, represents the sadistic totalizing side of his anality. In a sense we can interpret Argan's tyrannical abuse of his daughter as but one more metaphor for the control of his feces which is so vitally important to him—staving off as it does the undoing of his being, its total collapse into death. On another level, a level that Freud also analyzed and that we have already seen operative in Argan, his interest in feces is displaced (but only partially) onto that other currency, money.[53] Argan, although wealthy in his own right, has not forgotten what this exchange of his daughter for a doctor son-in-law will also bring him financially:

> le parti est plus avantageux qu'on ne pense. Monsieur Diafoirus n'a que ce fils-là pour tout héritier; et, de plus, Monsieur Purgon, qui n'a ni femme, ni enfants, lui donne tout son bien, en faveur de ce mariage; et Monsieur Purgon est un homme qui a huit mille bonnes livres de rente. . . . Huit mille livres de rente sont quelque chose, sans compter le bien du père. (I.v; 4:396)

This obsessive intrusion of Argan's anality into the general economy of marriage as it was practiced in the seventeenth century (an "unnatural" institution in Molière's terms, repeated in comedy after comedy) is precisely society's desire to confuse the libidinal (i.e. natural) economy with the economy of the marketplace. In his defense of young lovers against aged, maniacal fathers, Molière at first appears to be defending a liberatory position, which is radically disruptive of the patriarchal economy of his day. Argan's case, however, is complex: in either its passive or active forms, his anality clearly situates Argan on the near side of phallic sexuality, the sexuality of the emergent bourgeois family.[54] For, although by his insistence on the continued heartless exploitation of his daughter he participates in an economy of patriarchal aggrandizement, this very economy is corrupted by the intrusion of his lower bodily stratum into the integrity of his position as father. It undoes the orthopedic rigidity necessary to support the economic law of marriage he would, as *oikodespotès*, impose. We might say that his own fascination with his bowels, with his anal economy, precludes his phallic

[53] As Freud writes, "In reality, wherever archaic modes of thought predominate or have persisted—in ancient civilizations, in myth, fairy-tale and superstition, in unconscious thoughts and dreams, and in neuroses—money comes into the closest relation with excrement" ("Character and Anal Erotism," Standard Edition, 9:174).

[54] Kaja Silverman has recently written on the different possibilities of "male subjectivity" that would not be based on a phallic (i.e, oedipal) model all while defining phallic model as the dominant cultural mode of sexuality in (patriarchal) modern culture: "our present dominant fiction is above all the representational system through which the subject is accommodated to the Name-of-the-Father. Its most central signifier of unity is the (paternal) family and its primary signifier of privilege the phallus." See her *Male Subjectivity at the Margins* (New York: Routledge, 1992), 34.

valorization as father—that is the *Aufhebung* by which biology (Argan as *genitor*) becomes one with ideology (Argan as *pater*).[55]

His own marriage is striking precisely because it is peculiarly unphallic. His relation to his wife, who we know from the very outset of the play is interested only in inheriting his wealth, corresponds to the passive infantile side of his anality. She caters to his mania, to his hypochondria, in a blatantly hypocritical way that fools no one but Argan. Argan adores his wife because in his relation to her he can safely regress to the position of the infant. (We might remark that this marriage is childless, the sign, perhaps, of a lack of genital sexuality?) Their sexual relation consists of his moaning to her about his maladies, about the indignities of his body (i.e., offering up to her his body in its "femaleness" rather than, following "humoral" theory, its "maleness") and her responses, couched significantly in infantilizing terms of endearment: "mon fils," "mon petit fils." We can assume that in his relation to his wife, Argan must find a pleasure similar to the one he achieves through his constant purges, a pleasure in which he regresses to an infantile state of indifference, a pregenital state of the child for whom the distinction between outer and inner worlds and thus between a sense of self and a sense of other is only barely beginning to be formed.[56] He regresses (or exists) precisely in a body without limits, a body of constant flux, a body that for him must be highly eroticized and thus both extremely pleasurable and extremely dangerous—the grotesque body of the carnival.

Yet, for the economy of the play, it is this body that threatens, as it has threatened the happiness of his daughter, the economic well-being of the family unit. Lost as he is in the pleasurable illusion of his marriage, lost in the anal pleasure of Béline, he is ready to sacrifice his family's financial security. We might even suggest that unaware of phallic jouissance he has no qualms about handing over to his wife the "family jewels," which in this case are much less valuable to him than his wife's tender (verbal) ministrations to his erotically more invested intestinal tract. It is only because of the cunning of his servant, his brother, and his daughter, of his "household," that is, that Argan is saved from this act of financial auto-castration. It is their economic interests that seem to be rational and not libidinalized ("mature," according to Freud), that reassert themselves at the hour of their destitution and rally the cunning necessary to unmask Béline as the ruthless fortune hunter she is. Argan's family is saved in extremis and saved in spite of the master of the household, who is unable to see reality until he feigns, acts

[55] For this interesting distinction within the economy of patriarchy of "genitor/genitrix" and "pater/mater," see Jean Joseph Goux, *Freud, Marx, économie et symbolique* (Paris: Seuil, 1973), esp. "La génération matérielle," 239–56.

[56] Paster's comment on the double valency of purging is relevant for Argan: " Purging recalls the deeply pleasurable ministrations of passive early experience, but it also threatens the bodily boundaries of self-mastery of the subject" (*The Body Embarrassed*, 21).

out what he most fears—his own demise. Like a comic Lear, Argan passes through death to find his right, that is paternal, place in the reactions of his anal-sadistic wife ("Le ciel en soit loué! Me voilà délivrée d'un grand fardeau. . . . Un homme incommode à tout le monde, malpropre, dégoûtant, sans cesse un lavement ou une médecine dans le ventre, mouchant, toussant, crachant toujours, sans esprit, ennuyeux," III.xiii) and his dutiful daughter, ready to renounce her own hopes of erotic fulfillment to please her dead father ("O ciel! quelle infortune! quelle atteinte cruelle! Hélas! faut-il que je perde mon père, la seule chose qui me restait au monde?" . . . Ah ! Cléante ne parlons plus de rien. Laissons-là toutes les pensées du mariage. Après la perte de mon père je ne veux plus être du monde," III.xiii, xiv).

The play ends, appropriately enough, by dissolving into a carnivalesque charivari, where Argan is duped by his entire entourage into submitting to a mock-heroic induction into the ranks of the physicians. Through the comic use of "un latin de basoche," through infantile chanting and rhymes (can we see this as a parody of the infants' induction into language, and therefore, according to Kristeva, the superseding of the anal stage for an entrance into the "symbolic" of language, into castration, and thus "phallic desire")?[57] Argan "becomes" a doctor, achieves narcissistic self-sufficiency and self-enclosure—he is at once patient and healer, a closed economy of supply and demand, an auto-erotic circle of a suffering body/soul and its healer/lover.[58] But, and this is equally important, there does not seem, despite the (mock) initiation into the symbolics of medicine a going beyond the body, but rather a total, "grotesque" acquiescence to the body, its quiddity, its ever-present and never ending demands. The *Malade imaginaire* offers no sublimated economy that would place the body in another (repressed) locale. Rather the body seems to end the play as triumphantly present as ever, only more ominously so, for the body's triumph in the *Malade* signals, as we know from Molière's biography, quite literally the death of its author.

When we step back in time to *L'avare,* written and performed five years prior to the *Malade,* we appear to have advanced in the development of the bourgeois family and its precapitalist milieu. This step back from the carnival to the fair indicates, it seems to me, a certain cultural indeterminacy that lends itself equally to different comic treatments. For although it has been claimed that *L'avare* is a very physical comedy, for our purposes this earlier play seems to be already situated on the far side of the divide where the body in its quiddity is no longer present.[59] What we have in its stead is precisely

[57] See Kristeva, *Powers of Horror*, 56–89.

[58] François Dagognet in his *Le corps multiple et un* (Paris: Les empêcheurs de penser en rond, 1992) reminds us that for the Greeks "Medicine, according to Erixymacus, is entirely governed by Eros" (18).

[59] Will Moore in his *Molière, a New Criticism* (Oxford: Oxford University Press, 1949) underlines what is for him the physicality of the play (30) "*L'avare* is full of concrete illustrations

"Classical representation," in which and for which the body exists, if at all, as an object of discourse, as a discursive, that is, absent reality.[60] In its place we find, however, an entire play structured around the symbolic systems of exchange—sex and money—which although they never make any direct mention of the physicality of the body, all in one way or another bear its traces.

I would like to propose simply that when the grotesque body of free-flowing excreta is suppressed—a suppression that both Foucault and Elias, each in his own terms, map out for us—what is repressed returns in the sublimated, symbolized form of another currency. When we pass from Argan's *chaise percée* to Harpagon's *cassette*, the feces that was so amply apparent in the carnivalesque world of *Le malade imaginaire* continues to exist in the libidinalized fetishization of money (*trésor*) of *L'avare*. Despite the long tradition that traces the play's plot to Plautus and the *Aulularia,* I think that the *Avare* can be properly understood—not only as a reflection of the seventeenth century's economic and cultural turmoil but in our own terms as well as a harbinger of modern subjectivity, by which I mean, modern sexual, "oedipal" economy—only if we see it in relation to the *Malade*. The anal economy of Molière's last play resurfaces in/as the Classical economy of representation of *L'avare*, where the symbol stands in for (thus kills) its missing (repressed) referent. As I have already mentioned, one of Freud's most shocking but by now sufficiently banalized insights suggests that in the unconscious there exists a contiguous relation between feces and money ("in unconscious thoughts and dreams, and in neuroses—money comes into the closest relation with excrement").[61] When we move in Molière's universe, a convoluted, conflicted, and often contradictory universe, from the farces to the "high" (i.e. "Classical") comedies, we move, in a sense, from a subaltern to a hegemonic discourse. Ideologically speaking "the Classical" (despite the resistances to it) was becoming the master narrative of the emerging absolutist/ mercantilist state. But, as Stallybrass and White point out, the grotesque remains the hidden, underside, informing Classicism's self-definition.[62] In a sense then, the body so flagrantly present in the

---

of moral qualities; nothing is described, everything is shown in many physical acts: Harpagon searches his man's clothes, runs after his money, wears glasses and a ring on his finger, crawls under the table."

[60] Barker writes in *The Tremulous Private Body* (62), "the carnality of the body has been dissolved and dissipated until it can be reconstituted in writing at a distance from itself."

[61] Freud, "Character and Anal Erotism." See also Ilana Reiss-Schimmel *La psychanalyse et l'argent* (Paris: Odile Jacob, 1993), 51–52: "Thus from the perspective of the theory of symbolism money is considered a sexual symbol, the equivalent, both univocal and universal of excrement," and Jean Laplanche *Problématiques, vol.5, Le baquet: Transcendence du transfert* (Paris: P.U.F., 1987), 174:"Money has a libidinal value. Here we are obliged to push our thought to the extreme and to remind ourselves that the libidinal value of money is above all anal: excrement, penis, anus, or ass-wipes."

[62] Stallybrass and White, *The Politics and Poetics of Transgression*, 113:"The Classical body . . . rediscover[s] in itself, often with a sense of shock or inner revulsion, the grotesque,

Malade, disappears here, and in its stead we have a new "grotesque," the mental grotesquery of Harpagon's fetishization of money which threatens, for very different reasons, the household of which he is the head.[63]

What I am suggesting is that we are dealing with a chiasmatic reversal in our comparison of the two comedies which is perfectly consonant with the idea I put forward at the beginning of this chapter—the theater is a mediating locus that contains in itself the conflicting forces of competing ideologies that are particularly active in seventeenth century France. While in the *Malade* we had the predominance of anality that is allied to the carnivalesque, over "genitality, in the *Avare* we have a reverse situation the dominance of the "phallic" (i.e. the "genital") over the anal. In each case, however, one does not exist without the other: they exist in a dialectical codependency with different, but weighted, valencies defining the comic of each play.

In a series of essays Freud returns to the problem of anality, to the importance of the anal zone in the development of our sexual (in the widest sense) subjectivities.[64] Now, before going further, I must stress that the body that Freud presupposes in his discussion is the "classical" "closed" (socially, ideologically, sexually) body. But rather than see that as being only the fully formed body of nineteenth-century bourgeois Vienna, we can see it already as the emerging hegemonic bodily structure toward which, as Foucault and Elias have shown, the society of late seventeenth-century France was moving—the body of Harpagon, for instance, especially as he/it exists in a tendentious relation to Argan and the grotesque. In both "Character and Anal Eroticism" and "On the Transformation of Instincts with Special Reference to Anal Erotism" Freud comes back to the anal stage to suggest how certain character traits met with in adults—traits of "orderliness, parsimony, and obstinacy"—can be seen as the result of a particularly ill-navigated passage from (in his own normative description of sexual chronology) the predominance of the anal to the genital zone. This "ill-navigation" (another term would be "neurosis") can take several different forms in the constitution of the mature character: "the permanent character-traits are either unchanged prolongations of the original impulses, or sublimations of them, or reac-

---

the protean, and the motley, the neither/nor, the double negation of high and low which was the very precondition for its social identity."

[63] Goux, *Freud, Marx, économie et symbolique*, 35, insists on the importance of symbolic exchanges in defining the human subject: "What Marx teaches us, just as what Freud teaches us, is that the subject is made up of only an ensemble of social relations. Either as the subject of ideology or the subject of neurosis (a private ideology), the subject is constituted as one pole in a relation of complex exchanges, exchanges of vital activity. The subject is always a subject of exchange."

[64] "The multifarious instinctual impulses which are comprised under the name of anal erotism play an extraordinarily important part, which it would be quite impossible to over-estimate, in building up sexual life and mental activity in general" (*From the History of an Infantile Neurosis*, Standard Edition, vol. 17:72).

tion-formations against them."[65] In the case of our protagonist we have no trouble recognizing both parsimony and obstinacy which seem to predominate while orderliness can be seen clearly peering through his tyrannical desire for control of his children and household. They are all intertwined with his retentive delight in acquiring and holding onto his money (but not only money: according to the list of usury conditions La Flèche reads Cléante in the contract Harpagon has drawn up (II.i), we see that he hoards, pack-rat style, objects of all and sundry provenance). The people in whom these traits predominate, according to Freud's speculations, are those who as children experienced a particularly intense erotogenic pleasure in the act of withholding or releasing the contents of their bowels.[66]

Freud goes on to speculate that in those people who retain, consciously, the erotic pleasure of their anal zone, these traits do not develop. Rather, it is only by the ego's giving in to ambient social pressure and renouncing the infantile pleasure associated with defecation that pleasure remains in the unconscious, transformed into these character traits.[67] At the same time that the pleasure becomes attached to the character trait, the object of that pleasure, the feces, is itself transformed.

The relation that Freud draws between feces and money, as shocking and seductive as it may seem, is only one small part of a complicated chain of symbolic displacements that can, he hypothesizes, exist in the unconscious of the infant and that can later continue to exist in sublimated form in the adult. In the essay "On the Transformation of Instincts with Special Reference to Anal Erotism" Freud continues to refine, this time with relation to the object (feces) of anal erotism, the symbolic displacement from infancy to adulthood. Here Freud suggests that for the infant, at a very early stage of his development, a chain of symbolic displacements is elaborated, infused already with erotic pleasure, wherein the equation "feces (money, gift), child and penis are seldom distinguished and are easily interchangeable."[68] Freud goes on to offer a distinct evolution of this signifying chain for the normal development of women and men. Here I focus only on what he has to say about male evolution:

> A different series of relation can be observed much more distinctly in the male. It is formed when the boy's sexual curiosity leads him to discover the absence of a penis in women. He concludes that the penis must be a detachable part of

[65] See "Character and Anal Erotism," Standard Edition, 9:175.

[66] "Character and Anal Erotism", 9:170. "As infants they seem to have been among those who refuse to empty the bowel when placed on the chamber, because they derive an incidental pleasure from the act of defecation; for they assert that even in somewhat later years they have found a pleasure in holding back their stools. . . . From these indications we infer that the erotogenic significance of the anal zone is intensified in the innate sexual constitution of these persons."

[67] "On the Transformation of Instincts," Standard Edition, 17:128: "the organic sources of anal erotism cannot be buried as a result of the emergence of the genital organization."

[68] Ibid., 204.

> the body, something analogous to faeces, the first bodily substance the child had to part with. Thus the original anal defiance enters into the composition of the castration complex.[69]

Ilana Reiss-Schimmel glosses Freud's dense essay to point out the following predominant traits: feces as it is transformed into "gift" already bears the impress of desire—the child's desire to please its mother and receive her love in return—as such the object (feces/gift) is already an ambivalent object.[70] Freud's symbolic chain of displacements is established, she says, on an analogy of separation that is understandable only in relation to an originary fantasy of castration, which alone allows for the substitution of one element for another. Underlying, therefore, this substitutive chain (for the male subject) is, as we have seen in Freud, the castration complex which, will retroactively determine the libidinal intensity of the invested object ("money," "penis").[71]

In his study of the "Wolfman" (*From the History of an Infantile Neurosis)* Freud returns to his speculations on anal sexuality and its effects on psychic life and offers the following summary:

> Since the column of faeces stimulates the erotogenic mucous membrane of the bowel, it plays the part of an active organ in regard to it; it behaves just as the penis does to the vaginal mucous membrane, and acts as it were as its forerunner during the cloacal epoch. The handing over of faeces for the sake of (out of love for) some one else becomes a prototype of castration; it is the first occasion upon which an individual parts with a piece of his own body in order to gain the favor of some other person whom he loves. So that a person's love of his own penis, which is in other respects narcissistic, is not without an element of anal erotism. 'Faeces,' 'baby,' and 'penis' thus form a unity, an unconscious concept (sit venia verbo)—the concept, namely, of 'a little one' that can become separated from one body.[72]

A relation is thus clearly established by Freud which intermeshes anality, the castration complex (itself directly related to the outcome of the oedipal development of the child), and the establishment of adult character traits that bear the mark of these differently connected unconscious processes. For our present purposes what is particularly important to "retain" is first the idea of psychic transmutability (i.e. feces = money) and then the inherent fear of losing a part of one's self, a part that is highly invested with narcissistic libido.

While it was Argan's anality that presided over his familial economy, the

[69] Ibid., 208.

[70] Reiss-Schimmel, *La psychanalyse et l'argent*, 57: "The gift is not just the vehicle of amorous feelings, but may also be invested with hostile wishes."

[71] Ibid., 76–77 "For Freud it is the different ways of integrating anal eroticism that determine the symbolic value of money," and "the symbolic value that an individual attributes to money is a function of his level of libidinal organisation."

[72] Freud, *From the History of an Infantile Neurosis* Standard Edition, 17:84.

Harpagon household seems, at first, to be firmly situated in an mercantilist economy with a correlative dominance of oedipal (that is genital) sexuality. *L'avare* appears as probably the most glaringly oedipal of Molière's many conflicted familial comedies. The rivalry between the father and son for the sexual prize (Mariane), as comically ludicrous as it might appear to the audience, provokes at the same time as laughter a sense of unease. Sexuality reveals its hostilely aggressive side in the rivalry of Harpagon and Cléante, a rivalry intensely marked by death wishes on both sides ("Cléante—Voilà où les jeunes gens sont réduits . . . et on s'étonne après cela que les fils souhaitent qu'ils meurent" II.i; 3:342 "Frosine—Il faudra vous assommer, . . . et vous mettrez en terre et vos enfants, et les enfants de vos enfants. Harpagon—Tant mieux" II.v;3:345). [73] It is in fact this mortiferous rivalry ("mon père est mon rival") between father and son that forms the central plot device of the play. Only when we comprehend that this desire, the disruptive intrusion of the body into the world of mercantilism, is inseparable from the economy of the marketplace, can we understand that *L'avare*, even at this early date, presents us with a world where people are already in Marx's terms "fetishized commodities" and thus can we understand the seamless interweave between sexuality and avarice as structurally necessary in this comedy of the oedipal family.[74] This family from its very inception—here on the seventeenth-century stage—is shown to be dysfunctional: although the two economies, libidinal and financial, may overlap they cannot be made to coincide.

The comedy configures a clear sexual symmetry between the young members of the household—both of Harpagon's children are in love and wish to marry, and then immediately triangularizes that symmetry through the rivalrous relation between Harpagon and his son Cléante, and by the censorious pressure Harpagon brings to bear on Élise. The mediation for this triangularization of desire is financial. From the very outset the desire of the children is frustrated by the avarice of the father:

> Figurez-vous, ma soeur, quelle joie ce peut être que de relever la fortune d'une personne que l'on aime; que de donner adroitement quelques petits secours aux modestes nécessités d'une vertueuse famille; et concevez quel déplaisir ce m'est de voir que, par l'avarice d'un père, je sois dans l'impuissance de goûter cette joie, et de faire éclater à cette belle aucun témoignage de mon amour. (I.ii; 3:327)

[73] Georges Mongrédien, the editor of the Molière edition I am using, articulates this "discomfit" (we might call it a rather overdetermined and thus particularly interesting discomfit, coming as it does from one of the representatives of high French bourgeois culture) in the following way: "Without a doubt, the spectator feels a discomfiture, a feeling of being ill at ease spending two hours in the midst of the poisonous atmosphere of this family" *(Oeuvres complètes* 3:318). For a history of the critical reception of *L'avare* in general and of the relation of Harpagon and Cléante in particular, see Barbara W. Alsip, "*L'Avare*: History of Scholarship," in *Oeuvres et critiques,* 6/1 (summer 1981): 99–110.

[74] For Marx's classic definition of "fetishism," see "The Fetishism of Commodities and the Secret Thereof" (sect. 4 of chap. 1 "Commodities" in *Capital*, in *The Portable Karl Marx*, ed. E. Kamenka (London: Penguin Books, 1983) 437–61.

Cléante's opening declarations to his sister while couched in terms of desire ("goûter cette joie" and further on "nous ne serons plus dans le bel âge d'en jouir") and frustration ("impuissance") are also and as fully imbricated in an economy of mercantile exchange—in which his desire for Mariane can, he knows, be mediated by his family's wealth. His desire comes up against what he calls the "rigoureuse épargne" of his father and is frustrated. In a simple sense, therefore, the oedipal rivalry between father and child is mediated in and through money—the new law of emerging capitalist France. It is the "no" of the father but, here, transcoded as a question of financial tyranny. In this play Harpagon's controlling the family purse strings effectively controls the son's *bourses* as well. Élise fares no better with her father than her brother. She becomes a bartered bride. In the financial machinations of her father, where what counts is not to have one's estate diminished, not to lose what one has accumulated, she is given to the *moins coûtant*, to Anselme, whose chief claim to her in her father's eyes is that he is willing to take her as a wife without a dowry (*sans dot*) without, that is, there being any loss of property on the part of Harpagon.

This fear of loss is at the very heart of Harpagon's mania. From his first entrance on stage, Harpagon appears obsessed with the thought that everyone is trying to get the better of him, which becomes in his fantasy the idea that everyone is trying to rob him. His interchange with La Flèche sets the comic tone for the rest of the play:

> Va-t'en l'attendre dans la rue, et ne sois point dans ma maison planté tout droit comme un piquet, à observer ce qui se passe, et faire ton profit de tout. Je ne veux point avoir sans cesse devant moi un espion de mes affaires, un traître, dont les yeux maudits assiègent toutes mes actions, dévorent ce que je possède, et furètent de tous côtés voir s'il n'y rien à voler. (I.iii; 3:328)

The anxiety of being robbed is exacerbated for comic effect by the presence in the home of a large sum of money that Harpagon received the day before. He is frantically trying to hide it from all those prying eyes he imagines around him:

> Certes ce n'est pas une petite peine que de garder chez soi une grande somme d'argent; et bienheureux qui a tout son fait bien placé, et ne conserve seulement que ce qu'il faut pour sa dépense. On n'est pas peu embarrassé à inventer dans toute une maison une cache fidèle; car pour moi, les coffres-forts me sont suspects, et je ne veux jamais m'y fier: je les tiens justement une franche amorce à voleurs, et c'est toujours la première chose que l'on va attaquer. Cependant je ne sais si j'aurai bien fait d'avoir enterré dans mon jardin dix mille écus qu'on me rendit hier. Dix mille écus en or chez soi est une somme assez . . . (I.iv; 3:331)

Harpagon has buried the money, locked in the famous *cassette* in his garden. For the time being I want to point out only the obvious: if we can, for the moment, accept Freud's chain of equivalencies feces = money, Harpagon's choice of a "cache" is particularly rich in analogies. He buries his money, out of sight, in the ground. The only safe place he can find for his treasure is in the "bowels" of the earth. But even here, of course, the hiding place is not entirely secure; other eyes can peer into ground, discover and carry off the precious *cassette*. What is intriguing in Harpagon's mania is its monolithic intensity. In a sense Harpagon's avarice insofar as it reduces the entire world to a series of things that can be possessed (and therefore at the same time to a series of things of which one can be dispossessed) reflects a totalitarian psychic system that would constantly attempt to enclose the world in the same way the body is phantasmatically shut. If we remember that the original choice of the infant in relation to his bowel is presented as a dichotomy, either to retain his feces in the auto-erotic enclosure of narcissism, or to surrender it as a love offering to an object (person) in the world, we see that we are presented with a choice, *grosso modo*, between closing in on the self, or opening up the self to the world. We can understand the enormous tension that exists in Harpagon—the comic tension of a character who is situated on the horns of this one very crucial dilemma. He is presented as a totally self-enclosed (but paranoid) narcissist, a position that would seem to parody in a negative reversal the ideal of corporate/bodily integrity that underpins the evolution of absolutist patriarchy. And yet at the same time he is tempted by the opening up of this enclosed, defended structure as it reaches out for object-love. There is a conflict, I am suggesting, between these two very basic tendencies—the desire to retain, to remain in a self-enclosed tyrannical psychic structure that is in conflict with his genital desire for Mariane. It is this conflict that points to an impossible tension in the "father," his presentation as split being, and that, I believe, accounts in great part for the hilarity of Harpagon's character.

What could be more comic that a desirous "barbon?" What more perverse that the spectacle of a wizened, maniacal old miser (let us not forget the traditional iconographic representation of Avarice is a withered hag) who nevertheless is presented as concupiscent? The body returns, elliptically, in this comedy as that which resists the retentive psychic economy of sublimation. It is the conflict between the desire of the body and the resistance of sublimated retention that forms the comic nexus of the play.

We witness the reappearance of the body most pointedly in the interchanges between Harpagon and his procuress, Frosine. Although La Flèche warns her that she is dealing with a particularly obstinate case, that Harpagon is, as he strategically says, "le plus dur et le plus serré" of men (and I suggest that in the French "serré" there is the same sense we have in the English "tight-assed"), she maintains that she, desire's spokeswoman, knows how to loosen up the most obdurate cases. In a sense, Frosine (although she will meet defeat) is presented as a combination of all those cunning female servants who populate Molière's theatrical universe, but to her is added here the aura of a ministering mother. Like all those stereotypical figures of the go-between, these women, in relation to the "man/child" they are called upon to service ("il y a certains services qui touchent merveilleusement"), promise to supply those bodily comforts (sexual pleasure), and attend to their charges in a way that reproduces the mother's initial bodily ministration to the baby.[75] Frosine's description of herself as an expert in catering to men's innermost secrets is couched in terms of opening up the enclosed body of adult males. In a sense, therefore, she (Molière) creates the analogy that equates the "jouissance" of the body to "openness." Pleasure, the body's desire to be opened, to be available, to be made, so to speak, like a woman, is positioned as a feminization and thus, as the inverse of what the dominant ideology says a man must be—closed, "serré," bounded:

> Mon Dieu! je sais l'art de traire les hommes, j'ai le secret de m'ouvrir leur tendresse, de chatouiller leurs coeurs, de trouver les endroits par où ils sont sensibles. (II.iv; 3:345)

Desire, when it announces itself in this play in the body of Harpagon, declares itself as precisely what patriarchal Absolutism as it evolves toward ideological hegemony, had to suppress. It signals quite unconsciously that it desires the presence, as pleasure, as, once again in Bakhtin's terms, the "grotesque" (as female) of precisely what it has had to repress. It is this persistence, in the dominant discourse, of the fantasy of its own obverse which is being played out in the tension between Harpagon's retentiveness and the desire that is bred in that retention for release—the Classical body's yearning for its own grotesque.[76]

Frosine begins her attack on Harpagon where she thinks he is most vulnerable—his (bodily) vanity:

> FROSINE: Ah! mon Dieu! que vous vous portez bien! et que vous avez là un vrai visage de santé!
> HARPAGON: Qui, moi?
> FROSINE: Jamais je ne vous vis un teint si frais et si gaillard.
> HARPAGON: Tout de bon?

[75] In his article "Notre corps ou le présent d'une illusion" (*Nouvelle Revue de Psychanalyse*, 3[1971], 34), talking about the primordial importance of the infant/mother bond in forming the "phantasmatic" image of the subject's body, Jean-Claude Lavie says: "In relation to our body, it is less our body that counts than the relation it allows us to have with our mother."

[76] Talking about the imposition of Classicism in England in the eighteenth century, Stallybrass and White write (*The Politics and Poetics of Transgression*, 105): "The production and reproduction of a body of classical writing required a labour of suppression, a perpetual work of exclusion upon the grotesque body and it was that supplementary yet unavoidable labour which troubled the identity of the classical. It brought the grotesque back into the classical . . . as a vast labour of exclusion requiring and generating its own equivocal energies. Quae negata, grata—what is denied is desired."

FROSINE: Comment! vous n'avez de votre vie été si jeune que vous êtes ; et je vois des gens de vingt-cinq ans qui sont plus vieux que vous.
HARPAGON: Cependant, Frosine, j'en ai soixante bien comptés.
FROSINE: Hé bien! qu'est-ce que cela, soixante ans? Voilà bien de quoi! C'est la fleur de l'âge, cela, et vous entrez maintenant dans la belle saison de l'homme. (II.v; 3:345)

But his vanity is no match for his avarice. Although Frosine presents herself on one level as a ministering mother, catering to the bodily needs of her charges, on another level, these ministrations are themselves part of a financial system of exchange—sex for money—and it is here that her own vulnerability comes too directly into conflict with Harpagon's mania and is undone ("Que la fièvre te serre, chien de vilain à tous les diables! Le ladre a été ferme à toutes mes attaques" II.v; 3:350). Harpagon remains impenetrable to pleasure. His desire, after its destructive meandering through and across the desires of his children, gives way to the force of his own mania.

Of course, any attempt to divorce sexuality ("love") from economy is already precluded from the ideological universe of the play. Although there is a yearning for their separation especially in the gesture that would place passion on the side of the natural (i.e. youth, heterosexuality, and the like) and economy on the side of "perversion" (i.e. avarice), in truth, as we have seen, this is an untenable dichotomy in a world totally immersed in the bourgeois culture of the seventeenth century. For that (still primitive) bourgeoisie, marriage remains the most overinvested institution for the exchange of financial and sexual economies. For this reason the plot of *L'avare* can crescendo to a dizzying height of comic misprisions in the dialogue between Harpagon and Valère, the former panic-stricken over the loss of his "cassette," the latter pleading his "love." It is precisely because there is a *chassé-croisé* between Harpagon's relation to his hoarded treasure and Valère's desire for Élise, a chiasmus that comes to rest on the linguistic indeterminacy where passion and avarice overlap (such words as "treasure," "love," "engagement") that lends itself, indiscriminately, to entirely opposed economic interpretations depending on the code into which they are placed, the code of financial avarice, or the code of traditional passion. Despite or rather because of the blurring of (linguistic) codes, the risible of the play underlines and therefore puts into comic relief what otherwise would be obfuscated in the simply quotidian acceptation of either one of the codes in its home idiolect—that the woman as object of desire (in a bourgeois) economy is also a "treasure" (an economic investment) in the same (but parodically exaggerated) way the hoarded stash of money for Harpagon is an object of libidinal lust.

How can we understand the immensely comic (for us) displacement of lust onto his *cassette* if not precisely by seeing it as the highly overdetermined instance where libidinal energy is captured and fixed on a symbolic object of psychic exchange? The scene of Harpagon's distress upon discovering the theft of his cassette is among the most hilarious in Molière's repertoire. It is a bravura piece of writing (and of acting) that focuses in so concentrated a fashion all of the lines of contradictory tensions between market and libidinal economies in the play, into this one paroxystic moment where the symbolic systems of finance and the body come to rest in and on the miser's anguish over his loss—a distress that is figured most poignantly and most comically as a loss of one's self—Harpagon cries that his body has been attacked, that he has been murdered:

> Au voleur! au voleur! à l'assassin! au meutrier! Justice, juste Ciel! je suis perdu, je suis assassiné, on m'a coupé la gorge, on m'a dérobé mon argent. . . . Mon esprit est troublé, et j'ignore où je suis, qui je suis, et ce que je fais. Hélas! mon pauvre argent, mon pauvre argent, mon cher ami! on m'a privé de toi, et puisque tu m'es enlevé, j'ai perdu mon support, ma consolation, ma joie; tout est fini pour moi, et je n'ai plus que faire au monde: sans toi il m'est impossible de vivre. C'en est fait, je n'en puis plus; je me meurs, je suis mort, je suis enterré . . . (IV.vii; 3:374)

In the high comedy of this scene Harpagon describes the disintegration of his self. But, curiously this disintegration is metaphorized in a highly symbolic fashion, a fashion that, I suggest, allows us (some) entry into the phantasmatic system that underpins Harpagon's anxiety. He tells us that he has been "murdered," but this murder is significantly couched in particularly symbolic terms, "on m'a coupé la gorge" ("they've slit my throat), a cry that is immediately coupled with "on m'a dérobé mon argent" ("they've stolen my money"). I would propose that the equation of having one's throat cut and having one's money stolen allows us some insight into why Harpagon's psychic trauma is so comically intense and why, finally, it leads us back into the conflict between anal and genital sexuality we have been tracing through the two comedies.

In a simple way, if we take into account the "economic" phenomenon of psychic displacement discussed by Freud in relation to dream interpretation, we will be able to unravel what is at work in Harpagon's mania. Laplanche and Pontalis offer a succinct summary of displacement: "The psycho-analytic theory of displacement depends upon the economic hypothesis of a cathectic energy able to detach itself from ideas and to run along associative pathways."[77] In other words, an affect can be detached from its source and displaced onto another psychic or physical structure. In Harpagon's case I think we can assume that we have a "vertical displacement" from the lower bodily stratum to the higher, from the genitals to the throat (neck, head). In another searingly funny cry Harpagon reveals the profound investment at work in this psychic configuration, when after referring to the

[77] Jean Laplanche and Jean-Bertrand Pontalis, *The Language of Psychoanalysis*, trans, Donald Nicholson-Smith (New York: Norton, 1973), 121.

theft in abstract, that is legal-social terms, calling it a "un guet-apens," "un assassinat," where "les choses les plus sacrées ne sont plus en sûreté," he returns to the physicality of his attachment referring to his treasure as "mon sang," "mes entrailles"(V.iii; 3:379). He constantly oscillates from the abstract to the body, from the higher to the lower. In his impassioned cry at having his throat slashed I think we can hear a more primitive castration anxiety, an anxiety that returns us once again to the confusion we have already alluded to in Freud's discussion of the symbolic displacements of anality. But in this case, both the displacements and the affect are stronger and more complicated than we might first imagine.

On one level it is reasonably clear that in the passage from anality to genitality, from Argan to Harpagon, from "grotesque" to "Classical," Harpagon represents a snag in any clearly defined, unproblematic navigation from the one to the other. Let us recall (one of) the associative chains Freud proposed in his discussion of the persistence of the anal stage in the character traits of a mature individual "feces = penis = money", and then let us also remember that the passage from the anal to the genital stage is intimately connected to the "castration complex" and to the different traumatic avatars of this complex for the psycho-sexual development of the male child. Although it would be unproductive to offer an analysis of Harpagon, who is, after all, not a real psychic entity (not a person) but merely a character in a play, by considering him as a nexus of conflicting and conflicted social, sexual, and economic vectors, we can see how, through a "personal" analysis, we can arrive at a sociohistoric description.

Harpagon, in his obsessive miserliness, would represent a "misplaced" investment of libidinal energy onto his bowels—onto, that is, the pleasure of the retention of his bowels, onto money—or we could turn this around and say that there is the invasion of genital sexuality by the misplaced intensity of anality. In either case the vehemence of this displacement is explicable only if we concede that the intermediary term in the associative chain—penis—has dropped out, been displaced. It has been consigned to the invisibility of the unconscious, resurfacing as concentrated affect, the fear of loss, the fear of self-destruction, the fear of death. This fear of loss—the representative of the castration complex—has been, I believe, sutured into the psychic construction of Harpagon by and through the insistence on still another displacement, the metonymic displacement from money (viz. penis) to *cassette* (from a part to a whole, from contained to container). The cassette functions, on one level, as a fetish object, which allows Harpagon to have his money (feces/penis) and to relinquish it too (transform it into, in a sense, object love). The vehemence of his attachment to his cassette ("O ma chère cassette"), takes on the lure of another man's (Valère's, for example) attachment to a woman. In his essay "The Theme of the Three Caskets" Freud talks about how the casket (box, i.e. "cassette") is a symbol of "the essential thing in woman, and therefore of a woman herself" He goes on, however, to show how in folklore and fairytales, this "woman herself" is an ambiguous construction where the "casket" does not represent just woman in general, but a particular ambivalent projection of woman, both the figure of "Atropos," a symbol of death and (as a reaction formation) the image of woman as the youthful, life-giving goddess of Love.[78] This ambivalence functioning bivalently, I believe, acts as the hinge between the sexual and financial economies in the play, allowing their mutual displacement. As we have seen, especially in the stychomachia that opposes Harpagon and Valère, this ambivalence (essentially on the level of linguistic economies, between metaphor and metonymy) relays the sexual into the linguistic creating the comic quid pro quo of the double misprision in the dialogue, the sexual/economic chiasmus of woman and money.

But, as this dialogue also makes clear, while Valère talks about his love in more traditionally "metaphorical" terms, Harpagon understands these metaphors only metonymically, because for him, first and foremost, the cassette represents a displaced part of himself. So on one level we can see that the cassette might represent a woman but for Harpagon this is a special phantasm of a woman, the fetishistic "woman-with-a-penis." And, I would suggest, it is to this final displacement that Harpagon is most attached; one he cannot give up and that finally presides over his divesting himself of his genital/oedipal desire for Mariane—a desire in which, as in all desire, he risks (or so it appears to him) his annihilation in the woman-as-other, the woman as object and proof of castration (for the male psyche)—and remains in the protected, self-enclosed narcissistic position where as long as he has his beloved cassette (his feces/penis) he is protected from loss, protected from castration, protected from death.

With the restitution of his cassette, the play can end, as all comedies do with the promise of marriage—the marriage of the children. On an important level, therefore, the comedy ends by reaffirming a familial model of oedipal/genitality. The lost, good father has been found. The family is reconstituted: brother and sister are introduced to each other and all go off to gather around the silently, suffering absence of this play, the mother. While the stage is cleared by the exit of all the characters gone off to share the news of their impending wedding with this never-realized maternal presence, Harpagon, alone, returns to his obsession, returns to the position from which he was almost budged but which proved too obdurate. He returns to the contemplation of what completes and assures him of his integrity; he reverts to the closed circle where, with his cassette, he retains an entire libidinal economy, protected from the anxiety of risk and loss.

[78] Standard Edition, 12:72: "The goddess of Death was replaced by the goddess of Love." Freud goes on to generalize from these speculations (73): "The great Mother-goddesses of the oriental peoples, . . . all seem to have been both founts of being and destroyers: goddesses of life and of fertility, and death goddesses."

L'avare and *Le malade imaginaire* form a chiasmatic economy of their own, emblematic of the conflicted and contradictory economies, libidinal and financial, that Molière's theater mediates. On the one hand we have the predominance of the farce, of the carnivalesque grotesque body, the open, effluent body of Argan; on the other, "high comedy" of Classicism with its sublimation of the body, its disappearance in an economy of retention and symbolization. This dichotomy, of course, is too rigidly opposed here to account fully for the overlaps, exchanges, and interconnections that unite rather than oppose the multiple economies that coexist within Molière's theater and which finally come to rest in that ultimate economy, the economy of laughter, the laughter of the spectators of these, and other Molièresque comedies. How are we to understand this laughter, this "sideration of the body" in its voluptuous abandonment to its own pleasure? The history of laughter, of the comic, is long and complex. I do not wish to enter here into a long debate that begins with ancient Greece and continues down through the ages with important modern contributions by Bergson, Freud, and others. Here, as a coda, I add only a small note on what I believe is the role of the laughter spawned by Molière's comedy, spawned by Harpagon and Argan.

If we return to Bakhtin, who comments extensively on "carnivalesque laughter," he tells us that the laughter of the marketplace, the laughter of the premodern, nonindividuated ego is

> first of all, a festive laughter. Therefore, it is not an individual reaction to some "comic" event. Carnival laughter is the laughter of all the people. Second, it is universal in scope; it is directed at all and everyone, including the carnival's participants. The entire world is seen in its droll aspect, in its gay relativity. Third, this laughter is ambivalent: it is gay, triumphant at the same time mocking deriding. It asserts and denies, it buries and revives.[79]

Bakhtin's description of laughter, although nuanced at the end, remains nevertheless, like most of his description of the "carnivalesque," a paean to some utopian notion of the "people." What is repressed from his enormously rich contribution to the study of laughter, of the carnival, is precisely, as Stallybrass and White point out, the negative, destructive side of the grotesque, which rather than empowering as often as not authorizes itself by degrading, demeaning society's outcasts while maintaining its own complicitious relation with the dominant social structures.[80] Although Freud in his essay "Humour" claims that "Humour is not resigned; it is re-

[79] Bakhtin, *Rabelais and His World*, 11–12.

[80] Stallybrass and White, *The Politics and Poetics of Transgression*, 19: "the politics of carnival: its nostalgia; its uncritical populism (carnival often violently abuses and demonizes *weaker*, not stronger, social groups—women, ethnic and religious minorities, those who 'don't belong'—in a process of *displaced abjection*); its failure to do away with the official dominant culture, its licensed complicity."

bellious. It signifies not only the triumph of the ego but of the pleasure principle,"[81] the question for Molière remains, it seems to me, undecidable, situated somewhere between the unavowed repression inherent in Bakhtin's carnival and the structuring of the modern ego—as much product of what has been unconsciously repressed as what is consciously expressed.

What generates the laughter, the mirth of the spectators in the comedies we have been discussing? On the one hand we might say that it is the mania—the hypochondria, the fixation of Argan on his bowels, or the avarice of Harpagon fixated on his cassette (his money, therefore, also his bowels). In both cases we are made to laugh, our laughter is spawned by an *écart*, a split in the image we have of the main character, the father, head of the household (*oikodespotès*).[82] In the patriarchal world of seventeenth century France, in this world which ideologically tends ideally toward the order of the absolute, the order of the "one" which is "embodied" most tellingly in the persona of the king and of all his paternal declensions, declensions that span the celestial and terrestrial realms from "God the Father," to the king "father of his people," to finally the father, head of each individual household, the unacceptable, the monstrous is precisely a "split" in this unitary phantasy. For, as we have seen, in either the Galenic or Freudian schema the split in the subject, the subject that is not integral, is the sign of the intrusion into the world of masculine perfection of the "other"—the other coded as feminine.

We laugh at Harpagon/Argan, precisely because in the context of their world, they are excessive, split by their monomania which, rather than confirming them as absolute, has the contrary effect of revealing their flaw, and thus the flaw of their world. They reveal what all seventeenth-century culture in its hegemonic drive would keep hidden—that the king, the father, is not one, but two, that in other words under the austere reverence of the one, is the many, the multifarious, and this many is the other—the children, the wily servants, the submissive (and the plotting) women. Harpagon/Argan in their mania reveal what the culture of patriarchy would keep hidden, that the father's "split is showing." It is this split that causes our laughter, I believe, on one level the release of our pent-up economies of repression and control. We laugh at the ridicule that is not so much in the characters as in the system, in the system that controls us all.

So, on one hand, this laughter can be seen, as it often has been, as "liberatory," "rebellious," Molière as the underside of Classicism's repression.

[81] "Humour" Standard Edition, 21:160.

[82] Here I would seem to reach a similar but diametrically opposed view of mania in Molière from Glucksmann who in his *La bêtise* (228), when talking about this desire for the absolute writes: "The comedies of Molière take as their theme the thousand and one ways a hero, one and indivisible, begins to gravitate around his own person. Without ever allowing himself to be distracted or troubled he pursues, in a vertiginous spiral, his fetish object, a man, a woman, some strongboxes, or an enema—wherein the absolute and exclusive relation that makes him eternal plays itself out."

But on the other hand, bearing in mind the critique of the "carnivalesque," the thought that the carnival, that Molière, are inextricably involved in the dominant political narratives of their time, narratives in which his (their) social, economic, and sexual interests are invested, we might then think that rather then being disruptive of social order, the laughter spawned by his plays is simply recuperative rather than rebellious. For, when we look at the target of our laughter—Argan/Harpagon—we realize that we are laughing at the bad father, the father as *pharamakos*, the ritual victim led out onto the stage of our own repressive fantasies and sacrificed to them. But this sacrifice, like all sacrifice, tends to finally maintain in place an entire world-view: when we laugh at the bad father, when we see Argan/Harpagon as risible, "feminized," maniacal, we do so only because we can compare them, as failed fathers, to that image of the ideal father, the absolute father, who continues, in this comparison, to reign in our thoughts, in our repressions, in our fantasies. How else can we explain both the benign patronage of Louis XIV laughing at the antics of Molière's preposterous bourgeois, or the more enchafed reactions of the archbishop of Paris for whom Molière and his cast of characters represented a threat to the well-run order of seventeenth-century France? Both were surely right, but to his credit Louis XIV was probably more sanguine about the effects of Molieresque laughter: being directed as it was at those imperfect bodies of the father, knowing, in his own splendid isolation, in the impervious isolation of his body royal, that the real father, the state, Louis, were only enhanced by the raucous laughter spawned by the debasement of his imperfect earthly simulacra.

2 *Classicism's Pornographic Body:*

L'école des filles, L'académie des dames

> To read a pornographic novel and to be subject to its influence is perhaps in some way to experience something of the essence of literature.
>
> Jean-Marie Goulemot, *Forbidden Books*

> That fantasy is only a private matter is perhaps the supreme fantasy, fantasy par excellence.
>
> Jacqueline Rose, *States of Fantasy*

During the last decades of the sixteenth century the French body politic was rent by tumultuous religious and social upheavals. Writing during this period of momentous change, Montaigne describes the convulsions he witnessed in his world, and indeed that world itself:

> Le monde n'est qu'une branloire perenne. Toutes choses y branlent sans cesse: la terre, les rochers du Caucase, les pyramides d'Aegypte, et du branle public et du leur. La constance mesme n'est autre chose qu'un branle plus languissant.[1]

The image of a constantly writhing, heaving world, even if it implies a more politically self-conscious vision, has deep affinities with the Rabelaisian view of the universe as an ever-evolving living entity, constantly in process, copulating, birthing, and dying without beginning or end. Montaigne's description of a world in constant upheaval was used by him to express the multiple and violent changes to which he was witness and which had a profound impact on his daily existence. Nevertheless, his choice of an image freighted with corporeal echoes displays a continued, if skewed, apprehen-

[1] Michel de Montaigne, "Du Repentir" in *Les Essais,* ed. Maurice Rat (Paris: Garnier Frères, 1962), 2:222.

sion of the world in both its physical and metaphysical dimensions as a dynamic, paroxystic and universal movement, animating mankind, its sociopolitical institutions, and the surrounding cosmos.[2] It is a view that, mutatis mutandis, can be said to be almost universal in the sixteenth century. We find it either in its joyous or fearsome avatars in the poets of the Pléiade, in the work of Agrippa d'Aubigné and, of course, in Rabelais.

Despite what we know of the continued social upheaval of mid-seventeenth-century France, by the 1660s, a mere seventy-five years after Montaigne's famous depiction, the world, as it is represented in the texts that we have canonized as Classical, seems to have been reduced to a state of quiescence, if not stasis. The tumultuous (grotesque) body of the preceding century, but also that, of the *libertins*, those baroque *extravagants* of the early decades of the seventeenth century, has given way to a new esthetic. Slowly, not without resistance, Classicism imposes its stately, disembodied version of representation in the salons, in the ministries of those who have the responsibility of commissioning works for the royal court and on the stage. Although the first decades of the seventeenth century witnessed the ongoing skirmishes between the tenants of an esthetic that championed the linguistic virtuosity and inventiveness of preceding generations (de Gournay, Saint-Amant, Scarron) and those championing the more restrictive principles of Classical decorum (the "Malherbian revolution")—a purification of the French language with a concomitant program of social, esthetic, and ethical reforms—it becomes clear that by the 1630s with the triumphant reception accorded Corneille's *Le Cid* (1636) and *Horace* (1640) the latter was destined to carry the day in all those forms of "public art" that were brought into the service of the monarchy.[3]

When describing the gradual elaboration of the Classical doctrine it has become a commonplace to mention, as we have seen in our own discussion of the gradual shift from the grotesque to the Classical body, that all reference to the physical body becomes "obscene," that is, exiled from the realm of representation. The body becomes marginalized, pushed out into the periphery of discourse from where it continues, nevertheless, as Barker has

[2] For a discussion of Montaigne and his world in motion, cf. Jean Starobinski, *Montaigne en mouvement* (Paris: Gallimard, 1982).

[3] This is not the place to rehearse the never-ending Classical/Baroque controversy. Some books that treat the issue effectively are: Jean Rousset, *Circé et le paon: La littérature de l'âge baroque en France* (Paris: Corti, 1953); and Severo Sarduy, *Barocco* (Paris: Seuil, 1975): Verdun Louis Tapié, *Baroque et classicisme* (Paris: Plon, 1957). For the development of social attitudes, see Robert Mandrou, *Introduction à la France moderne, 1500–1640* (Paris: Albin Michel, 1961). See also for the elaboration of French neo-Classical doctrine, René Bray, *La Formation de la doctrine classique en France* (Paris: Hachette, 1927), Henri Peyre, *Qu'est-ce que le classicisme?* (Paris: Nizet, 1964), and Elbert Borgerhoff, *The Freedom of French Classicism* (Princeton: Princeton University Press, 1950). See also Mitchell Greenberg, *Corneille, Classicism and the Ruses of Symmetry* (Cambridge: Cambridge University Press, 1986), for a discussion of the controversies and triumphs surrounding Corneille's theatrical revolution.

written, to exert its own imperious pressure on those structures that have banished it.[4] While it is true that the body is gradually effaced from literary and social representation and that the discursive effects of this effacement will have profound consequences in the elaboration of both a new sociosexual habitus and the subject that emerges from that habitus, it is also true that this erasure of body, the body in and as representation but also as a sign of the material difference between the sexes, is compensated for in the elaborately spectacular mise-en-scène of one particular body.

One body becomes incorporated in and as the state in its physical and metaphysical dimensions. The displayed, observed and constantly adulated "corps glorieux" of the king comes to stand in for all those other, private bodies, exiled from polite discourse. We cannot but be struck by the immense chasm that separates the disappearance of the private body of Absolutism's subjects from the emergence of the body of the king as the obsessive focal point of not only his own subjects' persistent gaze, but of gaze of the known world. At the very moment when the body in all of its *kreaturliche* reality is being circumscribed, when any mention of bodily functions becomes a scandalous transgression, the body of the French king—and we see this starting with the journal kept by Héroard, physician to the infant Louis XIII, a journal obsessed with the child's body in all of its functions—becomes the object of constant spectacular display and minute delectation.

Although there is a long tradition of princely exhibition that the French inherited from the courts of the Italian Renaissance, Louis XIV transformed this celebration of the kingly body into a political fixation. We have only to recall the iconographic dissemination of the glorified portraits of the king throughout the realm and beyond, the medals coined in his honor, the different public ceremonies and court festivities where Louis emerges as a godlike apparition to understand that if all other bodies are "disappeared" by the onward march of Absolutism, Louis' body, at the same time, becomes, the absolute, unattainable standard that all of his subjects are compelled to adore. This adoration becomes a veritable ritual of the body in its most intimate functions. The court ceremonies and etiquette elaborated around the king's body in its most personal functions—its dressing and undressing, what it ingests and excretes, with whom it copulates—mark the paradoxical shift by which the "private" body of the king is made to be the most public of spectacles in which and through which, all the other "private" effaced bodies of the French find their ultimate grounding and meaning. It is as if, by a magisterial sleight of hand, a sleight of hand that is an imperious political gesture, the one spectacular body of France that is allowed into representation becomes by its very exclusivity the only body that can trans-

[4] Francis Barker, *The Tremulous Private Body: Essays in Subjection* (London; Methuen, 1984), 65: "Neither wholly present, nor wholly absent, the body is confined, ignored, exscribed from discourse, and yet remains at the edge of visibility, troubling the space from which it has been banished."

gress the laws of propriety and sociability. Thus a system of representation is founded which condemns an entire society to the sacrifice of individual bodies so that the sovereign body can exist as an object of unique and obsessive devotion.[5]

This body, on the one hand, becomes confused with, as it represents, the greatest example of the Classical body, bounded and male. In a sense we might say that Louis with an uncanny appreciation of the secular and religious tradition that preceded his reign constitutes himself, his body, as the sovereign body of absolutist France—an image-simulacrum of the Lacanian phallus, the object of devotion of all his subjects (pace Saint-Simon) of both sexes. Louis beams down on his subjects from his official portraits as this strangely self-contained being, decidedly male, and yet, with a more than a hint of female seductiveness—witness his own narcissistic delectation in his image, an image swathed in the symbols of majesty, voluptuous silks, soft velvets, and warm ermine from which emerges the long, well-turned legs of which we know Louis was so proud. In a sense, we return here to that image or rather imaginary projection of the androgyne. Louis projects his iconic mastery of his "corps glorieux" out into the world as the ultimate form of sovereignty that transcending sexual difference becomes the ultimate avatar of sexual potency and desire.[6]

The major representatives of the arts and sciences quickly came to realize that their economic well-being as well as their social standing depended on a close alliance with, or even a willed subservience to, those political architects (Richelieu, Mazarin, Fouquet, Colbert) working with the monarchy to construct the new absolutist regime. Through its artistic conventions, but also through its less easily defined repercussions in the areas of sociality (*préciosité*, for example), Classicism tends to impose a structure of rather strict decorum on the chaotic manifestations of daily life. Just as its principal ideal/model, the royal court, takes on ever more hieratic, rigid, and stratified symbolic practices in order to impose an image of stately harmony and control, so does Classical representation attempt to project an image of a world reduced to the merest flutter of movement. At its most triumphant (and of course, here I mean, in /as "representation") Classicism seems to reduce all outward manifestations of vitality to the murmur of an ambiguous phrase, to the fleeting apprehension of an ambivalent glance.[7]

[5] See Norbert Elias's discussion of the etiquette and ceremony surrounding the king's body in *The Court Society* (trans. Edmond Jephcott New York: Pantheon Books, 1983).

[6] Louis Marin, in *Food for Thought* (trans. Mette Hjort [Baltimore: The John Hopkins University Press, 1989]),offers a detailed analysis of Hyacinthe Rigaud's famous portrait(s) of the king, emphasizing the androgynous aspects of the represented kingly body.

[7] What I mean here is that one sees the "purest" form of an ideology's investments in certain dominant schema not in the hurly-burly of the quotidian but in the artistic projections of that quotidian into a fantasized "empyrean." In this I agree with Franco Moretti who writes about Absolutism's dramatic representations of sovereignty: "If the general culture of absolutism qualified the sovereign power it conferred upon the king with countless hesitations and uncertainties . . . tragedy surrenders such power to him wholly and without the slightest reserve. In

Trapped within the confines of an esthetic that is politicized and a politics that takes on, through the studied extravagances of court life, an ever greater spectacularity, Classical dogma seems to stymie its subjects in a willed immobility. The vitality of Montaigne's universe is frozen in static inaction. Movement is banished from the world of absolutist representation. In essence any motion in the world becomes synonymous with the collapse of Classical equipoise into fragmentation, disruption, and, eventually, death. The most famous examples of Classical stasis are found in the Racinian tragic dilemma; all those protagonists trapped in their own immobility, their inability to take any definitive action. When, finally, they are roused out of their torpor, either voluntarily or at the command of another (cf. Roxane's "Sortez!") they meet their end. Similarly, in the *Princesse de Clèves,* that culmination of Classical narration, where all movement is reduced to "une sorte d'agitation sans désordre,"[8] any impetuous motion leads inevitably to destruction. In the most pivotal scenes in the narrative, scenes highlighting masculine activity, the joust and the *jeu de paume*, the nighttime vigil at Coulommiers, action is an engagement with fatality, either actually or metaphorically: Henri II dies in the first, the duc de Nemours is believed dead in the second, and the prince de Clèves will pine away from jealousy in the last. All the remaining action in the novel (and we will come back to the importance of this in our discussion) is reduced to the darting movement of the eyes as they try to interpret a universe that in its immobility remains as impenetrable as death.

Would it be an exaggeration to suggest that beneath the stately grace of Classicism's most elegant creations we can detect the constant workings, in both its active and passive form of an imperious death drive? Could we then, in a sweeping generalization, see Classicism's intimate connection to Absolutism, as the first (dissembled) celebration of the death drive, the worshiping in extravagantly apposite models of perfection, of that underlying absolute, Death, which as Bossuet never tires of reminding his very aristocratic patrons remains their one and true master?[9] In this sense can we not also see, that the portrait of the king, the king as portrait serves the very complex function of representing, in the display of the hieratic image of the kingly body, the king as beyond the realm of quotidian existence? The king in his representation represents not only the ideal father, but also the dead father, the father who from beyond time and memory presides over the destiny of his people as both the supreme judge and supreme executioner. It is

---

the world of tragedy, the monarch is truly absolute. . . . Tragedy then stages not the institutions of absolutism, but its culture, its values, its ideology"("A Huge Eclipse," *Genre* 15 [1982]: 29).

[8] Marie-Madeleine de La Fayette, *La princesse de Clèves*, ed. Emile Magne, in *Romans et nouvelles* (Paris: Garnier, 1961), 253.

[9] "Vous êtes des dieux. . . . Mais ô dieux de chair et de sang, ô dieux de terre et de poussière vour mourrez comme des hommes." (quoted in Ernst Kantorowicz, *The King's Two Bodies* [Princeton: Princeton University Press, 1957], 409).

from the realm of the dead that Louis attempts, in his representation, which as Pascal tells us "is" the king, to materialize on his own body his sacred function as *père du peuple*. This paternal image conjures up, however, as much anxiety as desire. [10]

But *thanatos* of course is just one side of the coin. Eros, too, continues its work but, it would seem, with the impositions of Classical dictates regarding the unseemliness of the body, in more marginalized, if more virulently oppositional forms. In a strange twist of fate, the absolutist state exerting its influence over an ever greater portion of French public life succeeded in reducing the "branle public" of Montaigne's world to the infinitely more narrow confines of a "branle privé." Banished from the realm of acceptable representation, the body returns, both the represented body—in and as text—and, more insidiously, the actual bodies of the seventeenth-century reading public. In the 1650s, in that brief span that separates the final spasms of the Frondes, that series of nobiliary and merchant revolts, from the inauguration of Louis XIV's personal rule, this public finds itself interpellated by a spate of new texts that introduce a novel, embodied reading praxis. In the middle of the century, at the height of the précieux moment, the body, its urges, and its lusts have been subdued in favor of an allusive rhetoric and psychology of "love." Yet, simultaneously with such other founding texts of Classical representation as Descartes's *Les passions de l'âme* (1647), Pascal's *Lettres provinciales* (1656–57) and the *Logique* (1662) and *Grammaire* (1660) of Port Royal, we see the clandestine publication of the first pornographic narratives written in French, the anonymous *L'école des filles* and Nicolas Chorier's *L'académie des dames*.[11] Classicism's subjects (both male and female) are invited to reexperience the suppressed "branle du monde", through the experience of their own private "branlade"; masturbation as a literary activity makes its appearance on the scene of French letters:

[10] While, of course, it is Freud who in *Totem and Taboo* introduces the "dead father" in analytic theory, it is Guy Rosolato, following Lacan, who has elaborated the most sophisticated theoretical discussion of the role of the "dead father," cf. "Du père," and "Trois générations d'hommes dans le mythe religieux et la généalogie," in *Essais sur le symbolique* (Paris: Gallimard, 1969). For an understanding of the difference in the Lacanian concepts of the "symbolic father," and the "imaginary father," see Charles Shepherdson, *Vital Signs: Nature, Culture, Psychoanalysis* (New York: Routledge, 1999).

[11] In the following discussion I refer to both these works indiscriminately, although as it will become apparent the *Académie* as the more sophisticated, more elaborate work will be called upon more often. For an overview of the history of early modern pornography, see Lynn Hunt, ed., *The Invention of Pornography: Obscenity and the Origins of Modernity 1500–1800* (New York: Zone Books, 1993). Other interesting historical details are found in Jean Mainil, *Dans les règles du plaisir: Théorie de la différence sexuelle dans le discours obscène, romanesque et médical de l'ancien régime* (Paris: Éditions Kimé, 1996): Jean Marie Goulemot, *Ces livres qu'on ne lit que d'une main: Lecture et lecteurs de livres pornographiques au XVIII*^e^ *siècle* (Aix-en Provence, Alinéa, 1991), [trans. James Simpson, *Forbidden Texts: Erotic Literature and Its Readers in 18th-Century France* (Philadelphia, University of Pennsylvania Press, 1994), Robert Darnton, *Édition et sédition* (Paris: Gallimard, 1991), Peter Cryle, *Geometry in the Boudoir: Configuration of French Erotic Narrative* (Ithaca: Cornell University Press, 1994).

Nostre auguste père de Priape fulmine anathème contre tous ceux de l'un et de l'autre sexe qui liront ou entendront lire les préceptes d'amour, expliqués moralement en la célèbre *Escole des Filles*, sans spermatiser ou estre stimulés de quelque émotion spirituelle ou corporelle.[12]

Although there was no lack of licentious writings throughout the history of French literature and in particular during the early part of the seventeenth century (the uninhibited collection of verse *Le parnasse satyrique* for example) the publication of these two extended narrative fictions marks the emergence onto the stage of world literature of what can be properly called "pornography," if we accept (from the enormous and vexed range of possible meanings) as a working definition of pornography, the detailed and repeated "realistic" description of physical (i.e. genital) attributes and copulatory practices whose function, in the terms of Carter, is "that of arousing sexual excitement" (in the reader/viewer).[13] Pornography, as has been repeatedly noted, is essentially a "masturbatory machine."[14] Not the least of the many paradoxes that we will have to elucidate in our discussion is the emergence of this literature, a literature of the body, the body seized and exposed in its most physically intimate of postures during a period that is marked, as we have seen, notably, in philosophy, in esthetics (the *bienséances* of the Classical stage), and in "sociability"(e.g., the ever-increasing dominance in the civilizing process of the role of the women-centered salons of the Précieuses) by the effacement of body from representation.[15]

[12] "Bulle orthodoxe," *L'école des filles*, ed. Pascal Pia (Paris: La Bibliothèque Privée, 1969) LXI (All references to the *École des filles* are to this edition; in my discussion of the work I have adopted the modern orthograph of "école").

[13] Angela Carter, *The Sadeian Woman* (New York: Pantheon Press, 1978), "pornography's principal and most humanly significant function is that of arousing sexual excitement." Goulemot (*Forbidden Texts*, 10–11) notes, in relation to the seventeenth century's fascination with erotic literature: "Not that the seventeenth-century was entirely devoid of erotic literature. One need only recall the apparently insatiable demand for translations of the writing of Pietro Aretino and that some of the more marginal, more free-booting poets were quite happy to make abundant sacrifice at the altar of Venus." But he goes on to suggest (12) "that it was under Classicism that erotic literature was invented, with its rules of production, its means of distribution and the modes of consumption."

[14] Mainil, whose *Dans les règles du plaisir*, to my mind, and despite the differences in our theoretical approach to these texts, is the most elucidating study of early modern pornography and one to which my own reading owes much, writes, (25): "Obscene refers to any text that ostentatiously insists upon the physiological aspects of sexuality, any text whose principal interest lies exclusively in sexual coupling . . . or that pretends to lead to better sexual relations . . . or to the reader's masturbation. . . . I will call 'obscene' any text which in a more or less explicit way claims to invite its readers—both male and female—to 'spermatise.' " Carter in *The Sadeian Woman*, 12 says much the same thing.

[15] Here are two examples from literary historians. Writing about "libertinage érudit" (i.e., freethinking in matters of religion and philosophy as opposed to that freethinking associated with licentious behavior, although the two seem often to go hand in hand), René Pintard in *Le libertinage érudit dans la première moitié du dix-septième siècle* (Geneva: Slatkine, 1983) writes (86)" And this is why, as the years roll by, writers become more and more prudent. Those who continue to confront the thunderbolts of the justice system—the authors of the *Escole des filles* or of the *Bordel des muses* are inveterate debauchés. The literati, first among

On a very simple level one might suggest that the appearance of these texts that strip bare the body and expose it to view in its most asocial postures is merely a return of the repressed, an aggressive reaction to social, religious, and political dictates that prove too restrictive not to elicit rigorous resistance. But the question of pornography is too vexed, even here at its origin, to be met with any univocal answer. Despite the assertions of historians such as Lynn Hunt or Robert Darnton, who tend to see early-modern pornography as contestatory of the social status-quo, other commentators are quick to point out the inherently conservative political and social implications of pornography in general. Feminist critics, in particular, have attempted to analyze the duplicitous role pornography plays in simply reinscribing a patriarchal, phallocratic sexual division that always presents and represents a masculinist view of women, gender, and sexuality: the pornographic scenario of sexual liberation only serves to reinscribe a traditional subservience of women to men.[16]

Although I do not wish to enter into this debate, a debate that strikes me as a rather cacophonous *dialogue de sourds* between those who see pornography as essentially liberating and those who see it as a vicious degradation (of women, principally), I would like to situate my reading of France's early modern pornography on an admittedly slippery divide where the thematics

---

them Descartes, bend with an ever-growing ease to all the rules of a subtle diplomacy, as they learn the art of mitigation . . . and discover ways to outwit the censors)." Erich Auerbach, commenting in *Mimesis* on the aporia of passion and the body in French Classical tragedy states: "French tragedy took over the sublime conception of love which the Middle Ages had developed in courtly culture, not without the collaboration of mysticism and which Petrarchism had carried still further. . . . But in all this there is hardly a trace of the physical and sexual, which the taste of the time considered base and improper" (*Mimesis, The Representation of Reality in Western Literature*, trans. Willard Trask, [New York Doubleday, 1957], 340).

[16] Hunt, in the preface to *The Invention of Pornography*, (10), states that "in early modern Europe, that is, between 1500–1800, pornography was most often a vehicle for using the shock of sex to criticize religious and political authorities." Darnton, in his *Édition et sédition* writes (v–vi): "I claim that the illegal book, philosophical treatise, political tract, scandalous gossip corrode monarchical ideology and its pillars—the king, the church, and morality—by the systematic and unrestrained use of these arms: mockery, folly, critical and historical logic, pornography." On the other side, among the enormous amount of work done by the students of pornography, one could cite Carter (*The Sadeian Woman*, 17), who states that "most pornography remains in the service of the status-quo," or Michael Kimmel (*Men Confront Pornography* [New York: Crown Publishers, 1990], 15): "Pornography . . . does not represent a liberatory breath of free sexuality in the morally stale and fetid air of conservative censoriousness; it is only the sexualization of that traditional patriachal world. Pornography is not rebellion; it is conformity to a sexist business-as-usual." The bibliography on pornography is immense. Some of the works that have been instructive to my thinking are: Frances Ferguson, "Pornography: The Theory," in *Critical Inquiry* (spring 1995), 670–95; Michael Goldstein and Harold Kant, eds. *Pornography and Sexual Deviance* (Berkeley: University of California Press, 1973); Susan Gubar and Joan Hoff, eds., *For Adult Users Only* (Bloomington: Indiana University Press, 1989); Susan Griffen, *Pornography and Silence: Culture's Revenge against Nature* (New York: Harper and Row, 1980); Walter Kendrick, *The Secret Museum: Pornography in Modern Culture* (Berkeley: University of California Press, 1987); Berkeley Kaite, *Pornography and Difference* (Bloomington: Indiana University Press, 1995); Laura Kipnis, *Bound and Gagged: Pornography and the Politics of Fantasy in America* (New York: Grove Press, 1996). Other books and articles that have had a more direct influence on my argument will be cited.

of pornography (the conscious sociopolitical discourse of the text, a discourse constantly fragmented, interrupted, and also supported by the description of sexual acts) and the phantasmatics of pornography (precisely the multifarious unconscious fantasies and scenarios that exist in a transferential relation between reader and text and that are not easily amenable to thematic, that is sociopolitical univocity) collide. In the discussion here I am guided by the following questions: What is the political (i.e. sociosexual) role of the pornographic text in seventeenth-century France? How and in what ways do the fantasies for which these texts are the vehicles affect the reader—what, in other words, is the relation between the written text and the images—the visual/dreamlike scenarios evoked? What is the relation between vision and sexuality, how is the one imbricated in the other and what does that say for the origins of the modern subject? How do the fantasies that these texts produce work in contradictory and conflictual ways to shore up or undermine the dominant sexual discourse of Absolutism (what are the narrative strategies of the pornographic, and why, for instance, as has been so frequently noted, are the principal narrators "women")? Finally, how and in what ways does sexual excitement, the body engaged by these texts, these texts embodied in the masturbatory responses of the reader, reflect both the private but also the very public pleasure and anxiety of Classical France?[17] To put it in other terms, what is the role of (sexual) fantasy in the ongoing construction of the absolutist state and its subjects?

It has often been noted that although these two texts of the French seventeenth century are regarded as the founding novels of the modern pornographic genre, their own origin can be traced to the pervasive influence of an earlier text, that is itself a distillation of Italian Renaissance humanism, Pietro Aretino's *Ragionamenti* (or *Sei giornate*) published in 1534. Aretino's book went through myriad editions and was translated into all the major European languages during the sixteenth and seventeenth centuries. It was a text that, according to Jean-Marie Goulemot, was in particular demand in early seventeenth century France.[18] Without going into comparative detail I want simply to underline what are the two most distinctive features of the Aretin text which decisively influenced the *École des filles*, the *Académie des dames*, and their progeny.

On the one hand, Aretino, true to but also critical of the entire Renais-

[17] For a compilation of psychoanalytic theories of and on masturbation, see *Masturbation from Infancy to Senescence,* Ed. Irwin Marcus and John Francis (New York: International Universities Press, 1975). Masturbation was the central topic of discussion at the meetings of the Vienna Psychoanalytic Society from February to April of 1912. See vol. 4 of *the Minutes of the Vienna Psychoanalytic Society*, ed. Herman Nunberg and Ernst Federn (New York International Universities Press, 1975). Freud briefly commented specifically on the subject of masturbation, see "Contributions to a Discussion on Masturbation," (the Standard Edition [introduction, n. 2], 12: 239–54).

[18] Goulemot, *Forbidden Texts*, pp.10–11, "Not that the seventeenth century was entirely devoid of erotic literature. One need only recall the apparently insatiable demand for translations of the works of Pietro Aretino."

sance humanist tradition, couches his narrative in the form of Platonic dialogue between an older, experienced woman and a younger, sexually but also socially naive adolescent. In the *Sei giornate* it is the experienced prostitute, Nana, who instructs her daughter not only about sexuality but also about how sexuality is inextricably tied to ambient social and economic inequalities. Already we see in Aretino the analogy between sexuality and knowledge, between sexual knowledge and societal power which will continue to be a theme in the seventeenth-century texts. In both the *École* and the *Académie* sexual experience is equated with intellectual awakening, especially for the young girl, from a socially imposed, torpid ignorance:

> Ma cousine, cela est estrange; depuis que Robinet a couché avec moy et que j'ay veu et senty les choses, en examinant les raisons, tout ce que m'a dit par cy devant ma mère ne me paroist plus que sottises et des contes pour amuser les petis enfants. Je n'estois bonne auparavant qu'à filer et me taire, et à présent je suis bonne à tout ce que l'on voudra. Quand je parle maintenant avec ma mère, je me fonde en raisons et je discours comme si c'estoit une autre, au lieu qu'autrefois je n'osois desserrer les dents. Pour ce qui est de cela, l'esprit commence à me venir, et je mets mon nez dans les affaires où à peine aurois-je pu rien connoistre auparavant.[19]

The same message is relayed in the *Académie des dames*, initiation into sex initiates the young virgin into knowledge, into, that is, the universe of the intellect, the world of men:

> Octavie—Chez nous, on pourrait le dire, en un même endroit résident notre virginité et raison les deux plus précieuses choses de la vie. En prenant notre virginité l'homme nous ouvre aussi la raison.[20]

Aretino, following Plato's introduction of Diotima in the *Symposium*, reinscribes the tradition of the older, experienced woman who is called upon to explain, to the (reading) public at large, the relation between sexuality and power and, more important, the true nature of desire. "Why is Diotima a woman?" asks David Halperin at the beginning of an essay on the sexual politics and rhetorical strategies of the Platonic dialogues in general and of the *Symposium* in particular.[21] For it this latter work that is the ancestor of all those Renaissance Humanist treatises on love which in turn will serve the authors of licentious literature as the model for the ironic displacement of philosophy by pornography. And from the very beginning, in ancient Athens, the male author seduces his audience into the mysteries of

[19] *L'école des filles*, 61–62.
[20] *L'académie des dames*, a, 115. For a complete reference to this text, see n. 56 below.
[21] David Halperin, "Why Is Diotima a Woman? Platonic Eros and the Figuration of Gender," in *Before Sexuality* , ed. David Halperin, John Winkler, Froma Zeitlin (Princeton: Princeton University Press, 1990).

love by donning women's clothes. It would seem that in order to present the "truth" of desire, even if this desire is, as Halperin points out, "pederastic," it is only by becoming the other, by appearing in female drag, that an accurate accounting of sexuality can be revealed to men. Left to themselves men are bereft of true wisdom, of true philosophy and, one must assume, of any authentic knowledge of desire/sexuality.[22] The secrets of desire are known only to (old) women, or to those old men who, like Tiresias, are also women. But as Tiresias's sightlessness reminds us, this man can be a woman only by paying the ultimate price of castration. Tiresias's blindness, which enables him to speak of desire, equates the mysteries of femininity with the unseeable.

Rather than face the anxiety of castration, rather than risk losing their sight, male authors from Plato onward have preferred the "perverse" solution of transvestism.[23] While Plato cross-dresses as Diotima in order to expound the true nature of desire to men, he thus establishes several narrative but also ideological strategies that will have a long progeny. These narrative techniques will be incorporated in almost all the philosophical and pornographic treatises that are indebted to him.

Diotima is a "wise woman" who also, we must remember, is presented by Plato as a "prophetess," that is, her knowledge is not merely garnered from the quotidian experience of common humanity.[24] Through her gift of prophecy, Diotima communes with divine mysteries. It will take only the slightest misogynistic twist to distort her heavenly gift into an unnatural one, making her the ancestor of all those medieval and Renaissance experts in love, in love potions and philters, of all those old women from " la Celestina" on whose knowledge of carnality is intimately connected with their relation to the illicit, with the irreligious, and ultimately (for the Christian world) with the Satanic.[25] The character of Diotima as it evolves through the Middle Ages and the Renaissance, serves as the double font, the origin

[22] Ibid., 258: "Diotima is better informed about the desires of men than are men themselves. Without her expert intervention in their affairs, men would never be able to uncover the true sources, objects and aims of their own desires. It takes a woman to reveal men to themselves." See also, for another discussion of the function of Diotima in the Symposium, Luce Irigaray, "L'amour sorcier (Lecture de Platon, *Le banquet*, 'Discours de Diotime')," in *Éthique de la différence sexuelle* (Paris: Minuit, 1984), 27–41.

[23] I am referring here to Freud's distinction in his article "Fetishism" (Standard Edition, 21, 149–57): "for if a woman had been castrated, then his own possession of a penis was in danger; and against that there rose in rebellion the portion of his narcissism which Nature has, as a precaution attached to that particular organ" (153). It is that "rebellion," a spliting of the ego and a consequent denial of the reality of sexual difference, that the "fetish," a compromise solution, represents. See also my extended discussion of castration anxiety, fetishism and transvestism in chap. 3, "Absolutism and Androgyny."

[24] Halperin, "Why Is Diotima a Woman?" 264.

[25] Suzanne in the *École des filles* takes on, at the very end of the novel, the traditional role of go-between, allying herself with the Celestina tradition of marriage brokers, purveyors of illicit sex (168): "Laisse moy gouverner cest affaire [i.e. marriage] car c'est mon mestier cela. . . . J'ay faict des mariages plus d'un . . ."

of the figure of Sapientia, but also of Luxuria—of the wise woman and the sexually dangerous witch.

But the question remains "why is Diotima a woman?"—that is, why from the beginning, but even more intensely why on the threshold of modernity, is there the desire for the male author to chose the "perverse," one might say the fetishistic, solution to the fear of castration and to cross-dress as a female narrator? Halperin responds that Diotima is a "woman" because, at the dawn of philosophical discourse, Plato has recourse to the illusion, the masquerade of femininity, in order for men to form a homosocial network in which and through which masculinity can be "culturally reproduced."[26] This is surely true, but if we think of other more primitive, more "sacred" rites where, in the tradition of priestly tranvestism, shamans cross-dress as women in order both to endow themselves with what is most foreign in the female—the procreative power of the womb—and to ward off apotropaically the threat that this procreative power has to male hegemony, we can see that the desire to combine on one body the attributes of femininity while warding off the its threats, reinscribes on the body several layers of overdetermined cultural and psychic meaning.[27] On the one hand, and I will return to this, the cross-dressed narrator is an inscription of androgyny in the text which functions as both a fantasy of existential plenitude and the mythic representation of this fantasy. This myth/fantasy is an attempted response to the unanswerable enigma of sexual difference and desire. On the other hand, the cross-dressed narrator serves a simple discursive ploy which is to establish the narrative as gyneceum, where the secret of femininity is recast as the very founding fiction of the text itself. Here we are in a world of women from which men have been a priori excluded. It is this fictitious exclusion which sets up the very limits (the text as seraglio) that, on the first level of erotic titillation, the reader is invited to transgress.

[26] Halperin, "Why is Diotima a Woman?" 288: "Diotima's feminine presence at the originary scene of philosophy, at one of its founding moments, contributes an essential ingredient to the legitimation of the philosophical enterprise; her presence endows the pedagogic processes by which men reproduce themselves culturally—by which they communicate the secrets of their wisdom and social identity, the 'mysteries' of male authority, to one another across the generations with the prestige of female procreativity. Diotima is a woman because Sokratic philosophy must borrow her femininity in order to seem to leave nothing out and thereby to insure the success of its own procreative enterprises, the continual reproduction of its universalizing discourse in the male culture of classical Athens." In another context Nancy Miller, writing about the techniques of eighteenth-century novel (both traditional and pornographic novels), says that "female drag allows the male 'I' not so much to please the Other—by subscribing or capitulating to women's 'taste'—as to become the Other. . . . By this I mean that the founding contract of the novel as it functions in the phallocentric (heterosexual) economies of representation is homoerotic: 'women' is the legal fiction, the present absence that allows the male bond of privilege and authority to constitute itself within the laws of proper circulation" ("I's in Drag," in *French Dressing: Women, Men and Ancien Régime Fictions* [New York: Routledge, 1995], 93–105).

[27] For an encyclopedic overview of the cultural phenomenon of cross-dressing, see Marjorie Garber, *Vested Interests*: Cross-Dressing and Cultural Anxiety (New York: Routledge, 1992), and my discussion of transvestism in chap. 3.

Taboo and transgression exist, therefore, as the initial contract the text establishes with its reader. The voyeuristic pleasure and anxiety of the reader is instituted as the founding contract of pornographic reading. Freed from the controlling presence of men, women left to themselves can at last reveal their true nature, reveal their secrets. This strategy of narrative drag serves a constantly double purpose: on the one hand it establishes the taboo limit that the readerly gaze is constantly solicited to transgress, and at the same time it establishes this transgression as a vision, thus locking the pornographic text into a constant relay between discourse and vision, between, that is, the inextricable imbrication of the symbolic and the imaginary registers.

The narrator is in drag to give the illusion of a world of women from which the male is excluded, only to assure all the more that its secrets will be exposed to an intrusive, penetrating gaze.[28] The masquerade of the text, the masquerade of femininity, is the founding predicate for what is most essential in the pornographic scenario: the text in drag functions as the exhibitionistic pole that solicits and teases the voyeuristic gaze of the reader by a game of hide and seek. What is seen is never what is really there, and what is there is never what is actually shown.

The second of Aretino's innovations is directly connected with the first. He introduces *ekphrasis* as the vehicle for his narrative. It is this rhetorical trope that, from the beginning, colludes most pervasively with the elaboration of sexual excitement. Ekphrasis is the writerly attempt to visualize the written, to make what is written appear to be an unmediated vision.[29] The representation of sex, in the *Sei giornate* is inseparable from a certain narrative theatralization, which betrays the forceful presence of a *Schaulust* that is inseparable from the textual representation of sexuality and that will accompany with ever greater verve the French texts of the seventeenth century. In a sense the pornographic specificity of vision that these texts, imitating Aretino's lead, will make the centerpieces of their erotics is directly related to development of Renaissance painting, where the body is effaced by the marvelous perspective of the canvas. The geometry of the painting reduces the viewer's body to the confines of a disembodied eye which in

[28] Goulemot (*Forbidden Texts* p. 49) writes: "The erotic novel is then in essence a novel about voyeurism."

[29] Carlo Ferroni, in *Le voci dell'istrione: Pietro Aretino e la dissoluzione del teatro* (Naples: Liguori Editore, 1977), especially in chapter 4, "Il teatro della Nana," emphasizes the importance of theatricality, that is, a rhetoric of vision, for the textual construt_ion of the *Ragionamenti:* "The writing of the *Sei giornate* leads us to underline its specifically spectacular nature: the chattering of Nana is not simply the object of a reading or a listening, but it appears as something 'seen' and that makes crowds of spectators come running" (137). See also Peggy Findlen, " Humanism, Politics and Pornography in Renaissance Italy." In Hunt, *The Invention of Pornography*, (49–109), Findlen also comments: "Aretino's dialogues make full use of visual currencies." (74). For a discussion of the use of *ekphrasis* in classical texts, see Sarah Goldhill, "Refracting Classical Vision," in Teresa Brennan, and Martin Jay, ed., *Vision in Context* (London: Routledge, 1996).

turn seeks (in Linda Williams's phrase) the "frenzy of the visible" to revision its own disappearance in the constantly evoked scenarios of the body unveiled and infused with an overwhelming sexuality.[30] This textual *Schaulust* will go on to infuse ever more descriptive, voyeuristic detail in the eighteenth century (cf. Sade's complex, almost Piranesian tableaux) and will ultimately realize its own potential in the final transformation (inversion) of contemporary pornography, where the visual (in the form of film and video) now entirely dominates pornographic representation. Where previously the eye had to satisfy itself, because of the technological inadequacies of the printed narrative, with the illusions of rhetoric, it can now gorge itself (without apparently ever reaching satiety) in the seemingly never-ending production of visual pornography. Our contemporary plethora of pornographic videos can be seen as the ultimate apotheosis of the eye as sex organ which was given its first definition during the Italian Renaissance.

> Pornography is profoundly and paradoxically social, but even more than that, it's acutely historical. Pornography's favorite terrain is the tender spots where the individual psyche collides with the historical process of molding social subjects.[31]

Laura Kipnis, whose work on this subject is indebted to psychoanalysis and the emphasis analysis places on the role of fantasy in the construction of both individual and collective identities, makes a compelling case for understanding pornography as intimately mimicking, in its very essence, the instabilities and anxieties of the dominant culture inside of which it flourishes.[32] In other words, according to Kipnis and also to many other theorists of the pornographic conversant with psychoanalytical theory, the fantasmatic space opened by pornography not only engages the reader as an isolated sexual subject but situates that sexuality within a sociocultural context. The pornographic universe perhaps more acutely than other forms of representation underlines both the political aspects of sexuality as well as

[30] Linda Williams, *Hard Core: Power, Pleasure and the "Frenzy of the Visible"* (Berkeley: University of California Press, 1989).

[31] Kipnis, "How to Look at Pornography," in *Bound and Gagged*, 167. Carter has a similar take on the imbrication of sociality and pornography: "sexual relations between men and women always render explicit the nature of social relation in the society in which they take place and, if described explicitly, will form a critique of those relations" (*The Sadeian Woman*, 20).

[32] Carter (*The Sadeian Woman)* has, with an emphasis on the inequitable economic relations in a bourgeois society pointed to the same rootedness of pornography in social and economic structures of the society its fantasies reproduce: "relationships between the sexes are determined by history and by the historical fact of the economic dependence of women upon men" (6). She continues: "Although the erotic relationship may seem to exist freely, on its own terms, among the distorted social relationships of a bourgeois society, it is, in fact, the most self-conscious of all human relationships, a direct confrontation of two beings whose actions in bed are wholly determined by their acts when they are out of it" (9).

the sexualization of the political (how an individual is subjected to the laws governing the social conventions of the world into which she or he is born).

We have already seen how, in another, anthropological register, Mary Douglas has discussed the ways the body can be used to symbolize social anxieties, anxieties of dissolution, fragmentation, chaos: "The body is a model which can stand for any bounded system. Its boundaries can represent any boundaries which are threatened or precarious."[33] Discussing the importance of Douglas's work for an understanding of the interrelatedness of the individual body and the body politic, Judith Butler underlines, with her own reading of recent French psychoanalytical theorists, what can be seen as a first step in understanding the interrelation among infractions of bodily openings ("margins"), anxiety, and pornography: "all social systems are vulnerable at their margins, and all margins are accordingly considered dangerous. If the body is synecdochical for the social system per se or a site in which open systems converge, then any kind of unregulated permeability constitutes a site of pollution and endangerment."[34] Anxiety is introduced into the social fabric at those insecure points where distinctions between inside and outside, self and other, male and female are maintained with only the greatest vigilance. Despite this watchfulness (both individual and communal) these distinctions, which paradoxically are fueled by the libidinal charge that unconscious fantasies carry, are always destined—by the very fact that their own force comes from what they are trying to repress—to remain vulnerable, more or less secure, more or less anxiety provoking.

Psychoanalysis since Freud has emphasized the importance of the same bodily openings/ margins that Douglas describes in symbolic, anthropological theory. From the *Three Essays on the Theory of Sexuality* and continuing throughout his work, Freud situated these bodily sites as the physical ground upon which, or rather through which sexuality, first as inchoate physical pleasure, then as the fantasies of pleasure, is introduced into the infant. Pleasure and thus sexuality are introjected, by the ministrations ("seductions") of the mother (or her substitute) "into" the infant. By extension, however, given the parents' own psychic imbrication in their culture's taboos (law), customs, and prejudices, this "seduction" of the infant into sexuality, is also and co-terminously freighted with moral injunctions, guilt, and fear.[35] Jean Laplanche has been the most articulate contemporary theoretician to reaffirm Freud's founding discussion of the role of seduction, "seduction at the bodily borders" in and through which, according to Laplanche, sexuality as fantasy is introduced into the infant:

> We recall that these zones, sites of transit and exchange, are above all and primordially the focal points of maternal ministrations. This hygienic care is mo-

[33] Douglas, *Purity and Danger*, 115.

[34] Judith Butler, *Gender Trouble: Feminism and the Subversion of Identity* (New York: Routledge, 1990), 132.

[35] Freud, *Three Essays on the Theory of Sexuality*, (Standard Edition, vol. 7).

tivated consciously by hygienic solicitousness, but in this solicitousness wishful unconscious fantasies are everywhere at work.[36]

If we thus compare the anthropological and psychoanalytical theories of the importance of the body, and particularly of bodily orifices for serving as hot spots that relay, through symbolizations, inner and outer realities, the space through which the outside world enters into the infant's reality as saturated sensations—saturated with both a physical and psychic charge, a charge that overwhelms the very primitive and limited receptive system of the child—we can understand how these highly charged zones will become the sites of intense and often contradictory fantasies that inhabit the child without his or her ever being able to fully metabolize them into an entirely successful defensive system. These fantasies are rarely consonant with the normative and prescriptive discourses that greet the child and lead him/her down the paths of acceptable social/sexual gender adaptation.[37]

The political structures with their concomitant discursive networks that ensure the maintenance and survival of any society present themselves as the elaboration in the present of eternal truths discovered or enunciated in the distant past. These verities must be embodied in each new generation. It falls to those social institutions, marriage, family, religion, to mold ritually the individual to the laws, to the practices, and, more important to the acceptable forms of desire of that society into which he or she is born. It is through these institutions that the newborn subject of the state is sutured into all those sociosexual roles that give him/her a social meaning and status. In return, the subject is called upon to ratify, by his/her participation in the rituals of society, those institutions that by this participation are reaffirmed as "natural."[38] The political seeks its auto-justification by a constant appeal to have its own "naturalness" validated by its subjects' willing acquiescence to whatever roles it pre-assigns them—social roles, gender roles, economic roles. That these roles are infused with a fantasy life of their own is what is not allowed into rational discourse. When, however, a form of representation arises that gives precedence to fantasy over quotidian reality, that reasserts the role of the margins, the "holes" in the corporate fabric

36 Jean Laplanche, *Nouveaux fondements pour la psychanalyse* (Paris: P.U.F., 1987), 127.

37 Kaja Silverman in her continued explorations of the importance of the "gaze" in cinema and culture (*The Threshold of the Visible World* [New York: Routledge, 1996]) refers to Laplanche's theoretical importance "Laplanche . . . maintains that bodily openings enjoy their powerful status because they represent the points at which fantasy is introduced into the child" (14).

38 Clifford Geertz, "Centers, Kings, and Charisma; Reflections on the Symbolics of Power," in *Local Knowledge: Further Essays in Interpretive Anthropology* (New York: Basic Books, 1983), quoted in Eric Santner, *My Own Private Germany*: *Daniel Paul Schreber's Secret History of Modernity* (Princeton; Princeton University Press. 1996), xiii, writes "At the political center of any complexly organized society . . . there is both a governing elite and a set of symbolic forms expressing the fact that it is in truth governing. . . . It is these—crowns and coronations, limousines and conferences—that mark the center as center and give what goes on there its aura of being not merely important but in some odd fashion connected with the way the world is built."

rather than to the image of the constructed and bounded body, then anxieties that have been suppressed resurface in the body politic bringing down the wrath of those institutions whose role of guardian of the social order is inevitably put into question.

One of the imputed dangers of pornography is the arousal of sexual fantasies whose power is "ecstatic": the sexual arousal induced by the representation carries the reader out of the bounds of his/her socially defined self. By revealing the precariousness of that self's construction, it at the same time calls into question, if only for one spasmodic moment, the stability of all those symbolic institutions whose role it is to shore up the self-conscious identifications that made that self a viable social entity. We can understand, therefore, how the pornographic representation of sexual acts and practices will have a heated resonance as they inevitably trigger larger political anxieties in the world.

It can only be assumed that the greater the social insecurities of a particular society the more hostile will be the reactions of those institutions to which are entrusted the defense of political, psychic, and bodily borders. France during the period of the Frondes was politically and socially a society going through rather stormy changes in polity. The regency of Anne d'Autriche, like all previous regencies, marks a moment of great vulnerability: the consolidating work of Absolutism carried out under the regimes of Louis XIII and Richelieu is threatened during the minority of Louis XIV. The *Frondes*, bear witness to the underlying instability of the monarchical regime. At the same time dissensions in religion (the rise and conflict of Jansenism, the continued resistance of Protestant communities) further threaten the stability of the realm. Finally, discussions in science and philosophy, changes in esthetic values, mark the midcentury as a period of intense social realignments.[39]

When in the middle of this period *L'école des filles* appeared, it was quickly embroiled in a scandal that was symptomatic for what it reveals about the anxieties and vulnerabilities of mid-seventeenth-century France. We have a rather complete juridical record of the arrest (or attempted arrest), interrogations, judgment, and punishment of the two principal "producers" (the word "author" is inappropriate) of the text, Jean L'Ange and Michel Millot.[40] Upon its publication in 1655 the book was seized, all copies of it were destroyed (except for some that were supposedly in the possession of Scarron but which have not come down to us) and the two

[39] Joan DeJean, in "The Politics of Pornography: *L'école des filles*," in Hunt, ed., *The Invention of Pornography*, 120, writes "it is important to remember that it [*L'école*] is the product of a true transitional moment."

[40] I am following Pascal Pia's narration of the case in the introduction to the above-cited (n. 12) edition of the text. All the relevant material to the trial of the two defendants is included at the end of this edition. See also, DeJean, "The Politics of Pornography," for a discussion of the political implication of the novel's publication.

culprits condemned.[41] The royal prosecutor demanded the following sentence:

> Sçavoir ledit Millot estre pendu et estranglé à une potence plantée au mesme lieu où lesdits exemplaires seront bruslez et à l'esgard dudit Lange faire amende honorable devant le portail de l'eglise Nostre-Dame teste et pieds nuz en chemise, ayant une torche ardante en la main du poidz de deux livres, ce fait condamné à servir le Roy dans ses galleres comme forçat le temps et espace de cinq ans.[42]

The sentence strikes us as extreme, even given the harsh climate of the period.[43] The book was condemned by the court as being "contre l'honneur de Dieu, de l'Eglise et fort contraire aux bonnes moeurs et discipline chrestienne."[44] It is not particularly surprising that a book that purports to be a marriage manual but that cynically undermines the sacramental aspects of marriage and that, rather than offering marriage as a holy act that founds society, presents it simply, and uncomplicatedly, as a cover allowing women precisely what society prohibits, free sexual choice, would obviously call down the wrath of those institutions it surreptitiously threatens. What impresses me as more intriguing is not so much the official, if extreme reaction to *L'école*, but rather the strange rumors about its provenance, about its assumed authorship, and therefore about the anxieties (political and sexual) to which the book gave rise. These rumors reflect an entire epoch's concern with "la chose sexuelle" embodied in and as a heterosexual (and quite traditional) battle between the sexes.

Two anecdotes about the book pique our interest. The first concerns the acknowledgment, by Jean L'Ange during his interrogation, that he had given "eight or nine" copies of the book to Paul Scarron.[45] The allusion to Scarron is intriguing for several reasons not least of which is that the mention of Scarron broadens the scope of the *L'école*'s literary genealogy, enlarging its aire de réception by associating it, through the person of Scarron, with the entire libertine tradition (both philosophical and sexual) of the first decades of the French seventeenth century. This reference to Scarron

41 "No trace remains of the original edition of pornography's alleged original work; the earliest editions available, those on which all modern editions have been based, date from 1667 and 1668" (DeJean, "The Politics of Pornography," p. 112).

42 Pia, *L'école des filles*, xxviii–xxx.

43 Pintard, in *Le libertinage érudit*, 24, reminds us that the government did use greater physical force, that capital punishment increased (particularly after the Frondes) as the century progressed to punish crimes of "blasphemy." "Thus, one punished more and more invoking the crimes of impiety and sacrilege."

44 *L'école des filles,* "Les pièces du procès," 177.

45 Pia, Introduction to *L'école des filles*, xxvi. For other possible connections to the "libertins," he states "But, L'Ange himself, without being the author, had a taste for books and 'curiosities' of literary life. He had connections to Scarron and had even earned the gratitude of poor Tristan l'Hermite" (xviii).

extends the potential space of which the novel is the nexus back in time, encompassing by association the persecuted libertine writers, but also the by now banished baroque/grotesque body and its esthetic which we associate with them. It also and at the same time, however, through Scarron's relations first with Nicholas Fouquet (who also purportedly kept, well hidden, a copy of the book) but more importantly with Scarron's wife, Françoise d'Aubigné, later Mme de Maintenon, projects the book forward into the century and places it squarely, with all its subversive potential, at the heart of Absolutism's inner sanctum, at Versailles, and more curiously, through Maintenon's eventual morganatic marriage to the king, at the center of Louis XIV's family life.[46]

Even more compelling, and this final anecdote will bring me closer to what I believe is the potent phantasmatic imbrication of history, sociality, and sexuality, that may lie at the heart of both the *École* and the *Académie des dames*, is the rumor, more diffuse than real, that Françoise d'Aubigné was either (pick your version) the model for the novel's naive main character, Franchon, or even more symptomatic, the actual author of the work. Although Pascal Pia has sufficiently debunked the historical reality of this rumor, it is intriguing for what it reveals about the phantasmatic aura that surrounded Françoise d'Aubigné. It is, I would propose, an aura that before her enveloped those other women accused of too-intimate proximity with the seat of French power, the royal throne, Catherine and Marie de Médicis, and as it was, with infinitely greater violence, to plague, both in life and death, that other symbol of female usurpation, Marie-Antoinette.[47]

Patriarchal monarchy, such as that of absolutist France (in its phantasmatic underpinnings), is subtended by many conflicting fantasies of the kingly, masculine body.[48] Chief among these is the fantasy of autochtho-

[46] We know, of course, that several of the ladies-in-waiting to the dauphine were caught reading *L'école* in secret at Versailles. When discovered they were summarily dismissed from their positions and sent back, in disgrace, to their respective homes in the provinces. "The ladies-in-waiting to Mme la Dauphine lent each other the *École des filles* to the annoyance of their governess, the marquise de Montchevreuil, who feared being reproached for the shamelessness of her charges. On this subject, Bussy-Rabutin wrote, 19 November 1687, to his cousin Sévigné: 'Mme de Montchevreuil having found in the bedchamber of the ladies-in-waiting to the dauphine a book entitled the *École des filles* went to complain to the king, telling him that she could no longer guarantee (their virtue). His majesty answered her by relieving her of this burden, saying that neither the queen his mother nor the queen his wife had been able to keep any of their ladies-in-waiting, he doubted that the Dauphine would have any greater success. Two months later, on January 17, all the ladies-in-waiting were dismissed" (Ibid. xl–xli).

[47] These rumors concerning Françoise d'Aubigné were revived at the beginning of this century by Pierre Louys. Pascal Pia in his introduction (xxvi–xxvi) demonstrates the improbability of any connection of the novel with Mme Scarron, either as its model or author. Nevertheless, what I find intriguing is not the reality of Françoise d'Aubigné's role or lack thereof in the novel, but the phantasmatic scenario that she induces both in her contemporaries and in modern commentators. Pierre Louys, we are told, admits to a "a feeling of instinctive horror" (xxxi) about her. It is precisely this horror, a mingling of loathing and desire, which is compelling.

[48] For an interesting study on the sexual fantasies associated with the king, his body, and that body's sexual prowess or lack thereof—but in this case more specifically Louis XVI—see

nous self-sufficiency, that is, the "sacred" power of the king to control the chaotic forces of nature, to keep nature under control. This fantasy/desire is grounded in the more primitve phantasm of a conflict between very powerful forces of concentration and dispersion that will become embodied, in an individual's early life, in sexed images of the primitive parental couple (the Urvater and the "phallic mother"). The principal attribute of the symbolic father is his extraordinary phallic power. Both anthropology, in studies of various "primitive" kingdoms, and psychoanalysis with Freud's own myth of the "primal father," a myth taken up and expanded upon by Lacan, associate masculine power (and anxiety) to sexual potency which is seen as one of the key qualities fantasized by the subjects of the charismatic leader/chief/king.[49] When, therefore, a woman, for whatever reason, is suspected of coming too close to that self-sufficiency and thus implying an unmanning of the king in his symbolic role—and this usually is facilitated by the "actual " king not being consubstantial with his symbolic potential, that is, not able because of age (too young, as during a regency) or too old (as at the end of an era, i.e., Louis XIV living on during the decline both of his regime's former splendor and his own body's youthful prowess) of representing in his real body, the symbolic body's fantasized potential—the woman is blamed for opening this breech in the body politic, for making that (masculine) body more like her own. Femininity is too contagious, too invasive not to create anxieties of dispersion and fragmentation in the political theorists of Absolutism. The demonizing fantasy of a woman in power is placed into phallocentric narratives as an apotropaic talisman. These become patriarchal morality tales, whose role it is to constantly warn the reader/spectator of the imagined threat to social (masculinist) order that this "unnatural woman" represents and to protect, by the same token, the image of the benevolent and potent charismatic leader, the "father of the nation."

Classical literature is rife with representations of these dangerous threats to phallic self-sufficiency. In a position of power, the woman is seen as unnatural because she has either usurped male prerogative (the haunting fantasy of Agrippine or Athalie in Racine's tragic rescription of this fantasy), or has stepped beyond the bounds of acceptable feminine behavior, Corneille's Camille or Chimène for instance, the latter of whom is branded by the learned members of the newly constituted French Academy quite simply as "unnatural" ("amante trop sensible et fille trop dénaturée").[50] Any slippage

---

Antoine de Baecque, *Le corps de l'histoire: Métaphores et politique 1770–1800* (Paris: Calmann-Lévy, 1993).

[49] Cf. Freud, *Totem and Taboo* (Standard Edition vol. 13). Freud's initial speculations have been taken up recently by social/ political theorists. See particularly, Eli Sagan, *At the Dawn of Tyranny* (New York; Knopf, 1985), and the work of Eugène Enriquez, *De la horde à l'état: Essai de psychanalyse du lien social* (Paris: Gallimard, 1986), and more recently, *Les figures du maître* (Paris: Arcantère, 1991).

[50] Jean Chapelain, *Les sentiments de l'Académie française*, quoted in Paul Pelisson, *Histoire de l'Académie française* (Paris: 1700) 39.

in male potency, any usurpation of masculine prerogative is immediately blamed on the woman as excessive—excessively sexual, excessively perverse, excessively ruthless. All these accusations will be hurled against the two Medicis regents, against Maintenon, and of course, as all the pornographic pamphlets of the Revolutionary period attest, against Marie-Antoinette. It is fascinating therefore to see that in the continual tug-of-war that exists between the sexes, as soon as male authority wanes, as soon as that authority can no longer be seen as a sufficiently powerful to bolster the integrity of the state, that state's decline either economically or militarily will be blamed on the flip side of the sexual coin—on female duplicity, which always reveals itself to be inextricably tied to the mysteriously dynamic, yet forever irrecuperable, power of the womb. In the last resort the battle of gender (and political) hegemony comes down to a sexualized fantasy, to "le combat du vit et du con," as the title of the satirical poem that closes the *École des filles* so unambiguously puts it.

It is this battle, or rather the fantasies that are evoked by it, that underlies the pornography and the concomittant sexual excitement of both the *École des filles* and the later, more elaborate, more complex, *Académie des dames*.[51] We must not forget that at the deepest psychic level, masturbatory fantasies reveal both the intensity of primitive, infantile sexuality and the anxieties attached to this sexuality and inseparable from it.[52] In a sense we must even see the fantasies as a defense against the disruptive power of the anxiety.[53] These anxieties almost always include threats to corporal integrity and to gender identity. They express the fear of and yet the desire for disintegration, for fragmentation, for reabsorption into the maternal body, the return to the womb. Seventeenth-century pornography will always present itself, therefore, as both a transgression and the immediate recupera-

[51] Many of the commentators of this latter work are struck by what they perceive to be its violently misogynistic tone. Cf. Lise Leibacher-Ouvrard, "Pseudo-féminocentrisme et ordre (dis)simulé: La *Satyra sotadica* (1658–1678) et l'*Académie des dames* (1680)," in *Ordre et contestation au temps des classiques* (Tubingen, *Papers on French Seventeenth-Century Literature*, 1992), 193–202. Although the misogyny of the text is an interesting phenomenon and perhaps even worthy of indignation, we should remember that according to the psychoanalyst who has worked most extensively in the field of pornography, Robert Stoller, (*Sexual Excitement: The Dynamics of Erotic Life*, [New York: Pantheon, 1979], 6), "it is hostility—the desire, overt or hidden, to harm another person—that generates and enhances sexual excitement." In this he comes close to allying his own clinical observations with Georges Batatille's theoretical speculations about the complex interweaving of sadism and masochism in erotic excitement; see *L'érotisme* (Paris: Minuit, 1957).

[52] Joyce McDougall, for instance, writes in *Théâtres du je* (Paris: Gallimard, 1982), 88: "Masturbatory fantasms . . . conceal in condensed fashion the entire history of the analysand's infantile sexuality and they indicate to us, at the same time, where the greatest concentration of anxiety lies."

[53] See Stoller (*Sexual Excitement*, 21) "Excitement, then, is a defense against anxiety, a transformation of anxiety into something more bearable, a melodrama. The ultimate danger that I believe lies at the heart of sexual excitement is that one's sense of existence, especially in the form of one's sense of maleness or femaleness, can be threatened."

tion of that social/sexual violation, both a liberation and a constantly recycled frustration. As a first step in trying to elucidate the role of the pornographic in early modern France, we might start by seeking to understand it as an ambiguous mise-en-scène of primitive anxieties. These anxieties are then expressed as sexualized representations that are freighted with and informed by the power relations that pertain between the sexes in that society, with their constant instabilities and possible realignments. In a sense the political insecurities of corporate integrity, an integrity that is symbolized in the kingly "corps glorieux," get reflected back in the anxieties manifested in the underlying sexual scenarios of pornography. Threats to the integrity of the realm are reproduced in the two novels as the never-ending duel between the rampant penises and the insatiable wombs.

The relation between the penis and the vagina ("le combat du vit et du con") can be reduced in its essential to a relation between the visible (perhaps, as I've said, the omnipresent vision of the king as phallus) and the invisible (the female sex, which in phallocratic relation to the portrait of the king, is seen as an absence, a lack), between that which can be seen and what always remains at a remove, always hidden. Despite both books' having been described most recently by Jean Mainil as celebrations of the phallus and of phallic power, what I believe is more essential is not so much the omnipresence of the penis—the detailed descriptions of the male organ, "en long et en large"—although the fantasies attached to the male organ are important and will be discussed in due turn—but rather the invisibility of the female organ, and the impossibility to "see," to know, to describe, and, therefore in some sense, to contain it.[54] In *L'école des filles* the expert Suzanne goes into rather graphic detail as she explains to Franchon the anatomy of the male member:

> Premièrement, tu doibs sçavoir que cest engin du garçon a une peau par dessus, douillette et unie, qui donne du plaisir à la fille quand elle y touche avec la main. Il est dur et plein de ners par dedans, et l'on sent cela par dessous la peau, qui est mouvante. Par dessous et le long de cest engin, il y a un tuyau qui paroist enflé comme une grosse veine et qui aboutit à la teste, là où il y a une petite fente en long, comme d'un coup de lancette. (19)

But, when it comes to describing the corresponding female member, Suzanne can say nothing. All she can do, true to the "monosexual" theory of her time, is to offer a cursory explanation that the female genital is simply an

[54] Mainil in *Dans les règles du plaisir* reads the two pornographic texts in conjunction with medical and philosophical treatises of the day. Despite what appears to be the "female-centered" status of the novels Mainil correctly reads the texts against themselves to prove that they are, indeed, "phallocentric" celebrations of the male organ and masculine power politics. Having said this, and being in agreement with him, I also want to stress that where I differ, is in the more ambivalent role of fantasy, which Mainil does not address, remaining as he does on the level of a thematic analysis of the texts.

inverted version of the male: "Pour la fille je ne sçais comment elle est faite, mais on dit qu'elle a un engin par dedans, fait comme celui du garçon (19).[55]

For Suzanne, her creator and her readers, the female sex is unknown and unknowable, either because it is simply, at one and the same time, exactly like the male organ and exactly unlike it. By the time we come to the *Académie des dames,* however, written in a much more elaborate, narratively self-confident style, what appeared unknowable in the *École*, gives way to a detailed anatomical description of the female organ. Despite the clinical depiction of the external sexual organ of the woman, however, as this delineation comes closer to the mysterious interior of the female body, anatomical detail gives way to metaphor, the rhetoric of approximation, of comparison, of fantasy. The female body becomes a "garden," a "dark profundity of nothingness (emptiness)", a "flower," a "grotto," and so forth:

> Tullie—Enfin, l'intervalle qui s'étend de l'entrée au fond du jardin a reçu le nom de gaine; c'est là que l'organe s'introduit, lorsque la femme reçoit le choc. Les médecins l'appellent tantôt col ou canal de l'utérus, tantôt sein de pudicité. Cette gaine entoure, étreint et serre le membre viril dès qu'il y pénètre et s'y insinue: elle est, Octavie, comme le conduit par lequel le genre humain est amené des obscures profondeurs du néant à la lumière du jour.
>
> Octavie—Tu sais si bien dépeindre, qu'il me semble moi-même voir tout ce qui se cache au fond de mes entrailles, comme si c'était placé devant mes yeux. (*Académie*, a, 71–72)[56]

But, Octavia is both prescient and wrong. She is correct to focus her (and the reader's) attention on the descriptive, visual quality of her tutor's lessons, but she is naive in thinking that these descriptions present a pristine vision of her body's interior. The very formula she uses ("il me semble") both hides and reveals the desire to visualize the body's interior and the imaginary quality of that vision. The phrase " it seems to me" indicates precisely this ambiguity it "appears," or rather "I have the impression that," involves us in an entire baroque play between "seeming and being," between objective fact and subjective fantasy.

One has only to look at any of the myriad anatomical engravings of the period to see how the attempts to objectify the body's organs are inextricably linked to, and inseparable from cultural and personal fantasies.[57] In

[55] Thomas Laqueur has argued in *Making Sex: Body and Gender from the Greeks to Freud* (Cambridge: Mass.: Harvard University Press, 1990) for the predominance of the "one sex" view of anatomy in early modern Europe.

[56] I have read two versions (of the many that exist) of the *Académie des dames*, referred to as version a and version b in the text. Version a is *L'oeuvre de Nicolas Chorier*, "Satyre sotadique de Luisa Sigea," introduction and notes by Bagneux De Villeneuve (Paris: Bibliothèque des Curieux, 1910); and b is *L'académie des dames* in *Oeuvres érotiques du XVIIe siècle,* "L'enfer de la Bibliothèque nationale," ed. Michel Camus (Paris: Fayard, 1988) 393–639.

[57] Jonathan Sawday, (*The Body Emblazoned: Dissection and the Human Body in Renaissance Culture,* London: Routledge, 1995) offers ample iconographic evidence of this inability to separate "objective reality" and fantasy.

this regard we should perhaps remember that the seventeenth century was not particularly idiosyncratic in its inability to separate clinical knowledge of the body from fantasies about this same body. As Jean Laplanche reminds us, there is always a large divide separating objective, scientific knowledge of the body on the one hand and, on the other, the fantasies that individuals retain, regardless of their rational information about the interior reality of their own and others' bodies.[58] It is the phantasmatic aspect of the body, and here, essentially the fantasies about the unknowable sex of the woman, that poses the central enigma of the pornographic text and functions as the focal point of the characters' and the readers' aroused curiosity.

The theoretical and practical sciences of the seventeenth century made great strides in two mutually interrelated domains, the study of optics and the practice of anatomy. Many of the major scientific discussions of the day, from Galileo and Newton to Leibnitz and Descartes, dealt in one way or another with perfecting the different apparatuses of vision and the consequences of such innovations for scientific progress.[59] In the heady atmosphere of philosophical and scientific debate it is difficult to sort out the role of *Schaulust* as a sexualized instinct-driving fantasy from the apparently more objective quest for scientific knowledge. In an area that is of more direct interest to me here, however, we can point out that anatomy, especially the direct viewing of the body through clinical dissections, achieves, if we are to believe recent historians, almost a cultlike following in all the major intellectual centers of Europe.[60] Public dissections, performed in the amphitheaters of Europe's leading universities, probed the body in order to uncover and reveal to the curious eyes of physicians and of the lay public at large its inner workings, its best-kept secrets.

Although the bodies opened and revealed to the gaze of an insatiable public's eyes were clearly of the both sexes, we can suppose, from the engravings that were reproduced to illustrate the learned anatomical disquisitions, starting with Vesalius' 1543 treatise *De humani corporis fabrica* which has on its cover the dissected body of a woman, that the iconographic focal point seems to zoom in, once again, on the mysterious insides of the female anatomy. Jonathan Sawday reminds us that it is possible "to think of the 'new science' of the latter seventeenth century as a determinedly 'masculine' creation." He goes on to state, however, that the aim of the "major scientific, i.e. biological inquiry of the seventeenth century was the

[58] Jean Laplanche, *Castration/Symbolisations* (*Problématiques,* vol. 2, [Paris: P.U.F., 1980], 51): "Psychoanalysis . . . underlines the idea of an anatomy or an imaginary body, a body where notably everything that is on the inside is fantasized in the most extravagant way without any relation to scientific discoveries.

[59] For an overview of the importance of optics in this period, see Françoise Siguret, *L'oeil surpris* (Tubingen: Biblio 17, 1985).

[60] See for instance the work of Barker (*The Tremulous Private Body*), T. Laqueur (*Making Sex*), and especially, Sawday (*The Body Emblazoned*).

exploration of the 'reproductive body.' "[61] The desire to explore the procreative body strikes us as intimately connected to sexual fantasies about the powerful, mysterious womb in its opposition to the potent penis, fantasies in which are imbricated a whole series of political and sexual issues, issues of power and control. The field of reproductive inquiry fueled and continued a scientifico-philosophical debate that pitted an outmoded Aristotelianism with its self-assured male-centered view of reproduction (the "animaculists") against the more modern *ovaristes* those defenders of the theory of the predominance of the ova over the sperm in the reproductive process. At stake, in this struggle, was the natural scientific rock upon which could be eternally fixed the triumph of masculine activity over feminine passivity, of ideality over materiality, of, finally, the ideological predicates of patriarchy over any usurping feminocentric theory.[62]

It is this struggle that surfaces in the fantasies and anxieties of the pornographic texts as they both hide and reveal their own desire to see the invisible ("where babies come from") by focusing on the sex of the woman, as a surrogate for the unknowable maternal womb. Guy Rosolato, the French psychoanalyst and theorist, has elaborated a concept—the "objet de perspective"—that strikes me as useful for understanding the complex conundrum in which the strands of sexuality, vision, and knowledge are knotted. Rosolato defines the "perspectival object" in the following way:

> It is possible to detect in any material or mental object where focalization in/on a vanishing point is elaborated in relation to a specific organization, an area in which a question, an opening, or a mystery is concentrated in the very space where a proliferation of cover-ups or disguises is being simultaneously constructed. It is thus a question of a localized manifestation of a limit, of an interface between the visible and the invisible, or, in a more general sense, between the known and the unknown.[63]

Tom Conley has glossed Rosolato's description of the "perspectival object" writing that "it figures a concentrated point of attention that captures what a subject chooses to see, simply because in it resides what cannot, because

[61] J Sawday, *The Body Emblazoned*, 231. Freud, of course, equates the desire to "see" with the desire to "know." In his discussion of childhood sexual fantasies (*Three Essays On the Theory of Sexuality*) he remarks that the child's initial question, "is not the question of the distinction between the sexes but the riddle of where babies come from" (Standard Edition, 7: 195), the desire to explore the interior of the mother's body, to "see" where babies come from precedes, but is related to, the problem of sexual difference.

[62] For an extended discussion of this debate see Marie-Hélène Huet, *Monstrous Imagination* (Cambridge, Mass.: Harvard University Press, 1994), and Mainil, *Dans les règles du plaisir*, chap. 4, who writes (44): "Having become active in procreation and indispensable because she bears within her the fecundable egg from which the world will develop 'ab ovo' woman will be forever accused of being too curious. Education alone, or rather its absence, will be able to guarantee the submission of woman to the ideological status quo."

[63] Guy Rosolato, "L'objet de perspective dans ses assises visuelles," in *Pour une psychanalyse exploratrice dans la culture* (Paris: P.U.F., 1993), 29.

of its paradoxical evidence and accessibility, be seen.[64] It is, in other words, a visual or discursive device that, rather like the geometrical "focal point" in Renaissance painting, fixes the viewer in a certain position, allowing a vision informed by precisely what is not visible, what is kept by this one view unseeable and unknowable. It is, however, the unseen, that informs by its very absence the power and fascination of what is perceived, and believed. It is important to remember that for Rosolato, what is unseen, what remains in an analytic perspective, unseeable and yet what informs infantile sexual fantasies is the unknowable fantasy of the "maternal womb."[65] It is, he hypothesizes, this initial infantile curiosity/fantasy that will continue to exert an intense pressure in the elaboration of the child's "theories" of sexual difference as these theories evolve in and through primal fantasies.[66] Rosolato's joining of the visual and the sexual is indebted to both Freud's and Lacan's discussion of the importance of vision in the elaboration of sexual fantasies and identities, and yet, as we will see, it offers a particularly novel way of understanding the way subjectivity as a particular confluence of sexuality and discursivity is produced—in both its covert and overt forms in the pornography of mid-seventeenth-century France. For, one of the questions that must intrigue us with these pornographic texts, is not so much what does this pornography show us but rather what is this vision of sexual activity keeping from our view, what in other words is the vision of sex not allowing us to see?

In a way that is strikingly reminiscent of Freud's discussions of the importance of visual perception in the child's discovery of sexual difference ("Some psychical consequences of the anatomical difference between the sexes"),[67] both pornographic texts pose the problem of sexual difference in prominently visual terms. In the *École des filles* the male organ is perceived and described in a classic scenario of voyeurism/exhibitionism. To Suzanne's question of whether or not she knows what men have that they as women do not possess, if, in other words, she has ever seen a male member, the naive Franchon responds:

> J'en ay une fois vu un dans la rue qui pissoit contre une muraille, et qui tenoit quelque chose en la main que je ne pouvois deviner, et comme il me vit venir du long du mur, il se retourna vers moy, et me fit voir comme un bout de boudin

[64] Tom Conley, *Film Hieroglyphs: Ruptures in Classical Cinema*, (Minneapolis: University of Minnesota Press, 1991) xxiii.

[65] Rosolato, "L'objet de perspective," 29: "We know since Freud that the visual and mental curiosity of the child is developed through an always differed observation of the mother's sex."

[66] Ibid, 30: "The perspectival object is constituted in that intimate passage, in the very experience of sexual theories, and in phantasms of castration. We will therefore claim that the connection between the visible and the invisible, between the known and the unknown is made quite especially in relation to sex."

[67] Standard Edition 19: 243–61, at 252: "A little girl behaves differently. She makes her decision in a flash. She has seen it and knows that she is without it and wants to have it."

> blanc qui estoit assez long, dont je m'esmerveillai que je n'en avois point de pareil. (9–10)

Franchon here seems to confirm, with an advance of almost three hundred years Freud's (in)famous description of how the young girl, seeing the organ of a male relative, realizes that she hasn't got one ("je m'esmerveillai que je n'en avois point de pareil") and that she wants one (this "want" is what, of course, the entire ensuing narrative attempts to both affirm and fulfill). Both novels, but particularly the *Académie des dames,* will devote studied passages reproducing this initial, founding moment of wonder—the penis is described, extolled, constantly present throughout the narrative. Its very ubiquity serves discursively as a constant reminder of the anxiety that its absence provokes in the narrative and, we must assume, in the society that narrative both challenges and affirms.

But in the *Académie des dames*, confronted with the omnipresent penis, the vagina, as we've already mentioned, persists in remaining inscrutably beyond sight:

> OCTAVIE: Ah! tu m'étends un peu trop les lèvres de cette partie; eh bien! Que vois-tu au-dedans?
>
> TULLIE: Ce que j'y vois ? ah! j'y vois une fleur dont la couleur et l'éclat l'emportent sur la pourpre et sur l'écarlate. (*Académie*, b, 422)

What is even more interesting is that, most pointedly, the maternal womb defies any attempt to "see" its mysteries:

> OCTAVIE: Elle [the mother] s'inclina pour le prendre, et cependant je considérais attentivement toutes les beautés que cette posture exposait à mes yeux: j'admirai les fesses blanches, fermes, polies; il ne se peut rien voir de plus beau.
>
> TULLIE: Tu ne dis rien du bel endroit?
>
> OCTAVIE: J'eus un peu de peine à le voir; je l'aperçus néanmoins.(b, 526)

Rather than the too-obvious, too-present penis, therefore it is the vagina particularly, the fascinating, procreative but unknown and unknowable, maternal womb, which is the motor force driving the novels forward. The desire to see, to "know," and to contain the power and mystery of the female genital fuels the repetitive pornographic descriptions with a sexuality and an anxiety (and not just a male anxiety) of the unseen and the unknown. The vagina remains always out of sight, beyond the realm of the visible. It is the obscene of seventeenth-century France and the impetus of its drive to know. The origins of all modern pornography lie in the *Schaulust* of the text, an obsessive drive to see and thus control, the hidden, unfathomable female genital.

From the beginning, then, the desire to see is presented as inseparable from the desire to know, to possess, and to colonize which stands at the threshold of modern sexual subjectivity and which is crystallized in the very form pornography takes. From its inception, in the constant scenic evocation of sex, of sex as a mise-en-scène, of tableaux, sexuality (that is, genital sexuality) is presented as absolutely coterminus with vision. The eye—that organ, which according to Lacan, most successfully "eludes castration," appears as an already "there", inseparable from genitality, in the elaboration of sexuality in its most intimate, phantasmatic, aspect.[68]

Instead of perceiving these two aspects of the texts—the narration cast in the form of a dialogue between women and the ekphrastic rhetoric that creates the illusion of vision—as separate entities, we should bear in mind that they are inextricably interwoven. They are but two sides of a rather complex coin: discourse, particularly the pedagogic philosophical narrative, continually fades into sexual tableaux, while the tableaux, once their scenes are played out, devolve once again into the discursive narrative. In other words, *narratio* and *descriptio* form a seamless roundelay in which knowledge and sexuality continually fade in and out of each other.

On one side we have in the narrative, the narrative embodied as a "woman's discourse," the thematic, supposedly subversive, attack on the social and sexual institutions considered (by the text) repressive of the day. This liberatory discourse is what is most easily, through a classically thematic analysis, recoupable by those critics who simply read contradictions between what is expounded as theory and what is sexually practiced against each other. On this level, one can rightly claim that despite their overt intentions, these pornographic texts merely repeat the dominant, masculinist, and thus repressive structures the texts are purportedly criticizing.

Chief among these structures are marriage, the church, and maternity. Both texts present themselves as marriage manuals, the *École* explicitly and the *Académie* implicitly.[69] In each instance there is an older, wiser, sexually experienced, woman who serves as the mentor (sexual and intellectual) of the younger, virginal, about to be married adolescent. In the case of the *Académie*'s Tullie, we have a prodigious "femme savante": "Vous avez toujours passé pour une fille des plus éclairées de notre sexe, que vous vous êtes rendue savante dans l'histoire et dans les langues étrangères et la connais-

[68] Jacques Lacan, *Les quatre concepts fondamentaux de la psychanalyse, Séminaire XI* (Paris: Seuil, 1973) esp. chaps. 6–9. In the course of his seminars on the imbrication of vision and subjectivity Lacan returns to the seventeenth century to establish the relation between the geometric perspective of Renaissance painting and the institution of the modern "Cartesian" subject. Cf. for example, 81: "It is in Vignola and in Alberti that we find the progessive interrogation of geometrical laws and of perspective, and it is particularly in the research into perspective that we find concentrated a privileged interest for the visual domain with which we cannot not see the relation to the institution of the Cartesian subject who is itself a sort of geometric point, a perspectival point."

[69] "Je viens, ma très chère, me réjouir avec toi de la nouvelle que j'ai apprise de ton mariage avec Pamphile (*Académie*, b, 403).

sance des choses les plus cachées de la nature n'a pu échapper à la vivacité de votre esprit (b, 404). In each case, however, the knowledge and wisdom of the older woman serves as a dialectical foil of, we might say, "Cartesian" reason against received ideas. Each mentor cloaks herself in a knowledge that is the direct result of her own sexual experience in order to undo the elaborate social edifice of prejudices made up of tradition, superstition, fear, and intimidation which keeps women both in sexual and intellectual thralldom to men.

Marriage as we have already seen in Molière is, of course, the most highly invested of these social institutions. It is that institution where sexuality, economy, and politics are most tightly confounded. Instead of simply railing against the injustices that marriage as an institution inflicts on women, however, each text takes the same tack of attacking marriage at its most profoundly troubling center, the hidden knot where sexuality, honor, and property are all inextricably bound together under the rubric of monogamous "fidelity." Recognizing the inconvenience and probable danger of unwanted pregnancies, both novels extol the married state for a woman precisely because it affords her a cloak of respectability and an almost foolproof alibi should she become pregnant by a clandestine lover. Rather than an institution based on exclusive, sacramental fidelity, marriage becomes simply a convenient, protective cover for sexual profligacy and pleasure:

> Mais quand au lieu de fille ce sont des femmes, dame, le mary sert de couverture à tout, et on dit tousjours, quoy qu'il n'en soit rien, que c'est luy qui a faict la besoigne; outre qu'il ne faut point d'argent pour les entretenir, à cause que leur maison est desjà toute faicte, et pourtant on goute le plaisir d'une part d'autre avec moins d'embarras, et ils y prennent bien de plus grandes douceurs que s'ils avoyent quelque chose à craindre. (*École*, 170)[70]

In the *Académie,* basing her arguments on "natural" (i.e. Cartesian) reason rather than societal prejudices, Tullie also extols the virtues of (discreet) cuckoldry:

> Les lois civiles sont contraires en cela à celles de la nature; mais c'est seulement pour éviter les désordres qui pourraient arriver dans le monde. Apprends donc, Octavie, que le mal du cocuage, dont on nous prêche tant l'énormité ne doit pas nous effrayer, non plus que ce beau terme d'honneur qui n'est point une vertu réelle, mais un fantôme et une pure chimère. Ce n'est pas que dans nos petits commerces amoureux nous ne devions éviter l'éclat; ce serait une impudence extrême de faire hautement nos maris cocus; il faut sauver les ap-

[70] The same logic applies to the *Académie* where Tullie announces (b, 497): " Il n'en est pas de même quand nous sommes une fois engagées dans le mariage: il n'y a plus d'infamie pour nous, nous avons la liberté de tout faire; et ce beau manteau qui couvre tous nos divertissements nous met au-dessus de la calomnie la plus noire et la moins épargnante."

parences. Par une complaisance fausse ou véritable pour le pauvre homme, user un peu d'hypocrisie, faire quelques grimaces en temps et lieu, ne parler que fort peu ou point du tout de la personne que nous aimons, prendre à propos l'heure du berger, voilà les moyens de vivre heureuse dans la servitude du mariage en cachant le mystère de notre coeur, et de planter à nos maris des cornes d'abondance sans qu'ils s'en aperçoivent.(b, 432–33)

At the same time, women once married, in order to enjoy both social peace of mind and sexual pleasure, are forced into a strict code of hypocrisy:

Bien loin de mépriser les lois et les coutumes qui sont établies par un long usage, elle doit les avoir en vénération et les observer avec une si exacte régularité que sa vie à l'extérieur ne diffère en rien de l'honnêteté, pendant que, sous ce voile, elle cherchera ses divertissements. Il faut qu'elle paraisse un miroir de sainteté au dehors pendant que ceux qu'elle rendra heureux avoueront qu'il n'y a rien de plus lascif. (b, 493)

In the same vein, religion is criticized in both texts without any direct mention by name of the Catholic Church. The criticism, rendered always in allusive references is, nevertheless perfectly transparent. In the *École* God is introduced as a purely silent, nonjudgmental witness to the actions of mankind. When the naive Franchon expresses her fear that if it is known that a girl is no longer a virgin she will not find a man willing to marry her, and that even if she has kept her sexual activity a secret still God will be aware of it, Suzanne responds: "Dieu qui sçait tout ne le viendra pas dire et ne descouvre rien aux autres" (29). God is thus introduced at the very beginning of the novel to be immediately and expeditiously banished from the text. All of the reigning prejudices concerning virginity, fidelity, and honor are described as simply the invention of masculine jealousy and men's desire to keep women for themselves:

Et puis, à bien dire, ce n'est qu'une petite peccadille que la jalousie des hommes a introduite au monde, à cause qu'ils veulent des femmes qui ne soyent qu'à eux seuls; et croy-moy d'une chose, que si les femmes gouvernoyent aussi bien les églises comme font les hommes, elles auroient bien ordonné tout au rebours. (29)

In the *Académie* religion is satirized in a episode of ritual prenuptial flagellation. The unctuous flagellating monk "Théodore" is both a throw back to a long medieval tradition of libidinous clerics and a harbinger of all those eighteenth-century *abbés* from Dom Bougre to the acolytes of the dark Sadeian convents. While fulminating in traditionally overheated religious rhetoric against the weakness of the flesh and against the lasciviousness of women, he by his furious whipping brings Octavie, her mother, and himself to orgasm. The ambivalent horror of sexuality betrayed by the monk's religious rhetoric fuels his own and the women's pleasure with the force of a highly cathected libidinal repression. In the collision between the traditional but enchafed rhetoric of the "horror of the flesh" and the release of sadomasochistic pleasure lies revealed an hypocrisy that perversely undermines the entire history of the Church's attempt to bridle sexuality.

It is the attack on the sacrosanct institution of motherhood, however, which is potentially the strongest blow that these texts level against that most highly invested of state apparatuses, the family, and against the "natural" role and reproductive function of woman in society. At first it strikes us as strange that in these two works—which purport to be educational manuals, which, in other words, are entirely enveloped within those various economies, sexual and social, physical and metaphysical, that are most succinctly knotted in the conundrum of marriage, reproduction, and the family—the essential element, the keystone of the phallocentric oedipal unit, the father, is absent. In neither of these two novels is there any but a cursory mention of fathers. It may be very convincingly argued that the father is absent from these families, from these texts, only because he is disseminated throughout the textual universe in the relentless apparitions of his most significant of attributes—the powerful, inexhaustible penis. Perhaps the father functions all the more effectively when he is veiled, when instead of an actual paternal presence we have sitting in for him all those young lovers with their prodigious members. In a perverse gesture we can suggest that the absence of the father responds to an unconscious Medusan effect on the part of the narratives: to avoid the fear of castration that always threatens the father, the threat is parried by simply multiplying and disseminating across the entire textual universe the vision of a bountiful supply of phalloi, both the sign of the father's power and presence and the symbol of his unavowable lack.[71]

Mothers, on the other hand, are everywhere present in the text. This presence too may be seen to serve the same apotropaic function as the plethora of penises does for the absent pornographic father. On one level, the mother in these texts serves merely as the stand-in for the law of the father. In the *École*, in the absence of any actual paternal presence, it is the mother who embodies the threat of punishment if the taboos of sexual propriety are transgressed. Here the mother remains the father's surrogate. She oversees the family's honor as she oversees the economic and reproductive potential of her daughter. On another level, however, things are more complicated. If as I've said, it is precisely the maternal womb that remains the "obscene" of seventeenth-century culture, the *objet de perspective* controlling what we can and cannot see, if in other words the sex of the mother cannot be

[71] This of course is Freud's view of the apotropaic function of Medusa. See "Medusa's Head," Standard Edition, 18: 273–74.

known, her sexuality on the other hand can be put on display. In a narrative fueled by the very frustration concomitant with not being able to see, to know, and thus to control the mysterious female other, a discursive attempt will be made to circumscribe this difference by revealing another deeply guarded secret of femininity: mothers are sexual. This revelation is a double-edged sword, for, on the one hand, showing mothers as sexual beings debunks the myth of the virginal/maternal, it also by this same debunking debases. For here, mothers are shown to be sexual women who because of their sexuality are actually incomprehensible to an entire ideology that since Rome at least has presented mothers as matrons, sexless, selfless protectors of hearth and home. When they are revealed to be not that, to be merely giving the appearance of being that while secretly their true being is a voracious sexual appetite, then they are rather not like mothers at all but more like whores, only more hypocritical, more perverse.[72]

In the *Académie* all the mother's are finally *mères maquerelles*. They have a long and hypocritical history of sexual promiscuity (i.e. Sempronia, Octavie's mother), and they preside with voyeuristic delectation over their daughters' sexual initiation, participating in their deflowering to the point of aiding in the insertion into their daughter's vagina of the lover's penis. Constantly peeking through keyholes, they come bursting in through doors in order to observe sexual scenes in which they rush to be included. Their rhetoric of surprise and admiration is but a ploy to relay the sexual excitement to the reader. Mothers are strategically placed to advise prudence to the young lovers (advice that only heightens the reader's interest), especially to the hot-blooded overly endowed young men : "Surtout ayez égard à sa jeunesse. Je vous avertis de cela parce que j'ai appris que vous aviez un membre monstrueux, dont la longueur et la grosseur prodigieuses pourraient lui être nuisible si vous faisiez l'affaire avec trop de précipitation" (b, 462), thus serving as a constant intradiegetic relay for the reader, directing our vision, offering comments meant to render that vision more precise, more immediate, more stimulating: "Mais elle [Octavie's mother] fut bien plus surprise quand elle aperçut l'instrument de Pamphile, bandé d'une étrange manière. 'Ah! Bonté de Vénus! S'écria-t-elle , quel monstre! Ayez bon courage, ma fille' (b, 463). The *Académie* returns sexuality to motherhood but by so doing it also turns mothers into lascivious, insatiable succuba. The discursive function of the text whose role is to reveal the social and sexual hypocrisy of society thus constantly folds its thematics back into new tableaux denatu-

[72] Jessica Benjamin, in "The Alienation of Desire: Women's Masochism and Ideal Love," (*Psychoanalysis and Women*, ed. Judith Alpert, [Hillsdale, New Jersey: Analytic Press 1986], 113–14 writes: "The problem begins with the fact that the mother is not articulated as a sexual subject; she is the woman without desire. That is to say, in culture and theory alike, she is always refracted through the lens of the child's experience, in which passion, with all its implications of selfishness and independent subjectivity, is denied. Mother is there to serve the interests of the child; the image of her sexual power is too frightening for this denial to be challenged directly."

ralizing that supposedly most natural and ideologically nonsexual of social positions, motherhood. The sexuality of the mothers becomes simply a new provocation that refuels the pornographic pleasure of the reader.

At the same time, however, this sexualization of the mother is also a way of defeating what is most threatening in her, the reproductive power of the womb. In a sense, by making the mother sexual, the text reduces the menacing aspect of the womb, with all the phantasmatic fears that are attached to it. The fear of engulfment, the dread of and desire for reabsorption into the maternal body (although present in all children), takes an especially acute form in the young male who must in order to be a "man" detach from the primal attraction, the sirenlike call of the mother. By rendering the mother merely another sexually voracious woman the anxiety of male dissolution is parried by its displacement onto the valiantly erect, combative penis. Depicting all mothers as sexually active displaces both oedipal anxieties and fears of male inadequacies. Concomitantly, however, the pornographic strategies that the text's narrative machine is compulsively obliged to reenact as fantasies of genital dueling reveals the underlying and constantly upswelling anxieties about maternity, and about the mysteries of the female body that the text can never successfully work through but must always ward off by a repetitive, textual acting-out.

The "philosophy" that the characters expound with the same enthusiasm that they demonstrate for ever more complex couplings continues the pedagogical imperative to attack the dominant obscurantist discourse of sexual and intellectual repression. To this end, both of the young initiates' lessons include ever more detailed descriptions and analyses of sexual practices which would not be found in the contemporary spiritual/religious treatises preaching the duties of the perfect Christian wife and the mutual responsibilities of the ideal couple. As their experiences widen so too does their intellectual curiosity: questions are asked about strange sexual practices such as flagellation, anal intercourse, and (male) homosexuality. (Female homosexuality, or scenes of "girl-girl" sex, are presented, without comment, except for the implicit judgment that there is always something lacking in such encounters, always the expectation that a penis will appear and set things right).[73] Each of these topics is discussed in rather detailed and pedantic fashion, including "scientific," historical, and geographic appendices to explain the social and cultural origins of such practices, their paths of diffusion, and the present sexual state of the world. There are always some nations more receptive to certain practices because of climatic or physiological factors—that is, since Italian and Spanish women live in hotter climates, their vaginas are more "capacious." This "geo-climatic" observation explains why anal sex is a much more common practice in those climes than

[73] See Mainil's pertinent discussion of lesbianism in the *Académie*, *Dans les règles du plaisir*, 86–97.

in France or Germany where the colder climate prevents the distention of female genitalia.

While the *École* seems happy to remain in the quotidian world of the Parisian middle classes, simply expanding the range of sexual positions between the two partners, the *Académie* roams far afield in both geography and history. It contains the lengthiest and most elaborate discussion of various sexual deviancies. The text flirts with some of them, particularly anal sex, finally to reject them on spurious appeals to a certain "naturalness" that on other levels the same text attacks.[74] But, as long as the heterosexual contract is kept, the novel is strikingly liberal in its wide acceptance of the vast range of human sexual foibles:

> Toutes les inflexions et les contorsions du corps sont autant de postures différentes. On n'en peut point dire précisément le nombre, ni quelle est la plus luxurieuse. Chacun prend conseil de son gout, du lieu, du temps. Tout le monde n'a pas une manière d'aimer. (b, 602)

When, it comes, however, to dealing with the finer psychological points of human desire, of why there is this forceful attraction that impels the sexes to union despite social, religious, or physical obstacles put in their way, both the *Académie* and the *École* resort, each in its own way, to the myth of the androgyn in an attempt to explain the inexplicable:

> FRANCHON: Et pourquoi, est-ce, ma cousine, que le plaisir arrive de la sorte, et que tous deux, naturellement et sans sçavoir qu'il y en ayt, souhaictent tant de se joindre?
>
> SUZANNE: C'est qu'autrefois, remarque bien cecy, l'homme et la femme n'estoient qu'un, et ils estoient conjoints ensemble par ces deux membres qui estoient enclos l'un dans l'autre, en sorte que l'homme ne mouroit point et se reproduisoit continuellement en sa partie qui estoit sa femme et qu'il empeschoit de mourir. Et du depuis qu'ils ont esté séparé l'un de l'autre, la nature, qui se resouvient de sa désunion, veut toujours retourner à soymesme, pour avoir l'ancienne conjonction, et s'efforce, quand elle trouve, de deux corps de n'en faire qu'un. (*École*, 136)

This explanation of two separate but symmetrically opposed sexes tending naturally and inexorably toward the recovery of a lost primal unity is expressed more succinctly in the *Académie*:

> TULLIE: Quoi qu'il en soit, il mettra ce nerf qui le fait homme dans cette partie de ton corps qui te fait femme; vos deux sexes se mettront l'un dans l'autre, et de deux vous ne ferez plus qu'un. (b, 434)

[74] "N'est-il pas vrai, Octavie, que celui qui s'abandonne à c'est infâme plaisir tue un homme, puisqu'il en aurait pu former un? C'est un adultère, c'est un homicide, et il étrangle . . . par cette sale volupté un enfant qui n'est pas encore né" (b, 592).

Although it might strike us as unsurprising, even banal, for texts whose main focus is desire in its protean manifestations to appeal to our culture's most prestigious myth simply to repeat and reenforce the values and practices it upholds, nevertheless, in the context of pornography, several points seem particularly overdetermined. On a first level, as we have already seen in other discussions of the androgyn myth in the seventeenth century, the version invoked here is used to bolster a socially imperative, if perhaps vulnerable heterosexual bias. Sexuality is explained as the natural coupling of the two opposite sexes. What we have is an implicit appeal to biological, reproductive sexuality to explain psychosexuality (i.e. "desire"). We have seen that this rendition of the myth avoids what Aristophanes's version tells us: that in the androgyn myth two-thirds of the sundered bodies/couples were homosexual. The seventeenth-century versions of the myth confirm and reenforce the repression of a sexuality that discursively the novels also represent as anathema. On the other hand, when we examine the drive behind the myth, the drive toward a union that abolishes sexual difference, we are perhaps getting closer to a desire that is more primitive and more pervasive than the portrayal of either a hetero- or homo-sexuality. As Suzanne informs her pupil in the *École* (143) there is another way of looking at the androgyn myth: "C'est que l'homme et la femme estant considérés comme deux touts parfaicts, ils désirent, par la grande affection qu'ils se portent, de se transformer l'un dans l'autre."

The description of this transformation is particularly extravagant because to be accomplished there must be a strange reversal of gender roles: women must assume the active position on top during sex, and men, the passive position traditionally reserved for their partners:

> Or, en ceste posture où la femme est dessus et l'homme dessoubs, il y a une ressemblance de ceste métamorphose, par la mutation de devoirs qui est réciproque; au moyen de quoy l'homme se revest entièrement des passions de la femme, et ceste posture luy figure qu'il a changé de sexe, et la femme réciproquement s'imagine d'estre devenue homme parfaict dans la situation qu'elle luy faict garder, se sentant esprise du désir d'en faire les mesmes fonctions; tellement que l'un ne peut pas s'imaginer estre changée en l'autre, qu'il ne s'imagine aussi que l'autre soit changé en luy. Il faut adjouster à cela que si vous les voyiez de loin accouplés comme ils sont, vous les prendriez l'un pour l'autre . . . (*École*, p.143)

The wish to "transform" oneself into the other, to become the other sex, to in other words melt away from one's own fixed sexual identity is, it seems to me, the hidden, secret wish of these two novels, a wish to free gender from sexuality. This wish is probably unknown to the texts themselves. Yet it works surreptitiously and principally on the *ekphrastic*, nondiscursive level of the text, the level of sexual phantasm and excitement which is at cross-purposes to the more rigid, heterosexual, oedipal philosophy espoused and taught by the novel's liberated narrators.

The invocation of the androgyn myth functions in these texts, despite the limited and truncated version offered by the narrators, in a way similar to the way the "ombilic" of the dream, according to Freud, functions in dream interpretations. Freud tells us that there is always an unanalyzable part of the dream that exists like the "mushroom's thalmus" disappearing into the unconscious from which the rest of the dream emerges.[75] I would like to think of the androgyn myth functioning in the same way—it emerges from the philosophical, discursive level of the text, the level of social and sexual criticism, and yet, by the images it evokes, returns to some deeper, "unconscious" textual level where "thing images" and "word images" are constantly commingled. The androgyn myth opens the discursive level of the text onto the visual dynamics. By so doing it provides us an entry into the world of textual phantasms, a world where the power of pornography functions most forcefully but where the energy comes from the confusion of sexual roles and identities rather than from their rigidly produced and maintained separation.

On a discursive level (although it is becoming clear that is impossible to separate neatly "narratio" from "descriptio" in the pornographic text), the level that proved most threatening to the established, censorious agents of both civil and ecclesiastical authorities, the *École des filles* and *Académie des dames* can be seen, because of the condemnation of those social practices that would limit a woman's intellectual and sexual development, as allies of the same feminist movement that we see ridiculed by Molière in *Les précieuses ridicules* and *Les femmes savantes*. As much recent work on mid-seventeenth-century French society has demonstrated, there was a strong convergence of forces—social (the influence of the salons and salon literature), literary (the development and importance of the novel, of narrative fiction as primarily a woman-centered endeavor), spiritual (mysticism and particularly women mystics), and philosophical (the correspondence between the major male thinkers of the day and their important, noble, female interlocutors)—that leads us to appreciate the role of an important "proto-feminist" revolution in French life.[76] The force and the threat of these rather sweeping changes can be measured by the negative reactions that they inspired. The case of Molière is only one among many. Certainly both Boileau's rabidly mordant satires and Bossuet's equally hostile reaction to the increasing role women (especially Mme Guyon) played in spiritual guidance are equally telling.

Although it may, at first, appear egregious to equate pornography with

[75] For a discussion of the dream's thalmus see Samuel Weber in *The Legend of Freud* (Minneapolis: University of Minnesota Press, 1982).

[76] Among the plethora of work on the influential role of women, one could cite, Joan DeJean, *Tender Geographies: Women and the Origins of the Novel in France* (New York: Columbia University Press, 1991), Faith Beasley, *Revising Memory* (New Brunswick; Rutgers University Press, 1990), Erica Harth, *Cartesian Women: Versions and Subversions of Rational Discourse in the Old Regime* (Ithaca: Cornell University Press, 1992), Carolyn Lougee, *Le Paradis des femmes: Women, Salons and Social Stratification in Seventeenth-Century France* (Princeton: Princeton University Press, 1976).

the above-mentioned examples of high, if conservative, culture, we should not forget that obscenity, as Laura Kipnis writes, "traces, in effect, a very precise map of [a] culture's borders: pornography begins at the edge of the culture's decorum."[77] Pornography exists in an intimate dialectical relation with a given culture's most valued investments and prized intellectual accomplishments: it participates in the same social politics as its more chaste siblings, and by so doing serves as the negative shadow following the very predicates that would ignore it. It is no surprise, therefore, to have each text present and authorize itself by imitating, with the twist of satire, the platonic dialogues that are at the origin of the Western (masculine) tradition of inquiry and self-knowledge. Nor is it a shock that this satire's most virulent weapon would be the exploitation of images, the sexual tableaux, whose power is so heatedly condemned by these same dialogues.

Reading these novels on a thematic level confirms Lynn Hunt's definition of early modern pornography as a vehicle for attacking religious and political authority.[78] It provides a space for an alternative discourse, a discourse infused with a modern, Cartesian rationality and one that is, within the realm of the parameters of the period, opposed to the dominant theological, moral and political master discourses of the day .[79] It is also true, as Mainil has argued from a modern proto-feminist standpoint, that while these novels purport to offer a "liberatory" discourse of sexuality, they can be seen as merely reinscribing a masculinist view of sex and the role assigned to women by men in that view. We might say that this view is subtended by the normal oedipal scenario, the scenario of Classicism's conflicted familial representations, which is more comfortable with, even insists on, the preestablished division of the world into stable and fixed masculine and feminine roles. Each new subject is expected to journey from an initially confused, or chaotic, state, the state we might now compare to the "baroque" (grotesque) body, to the clear and distinct sexual (political, social) role/place that is naturally his or hers.[80] In other words, every subject is expected to become the clearly distinct masculine or feminine subject each corresponding to the emergent ideal of the Classical body.

On the other hand, when we consider the "ekphrastic" impulse of the texts, their constant metamorphoses into "tableaux," these phantasmatic

[77] Kipnis, *Bound and Gagged*, 164.

[78] Hunt, *The Invention of Pornography*, 10: "In early modern Europe . . . pornography was most often a vehicle for using the shock of sex to criticize religious and political authority."

[79] I am referring especially to the work of Mainil, *Dans les règles du plaisir*, where he insists on the persistent phallocratic scenarios that these novels continually stage for us. Cf. for example his comments on *L'école* (70) "A certain equalisation of the sexes, of their cultural and thus sexed role develops in the shadow of the hierarchies which are maintained, put into question, finally parodied and thus reinstated."

[80] David Rodowick *The Difficulty of Difference* (New York: Routledge, 1990) writes that "the theorization of the Oedipus complex attempts to establish a double track from the subject, a fork in the role to identity where the child must irreversibly choose either the route to maleness or femaleness."

productions open up for us the question of conscious and unconscious fantasies. These fantasies are not so easily recoupable by a system of binary sexual opposition, a system that insists on fixed gender identities and ignores the role of multiple and contradictory sexual and gender identifications which on the discursive level the texts, unbeknownst to themselves, reenforce. These two sides of the pornographic text are interwoven. Their interweave forms a textually strategic lure, guiding both the reading and the production of sexual fantasies around and within the overarching frame of a vulnerable heterosexuality. They consistently call attention to and yet elude any direct confrontation with the enigmatic (for patriarchal readers of both sexes) invisibility of femininity.

In order continually to reenforce what I am calling the "ekphrastic" imperative of the voyeuristic narrative, the text must insist on those intradiegetic signals that self-consciously call attention to themselves and by so doing reinforce the illusion of sight. The internal gaze of the characters relays the external gaze of the reader: "c'est un effect de ton désir qui te met aussi vivement les choses devant les yeux que si elles estoient en effect présentes" (*École* 151). The immediacy of sight is relayed by all the present-tense verbal references in the text, by the detailed descriptions that set the scene of the amorous encounters, by the constant references to candles which illuminate the sexual scenes assuring that nothing "remains in the dark" ("j'ai laissé tout exprès ces flambeax allumés afin que ma vue eût son plaisir aussi bien que les autres sens" [*Académie*, b, 458]), to keyholes through which the sexual action is viewed ("elle avait regardé par la serrure ce qui s'était passé" [b, 467]), to, in other words, the "lighting" necessary for setting the stage for the ensuing sexual tableaux ("Elle se retira après dans une chambre d'où on pouvait voir et entendre facilement ce qui se passait dans celle-ci" [b, 531]). Although there are references to former sexual exploits, stories recounted in the past tenses, the effective impact of the narration always remains in the present, in the present moment of reading. This reading is surreptitiously transformed by the above-mentioned internal markers into a viewing. The tableaux emerge, in a way that would seem to confirm Foucault's judgment, as the central element organizing both the conscious and unconscious structures of these novels as they are representative of the greater epistemic shift of the seventeenth century.[81]

Goulemot, discussing the pornographic novels of the Enlightenment, has talked about the absolute primacy of the "transgressive gaze" of the reader as the founding textual strategy.[82] In this primitive "virtual" universe, the

[81] Foucault, *The Order of Things*,(New York: Pantheon 1971) 75: "The centre of knowledge, in the seventeenth and eighteenth centuries, is the *table* [tableau]."

[82] Goulemot, *Forbidden Texts*, 43: "Everything turns on the gaze: the reader must be made to see, for the book can give rise to the desire for jouissance, for pleasure, only by describing those bodies offered up to stimulate desire or by depicting the gestures and postures of the moment of climax itself." And again, he speaks of "the key element of the erotic novel; the making of pictures, organized in order to solicit the gaze" (48).

gaze, among its many other functions, but perhaps in a sense in its most subtly perverse role, is a surrogate for the touch. The pornographic descriptions create images that can be caressed by the mind's "inner" eye, the eye of fantasy whose erotic potential is always heightened by the reader's own psychic configuration(s) and which is relayed in its evanescence by the masturbatory caresses of the reader. What is perversely striking about the descriptions in these two seventeenth-century novels, however, is that, true to their time and despite what we can consider their discursive rebellion against the dominant morality of Classicism, one would look in vain in these hundreds of pages to find a description that is in any sense naturalistic. These pornographic texts, no different from either their "legitimate" counterparts in drama or narrative fiction, paint their lascivious pictures with the brush of Classical abstraction, with, we might say, discursive *bienséance*. Although we are presented with repeated scenes of sexual couplings, these scenes are offered to our readerly gaze with the same rhetorical abstraction as the chastest descriptions in *L'Astrée*. Women are "perfectly beautiful" with alabaster or "olive"-toned skin, with blond, or raven dark hair. Their breasts are "perfectly symmetrical," their buttocks round and "delicious." Each man is "bien fait de sa personne." Each is "un hercule pour sa force et un adonis pour sa beauté," and is distinguished only by the size of his penis, which is always described as "d'une taille prodigieuse" "une veritable massue d'Hercule," and so forth.

Roland Barthes has written eloquently on the impossibility of a Classical text to ever describe "beauty" in a way that particularizes it . Only ugliness, according to Barthes, is scriptable. Beauty, on the other hand, can be described solely by circumlocution, by constant references to other cultural paradigms.[83] It would seem, if we follow Barthes, that the pornographic body, a body of pure fantasy, is in this sense the most beautiful of Classical creations, and the most perverse. For while the vision of the pornographic body, be it male or female, corresponds to the chastest descriptions of the beautiful in "legitimate" literature (*L'Astrée* or *La princesse de Clèves*), by its fascinating relation to the individual fantasies of the reader, it succeeds, nevertheless in producing a physical effect that the standard texts, except in the rarest of psyches, are incapable of inducing.

In other words, what is particularly striking in these pornographic texts, texts which depend absolutely on constantly appealing to the *Schaulust* of the reader, is that for all the stage props, for all the effects of lighting, and all the insistence on immediate vision, when we come down to it we realize that finally once more, there is "no there there," there is nothing to be seen—nothing, that is, except perhaps for the terrifying beauty of a sexuality that because it remains always phantasmatic is eternally proffered as an ideal precisely because it is always obscene, always out of sight, always be-

[83] Roland Barthes, *S/Z* (Paris: Seuil, 1970).

yond our grasp. Finally the vision of these seventeenth-century texts is a vision of nothing. Or perhaps we should say that the text's blank surface reflects a shining nothingness back at the reader, a nothingness in which he or she sees reflected his or her own immaterial fantasies.

Each text begins by placing a symmetrically paired heterosexual couple under the ever present gaze of the reader. This couple, we should remember, is always but a virtual couple. The sexually active participants in the pornographic scenarios are always figures conjured up in a dialogue between two women. It is this diegesis that disappears leaving us, one might say, our most "poetic" (in the sense of "produced") image of heterosexuality. Since the initial impulse of the texts, their founding fiction is the preparation of the young virginal girl for marriage, the vision of desire that the texts originally project is consonant with the underlying, patriarchal, view of sexuality. We might call this an orthopedic, or oedipal, view of sexuality, in that as a vision, it corresponds to and upholds the dominant founding (oedipal) fiction of the absolutist state. It is a view of sexuality founded on a supposedly natural understanding of erotic desire that corresponds to the (inarticulable) needs of the patriarchal family. In this view, the natural symmetry of male and female reproductive sexuality is posited as the grounding principle of erotic desire (psychosexuality). Despite what might be called the single sex view of anatomical difference, and although there are long and extended discussions trying to disassociate sexuality and reproduction, ideologically the textual universe of this early pornography is perceived as divided into two biologically symmetrical beings who come together to produce a new subject.[84]

In a very strategic sense this view of sexuality as inherently reproductive, although the "reproduction" is vehemently disavowed, is absolutely imperative for the elaboration of the mise-en-scène of the family as it is gradually evolving in the course of the seventeenth century to become the pillar of the modern state.[85] The "family romance," which begins to play so vital a role in the evolution of early modern society, which gradually becomes the dominant matrix for Classical representation, also serves as the enabling, if perverse parameters inside of which seventeenth-century pornography will launch its own attack on that society.[86]

[84] We know that ideologically speaking, a "single-sex" view of human anatomy prevailed, according to Laqueur, until the mid eighteenth century, a view in which the sexual organs of the female were seen as simply the same, but inverted, as those of the male. See Laqueur, *Making Sex*.

[85] The discussions in both novels tend, on one level, to downplay the reproductive function of sexuality as a way of calming the fears of unwanted, and potentially fatal, pregnancies. All sorts of reasons and authorities are invoked in an attempt to separate sex and reproduction morally and biologically. C.f. *Académie* (b, 586): "Il en est de même, disaient Socrate et Platon, de la semence de l'homme; c'est une folie de croire que l'intention de la nature soit qu'on l'emploie tout pour la génération."

[86] For the importance of the "family romance" in the elaboration of Classical culture, see Mitchell Greenberg, *Subjectivity and Subjugation in Seventeenth-Century French Drama and*

The wise-women narrators of these texts offer up for the century's illicit delectation, the "primal scene" of its dominant, familiarist, and heterosexist discourse. For what these marriage manuals summon us to witness is the impossible scene of the birth of the modern subject: the unattainable scene of that parental coupling that resulted in the origin of the spectator/reader. It was this scene, always beyond sight, beyond reality, that produced the reading/spectating subject as that subject was configured under Absolutism. At the same time, by the very tendentious relation that exists between the dominant oedipal narrative and the phantasmatic scenario, the visionary aspect of these tableaux can be seen to undo, or at least constantly to destabilize the hegemonic thrust of the dominant discourse.

On the most basic level, originary fantasies, of which the "primal scene" is one, can be seen both as being at the extreme opposite pole, in the psychic development of the subject, from the oedipal crisis and yet intimately related to it.[87] The fantasy of the "primal scene" is underpinned by the subject's narcissistic desire to be present at the scene of his/her own conception. This desire, according to Freud and his more recent commentators, corresponds to the early childhood query "Where do I come from?" or in other words, "How are babies made?" that is, it is in essence a question about sexuality, about sexual difference.[88] At the same time that the question may seem posed in seemingly innocent childish terms, the fantasized images are profoundly infused with infantile violence.[89] Although we will have to wait another hundred years for this brutality to appear full blown in the pornography of the marquis de Sade, already in these originary texts, violence is lurking in the background constantly intruding into the text through the use of martial metaphors to describe sexual encounters and organs. There are persistent references to copulation as a "champ de bataille" where the gen-

---

Prose: The Family Romance of French Classicism (Cambridge: Cambridge University Press, 1992).

[87] Guy Rosolato offers the most succinct (and contradictory) reading of the relation of the originary fantaisies (particularly the "primal scene") and the Oedipus complex: "The primal scene had the advantage of being centered on the Oedipus complex, . . . it serves . . . as a matrix for the triangulation" ("Paranoia et scène primitive," in *Essais sur le symbolique*, 204) and then in the essay "La Voix" in the same book, he writes (291) that "the phantasm is thus at the extreme opposite pole of the oedipal resolution of separation and of the acquired knowledge of sexual difference with its corresponding castration." Jean-Claude Lavie ("Excellence paradigmatique de la scène primitive," in *Nouvelle Revue de Psychanalyse*, 46, [1992]: (14) also reaffirms the connection between the primal scene and the Oedipus complex: "Oedipal rivalry and the primal scene are fatally linked together."

[88] Guy Rosolato summarizes the importance of the epistemophilia for the primal scene: "If we study the phantasm of the primal scene the quest that underpins it—to see the sexual coupling of the parents—really is asking for an answer to the question 'Where do we come from?' This question is asked from the earliest years in the form of 'How are babies made?' " "Les grands transparents: De la scène originaire au mythe de la création," in *Pour une psychanalyse exploratrice dans la culture* (Paris: P.U.F., 1993), 161.

[89] Rosolato, in "Les grands transparents," states: "The primal scene is generally imagined as a violent act between a castrating mother and a sadistic father, having, however, diverse possible combinations" (166).

itals are described in military terms; women's sexes are "fortresses" to be beseiged and taken. Penises are "battering rams," "swords," "daggers." Sexual encounters are described as "skirmishes," "battles," "victories," and "defeats." Under the coy rhetoric, under the constant metaphors that associate love-making to warfare, we can detect the displaced violence that is absolutely integral to the underlying fantasies and that betray, "avant la lettre," the sadomasochistic component of all infantile sexual fantasies. In a sense we can speculate that the sadomasochistic thrust that is quietly being revealed in the vocabulary of these scenes indicates the unconscious tensions created by the compulsive heterosexuality of the dominant textual narrative. The resistance to this hegemony surfaces in the allusions to warfare, to the mayhem of battle and the chaotic dispersion of bodies. The violence of the sadomasochistic scenario is disseminated throughout these texts, quietly working them over, splitting bodies from bodies and the body in itself. It is this muffled violence that reveals a more imperious, more perverse constellation of bodily positions and desires that attempt to break free of the ideological parameters inside of which the text initially traps its characters.

On a certain level one can argue that the entire pornographic enterprise is simply to reproduce in ever more elaborate forms the never-ending fascination with the quest for (one's own) origins. In the emerging "familiarist" culture of early modern Europe, the drive to uncover these origins condemn the subject to a *Schaulust* that can only ever want to "see" more and more, again and again, without ever being satisfied. Freud, in one of his more oracular pronouncements, declared that there was something innate in the sexual impulse itself that thwarted satisfaction. Frustration, rather than satiation is the ultimate destiny of the sexual *Trieb*. Pornography as a representation of the drives would seem to repeat on the level of ever more elaborate descriptions of sexual couplings, the force of a compulsive repetition that betrays the workings of a death instinct.[90]

These scenarios follow a seemingly preordained pattern which appears to defy time and all the changes brought about by social and economic revolutions, in the sense that we still find them, represented, *tels quels* in contemporary filmic pornography. We begin with the scenes of ill-defined feminine longing, of the young girl moved by bodily desires she cannot articulate. From there we move on to the initiation of the girl by an older woman into the (limited) pleasures of lesbian sex—women left to themselves excite and pleasure themselves while pining for the real and true source of their longings—the penis. These "girl-girl" scenes are followed by the tableaux of nuptial deflowering, where the virginal young girl is "made a woman" by her vigorous and powerfully endowed young husband. The wedding night is described in detail (often through the relay of maternal eyes) as the young

[90] S. Freud, *Beyond the Pleasure Principle* (Standard Edition, vol. 18).

man leads the young woman from the pain of the first penetration to, though his oft-repeated and herculean efforts, the paradise of sexual pleasure. The honeymoon period follows, where we are offered a long, detailed description of the new and varied positions that are essayed by the young couple. After the honeymoon, when we are assured that the woman is now fully awakened sexually and intellectually, and thus becoming both sexually and intellectually "voratious," we witness her escapades with men, singly and in groups. New lovers now enter the scene, which expands to include, ever more elaborate sexual acts (such as anal intercourse) and the discussions of those acts that are not directly practiced by the characters in the tableaux. Other tableaux are reported in what we might call a *mise-en-abîme* of sexual *ekphrasis*: the first tableau sees itself mirrored in another tableau describing acts that only heighten the excitement of the characters. Here, narration leads to description, which leads to heightened sexual excitement: "Ah! tu m'excites par ce discours! Il me semble que tout cela se passe chez moi, j'en suis toute émue" (L'Académie 516). Finally we move on to what we would now consider a scene of multiple partners—either several men having sex with one woman, or a combination of men and women in sexual frenzy.

Given the narrative, but also the psychic imperative of sexuality not to end, to leave the narrators and the reader/viewers *lassati nondum satiati*, the novels, rather then reach any sort of narrative closure simply stop in medias res. Since sexual closure is not possible unless it be, in the ultimate Bataillian sense, a *Liebestod*, the narrative, whose only reason for being is to continually renew sexual longing, can find no adequate, satisfying ending, either. The novels are, so to speak, open-ended (the *École* simply finishes with an interrupted conversation that we are led to believe will be resumed—"Adieu, jusques à revoir"—and the many variations of the *Académie* are indication enough of its impossibility to achieve a stable closure). We are left with the impression that these novels could—true to their investment in and representation of desire—go on forever. We will have to wait for the advent of the Sadeian novel for the pornographic text to find its only possible ending in death—an ending that these earlier texts avoid.

To return, as a way of an example to our initial point of departure, "le combat du vit et du con," the representation of the Classical body is reduced to the poignant opposition of the ultimate synecdochical signifiers of bimorphic sexual division, the penis and the vagina. In the scenes of ever more enchafed couplings, scenes which, as I mentioned, are framed as a battle, a joust for the ultimate victory of one or the other of the sexes over its opposite, in a curious fashion the only victory possible is always (of course) a stand-off, a tie. The orgasm that ends the encounter is startling however, because of the what I call, for lack of a better term, the "liquefication" of the subjects. There is, even in these early forms of pornography, an emphasis placed on what in modern filmic pornography has become known as the "cum" (or the "money") "shot."[91] The pornographic texts of the seventeenth century are, like their filmic counterparts of today, avidly interested in describing and extolling the moment of orgasm. But since, as we know, the orgasmic moment defies speech, exists outside of the representable, the novels must rely on the physiological consequences of the orgasmic moment (even if they be fantastical) to provide the ineffable with a degree of empirical physicality:

> Chose admirable, Tullie! Il ne fut pas plus tôt entré qu'il m'excita de nouveaux feux et me fit faire une si copieuse décharge qu'il me semblait que c'était plutôt l'urine qui coulait que de la semence tant elle sortait avec impétuosité. (*Académie*, b, 465)
>
> Je remuai avec une espèce de fureur toutes les parties de mon corps, et en même temps je fis une abondante éjaculation de sémence. (b,p. 548)
>
> Non, dit-il en regardant attentivement la semence que j'avais déchargée, ce n'est pas un simple écoulement, c'est un déluge! (b, p. 475)

> Toutes les filles de Rome et de Venise qui sont entrées en lice avec lui avouent que c'est le plus rude fouteur qu'elles aient jamais connu; enfin elles publient que jamais elles n'ont été si copieusement arrosées que par Médor. (b, p. 541)

What is striking about these descriptions, beside their remaining true to the scientific theory of the day which insists that both sexes discharge semen during orgasm, is the emphasis on the abundance of the flow of liquid. It is at the moment of the discharge that, it appears, all opposition between the hard erect penis and the receptive but evasive vagina, melt away. Difference dissolves in the instant of "la petite mort" and with it disappears a separate, sexed, male or female, being. Their difference has been liquefied. A moment of nondifference emerges in and as the orgasm. Although absolutely predicated on the stable opposition that the novels produce as the authorizing fiction for the sexuality of the characters, it would appear, if we are attentive to the insistence and repetition of these scenes of exultation in the overabundance of discharged seminal fluids, that the underlying drive of the texts is to melt away, to be changed into the other, to become both, or neither, the return to the androgynous indifference that both texts authorize, on their narrative level, as the fabled origin of desire/sexuality.

This fluidity of identity, of sexed and gendered position, is vehemently opposed by the ideological, oedipal parameters of the novels. But true to the ambivalent nature of fantasy it is the very prohibition of what is felt by the culture to be the too-dangerous, the too-unpredictable nature of desire, the suspicion that desire cannot be contained, that the texts also manifest as

[91] Linda Williams has dwelt at length on the importance of this shot, the vision of the ejaculating penis, in *Hard Core*, chap. 4, "Fetishism and Hard Core: Marx, Freud, and the 'Money Shot.' "

their transgressive drive.[92] Despite the entire censorious thrust of the narrative to protect stable and fixed gendered identities, there is an equally forceful move in the fantasies to transgress them. This transgressively fluid element also surfaces from time to time in the narrative, as for example, in the *Académie*, when in the middle of recounting to Octavie one of her Roman adventures, Tullie is overcome by the resemblance she "sees" between her female interlocutor and her former male lover:

> Baise-moi, Octavie, je ne puis te regarder sans me souvenir d'un gentilhomme français qui te ressemblait beaucoup de visage; il n'y avait rien de si aimable et je me suis divertie, étant à Rome, avec bien de la satisfaction. (b, p. 522)

In the moment of fantasy, when memory becomes saturated with desire, there is a fusion of the female interlocutor and the image of the male lover. In the swoon of desire sexed difference melts away into the desire for a non-difference that ignores the socially imposed limits of acceptable erotic longing and blithely transgresses those limits in the quest of some other, deeper satisfaction.[93]

In the ever renewed, ever thwarted quest for supreme sexual gratification, the novels trace the gradual undoing of the closed Classical body, that indescribable icon of Absolutist esthetics and ideology, and reveal the appearance of a body not of static biological difference but of fluidity, of multiple and imperious pleasure zones. In a sense, through the depiction of the voracious sexuality of the text, we have the foundering of the unitary subject and the (re-)emergence of the polymorphous, "baroque" body. It is the drives and pleasures of this body that reappear to efface the indescribable, perfectly beautiful but perfectly blank Classical body that the novels initially present to us. We may assume that it is precisely the unruliness of the drives that have been suppressed, quieted, pushed aside in the formation of a body that traverses in its glaring absence Classical literature from Corneille to the *Princesse de Clèves*. This absent body is born as the example of the "ideal" oedipal narrative, the society divided into a world of men and a gyneceum of women. All "indifference" has been effaced from the clear and distinct parameters of permissible Classical sexuality. In the fantasies of contemporary pornography, however, more insidious, more perverse desires surface and in their frenzy that refuses closure, just as surely as it confounds the predicates of its own appearance, the closed body of the unitary, separate Classical subject—in its masculine and feminine avatars—comes unraveled.

The ultimate refusal of the novels for any real closure—with the con-

[92] Rodowick , *The Difficulty of Difference*, 96. writes that "the narrative structure of phantasy is fundamentally paradoxical—the simultaneous expression and prohibition of desire."

[93] In his *Three Essays on the Theory of Sexuality* Freud talks about the difference between the aim of an instinct and the object of that instinct. The object is much more fluid, more labile than the aim, which uses the object(s) for its satisfaction.

comitant ever-widening circles of sexual tableaux, ever more varied positions, ever more arduous attempts to achieve orgasm—implies at the same time a greater and greater undoing of the unitary, Classical, subject the novels presented us with in the initial mise-en scène. The ever-expanding scenario, impelled by the desirous *Schaulust* moves away from individual bodies into a greater and greater depiction of body parts, penises, vaginas, breasts, buttocks, tongues, hair, and so forth. In this fashion, the individuated body is gradually exploded. It disappears in the dispersion of multiple parts, multiple points of penetration, multiple penetrating organs. In a sense, the greater the frenzy of the text, the greater the emphasis on ever more varied, more complex expressions of sexuality, the more we see emerge what Freud calls the polymorphous body, and which, as we have seen, Bakhtin announces as the grotesque, or "baroque" body. The more the Classical body/text attempts to break away from those bonds that circumscribe it, the more, in other words we experience the Bataillian leap into the erotic (even while stopping short of that ultimate leap into the supreme sensuality of death), the more the Classical body reveals its true yearning, which is precisely for what it had to repress in order to know itself as circumscribed, bounded, whole—its chaotic, fragmentary other.[94]

The desire of the sexed, closed, Classical subject, appears to be for a pleasure, a satiation that is available only by the elimination of precisely that bodily subjectivity. It is a satisfaction that is both reproduced, held at bay, and gradually undone in the ever more complicated scenes the pornographic text is obliged to offer its readers/viewers in their quest for an ultimate pleasure. The fantasies generated by the text, which we must recall are "conscious" fantasies rather like daydreams, collude with unconscious scenarios that are not, can never be, anchored in the representations of the text. Although the texts present us with a generalized heterosexual representation of sexuality, and although these representations fuel the masturbatory reveries of the readers/viewers, we know that these fantasies do not necessarily remain within the parameters of "conscious" representations, but elicit multiple and unconscious identifications and pleasures in the reading/viewing subject.[95]

It is important to remember, as Laplanche and Pontalis remind us in their seminal essay on fantasy, that fantasy is not the object of desire, but a scene,

[94] Georges Bataille, *L'érotisme* (Paris: Minuit, 1957). Bataille's work is essential for understanding, in a Hegelian sense, the interrelation between what Freud called eros and the death drive. Bataille, of course, uses as his main examples erotic literature since Sade. We can however find in even the more "lighthearted" pornography of the seventeenth century the workings, as I've tried to show, of violence, and its inextricable interrelation to sexual pleasure.

[95] Rodowick, *The Difficulty of Difference*, 136, states that "one cannot classify identification simply as masculine or feminine, active or passive, sadistic or masochistic. In all sexed subjects these processes comprise constantly permutable ratios between all these terms which can never be strictly aligned with biological gender."

a stage setting for the elaboration of desire.[96] In this elaboration the subject may well be disseminated across the entire setting, be an active or passive participant in the phantasmatic scenario, be an exterior observer, or even be identified with the setting itself. When dealing with a psychoanalytical rather than an ideological appreciation of subjectivity, of subjective positionings and social and sexual identifications, we should bear in mind that in the latter sexual difference is a "difference without," that is, it is predicated on a social imperative for stable gender differences, fixed masculine or feminine identifications that are entrenched, for instance, as the difference between male and female, straight and gay. In analytic theory, however, difference is always a difference within, an internal psychic split that is constitutive of the subject itself.[97] In other words, for Freud, sexual difference as David Rodowick reminds us "does not develop a priori from genital sex nor can it be understood as the teleological unfolding of a predetermined sexual division."[98] What this suggests is that there will always be dissonance between the level of lived ideological investments, investments where the human subject is inserted into certain predetermined gendered social roles that are explained as flowing unproblematically from his or her biological sex, and the realm of unconscious fantasy which profoundly ignores the division of the world into opposed fixed identities.[99] Seduced by the realm of the visual, trapped in the illusion of visual fantasies, the reader's/viewer's identifi-

[96] Jean Laplanche, Jean-Bertrand Pontalis, *Fantasme originaire, Fantasmes des origines, Origines du Fantasme* (Paris: Hachette, 1985), 74 "But the fantasm is not the object of desire, it is a scene. In the fantasm, the fantasm itself, the subject does not aim at an object or its sign, he figures himself in the sequence of images. He does not represent to himself the desired object but he is himself represented participating in the scene without, in the most primitive form of the fantasm, any specific place being able to be assigned him." Elizabeth Cowie, in "Pornography and Fantasy: Psychoanalytic Perspectives," (in *Sex Exposed: Sexuality and the Pornography Debate*, ed. Lynne Segal and Mary Mcintosh [New Brunswick: Rutgers University Press, 1993]), writes (140–41) "Whether the fantasy is a daydream . . . or an adult sexual fantasy, each, as in the 'original' or 'primal' fantasy visualizes a scene which presents a variety of positions which the subject of the fantasy may take up, whether he or she is also represented in the scene or not. The figures in the scene stand for positions of desire: to love or be loved from this place, to pleasure or be pleasured from this position. . . . The spectator identifies not with the figures, whether objects or subjects of desire within the narrative, but with different positions of desire."

[97] See Rodowick, *The Difficulty of Difference*, (69): "If psychoanalysis understands the development of sexual identity as an experience of division and loss, then any attempt to associate subjectivity with criteria of unity, coherence or mastery, especially as one side of a binary equation, is meaningless. The same is not true of an ideological representation of sexual difference which heavily invests in such dualism." (This is an excellent introduction to analytic theory, cinema criticism, and the question of sexual difference. I am indebted to Rodowick's work for some points made in the following discussion.)

[98] Rodowick, *The Difficulty of Difference* 70.

[99] "Freud's case studies, . . . his complex and contradictory analyses of phantasy militates against understanding sexual identification as opposition. . . . Sexual subjectivity can never be simply nor singularly aligned with femininity or masculinity. Indeed Freud's version of the acquisition of gender understands all subjectivity as divided within itself according to identifications that are continually traversed by sexual difference" (ibid., ix).

cations will always be multiple, contradictory, flowing across sex and gender lines of division.[100]

There is an irresolvable dilemma of course, at the heart of such an interpretation of the pornographic. While, on the one hand we are supposing that the role of pornography is to produce the masturbatory caress of the reader, in a sort of highly overinvested "reader response" theory of literature's efficacious influence on the world outside the text, it remains impossible for us ever (and this is the problem with "reader response" theory in general) to deduce a general theory of this response. The type of fantasies induced by the pornographic text are multiple, fractious, and contradictory. They involve hetero-, homo-, and bisexual identifications, as well as perverse and neurotic phantasmatic scenarios. The different proportions of all these infinitely interchangeable combinations can never be objectively enumerated to apply to all readers of whatever sexual proclivities, social positionings, or ideological investments of a given text, of any particular textual fantasy. And this might be in the last resort the ultimate but ambivalent "liberatory" gesture of these pornographic texts—they extend beyond their own time to ours, all the while holding out to us a desire born in another time, under very different skies, and yet they continue to work their erotic effect on us. We respond to their desire, a desire for plenitude, perhaps the infantile wish for perfect pleasure, that remains always and forever, by our very condition, foreclosed. At the same time by the spaces they open up individually and collectively, by the pedagogic imperative that they impose, which is a sexual "know thyself" they do uncover, even for a brief, furtive and pleasurably shameful moment, the space of desiring outside of the gendered fixities of everyday life. For their own period, for the conflicted seventeenth century where the collusion between the ideal images of a closed, protected state and a concomitantly closed, perfected body are constantly vying with forces that refuse just that closure, the fantasies of pornographic sexuality are perhaps more threatening to the authorities charged with protecting the state's internal and external borders than would at first appear. As we have seen throughout this chapter, pornography does not exist as an anomaly within a society's cultural production but rather is directly and precisely connected with its values and ideals. It mirrors its systems of sexual and social inequities. It is in this sense that we must understand the masturbatory excitement generated by these novels as not merely a personal, but a very public matter. It is of course, these "states of fantasy," as Jacqueline Rose would say, that respond precisely to the fantasies and the anxieties

[100] Linda Williams's work on pornography, specifically film and video porn, has been important in defining the fluid roles of fantasy. See *Hard Core*, and "Corporealized Observers: Visual Pornography and the 'Carnal Density of Vision'," in *Fugitive Images*, ed. Patrice Petro (Madison: University of Wisconsin Press, 1995) and "Pornographers On/Scene" in *Sex Exposed*, ed. Lynn Segal and Mary McIntosh.

of the (ideal) absolute state, that are, as it were, the shadow of that state.[101] Behind the elegantly hyperbolic portrait of the king, these pornographic texts constantly trouble the emerging distinction between the public and private spheres, crossing over from the one to the other, and negating, as they do the rigid lines of sexual difference, the image of a self-contained, self-sufficient patriarchy. The stately portrait of the king is undermined by the feminine in him that the portrait both hides and reveals. It is the motley that resurfaces in these texts, and it resurfaces as voracious femininity. In a sense, of course, the representations in these novels of a voracious, devouring womb constantly appealing to a rampant erect penis in a never-ending battle for supremacy can be seen as the anxious projection of a primitive male castration anxiety, which continually needs the image of the raging penis to reassure itself and the entire monarchal/patriarchal state against their fears of failure, of being overwhelmed by the feminine.[102] But, as we've seen, the pornographic fantasies of these texts abolish the distinctions between male and female, between the public and the private, between the seemly and the unseemly, and by so doing produce an image of the baroque body and of the body politic that will, under a system wedded to patriarchal unicity, continually fuel the very anxieties the masturbatory caress attempts to quell. It is not surprising that these texts—that reveal the anxieties and fears of the absolutist state and that by producing these anxieties as masturbatory fantasies uncover the cracks in the Classical edifice and the entire politico-sexual ideology that subtends it—will call down upon the pornographic the wrath of those whose interests and investments require the censorious surveillance of all those dangerous apertures and all those vulnerable borders that are forever threatening to collapse into scandalous abandon.

[101] Jacqueline Rose, *States of Fantasy* (Oxford: Oxford University Press, 1996).

[102] Lynn Segal, "Sweet Sorrows, Painful Pleasures: Pornography and the Perils of Heterosexual Desire," in *Sex Exposed*, 69, writes "Men's specific fears of impotence, feeding off infantile castration anxiety, generates hostility and panic towards women. Through pornography real women can be avoided, male anxiety soothed and delusions of phallic prowess indulged by intimations of the rock hard, larger than life male organ." In this same essay Segal comes to the interesting conclusion, which my own analysis of seventeenth-century pornography supports, that "pornography is not a means for men to achieve power over women, but proof that men lack power over women" (76).

3 *Absolutism and Androgyny:* The Abbé de Choisy and the Erotics of Trompe l'Oeil

> Sexuality lies less in the content of what is seen than in the subjectivity of the viewer. . . . The relationship between viewer and scene is always one of fracture, partial identification, pleasure and distrust.
>
> Jacqueline Rose, *Sexuality in the Field of Vision*

> To be a tableau: spectacle, lure, disguise, imaginary entrapment, a relation to the feminine: man plays on all of this. The mask reflects desire, a moment where reality appears as simply marginal.
>
> Christine Buci-Glucksmann, *La folie du voir*

> J'ay tout vu, tout sceu, tout entendu: je suis oculaire . . .
>
> Abbé de Choisy, *La marquise/ marquis de Banneville*

IT SEEMS THAT WE, IN THE WEST, are condemned to thinking "difference" in terms of a binary opposition rather than in terms of diversity. As we have been taught with stunning clarity over the last few years, first by thinkers, notably French, influenced by structural approaches to philosophy, psychoanalysis, and anthropology, then more recently by scholars working in the fields of cultural history, feminism, gay and lesbian studies, the history of Western representation is grounded in strategies of exclusion. A same repeated and ideologically "naturalized" gesture sets up oppositions and then proceeds to hierarchize them into already existing systems of socially encoded practices. "Difference," a term so abstract as to be almost semantically empty can, nevertheless, attach itself to practically any domain of thought and colonize it so as to repeat the social, sexual, and political investments of the dominant hierarchy.[1] But, for as abstract a term as it may

[1] The distinction between "difference" and "diversity" is employed by Jean Laplanche in his discussion of the castration complex in *Problématiques, vol. 2, Castration, symbolisations*

be, "difference" always seems to return to the body, as to its own site of origin. The sexed bodies of human beings, their biological division into male and female, serve as an appeal to difference's own naturalization. Difference continually conjures up the body as sign and site of its own irrefutable claim to the visible "truth" that it is then called upon to verify. Can we, however, expect to find an invocation of the body in all those political, social, economic systems, those systems of subjectivity, representation, and history which, while appealing to a certain disincarnated "ratio" and therefore away from any simple biological quiddity, would appear to ignore the body, its uses and mysteries?

Conventional annals of the literary history of the seventeenth century, for instance, have often proposed a radical "Baroque-Classical" split to explain complex cultural manifestations that coexist, are juxtaposed and intermingled in a rich web of social, economic, sexual, and aesthetic practices. Nevertheless in this imposed division the "baroque," which is described as dominated by manifestations of excess, by the blurring of boundaries in the plastic and verbal arts, by the inmixing of differences, is, because of a certain prevalence of what is judged to be an extravagant materiality, often coded as "feminine," while the more stately productions of the Classical period, productions marked by an emphasis on symmetry, rationality, simplicity, are seen to represent, metaphorically speaking, a certain "masculine ideal." It is this latter ideal that imposed its mark first on French and then on European life in the second half of the century.[2] We will keep this difference in mind even as we will also attempt to work against it, to see it as part of an ongoing strategy that, up until very recently, dominated our way of conceiving of the period in unarticulated, but accepted, gendered terms.

Historians influenced by the work of psychoanalysis, the English school of social/historiography and cultural theorists have come to be mistrustful of seeing social transitions in so radically oppositional terms. Steven Mul-

(Paris: P.U.F., 1980), 47–58 in particular. Laplanche's important contributions to psychoanalytic theory of castration and sexuality will be reintroduced later in this chapter. For the present I wish simply to underline the concepts of "difference" versus "diversity" as philosophical tools. The preceding sentences, make obvious reference to the enormous effort of Jacques Derrida, whose impressive contribution to modern philosophy is familiar to all contemporary students of literature. I want however to stress those other domains (not foreign to Derrida's thought of course) such as psychoanalysis (from Freud to Lacan and onward) and cultural anthropology, which have also exerted an important influence on alerting us to the problem of binary systems of thought, logic, desire, and to their construction, and aporia.

[2] For a more elaborate discussion of the "Baroque-Classical" opposition transposed in terms of a "feminine-masculine" opposition, see chap. 1 " Molière's Body Politic."

I also refer the reader to my *Detours of Desire: Readings in the French Baroque* (Columbus: Ohio State University Press, 1984). This distinction appears to have been reinforced by no less an authority than Michel Foucault, whose early studies of "madness," of "epistemologies" also chose to separate the "analogic" universe of the late sixteenth and early seventeenth centuries from the transparency of Classical representation. See his *Histoire de la folie à l'âge classique* (Paris: Gallimard, 1961), and *Les mots et les choses* (Paris: Gallimard, 1966).

laney, for instance, in his work on English society of the late Renaissance, a society which like that of France was undergoing enormous changes in its economic system as well as in its familial and affective structures, a society exposed to shattering religious and social trials, has talked about how the once static oppositional descriptions of those societies have proven to be inadequate to describe the enormous energy at work in European cultures. Even though we can detect what are clearly hegemonic patterns that predominate at any particular moment, this predominance should not prevent us from seeing those oppositonal spaces and discourses that not only coexist with the dominant but are absolutely necessary for its own self-definition: cultures contain within them the very contradictions that the dominant discourse attempts to obfuscate. That obfuscation reveals, however, at the very same time the presence, the seduction of those forces that, coded as "other," are forced into positions of exclusion, pushed out into the margins of social life. But from the margins they continue to exert a centrifugal pull on the complex network of those discursive systems of power, creating scandalous, tantalizing breeches in the totalizing ideological wall that the dominant discourse tries to erect around itself.[3]

The imperious move that Absolutism traces can be described *grosso modo* as a flight from chaos to unity, from fragmentation to the order of the One. The proleptically desired integrity of the realm found its most suitable allegorical model in the body, the "corps glorieux" (male and paternal) of the king. The king in/as his "body royal" represented that integral, bounded consolidation, closed in upon itself, without fracture or aperture that, as an image of desire, both pointed to and yet waylaid the social anxieties that an "unbounded" geopolitical openness inspired. Attacks on the integrity of the kingdom, coming from its open frontiers, borders through which flowed political, religious, and sexual dissidence, through whose porousness rebels (the great nobles, the queen mother, the king's brother, but also those rebellious, political, and religious tracts—those fomenters of civil strife) easily slipped to continue their rabble-rousing, found its ideological defense in the ideal image of the "Classical" body (closed, bounded, male). As we have seen, this body, in the terms of the Galenic medical knowledge of the day, would be the opposite of the leaky vessel of femaleness. The Classical male body, invulnerable to corruption, raised to its ultimate avatar in the king,

[3] Steven Mullaney, *The Place of the Stage: License, Play and Power in Renaissance England* (Chicago: University of Chicago Press, 1988), 130: "Hegemonic culture is . . . a historical dynamic, an ongoing, diachronic negotiation between the old and the new. The dominant culture in any given period cannot hope to include or even account for all human aspirations and energies; present culture is continually limited, challenged and modified by culture past and culture yet to come."

For a discussion of these revolutionary changes in the French and broader European context, see Mitchell Greenberg, *Subjectivity and Subjugation in Seventeenth-Century Drama and Prose: The Family Romance of French Classicism* (Cambridge: Cambridge University Press, 1992), and *Canonical States, Canonical Stages: Oedipus, Othering and Seventeenth-Century Drama* (Minneapolis: University of Minnesota Press, 1994).

could be seen to serve as an apotropaic talisman warding off the actual threats of invasion and dissolution feared at and through the borders.[4]

Is it just a felicitous coincidence that this integral body finds as its most adequate partner, what completes it in the scheme of Classical subjectivity, the Cartesian *ego* (i.e., "moi")? In one of his attempts to circumscribe his conception of it more clearly, Freud pointed out that the "ego is the projection of a surface."[5] If by this we understand that the ego is in a certain sense a mental perception (image) of the body and that the body is perceived (desired) as a closed, bounded entity, then we can understand how the Classical subject, body and ego, forms a seamless, totalizing roundelay where the image of the one subtends and grounds the formation (production) of the other.[6] Difference, therefore, for the Classical subject can only ever be figured as a difference "between," an external difference between the subject and his other. The absolutist subject can never see a "difference within": any experience of anxiety welling forth from within is denied in the Classical subject's immediate reaction, which is to *visit the anxiety he feels on the other this same anxiety creates*—the religious, colonial, but most especially for the French masculine subject of the Classical period—the other that pervasively haunts his reason—the feminine.[7]

That the unity and, therefore, the peace and prosperity of the realm depended on the exclusion of this seductive but turbulent and troublesome other, gendered as feminine in opposition to the transcendental masculinity of the father/monarch, is vividly expressed in the words of Louis XIV himself. In his *Mémoires,* a collection of instructions on the art of kingship addressed to the dauphin, the king specifically enjoins upon his heir to flee the contaminating influence of women, to be aware that if a monarch be moved

[4] Ernst Kantorowicz's classic study, *The King's Two Bodies: A Study in Medieval Political Theology*, is at the origin of a plethora of studies on the allegorical representations of kingship in England and France. See also Louis Marin, *Le portrait du roi* (Paris: Minuit, 1981) and *La parole mangée* (Paris: Méridiens Klincksieck, 1986); and Jean Marie Apostolidès, *Le roi machine* (Paris: Minuit, 1981).

[5] "The ego is first and foremost a bodily ego; it is not merely a surface entity,but is itself the projection of a surface" (*The Ego and the Id*, Standard Edition [see introduction, n.2], 19:26). Guy Rosolato glosses Freud's remark in the following way ("Recension du Corps" in *Nouvelle Revue de Psychanalyse*, 3 [spring 1971]:15): "The Ego remains tributary to the optical surface from which it emanates. Thus would we explain the phrase of Freud's in the *Ego and the Id* 'the ego is first and foremost a bodily ego.' Which is to be understood also as the result of this projection, the distance taken from the projected surface." See also Didier Anzieu, *The Skin Ego*, (New Haven: Yale University Press, 1989), for an extended elaboration of this concept of the "ego" as surface in post-Freudian thought.

[6] Jacqueline Rose in *Sexuality in the Field of Vision* (London: Verso, 1986), speaking of the formation of the Lacanian subject, has a critique of the "self-sufficient" ego that I find interestingly consonant with my adumbration of the interconnection of the absolutist imperative and the Cartesian ego: "The critique of autocracy and the critique of the ego should be taken together, since an ego in place which has held off the challenge from the unconscious or transformed it into something that can simply be known and controlled will be autocratic above all else"(5).

[7] For a detailed analysis of the Classical subject and his other, see Greenberg *Canonical States, Canonical Stages*, particularly introduction, xvii–xxxix.

by the "seductions " of the feminine, he exposes himself and his people to catastrophe. It is precisely by rejecting the temptations of the feminine, by resisting desire through arduous efforts that the king's masculine essence (his *vertu*) triumphs. History alas, Louis warns his son, is replete with men who were not strong enough to resist the siren's call. Succumbing to the lure of the other, these kings were led to their doom and their kingdoms plunged into chaos:

> "Je vous avouerai bien qu'un prince dont le coeur est fortement touché par l'amour, étant aussi toujours prévenu d'une forte estime pour ce qu'il aime, a peine de goûter toutes ces précautions. Mais c'est dans les choses difficiles que nous faisons paraître notre vertu. Et, d'ailleurs, il est certain qu'elles sont d'une nécessité absolue et c'est faute de les avoir observées que nous voyons dans l'histoire tant de funestes exemples des maisons éteintes, des trônes renversés, des provinces ruinées, des empires détruits."[8]

The traditional necessity for a keen division between the world of men and the world of women, the necessity for a clear separation of the sexes based on the rigid maintenance of ideas of sexual difference and thus superiority and inferiority, reemerges with renewed vigor as a forceful founding principle in the elaboration of the absolutist subject and state. As the recent work of historians and feminists critics suggest the sociopolitical status of women moves throughout the century from a position of *relative* subjective empowerment to a more passified position of objects of social exchange(s).[9]

In its dominant cultural manifestations, this same state created, as integral to its view of itself, a highly refined psychology of love. The relation between the sexes, how they differ radically from each other, and the strategies each employs in order to achieve some sort of meaningful, enduring connection, and the possibilities or impossibilities of such an achievement figures prominently in the plots of the century's great playwrights, Corneille, Molière, Racine, as it does in the moralists Pascal, La Bruyère, La

[8] Louis XIV, *Mémoires,* ed. Jean Longnon, (Paris: Tallandier, 1978), 260. For more detail, see 259: " Dès lors que vous donnez la liberté à une femme de vous parler des choses importantes, il est impossible qu'elles ne nous fassent faillir. La tendresse que nous avons pour elles, nous faisant goûter leurs plus mauvaises raisons, nous fait tomber insensiblement du côté où elles penchent; et la faiblesse qu'elles ont naturellement, leur faisant souvent préférer des intérêts de bagatelles aux plus solides considérations, leur fait presque toujours prendre le mauvais parti. Elles sont éloquentes dans leurs expressions, pressantes dans leurs prières, opiniâtres dans leurs sentiments, et tout cela n'est souvent fondé que sur une aversion qu'elles auront pour quelqu'un, sur le dessein d'en avancer un autre, ou sur une promesse qu'elles auront faite légèrement."

[9] I am thinking of the work of Joan DeJean, most specifically her tracing of the gradual political effacement of women out of the social realm and into the more contained space of the salon, and then of narrative fiction. See her *Tender Geographies: Women and the Origins of the Novel in France* (New York: Columbia University Press, 1991). See also Timothy Reiss, "L'invention de la littérature et la question des femmes," in *Rhétoriques fin de siècle*, ed. Mary Shaw, François Cornillart (Paris: Christian Bourgois, 1992), 97–117, and Faith Beasely, *Revising Memory* (New Brunswick: Rutgers University Press, 1990).

Rochefoucauld, and, of course, in the fiction of La Fayette, the "inventor" of that most modern of narratives, the psychological novel of love. Perhaps nowhere better than in the latter's *Princesse de Clèves* are we, like La Fayette's contemporary readers, seduced by the perfectly symmetrical and harmonious image of sexual difference that La Fayette creates for us. The following passage narrates the first encounter of the two protagonists; it is a fairy-tale-like scene in which each of the two partners is described as the most perfect example of his/her sex. Each mirrors the other in a symmetrical pas de deux:

> Elle se tourna et vit un homme qu'elle crut d'abord ne pouvoir être que M. de Nemours, qui passait par-dessus quelques sièges pour arriver où l'on dansait. Ce prince était fait d'une sorte qu'il était difficile de n'être pas surprise de le voir quand on ne l'avait jamais vu, surtout ce soir-là où le soin qu'il avait pris de se parer augmentait l'air brillant qui était dans sa personne; mais il était difficile aussi de voir Mme de Clèves pour la première fois sans avoir un grand étonnement. . . . Quand ils commencèrent à danser, il s'éleva dans la salle un murmure de louanges. Le roi et les reines se souvinrent qu'ils ne s'étaient jamais vus, et trouvèrent quelque chose de singulier de les voir danser ensemble sans se connaître.[10]

In *Subjectivity and Subjugation* I discuss the importance of this scene for the elaboration of absolutist subjectivity. I would like to quote a few words from that analysis which I find pertinent to the discussion I will be elaborating regarding the abbé de Choisy (who, as we shall see, was a member of La Fayette's circle), sexual symmetry, and fairy tales:

> It is the apposition of their difference, their exclusive and mutual "perfection," and then the harmony of the ensemble that surprises. It surprises them and it surprises the court. Their appearance is an epiphanous moment that transcending the narrative level carries us back to the rapturous world of myth. It is as if two demi-gods, each realizing in his/her person the aesthetic and metaphysical desires of an entire society, suddenly appeared in its midst: grace descends upon the world confirming its metaphysical desires as a physical reality.[11]

What is strikingly emblematic about this scene is that it could serve as the "Urszene" of Classical desire, a desire predicated on the "vision" of a strict separation of the sexes into a "naturalized" symmetry. This symmetry informs the desire that impels the narrative flow of the entire novel on to its melancholic conclusion. This conclusion, as we know, perversely undoes, or refuses that very desire and, therefore, the predicates which underpin it and with which the entire novel had seduced us.

[10] *La princesse de Clèves*, ed. Émile Magne, in *Romans et nouvelles* (Paris: Garnier, 1961), 261–62.

[11] Greenberg, *Subjectivity and Subjugation*, 25.

The society seduced by this narration of difference, of a world politically, sexually, and aesthetically grounded in a supposedly natural, symmetrical (but unequal) division of the sexes, a society often seen as the origin of our own discourses on love, seems therefore to be, on one level, a curious candidate for an equally persistent scenario of nondifference, the myth of another desire. I am referring, of course, to the presence—hidden and revealed in all those countless tragicomedies, in the burlesque narratives, and in those "fairytales" so in vogue—of the indiscriminate cross-dressers, the Celadons and Astrées who, slipping from gender to gender with seamless ease, pass from land to sea, from country to country, from class to class, signaling by their very ubiquity both the nostalgia for and the resurrection in narrative and dramatic disguise of the androgyn. The myth of the androgyn circulates on the margins of Classical culture, haunting its world of sexual (and thus economic, political, and familial) organization as a strangely tantalizing if troubling other.

Myth, as Claude Lévi-Strauss has suggested, functions to mediate those contradictions that appear irreconcilable in the actual lived dynamics of society.[12] When we pass from the social role myths play in society to an explanation of how this role operates with a peculiarly powerful individual and collective resonance, it is less to anthropology that we must turn than to psychoanalysis. The French psychoanalyst Guy Rosolato, for instance, who has worked extensively on some of our civilization's most powerful religious myths, stories of sacrifice and redemption that our culture has told to and about itself, discusses the way individual psyches with their own "(hi)stories" are sutured into overarching cultural narrations ("myths"), forming thus a sort of möbius knot in which the personal is imbricated in the political, while the political reinscribes its interests, interdictions, desires in the personal in the following way:

> The particular antidotal quality represented by the myth comes from a sort of unification, an attraction even, of the differences that each individual discovers in relation to the myth, and which, finally, flow together into a common stream. So that starting from a "singularity," with no future, which might even be thought of as nefarious, the subject can maintain a fascination or identification with a communal endeavor. By this process, the individual subject becomes able to accept without knowing it the social and in particular the moral laws for which his or her psychic structure is not suited. We can interpret this identification process as a fetishistic effect of the myth in relation to the drives of the subject.[13]

[12] Claude Levi-Strauss, *Anthropologie structurale* (Paris: Plon, 1967), trans. Claire Jacobson and Brooke Schoepf, *Structural Anthropology* (New York: Basic Books, 1976), chap. 9, 2: 146–97.

[13] Guy Rosolato, *Essais sur le symbolique* (Paris:Gallimard, 1969), p. 92. Jean Paul Valabrega, in his *Phantasme, mythe, corps et sens* (Paris: Payot, 1980), insists also on the transin-

Of course, the very interesting question remains of why certain myths at different historical moments find a particularly invested resonance in a given culture. It should be clear that I am not speaking here about those myths that the court propagandists of the seventeenth century reduced to the role of enlightening allegories. Chosen to enhance a particular political agenda, a particular socioeconomic policy, a particular foreign alliance (i.e. dynastic marriage), the allegorical exploitation of the pantheons of ancient Greece and Rome—Hercules, Apollo, Mars, Venus, or of such ideals as Justice, Charity, Plenty, that a post-Tridentine Catholicism informed with renewed vigor—invaded with their concomitant iconographic, poetic, and historical productions all aspects of seventeenth-century culture.[14] I am referring to those more insidious myths, more pervasive and less punctually inscribed in a circle of self-reflexive power, that nevertheless succeed in captivating, in their ambivalence, the cultural aporia of the period—the myths of Oedipus, of Narcissus, of the androgyn.[15]

But what does the myth of the androgyn, a myth first given to us by Aristophanes in Plato's *Symposium*, have to do with Absolutism, have to do with the sexual politics, the policing of bodies in Louis XIV's France? Furthermore, what connection can there be between an overarching cultural "mythos" and the life and writings of the abbé de Choisy, an eccentric, but bit player on the seventeenth-century stage?

Jacqueline Rose, in *Sexuality in the Field of Vision*, takes as her starting point Freud's comments on Leonardo to elaborate a theoretical essay on sexual subjectivity as informed by the scopic drive (a relation that we will see is essential for any understanding of Choisy). In that essay she writes about society's vulnerability to its conceptions and imposition of the laws of "sexual difference"—"The lines of that division"(i.e. sexual difference), she suggests, "are fragile in exact proportion to the rigid insistence with which . . . culture lays them down; they constantly converge and threaten to coalesce."[16] In this passage, I believe Rose is talking about the way sexuality-as-symmetrical-difference is always constructed as a repression of the bisexual dimension of psychosexuality that Freud hypothesized (but which

---

dividual role of myth, 118: "myth, truthfully speaking . . . is neither one nor the other, neither individual nor collective, but precisely both at once."

[14] In his notes to *Pierre Corneille, Oeuvres complètes*, 3 vols.(Paris: Gallimard, 1987), Georges Couton describes the importance of allegory for the seventeenth century in the following terms: "Allegory is one of the most obvious forms of thought and expression in the seventeenth century: one thinks and one speaks in models, exempla, emblems, and figures. The heroes, the characters of fable, of history, of literature, offer themselves as models, as precedents for the living and lend their names, which remind us of their vital choices and of their lives" (3:1604).

[15] I have written about what strike me as the two of the principal guiding myths of absolutist Europe, Oedipus and Narcissus, both of which, obviously, will be playing an important role in this reading of Choisy. For Narcissus, see my *Subjectivity and Subjugation*; for Oedipus, see *Canonical States, Canonical Stages*.

[16] Rose, *Sexuality in the Field of Vision*, 226.

the ancients had already identified in their myths and legends of the androgyns and the hermaphrodites).[17] It is the ambivalence of psychosexuality that is repressed in society's attempt to fit socialized sexuality into those supposedly natural (because visible) biological differences. The stronger the social demands to have sexuality conform to an apparent biological difference, the more imperiously will the repressed element of "indifference" (bisexuality) emerge in the phantasmatic constructions (dreams, myths, fairy tales, theatrical plots) of the time.[18] Existing on the margins, at the interstice of desire and reality, in their impossible separation, these phantasms inform by their very repression/presence the dominant discourse that would ignore them.[19]

On the one hand, to return to Plato, we might say that the ostensible aim of androgyn myth appears to be an explanation: the narrative explains the coming-into-being of desire. It functions as a myth of origins, the origins of a desire that the present of narration takes for granted, that is, desire is impelled by splitting and lack. The present is thus, projected backward and grounded in the past—*in illo tempore*. Further, the myth suggests that this splitting and lack are imposed by the father: Zeus, angered (threatened) by the androgyns' "pride" decides to punish them:

> At last after a good deal of reflection, Zeus discovered a way. He said: 'Methinks I have a plan which will humble their pride and improve their manners; men shall continue to exist, but I will cut them in two and then they will be diminished in strength and increased in numbers. . . . He spoke and cut men in two, like a sorb-apple which is halved for pickling, or as you might divide an egg with a hair; and as he cut them one after another, he bade Apollo give the

[17] In his article "Sur la mère phallique" *(Revue Française de Psychanalyse*, Jan.-Feb. 1968, 1–38), André Green talks about bisexuality in stylistic terms that send us back to the Platonic description of the androgyn: "It is the bisexual disposition which allows for the coexistence of desire and of identification. But this bisexuality would make the subject spin around, if nothing intervened to drag him out of this vicious circle. The primacy of the phallus commands the exchanges of bisexuality"(32).

[18] The essentially "hermaphroditic" conception of the body in Galenic theory and the eventual evolution toward a modern conception of sexual bimorphism is discussed by Peter Stallybrass and Ann Rosalind Jones in their chapter "Fetishizing Gender: Constructing the Hermaphrodite in Renaissance England," in *Body Guards*, ed. Christina Straub and Julia Epstein (New York: Routledge, 1991), 80–112. For France see Lise Leibacher-Ouvrard, "Tribades et ghyanthropes (1612–1614): Fictions and fonctions de l'anatomie travestie," *Papers on French Seventeenth-Century Literature*, (Tubingen: vol. 24, no. 2 [summer 1995]), 51–66; and Kathleen Long, "Hermaphrodites Newly Discovered: The Cultural Monsters of Early Modern France," in *Monster Theory: Reading Culture*, ed. Jeffrey Jerome Cohen, (Minneapolis: University of Minnesota Press, 1996).

[19] Talking about an analogous move in the social corpus Peter Stallybrass and Allon White *(The Politics and Poetics of Transgression* [Ithaca: Cornell University Press, 1986]) describe the repressive/constitutional factor of the grotesque/classical split in the following way: "The classical body splits precisely along the rigid edge which is its defense against heterogeneity: its closure and purity are quite illusory and it will perpetually rediscover in itself, often with a sense of shock or inner revulsion, the grotesque, the protean, and the motley, the neither/nor, the double negation of high and low which was the very precondition for its social identity" (113).

face and the half of the neck a turn in order that man might contemplate the section of himself.[20]

For the time being three things bear underlining in this passage: first, androgyns and "men" (i.e. mankind) appear to be synonymous; second, the origin of sexuality as difference, as "cut" is, as I've mentioned, an imposition of the father (the paternal function); finally, the awareness of difference of the split state passes through vision ("give the face and the half of the neck a turn in order that man might contemplate").

Before their fall into difference, the androgyns were divided into three, not two, sexes ("The sexes were not two as they are now, but originally three in number; there was man, woman, and the union of the two"). All three types are, nevertheless, somewhat indiscriminately jumbled together in the following description:

> the primeval man was round, his back and sides forming a circle; and he had four hands and four feet, one head with two faces, looking opposite ways, set on a round neck and precisely alike; also four ears, two privy members, and the remainder to correspond. He could walk upright as men now do, backwards or forwards as he pleased, and he could also roll over and over at a great pace, turning on his four hands and four feet, eight in all like tumblers going over and over with their legs in the air. . . . Terrible was their might and strength, and the thoughts of their hearts was great.[21]

Clearly, this description of the androgyns allows us to see that they are punished because they represent a threat to the Gods (i.e. the father /Zeus). Their defiance is, in a sense, the power and lure of their self-sufficiency. Theirs is the beatitude, strongly, pervasively, defiant of the law of paternal prerogative. Their force and their pleasure (the one is coterminous with the other) are not based on a debt to the father, but simply on an ecstasy of plenitude, a bodily jouissance not based on difference, but on "indifference." In this they represent, rather perversely for any patriarchal society (the world of ancient Greece, but also for that society of regrouping patriarchy, absolutist France), another subjective conundrum:—they are what desire desires—a state of narcissistic self-enclosure, a sublime union not founded on castration/ death but on an entirely different economy, beyond the laws of (sexual) difference as our Western societies have laid them down, and more akin, perhaps to the Tantric incantations of the East.

But, sundered, punished by the father they defied, the image of the androgyns still retains in the very élan vital of desire that they are made to represent the nostalgic power of a past they have lost, while at the same time

[20] Plato, *Symposium*, in *The Dialogues of Plato*, trans. Benjamin Jowett, 2 vols. (New York: Random House, 1937), 2:317.
[21] Ibid.

they are propelled by that very nostalgia toward a future that eludes them. In other words, the myth figures both the origin and end of desire—it is the origin of the desire of a patriarchal society that is narratized in the myth, at the same time that the myth figures as its origin, the end to that desire—the end to the difference of a sexuality that is imposed by the father, the end to a desire based on lack and death.[22] In a strangely proleptic way the myth of the androgyn seems to figure the model of Freudian sexuality that Lacan would expound: an originary monad (mother/child) is sundered by the imposition of the law of the father ("castration") which plunges the child into sexual difference and thus desire, the goal of which would be a "return" to a state of nirvana like quiescence. At the same time the myth also figures an alternative (a threatening alternative to patriarchal sexuality): a desire not based on lack (death) but on plenitude—Irigaray's image of a pair of self-embracing lips come to mind—a desire beyond the law of the father.[23]

This ambivalence proves seductive, I would suggest, to seventeenth-century France because it allows society to have a self-validating model for its own investments in its dominant (sexual) fiction, while at the same time pointing to another, more perverse, more threatening (utopic) model of sexuality not based on castration which would undermine the naturalized structures of patriarchy—the state apparatuses (religion, economy, marriage, class) that all are subtended by the myth's end product, which is the separation of the world into sexual difference.[24] I propose that it is precisely this *va et vient* between these two interpretations, an oscillation between these two poles, which represents different subjective positions, an oscillation that is a continuous and integral part of the narration itself, the end constantly inscribed in the beginning, the beginning continually projected into the ending, that the seventeenth century mediates for itself and for us, by and through the very locus of androgyny, the mark of desire in/as/on the body. Of course, the question remains for the seventeenth century as it does for us, "Quel corps?" for the myth of the androgyn raises more questions

[22] In her discussion of androgyny Kari Weil makes a similar point: "To figure ideal androgyny is complicated by the fact that the androgyne is assumed to transcend, if not to exist prior to, the terms that define and constitute it, specifically the terms characterizing male and female. Defined through this distinction, it reinscribes the sexual difference that it seeks to efface or to dissolve into a synthetic wholeness" (*Androgyny and the Denial of Difference* [Charlottesville: University Press of Virginia, 1992], 33). Weil, as most commentators of the myth tend to focus on the heterosexual (male/female) split while ignoring that desire, in the myth, is both hetero- and homosexual. Of the three types of androgyns described only a third is "heterosexual."

[23] For Lacan, a good place to start would be "La signification du phallus," in *Écrits* (Paris: Seuil, 1971), 103–18. Irigaray's celebrated image of the self-embracing lips—"Quand nos lèvres se parlent," 205–17—in Luce Irigaray, *Ce sexe qui n'en est pas un* (Paris: Minuit, 1977).

[24] I am borrowing the term "dominant fiction" from Kaja Silverman. See her *Male Subjectivity at the Margins* (New York: Routledge, 1992), 54: "The dominant fiction neutralizes the contradictions which organize the social formation by fostering collective identifications and desires, identifications and desires which have a range of effects; but which are first and foremost constitutive of sexual difference. Social formations consequently depend upon their dominant fictions for their sense of unity and identity."

than it answers, questions of the social/sexual production of the image of the body, questions of the role of castration in the etiology of sexuality and perversion, questions of the part played by vision (the scopic drive) in the elaboration of sexuality/pleasure (narcissism, fetishism), questions of "being and seeming" of a certain mise-en-scène of the self, a staging of the body that is always a form of trompe l'oeil, questions that all seem both to originate and to return to the enigma of the androgyn. And it is here that we must turn to François Timoléon de Choisy as he creates himself, in his memoirs and his fiction, as both "le berger et la bergère" to begin to confront these issues.[25]

> Quand je me suis trouvé à des bals et à des comédies, avec de belles robes de chambre, des diamants et des mouches , et que j'ai entendu dire tout bas auprès de moi: "Voilà une belle personne," j'ai goûté en moi-même un plaisir qui ne peut être comparé à rien, tant il est grand. (Abbé de Choisy, *Mémoires*)

> For me it has nothing to do with sex. I don't get turned on by it. It's just *fun*. (Neil Cargile, answer to why he cross-dresses, *The New Yorker*)

Despite his rather large corpus of historical writings, the abbé de Choisy, if he is remembered at all today (and he is with greater and greater interest), is recalled for his slim volume of personal memoirs—*Mémoires de l'abbé de Choisy habillé en femme*—in which he presents himself to history in the first rather fully documented case of male cross-dressing. Although the manuscript of the abbé's memoirs is fragmentary, the fragments have been collated into a cohesive narrative, with more or less lengthy sections describing his life during a period of his youth when he periodically (and often for extended periods) cross-dressed. We are told by the executor of his estate, however, that even into advanced old age the abbé enjoyed putting on women's accouterments to compose his austere histories of the Catholic church and of the kings of France. It appears that this was an inveterate habit he just could not give up. At his death his testamentary executor, the marquis d'Argenson finishes a rather stern portrait of the departed with the following words: "n'étant plus d'âge à s'habiller en femme, il ne s'est jamais trouvé capable de penser en homme."[26] I bring up this nasty quip because rather than focus our attention on the fairly outrageous cross-dressed career of Choisy, d'Argenson seems to point beyond the outfits, the makeup and the *mouches*, to what for the Classical period must have seemed even more shocking: the abbé appeared at the very height of the Classical moment as a strange, hybrid, a split being. Choisy was a negative cipher, having neither the mental qualities of a man, nor the physical attractions of a woman. In

[25] François Timoléon de Choisy, *Mémoires de l'abbé de Choisy habillé en femme*, in *Mémoires de l'abbé de Choisy*, ed. Georges Mongrédien (Paris: Mercure de France, 1966), 307.
[26] Quoted in Mongrédien, *Mémoires de l'abbé de Choisy* 14.

other words, in his extravagant self-production, a mixture projected out into the world as a spectacular mise-en-scène of an undecidable psychosexual persona, Choisy is the very embodiment, in both a literal and a phantasmatic sense, of the baroque (as a form of the grotesque) which persists at the center of Classicism's inner sanctum: let us remember that Choisy was elected to the Académie française in 1687, taking his place alongside those paragons of French Classicism, Racine and Boileau.[27]

What is fascinatingly scandalous about Choisy was his celebration of this split. While the Cartesian subject by definition will refuse to see the split in himself and project it outward, Choisy, although unknown to him consciously, nevertheless strategically manifests on his body, in his person, the "splitting of his ego." Although Choisy is careful to present his/her life as innocuous, as "bagatelles" or of no more importance than "une coquetterie de petite fille"(25), nevertheless in the greater scheme of his work, his "caprices" can be seen to offer an oblique attack on seventeenth-century France in its tremulous self-sufficiency.

Choisy was both central and eccentric to the Classical world of seventeenth-century France. First and most obviously he produces himself as a body that incorporates in and on itself the split that Classical society projects out and between the sexes. Then, in another sense, he moves between the social strata of the century, between his bourgeois ancestry and his (mother's) nobiliary pretensions, a move we see reflected in the spatial shifts in his domestic living conditions between the aristocratic Luxembourg Palace and bourgeois (and *populaire*) St. Marceau quarter where s/he takes up residence.[28] Finally, perhaps the most spectacular example of Choisy's oscillation between centrality and eccentricity is his famous voyage from the center of the universe (Versailles) to the ends of the world—to Bangkok, as he accompanies an embassy sent by Louis XIV to the king of Siam. Choisy in his life and writings becomes a perfect example of a crossroads, uniting in this person all that absolutist France would keep neatly (and strategically) separated. He is the motley, the "both/and (both man and woman, both inside and outside, both aristocrat and bourgeois), the

[27] Cf. Mongrédien, who enumerates the many interconnected relations Choisy maintained with the centers of power in Louis XIV's France. " Himself a childhood playmate of Monsieur, he was quickly involved in politics. He was sixteen years old when Louis XIV seized power, and was then well acquainted with such ministers as Le Tellier, Fouquet, Brienne, Colbert, and later on with Pomponne, Croissy, Pontchartrain. He came to know Condé, knew intimately Turenne, nephew of his childhood friend the cardinal de Bouillon; he was a friend of Bussy-Rabutin, of Bossuet, of La Rochefoucauld, and of Mme de La Fayette, the colleague of Racine and of Boileau at the Académie française, an intimate of the duke de Bourgogne, of the duke de Beauvilliers, of the duke de Saint-Aignan and of Mme de Maintenon at court" (15).

[28] It is hard to decide what pronoun to use when talking about Choisy cross-dressed. It is a decision of grammatical gender made all the more difficult by the text's own oscillation between referring to Choisy in both the masculine and the feminine. For the purposes of this essay, therefore, I will adopt the formula "s/he" when talking about Choisy as a production, that is cross-dressed, in the texts.

hybrid "monstrosity" that is anathema to Absolutism's compulsion for the "either /or."

Choisy, as he moves about the very centers of Absolutism's most invested institutions, the court, the army, the Church, the world of arts and letters, constantly collapses these institutions onto his own person—onto his persona—and makes of his life, which he calls "une comédie," a carnivalesque parody of all the founding predicates of Classical culture. If we believe Marjorie Garber who tells us that "transvestism is a space of possibility structuring and confounding culture: the disruptive element that intervenes, not just a category crisis of male and female, but the crisis of category itself," then we must pay serious attention to the abbé's "comedy" because it was an act that confounds and threatens to undo by aspirating into its spiraling sexual conundrum the very predicates of Absolutism.[29] That Choisy was able to do this without encouraging the wrath of the powers that be is one of the great mysteries of cultural history.[30] Perhaps he was thought too harmless? Perhaps, as Garber argues, culture creates (and thus needs) the transvestite as much as the transvestite puts culture into question? Or perhaps his most troubling transvestitic acts occur only in his writings/phantasies? In any case the difficulty we have with trying to fix Choisy into a discursive narration is that by whatever criterion we try to approach him, he escapes our grasp. Whenever we think we have a hold on him, his defining undecidability allows him to slip away. This man who claims to never have had an enemy in the world becomes the enemy of any interpretive gesture that by defining him would confine him.[31]

The only body of Choisy that we have, the only corpus left to dissect, is textual—and it is to these diverse texts that I turn, not to discover some sort of historical reality to the person, the transvestitic body of Choisy, but rather to examine his embodiment in a series of texts that reflecting each other in a dance of contradictions reveal, in negative reversal, a certain truth of the construction of sexual subjectivities in seventeenth-century France.[32] In order to do this, to set out some modern guideposts, I shall first

[29] Marjorie Garber, *Vested Interests: Cross-Dressing and Cultural Anxiety* (New York: Routledge, 1992), 17.

[30] We should not forget that French law punished transvestism with death by fire until 1760. Cf. Peter Ackroyd, *Dressing Up, Transvestism and Drag: The History of an Obsession* (New York: Simon and Schuster, 1979), 57.

[31] Choisy confirms this, "car pour des ennemis, grâce à Dieu je n'en ai point, et n'en eus jamais; et si je savais quelqu'un qui me voulût du mal j'irais tout à l'heure lui faire tant d'honnêtetés, tant d'amitiés, qu'il deviendrait mon ami en dépit de lui" (*Mémoires pour servir à l'histoire de Louis XIV*, in Mongrédien, ed., *Memoires de l'abbé*, 34).

[32] The distinction between "reality" and "truth" I am making here refers to Lacan's use of the two terms in psychoanalytic discourse. Cf. "Function and Field of Speech and Language," in *Écrits: A Selection*, trans. Alan Sheridan (London: Tavistock. 1977) where Lacan talks about "rememoration" (that is, the narrative by which the analysand re-creates his or her past) and distinguishes between truth (*vérité*) and reality (*réalité*): "In psychoanalytic anamnesis, it is not a question of reality, but of truth, because the effect of full speech is to reorder past contingencies by conferring on them the sense of necessities to come, such as they are constituted by the little freedom through which the subject makes them present"(48).

suggest some of the ways psychoanalysis has tried to understand the transvestite.

Freud locates the castration complex at the very center of the subject's entry into sexual difference by situating him or herself on one side or the other of a symbolic divide. For Freud, as is well known, this entry into symbolic difference is precipitated by the young child's sight of an anatomical distinction that becomes infused with anxieties of mutilation (for the boy and the girl) and disappointment and envy (for the girl).[33] In a sense, as Jean Laplanche reminds us, the castration complex is a nexus in which the two paths of anxiety and societal law are knotted in a blinding vision.[34] It is this vision of threatened (or accomplished) loss of an object highly cathected with narcissistic libido that sets the child off on the path to a "sexed" identity: either he or she identifies with the agent of castration and renounces his or her libidinal desire for the parent of the opposite sex with the hope one day, through this renouncement, of being able to assume the place of the threatening parent, and thus have access to the denied love object, or (and there are many other possible paths), he or she refuses the "sight" of difference, overcome by the anxiety of losing so highly invested part of his or her being and retreats into several "neurotic" or "perverse" libidinal positions.[35] One of these perverse positions, the fetishist, consists of course of a complicated set of anxiety disavowals of castration on the part of the young boy who, at the sight of the female genitals both admits and denies castra-

[33] The classic Freudian texts that present a succinct summary of the castration complex in its inextricable relation to the Oedipus complex are: "Some Psychological Consequences of the Anatomical Distinction between the Sexes" (Standard Edition, vol. 19); "The Passing of the Oedipus Complex" (ibid.); "Female Sexuality," (Standard Edition, vol. 21); "Femininity" in *New Introductory Lectures on Psychoanalysis* (Standard Edition, vol. 22).

[34] Cf. Laplanche, *Castration, symbolisations*, 9: "We now find ourselves at the crossroads of two developments, one concerning anxiety and the other concerning legality or social norms. Now, this point of articulation is precisely for psychoanalysis centered in the problem of castration." He continues (66): "It goes without saying that castration is precisely not a reality but a theorization of reality. It is a certain theorizing about reality that for Freud is so entirely anchored in perception that to deny castration would be the same thing as denying the experience of perception itself." Freud described this vision (in a much decried text): "There is an interesting contrast between the behavior of the two sexes. In the analogous situation, when a little boy first catches sight of a girl's genital region, he begins by showing irresolution and lack of interest; he sees nothing or disowns what he has seen. . . . A little girl behaves differently. She makes her judgment and her decision in a flash. She has seen it and knows that she is without it and wants to have it" ("Some Psychological Consequences," 19: 187–88). I quote these passages not as evidence of some theoretical truth but merely to insist on the importance of vision in the Freudian scenario.

[35] I am only describing in the broadest terms the dynamics of the castration complex, leaving to one side an account of the possibilities of the "negative oedipus" configuration. At the same time, to serve as a counterweight to what we know are the objections of certain feminists scholars to any theoretical use of the Oedipus/castration complex, I appeal to Teresa de Lauretis's comments on the problem: "The value of Freud's theory of sexuality far exceeds the normative Oedipal fantasy that grounds it. For in analyzing how subjectivity . . . is constructed from the ground of a dominant—social and psychoanalytic—fiction, he intimated and opened the critical path to understanding the semosic nature of fantasy as that which links the subject to the social through sexuality." *The Practice of Love: Lesbian Sexuality and Perverse Desire* (Bloomington: Indiana University Press, 1994), 108.

tion in the attempt simultaneously to safeguard his own penis and the idea of sexual difference.[36] Despite the fact that there is an infinite variety of possible fetishists, fetishism has become, since Otto Fenichel's classic study, to be seen as an essential component in the construction of a transvestitic personality.[37]

Although Robert Stoller, the psychoanalyst who has most thoroughly studied and published on the phenomenon of transvestism, has been recently accused by feminist and gay and lesbian critics of being too blatantly "essentialist," and although I would not like to reduce a character of Choisy's obvious complexity of accomplishments and phantasies to a simplistic formula, several coincidences that might usefully provide us with an entry into the conundrum of Choisy's life/texts jump out when we compare our seventeenth-century academician to the patients treated by Stoller in contemporary Los Angeles.[38]

Let me briefly summarize Stoller's theories in a few sentences. Stoller strongly suggests that the one consistent pattern in the psychosexual development of (male) cross-dressers is the overbearing presence during the child's infancy and childhood of a narcissistically depressive mother who is herself unhappily situated in her gender identity. By this Stoller supposes an

[36] Freud, "Fetishism" (Standard Edition, 21:154): " It is not true that the child emerges from his experience of seeing the female parts with an unchanged belief in the woman having a phallus. He retains this belief but he also gives it up. . . . In the world of psychical reality the woman still has a penis in spite of all, but this penis is no longer the same as it once was. Something else has taken its place, has been appointed its successor, so to speak, and now absorbs all the interest which formerly belonged to the penis." In "Splitting of the Ego" (Standard Edition, 23:277), Freud returns to this scenario and states that in "creating a substitute for the "woman's penis" the boy "had saved his own penis. . . . The boy did not simply contradict his perceptions and hallucinate a penis where there is none to be seen; he effected no more than a displacement of value—he transferred the importance of the penis to another part of the body. . . . This displacement, it is true, relates only to the female body: as regards his own penis nothing was changed." See also Leo Bersani's remarks about, once again, the coupling of "vision" and the construction of fetishistic fantasies: " Freud's essay on fetishism is all the more interesting . . . in that it describes a visual process. The drama of fetishism is a perceptual drama: it consists of a fundamental adventure in human seeing (Leo Bersani and Ulysse Dutoit, *The Forms of Violence* [New York: Shocken Books, 1985], 72).

[37] Otto Fenichel, "The Psychology of Transvestism" (1930), in *Collected Papers of O. Fenichel*, 2 vols. (New York: Norton, 1953).

[38] Among Stoller's many works the reader could consult with profit Robert J. Stoller, *Sex and Gender: On the Development of Masculinity and Femininity* (New York: Science House, 1968), *Presentations of Gender* (New Haven: Yale University Press, 1985), *Splitting* (New York: Quadrangle, 1973). As for a critique of Stoller's "essentialism," cf. Jacqueline Rose's introduction in Juliet Mitchell and Jacqueline Rose, *Feminine Sexuality: Jacques Lacan and the École freudienne* (New York: Norton, 1985), 37 n. 4, where the idea of "gender identity" is said to side-step "the acquisition of sexual identity and its difficulty" (the book under criticism is Nancy Chodorow's *Reproduction of Mothering, Psychoanalysis and the Sociology of Gender* (Berkeley: University of California Press, 1978); and Judith Butler, *Gender Trouble: Feminism and the Subversion of Identity* (New York: Routledge, 1990). Laplanche, (*Castration, symbolisations*, 33, n. 1) also decries what he calls "the presuppositions and finally the confusion introduced by Stoller." One could also consult the recent article by Jessica Benjamin, "Sameness and Difference: Toward an 'Overinclusive' Model of Gender Development," in *Psychoanalytic Inquiry*, 15 1 (1995): 125–42.

underlying unresolved desire for, if not the phallus, at least a fantasized "phallic empowerment" which informs the mother's depression. Coupled to this depressive mother Stoller discerns the presence of an absent or passive father and thus the lack of any compensating active paternal presence.[39] Stoller believes that if the father does not actively intervene in the relation between the mother and her child that child (of either sex) is headed for an unstable gender identity. Analytic theories of development see conflict both internal (caused by the innate internal drives) and external (i.e. the intervention of the father leading to dissonance in the child/mother monad) as the necessary impetus to psychic development. In the case of the cross-dresser, however, Stoller proposes that rather it is (first) the too-great a gratification of an Edenic closeness with mother who never allows the intervention of paternal (i.e. phallic) authority that sets the stage for this particular personality/gender configuration. In this configuration Stoller examines also the particular pattern of neurosis in the mothers of cross-dressers. He suggests that part of their depression stems from their own dissatisfaction with unresolved gender conflicts. Most of these women are described as having themselves demonstrated the prevalence of a tomboyish attitude in their own youth. Their passage into adult femininity has been marked by bitterness and reserve. In classic Freudian terms they are dispossessed of the phallus ("castrated"): their depression is their mourning for that phallic loss. In other words, the conundrum of the cross-dresser and his mother turns, as we might have suspected, around the dyad phallic-castrated. The castration complex with its anxiety and (possible) resolutions will thus always appear at the center of any discussion of "gender dissonance."[40] The question, therefore, of "castration," of the presence or absence of the phallus is, of course, according to Freud the single most pressing question in the formation of all psychosexual constructions. The particular twist that cross-dressing brings to this "universal phenomenon" is the fetishistic refusal of the child to relinquish his belief in the phallic-mother, the woman-with-a-penis, with whom the young child identifies and against whom he must struggle.[41] Finally, Stoller remarks that in most cases of transvestism, the cross-dress-

[39] Stoller here returns, as does most psychoanalytic theory, to the idea of an initial monadic state (comparable to the androgyn?) which must be split by the intervention of the father. If the child (the boy) is to navigate adequately the very rocky path that goes from the society's initial determining pronouncement at birth, "it's a boy" (or "it's a girl"), which lays out the long (and unique) path that the baby will have to travel so that biological sexual identity and "healthy" gender identity will, it is hoped, coalesce, forming what that society's ideological constructions label a successful "man" or "woman" (in other words, a construction in which sex and gender form a seamless whole), there must be the intervention of the father or his societal substitute.

[40] The details of this brief summary can be found in Stoller, *Sex and Gender*, 89–131.

[41] Fenichel, "The Psychology of Transvestism," 169: "The transvestite . . . has not been able to give up his belief in the phallic nature of women and, in addition, he has identified himself with the woman with the penis. Identification with the woman, as a substitute for, or side by side with, love for her is so plain in the manifest clinical picture that Ellis . . . regarded it as the essence of transvestitism. But the woman with whom the transvestite identifies is conceived of by him as phallic and this is the essential feature in the situation."

ing was initially imposed by an outside female presence to humiliate the little boy. In a sense, therefore, one of the functions cross-dressing serves for the adult is that of a fetishistic defense: it turns an initially humiliating and degrading situation (a situation of passivity) into an active affirmation wherein the male transvestite takes enormous pleasure in having kept intact, under his women's attire, a powerful penis.[42]

But what of Choisy in all this? At the beginning of the *Mémoires pour servir à l'histoire de Louis XIV*, the abbé offers us an intriguing image of his mother and the relation she constructed with the last, and most beautiful, of her sons:

> Ma mère par son esprit plus que par l'état de sa fortune, était fort avant dans les secrets de la cour: la reine Anne d'Autriche l'avait fort aimée, et le Roi lui-même la distinguait de toutes les femmes de son âge par ses bienfaits et par des marques de son amitié, jusqu'à lui donner des audiences réglées toutes les semaines. J'étais le dernier de ses enfants, et par conséquent le plus aimé. A l'âge de dix ans, elle me faisait écrire tous les matins deux ou trois heures au chevet de son lit, et toutes ses lettres parlaient d'affaires ou de nouvelles . . . par là j'ai été initié de bonne heure aux mystères de la politique.[43]

Mme de Choisy was, he adds, "une maîtresse femme qui voulait être obéie"(26). The image Choisy paints of his mother reminds us of those other politically manipulative women who are so carefully depicted in *La princesse de Clèves* vying for power at the court of Henri II. We know, of course, that La Fayette transposed backward to the world of Renaissance intrigue her visions of the courts of Louis XIII and Louis XIV: " Il y avait tant d'intérêts et tant de cabales différents, et les dames y avaient tant de part que l'amour était toujours mêlé aux affaires et les affaires à l'amour."[44] The inseparability of "desire and politics" that forms the central narrative knot in La Fayette's novel is reflected in Mme de Choisy, who serves as her son's initiator into politics. In this case, as for La Fayette's powerful women, politics remains inseparable from sexuality: at court (and this is only an exaggerated version of society at large) they are inextricably intertwined. Although we have no direct evidence (from her son's account) of amorous/political intrigues of her own, we do know that it was her political sense, her

[42] Stoller, *Sex and Gender*, 214: "It takes little imagination to recognize in the transvestite man's erotic daydream the little boy's impressions of the woman or older girl, who, in her greater power, so damaged his masculinity. By a remarkable tour de force he takes the original humiliation and converts it into an active process of sexual mastery and pleasure. He thus salvages some sexual potency, power, and masculinity from an originally castrating event." Or again, *Presentation of Gender*, 22: "one frequently finds that in early childhood the boy was cross-dressed by a girl or woman for the purpose of humiliating him. In time, the humiliation is converted, via the perversion, to a triumph, especially as manifested by the ability to achieve an erection and orgasm despite being in women's clothes."

[43] Choisy, *Mémoires pour servir*, 25.

[44] La Fayette, *La princesse de Clèves*, 252.

desire to maintain an emotional hold on the royal family, that initiates Choisy into the mysteries of politics and those mysteries into which he was initiated were the seductive pleasures of cross-dressing:

> j'ai été initié de bonne heure aux intrigues de la cour. . . . Ma mère avait tant de faiblesse pour moi, qu'elle était continuellement à m'ajuster. Elle m'avait eu à quarante ans passés; et comme elle voulait absolument encore être belle, un enfant de huit à neuf ans qu'elle menait partout la faisait paraître encore jeune. On m'habillait en fille toutes les fois que le petit Monsieur venait au logis, et il y venait au moins deux ou trois fois la semaine. J'avais les oreilles percées, des diamants, des mouches, et toutes les autres petites afféteries auxquelles on s'accoutume fort aisément, et dont on se défait fort difficilement.[45]

This passage informs us that from his earliest years his mother's ambition focuses almost exclusively on the use she could make of her son's erotico/political potential, both to bolster her own narcissism ("ma mère m'avait eu dans un âge assez avancé, je la faisais paraître encore jeune") and consequently his ("ce qui faisait sans doute qu'elle m'aimait plus que mes frères," 218) and to advance her (their) position at court. The young Choisy dressed and made up by this mother was the bait with which to trap that more interesting, more promising, and infinitely more powerful, prey—Philippe d'Orléans:

> Monsieur, qui aimait aussi tout cela, me faisait toujours cent amitiés. Dès qu'il arrivait, suivi des nièces du cardinal Mazarin et de quelques filles de la Reine, on le mettait à sa toilette, on le coiffait. Il avait un corps pour conserver sa taille (ce corps était en broderie): on lui ôtait son justaucorps, pour lui mettre des manteaux de femmes et des jupes.[46]

Choisy's description of his playing "dress-up" with Philippe creates a sensation of discomfit, particularly when we consider the full and painful import of that extra detail Choisy adds of the "corps" designed to inhibit the child's normal physical development.[47] This discomfit turns to a sense of indignation, however, when we discover that the children's play is (according to Choisy) a carefully orchestrated scenario of castration: "tout cela se faisait, dit-on, par l'ordre du cardinal qui voulait le rendre efféminé, de peur qu'il ne fit de la peine au Roi, comme Gaston avait fait à Louis XIII," 219). Choisy's version of Mazarin's machiavellian plot to emasculate Philippe has

[45] Choisy, *Mémoires pour servir*, 219.

[46] Ibid.

[47] There were many different devices used to inhibit, reshape, or otherwise "correct" nature in the seventeenth century. One of these devices was used on Choisy himself, as we shall see and in his "fairy tale," the little marquise is also subjected to it. Cf. Lawrence Stone, *The Family, Sex, and Marriage in England, 1500–1800* (New York: Harper and Row, 1977), talks in his chapter on educational techniques of these "orthopedic devices."

been disputed by most modern biographers of the prince.[48] What I find significant, however, is not whether Choisy's version is historically accurate, but what this anecdote reveals about his own perception of (political/sexual) reality—that is, how his own fantasies are inextricably interwoven with his perception of the world.[49] And what, we might speculate, the young Choisy "perceives" is the pleasure (how is a child to interpret cynically this pleasure) of an entire little court, reflected in his mother's eyes. In a sense, Philippe is but a double for Choisy, both children are sacrificed to the desires of their parents, a desire whose object is the king.

Mme de Choisy certainly had a husband and the abbé a father. This phantom father/husband, however, nowhere appears in the *Mémoires*. At first glance, it might seem that in the young Choisy's imaginary oedipal constellation the place of the father is empty. When we consider, with Lacan, however, that the " place of the father" is a structural rather than physical necessity (that is, the father is coterminus with the object of the mother's desire), and when we know Mme de Choisy has her sights constantly directed on more sublime objects of desire than her absent and bourgeois husband, we can suspect that the place of the father is occupied by a more threatening image.[50] As a political intriguer, as a woman who lives only in a manipulative game of power, wealth, and prestige, Mme de Choisy can have (at least as her son perceives her) but one transcendental object of desire—the "corps glorieux" of the king. [51] Louis figures (as he does for absolutist France in general) as Mme de Choisy's object of desire: "Le roi est si grand, qu'on peut dire, sans le flatter, qu'il est grand jusque dans les plus petites choses."[52] Louis is made to represent, for Choisy, the paternal phallus that in his identification with his mother Choisy will have to both worship and denigrate in his attempt to forge his own sense of independence. It is only once we understand the place the king occupies in his mother's desiring fan-

[48] See most recently Nancy Barker, *Brother of the Sun King, Philippe, duke of Orléans*, (Baltimore: Johns Hopkins University Press, 1989), who thoroughly dismisses Choisy's version of the events arguing that it would be unthinkable for any politically astute adviser to purposely endanger the mental or physical well-being of the prince who was, for more than eighteen years, the only heir to the throne.

[49] Laplanche, *Castration, symbolisations*, 66.

[50] It should be clear as, Rose points out, that the "father" in the Lacanian schema is a "role," not an actual "biological" progenitor. Cf. Introduction to *Feminine Sexuality*, 39: "when Lacan calls for a return to the place of the father he is crucially distinguishing himself from any sociological conception of the role. The father is a function and refers to a law, the place outside the imaginary dyad and against which it breaks."

[51] Cf. Jacques Lacan, "La signification du phallus," in *Écrits* 2 ([Paris: Seuil, 1971], 103–18) for a reading of the castration complex as I am using it here. Rose (*Feminine Sexuality*, 38) offers the following helpful gloss: " Castration means first of all this—that the child's desire for the mother does not refer to her but beyond her, to an object, the phallus, whose status is first imaginary (the object presumed to satisfy her desire) and then symbolic (recognition that desire cannot be satisfied)."

[52] *Mémoires pour servir*, 31.

tasies that we can understand that on some very primitive level it is the king as object of his mother's desire, embodied as "Louis," who assumes the place of the castrating father. Behind Mme de Choisy, behind her manipulative presence, a presence that is nonetheless seen as beneficial (c'était une maitresse femme, qui voulait être obéie, et qui faisait ma fortune" is repeated twice in the *Mémoires pour servir* [26 and 218]) looms as the actual, terrifying agent of castration, the father/king. [53]

But what makes Choisy particularly interesting, and particularly troublesome, is that for no matter how complicated or terrifying his castration fears might (or might not) have been, they were obviously (and this is the point of fetishism) strong enough to "split" his ego: he both renounces the maternal phallus (that is, he cannot have the phallus/king) and affirms it too, his identification with his mother's desire fetishizes his body as female—thus becoming in an imaginary scenario the phallus for the king.[54] This enables (forces) Choisy to "dress up," to be the woman, but always the "woman-with-a penis."[55] In other words, Choisy's entire body, and the projection of that body's image into the world and its reflection back onto the subject (Choisy) has the dual function of both acknowledging the split (i.e. castration) and denying it. Difference is both proposed, only to be confounded. Beneath the skirts and the make up, he tells us, the little girls with whom he played sensed something "different," something masculine. They knew, and we must assume that their knowing was only a reflection of his own knowledge, that his penis was safely hidden:

> Quand Monsieur était habillé et paré, on jouait à la petite prime . . . et sur les sept heures on apportait la collation. . . . Madame de Brancas y amenait souvent sa fille, qui a été depuis la princesse d'Harcourt. Elle m'aidait à faire ce pe-

[53] See Laplanche, *Castration, symbolisations*, for a detailed analysis of the importance and intricacies of the castration complex. In his discussion of Freud's elaboration of this complex, Laplanche points out (67) that "in any case, to whomever is attributed the formulation [i.e. the "menace of castration"] in the final analysis it is always the father who will be [perceived as] the agent of the threat."

[54] Fenichel, writing about the young (transvestitic) boy's "identification" with his mother, points out that it is always to the phallic woman that the boy identifies ("The Psychology of Transvestism," 169). Giorgio Agamben, in *Stanzas: Word and Phantasm in Western Culture*, (trans. Ronald Martinez (Minneapolis: University of Minnesota Press, 1993), writes of the contradictory space of the fetish (146) "The space of the fetish is precisely this contradiction; the fetish is simultaneously the presence of that nothingness that is the maternal penis and the sign of its absence. As both a symbol of something and its negation, the fetish can maintain itself only with the provision of an essential laceration, in which the two contrary reactions constitute the nucleus of a true and proper splitting of the ego (Ich spaltung)."

[55] Almost all the authors who have written on transvestism, despite their many differences, all agree on this one point. Cf. Stoller, *Sex and Gender*, 188: "one cannot be a male transvestite without knowing, loving, and magnificently expanding the importance of one's own phallus"; Ackroyd, *Dressing Up*, (29): "The female clothes which the transvestite wears might in themselves be seen as a symbol of castration—they are flowing not bifurcated and yet his penis, the real centre of his obsession is secure beneath."

tit ménage; mais quoiqu'elle fût fort belle, les filles de la Reine m'aimaient mieux qu'elle: sans doute que, malgré les cornettes et les jupes, elles sentaient en moi quelque chose de masculin.[56]

I have dwelt on these passages in the early life of Choisy because I believe that they offer some necessary clues for understanding the construction of his image of himself. This construction of a double persona, a "boy/girl," strikes me as particularly baroque in the sense that the personal psychic structures (of which we can only hope to catch a fleeting glimpse) are so intertwined with what we have come to recognize as the dominant structural and philosophic components of a baroque esthetic: a certain emphasis on vision, a vision that creates the circumscribed arena in which sexuality attaches itself to particular images, images that receive their consistency only in the spiraling relay of reflection which at the same time that it creates a grounding for the image, by the very fact of being a reflection, also undermines any possible constancy.[57]

This double persona is constantly present on multiple levels in all of Choisy's literary productions. It is an indication of a unresolved, perhaps unresolvable dilemma that refuses, and by this refusal can be seen as actively undermining, the dominant semiotic system to which on one level it pays homage. When reading the *Mémoires pour servir à l'histoire de Louis XIV,* for instance, we are struck by what, given the memoirs genre, could at first reading simply appear as another in the long series of typical panegyric histories produced by the propagandists of Louis's reign:

J'entreprends d'écrire des Mémoires sur la plus belle de toutes les vies, la plus remplie d'évenements extraordinaires, la plus digne de passer à la postérité: on n'y verra que villes prises, batailles gagnées, Etats conquis, et toutes les horreurs de la guerre suivies plus d'une fois de la paix, mère de l'abondance et des plaisirs; et, pout tout dire en peu de paroles, j'entreprends d'écrire la *Vie de Louis XIV*, roi de France, à qui ses peuples ont donné le surnom de *Grand*, nom glorieux que ses vertus, que ses actions lui ont acquis avec justice, et que l'équitable avenir lui confirmera.[58]

Choisy devotes considerable time, in his *Mémoires* to the expansionist campaigns of the French monarch, campaigns that, as we have seen in the introduction, were designed to expand the boundaries of the kingdom to its natural and (politically) invulnerable limits: " Le roi Louis-le-Grand, en

[56] *Mémoires pour servir*, 219.

[57] For a brilliant reading of the analytic (i.e. Lacanian) reading of the baroque, especially for the importance accorded to the scopic drive, cf. Christine Buci-Glucksmann, *La folie du voir: De l'esthétique baroque* (Paris: Galilée, 1986). "The generalized scopic drive hides a true work of cultural mourning, an implementation of the death drive that undermines and fragments any signifying intention, any immediacy of meaning, any self-evident empiricism" (47).

[58] *Mémoires pour servir*, 22.

faisant la paix de Nimègue, était parvenu au comble de la gloire humaine. . . . Il avait reculé toutes les frontières de son royaume"(114). Once again I insist on the importance, for seventeenth-century France, of the safeguarding of the borders of the state as an analogy for the "securing" of a certain image of the body and of the ego that is buttressed by that body image (of course, the analogy works both ways). In other words by synecdochal relay, Louis secures the limits of the political "body" of the state. This bounded body is represented as his own "corps glorieux," which in turn becomes the object of desire of his people, their own ego ideal. But, as recent theorists writing in the wake of Mary Douglas have suggested, this bounded (social) body is vulnerable at precisely those points of passage, those "borders" that are "conquered " and controlled with such difficulty.[59]

What precisely is intriguing in Choisy's narrative is that at the same time that he is celebrating, by elaborating this history of Louis's construction of his own and France's corporal integrity, an integrity subtended by a masculinist ideology of closure, unicity, and "difference," he is, through a parallel narration of his own life, undermining the image of an integral (masculine) state/subject:

> Au reste, j'avertis le lecteur qu'en écrivant la vie du Roi j'écrirai aussi la mienne, à mesure que je me souviendrai de ce qui m'est arrivé. Ce sera un beau contraste, mais cela me réjouira, et je veux bien courre le risque qu'on dise: *Il joint à tous propos les louanges d'un fat à celle d'un héros.*[60]

Choisy is good to his word: the *Mémoires* constantly oscillate between the narration of the king's heroic, military feats, victories that consolidate France's territorial borders and Choisy's own more domestic, more "effeminate" life. If we then read these *Mémoires* as a parallel history of the period, we can a detect a decidedly different or at least continually contradictory view of the king. The narration is a "split" narration, split between the projection of grandiose masculinity, and the *badineries* of a life given over to a man *habillé en fille*, who describes himself as "méprisable par une coquetterie de petite fille, . . . toujours gouverné par le plaisir"(25). If we wish to extend Douglas's analogy further, from the physical to the geopolitical and then to the rhetorical, we can say that the image of the corporal integrity of the king that is so important to underpin the ideological stability of the emerging Cartesian ego is continually riven, rent by the simultaneous image of Choisy, the image of the other that inheres in the "corps glorieux" of Classical France. As the traditional trope of the "mirror" as a metaphor

[59] Judith Butler, glossing the work of Mary Douglas, writes (*Gender Trouble*, 132): "Douglas suggests that all social systems are vulnerable at their margins, and that all margins are accordingly considered dangerous. If the body is synedochal for the social system per se or a site in which open systems converge, then any kind of unregulated permeability constitutes a site of pollution and endangerment."

[60] *Mémoires pour servir*, 25.

for his history tells us (21), Choisy reflects back to his reader (to *all* his readers present and future) an image of the king that functions almost as a psychic X-ray, exposing, under the martial valor of Louis, Choisy with his dresses and *mouches* as the underside of the Classical subject. It is an image that is exposed, he tells us, for all to see. Could we not also see the riven image of the king as a veiled gesture, the gesture of an attempted attack (castration) by Choisy, on Absolutism's inarticulable underpinnings? The history we are given to read (see) is the history of a hybrid subject, male and female, baroque and Classical, a history of the rent underside of Absolutism that Classical ethics and esthetics papers over in its constant "naturalizing" of sexual difference.[61] While the iconic image of the king shines in the reflection of his "two bodies," Choisy's own double body reflects back to the king what the Classical insistence on repression has attempted to erase: that all bodies are productions, traversed by different and often contradictory pleasures that cannot be accommodated by the dominant sexual fictions: the body is always excessive.

When Choisy is looking into his own mirror(s), what body does he see?

> J'avais une cravate de mousseline, dont les glands venaient tomber sur un grand noeud de ruban noir, qui était attaché au haut de mon corps de robe, ce qui n'empêchait pas qu'on me vît le haut des épaules qui s'étaient conservées blanches par le grand soin que j'en avais eu toute ma vie; je me lavais tous les soirs le col et le haut de la gorge avec de l'eau de veau et de la pommade de pieds de mouton, ce qui faisait que la peau était douce et blanche.[62]

> Mon corps était fort haut et rembourré par-devant, pour faire croire qu'il y avait là de la gorge, et effectivement j'en avais autant qu'une fille de quinze ans . . . On m'avait mis dès l'enfance des corps qui me serraient extrêmement et faisaient élever la chair, qui était grasse et potelée. J'avais eu aussi fort grand soin de mon col que je frottais tous les soirs avec de l'eau de veau et de la pommade de pieds de mouton, ce qui rend la peau douce et blanche.[63]

Two things immediately strike us in these brief descriptions. First it is impossible to separate the image of Choisy's body from that body's construction in and through cultural artifacts, clothes, makeup.[64] Second, as Paul

[61] Juliet Mitchell in her introduction to *Feminine Sexuality* helps us understand how this gesture of neutralizing "bisexuality" is part of the ideology of the self-present, transparent "cartesian ego;" p. 26 : " To be human is to be subjected to a law which decenters and divides: sexuality is created in division, the subject is split; but an ideological world conceals this from the conscious subject who is supposed to feel whole and certain of a sexual identity."

[62] *Mémoires de l'abbé de Choisy*, 291.

[63] Ibid, 332.

[64] Schidler, in his *Image and Appearance of the Human Body* (London: Kegan Paul, Trench and Trubner, 1935) talks about the importance of clothing in any construction of one's body image in the following terms (203): "Clothes become part of the body image. . . . Whatever article of clothing we put on immediately becomes a part of the body image and is filled with narcissistic libido."

Schidler has pointed out in his classic study of the body image, these cultural artifacts are invested with enormous narcissistic libido, which in Choisy's case makes him take his desires for reality. Choisy tells us that "actually" he does have breasts ("effectivement j'en avais autant qu'une fille de quinze ans"). The same type of orthopedic brace that we saw used on Philippe d'Orléans was also used on Choisy (as it is on Mariane, the "heroine" of Choisy's short "fairy tale").[65] The result was a "body" that was "female," at least as Choisy sees it. Choisy's vision would seem to confirm Lacan's remark that "in its relation to desire, reality appears only as marginal."[66] What Lacan means, of course, is that desire pays only very passing tribute to "reality," that, in fact, the distinction "reality/fantasy," a distinction so essential to Cartesian logic, is radically put into question as soon as we consider the way desire both is informed by and informs any subject's relation to the "objective world."[67] More interesting, the body that Choisy desires, the image of himself as body that he sees reflected back to himself when he gazes into his mirror, is the image of his twin, but in his case of his twin sister. Choisy is a new Narcissus, but not the Narcissus of the classical version of the myth: in a later rendition of the Narcissus myth, recounted by the geographer Pausanias, Narcissus, when he gazes into the pond and sees a reflection, it is the reflection of his twin sister who looks back at him. His sister "had exactly the same exterior appearance as he. Both wore their hair in the same way, had the same clothes. They share everything equally."[68] Choisy stares into his mirror's reflection and sees not a male self but a female double. In this way the myth of Narcissus doubles back and expresses, in one more twist, another version of androgyny—the androgyn here split into two symmetrical images that gaze longingly at each other across the abyss of difference that both joins and separates them.

Wherever Choisy goes, his mirrors (literal or figurative) are always close at hand. The comtesse des Barres episode is the longest and perhaps the most successful segment of the *Mémoires*. In this period of his life Choisy, having been publicly rebuked for his cross-dressing (I shall return to this incident shortly) decides to leave Paris for a life in the provinces. This is a particularly intriguing and complicated episode in the *Mémoires* for it is the only one where his public has no prior, no contradictory information about

[65] "Sa taille à douze ans estoit déjà formée. Il est vray qu'on l'avoit un peu contrainte dès l'enfance avec des corps de fer, afin de lui faire venir des hanches, et de luy faire remonter la gorge" *La marquise/marquis de Banneville,* in *Autour des contes de fées*, ed. Jeanne Roche-Mazon (Paris: Didier, 1968), 48.

[66] Jacques Lacan, *Séminaire II*, (Paris: Seuil, 1971), 99.

[67] For an interesting discussion on the impossibility of separating the world into any neat division between "reality" and "fantasy," see Jean Laplanche, *Probématiques, vol. 5, Le baquet: Transcendance du transfert* (Paris: P.U.F., 1987), 89–97, in particular, 93: "No memory is exempt from phantasmatic infiltrations, conversely, no phantasm is without an anchoring in, or at least without an intentional impulse towards, some real[ity]."

[68] Quoted in Pierre Hadot "le mythe de Narcisse et son interprétation pár Plotin" *N.R.P.* #13, 1976, 95.

his true (i.e. biological) sex. From the moment Choisy arrives on the scene at Bourges, he is a countess. There are no previous acquaintances, as in Paris, for instance, was the case of Mme de La Fayette and M. de La Rochefoucauld, who know the abbé first as a man and then as a woman.[69] Here Choisy /des Barres is a tabula rasa to the entire social world of Bourges. In order to offer herself properly as a dazzling spectacle to her new circle of admirers Choisy/des Barres sets about creating the necessary backdrop for the spectacular mise-en-scène of her persona. S/he buys a château and proceeds to furnish it. The most important element, the detail that is at first missing from this theater of illusions, is the mirrors:

> Ma grande chambre était magnifique: une tapisserie de Flandre des plus fines, un lit de velours incarnat avec des franges d'or et de soie, des sièges de commodité que j'avais faits de mes vieilles jupes, une cheminée de marbre; il n'y manquait que des miroirs . . .[70]

Without mirrors to reflect herself to herself Choisy/des Barres does not exist. Although, as we will see, it is infinitely more important for Choisy to be mirrored in the eyes of his public, the importance of having a constant reflection, a reflection that continually reaffirms from the outside the interior image he needs of himself, comes first and foremost by being surrounded by mirrors which, as we know, never lie. Luckily for Choisy, shortly after furnishing her home, a wealthy neighbor dies and s/he thus can acquire the finishing but essential touches for her décor:

> Madame la marquise du Tronc mourut dans son château, à trois ou quatre lieues de Bourges; ses meubles furent vendus, et j'achetai à fort bon marché deux trumeaux de glace, deux glaces de cheminée, un grand miroir et un chandelier de cristal. . . . On peut juger que ma chambre en fut bien parée.[71]

On the one hand, Choisy, in his "psyché," exists as a fe/male. The image reflected back to him disavows the symbolic castration that would place him in one or the other camp of sexual difference.[72] Lacan spent endless en-

[69] "Il arriva même que madame de La Fayette, que je voyais fort souvent, me voyant toujours fort ajusté avec des pendants d'oreille et des mouches, me dit en bonne amie que ce n'était point la mode pour les hommes, et que je ferais bien mieux de m'habiller en femme. . . . J'avais assez d'habits de femme, je pris le plus beau, et allai rendre visite à madame de La Fayette, avec mes pendants d'oreilles, ma croix de diamant: elle s'écria en me voyant:

Ah! la belle personne! Vous avez donc suivi mon avis, et vous avez bien fait. Demandez plutôt à M. de La Rochefoucauld. . . . Ils me tournèrent et retournèrent, et furent fort contents" (*Mémoires*, 224–25).

[70] *Mémoires de l'abbé de Choisy*, 331.

[71] Ibid. p. 331.

[72] As Rose puts it in her introduction to *Feminine Sexuality*, (49): "For Lacan, men and women are only ever in language. . . . All speaking beings must line themselves up on one side or the other of this division, but anyone can cross over and inscribe themselves on the opposite side from that to which they are anatomically destined."

ergy in his attempt to show that biological sexual difference can never be made to correspond to psychosexual difference; men and women are never merely complimentary terms of an ideologically freighted symmetrical dyad. Elaborating on Freud's insights Lacan proposed that the "error" in this attempt of achieving a heterosexual complimentary was explained in the terms of "having" or "being" the phallus for the Other: men supposedly "have" the phallus for women who "are" the phallus in their relation to men.[73] Refusing to choose between these terms, but projecting an image in which he both "is" and "has" the phallus, Choisy would exist in a third relation, something Lacan names an "appearing" ("par/être"), which, with all the implications of theatricality, dressing up, make-believe the term carries, I find particularly resonant for Choisy. Not only does it serve to explain the psychic image he projects out into the sexual world of Absolutism but it also resonates with this psychic dimension's inscription within the entire tradition of a baroque ethics and aesthetics. Choisy's making a spectacle of himself combines in one spiraling displacement both the "masquerade" that Lacan, following Joan Riviere, attributes as the "essence" of femininity with the "parade" that is its masculine equivalent.[74] In this way, Choisy situates himself as appearing both to "be" and to "have" the phallus in a spectacularly self-enclosed desiring network that allows him, in a perverse fashion, precisely to be what Absolutism wants—"tout." This is exactly what the compliment of one of her female admirers tells Choisy, when s/he is living as the comtesse des Barres: "Toutes les dames ne vous ressemblent pas, . . . votre miroir vous suffit et vous dit continuellement que vous avez tout par vous-même."[75] S/he has "tout." But, of course, the proof of this having, the proof of being both/and, is obtainable only as a reflection—it is only a play of mirrors. This play of reflections constantly reinscribes Choisy's narcissism, a narcissism that is inextricably tied to a fetishistic production of his body, as female. This fetishized narcissism constantly resurfaces in the *Mémoires* and in his fiction as the continual need for a never-ending "mirror-stage." As we know, the "mirror-stage" captures and seizes an "image" of corporal integrity that is essential for the formation of the subject's ego but, at one and the same time, that "ego-image" always acts as

[73] Jacques Lacan, "The Meaning of the Phallus," in *Feminine Sexuality*, 83: "Let us say that these relations will revolve around a being and a having, which because they refer to a signifier, the phallus, have the contradictory effect of on the one hand lending reality to the subject in that signifier, and on the other making unreal the relation to be signified."

[74] On more than one occasion in the *Mémoires de l'abbé de Choisy*, Choisy tells us that it was precisely his penchant for "making a spectacle of himself," rather than his cross-dressing per se that shocked his family. Cf. "Je ne me fis pas prier davantage, mais je m'y préparai comme à une fête qui devait me montrer en spectacle à tout un grand peuple"(295), or more to the point, (309): "J'y rencontrai un jour M. de Caumartin, qui est mon neveu; il se promena longtemps avec nous, mais le lendemain il me vint voir et me représenta assez vivement que je me donnais trop en spectacle."

[75] *Mémoires de l'abbé de Choisy*, 344.

an alienating fiction.[76] What Choisy mirrors in the production of his own persona and his own fictitious narrations is the production of femininity as a cultural fetish.

When as an author of fiction Choisy comes to depict his heroine, a perfect example of seventeenth-century beauty, he offers us the following description of Mariane:

> On estoit pris d'abord par un teint d'une blancheur éblouissante; un incarnat toujours renaissant surprenoit toujours; ses yeux étaient bleus, et n'en estoient pas moins vifs; ils sortoient de deux paupières épaisses qui rendoient leurs regards plus tendres et plus languissans. Le tour du visage estoit ovale, et sa bouche vermeille et rebordé presentoit dans le temps même qu'elle parloit le plus sérieusuement vingt petits trous creusez par les Graces, et vingt autres encore plus agréables qu'elle formoit en riant.[77]

Several things are remarkable about this description. First off, it strikes me as a "mirror-image" of the description La Fayette offers of her elusive princess:

> La blancheur de son teint et ses cheveux blonds lui donnaient un éclat que l'on n'a jamais vu qu'à elle; tous ses traits étaient réguliers, et son visage et sa personne étaient pleins de grâce et de charmes.[78]

In both of these examples (and this is not the only way in which *La marquise/marquis de Banneville* can be read as a parody of Classicism's most celebrated text of heterosexual desire), the heroines are offered to our readerly gaze as a perfect blank in representation. Instead of any detail that would distinguish them, we have a collection of stereotypes that simply disseminate them across the cultural landscape of feminine beauty. [79] They are offered up to our sight as its object, an object that captures the *Schaulust* of the gazes that are waiting for it. But what does it mean when a text appeals to an immediacy of vision, a glimpse of perfect (and totally undescribed) female beauty? In his article "Difference," Stephen Heath addresses precisely this question and suggests that:

[76] Jacques Lacan, " La stade du miroir comme formateur de la fonction du Je," in *Écrits 1* (Paris: Seuil, 1971), 89–100.

[77] *La marquise/marquis de Banneville*, 48. The authorship of this conte, which first appeared in the *Mercure galant*, had been variously attributed. The two most likely candidates were the abbé de Choisy and Charles Perrault. It is now admitted by most scholars that Choisy is the principal author. To what extent he was aided by Perrault is unclear. For a detailed account of the history and attribution of the text see Roche-Mazon, "L'histoire de la *Petite Marquise*," 21–44, in *Autour des contes de fées*.

[78] Mme de La Fayette *La Princesse de Clèves*, p. 248.

[79] Roland Barthes, in *S/Z* (Paris: Seuil, 1970), argued that only the ugly was scriptable because it is always particular that beauty is impossible to describe in any way that is not simply a reference to another cultural icon.

> where a discourse appeals directly to an image, to an immediacy of seeing, as a point of its argument or demonstration one can be sure that all difference is being elided, that the unity of some accepted vision is being reproduced.[80]

What is being reproduced in the appeal of/to the bodily image (even here in all its "aspecificity") is an ideology of sexual difference where the woman is looked at, upon, and seen to figure for the male viewer that difference that corroborates his own sexuality as superiority.[81] But this superiority is strategically undermined by both of these texts at the very same time they seem to be affirming it. For, while it is striking that in neither the *Mémoires* nor *La marquise/marquis de Banneville* is there a true portrait of either "heroine," Choisy does lavish infinite detail describing the outfits that s/he wears and the effect these clothes have on creating, in the eyes of her/his public, an image in which s/he pleasures. When, for instance, Choisy dressed as Mme de Sancy decides that s/he is going to offer the holy bread ("pain bénit") to her fellow parishioners, witness the great care in detailing her outfit:

> Je ne me fis pas prier davantage, mais je m'y préparai comme à une fête qui devait me montrer en spectacle à tout un grand peuple. Je fis faire une robe de chambre de damas blanc de la Chine, doublée de taffetas noir: j'avais une échelle de rubans noirs, des rubans sur les manches, et derrière une grande touffe de rubans noirs pour marquer la taille. Je crus qu'en cette occasion il fallait une jupe de velours noir . . .
>
> J'ai toujours depuis porté deux jupes, et j'ai fait retrousser mes manteaux avec de gros noeuds de rubans. Ma coiffure était fort galante; un petit bonnet de taffetas noir chargé de rubans était attaché sur une perruque qui était fort poudrée; madame de Noailles m'avait prêté ses grands pendants d'oreilles de diamants brillants, et dans le côté gauche de mes cheveux j'avais cinq ou six poinçons de diamants et de de rubis: trois ou quatre grandes mouches, et plus d'une grande douzaine de petites. . . . Je fatiguai beaucoup toute la journée, mais j'avais eu tant de plaisir de me voir applaudir de tout le monde, que je ne me sentis lasse que quand je fus couchée.[82]

I have quoted this rather extensive passage (and it is just one of many—all the detailed accounts in the texts are descriptions of clothes) because I think it points to the enormous *jouissance* the abbé experiences (even years later in the rescripting and the reviewing of these scenes) not in the reality of the body—its *Kreaturlichkeit*—but in its displacement, in the symbolic exchanges of the sexed body into and as the material construction of a body

[80] Stephen Heath, "Difference," in *Screen*, Nov.-Dec. 1978, 59.

[81] See my discussion of this issue in relation to *La princesse de Clèves* from where I borrow these few sentences in *Subjectivity and Subjugation*, 191–93.

[82] *Mémoires de l'abbé de Choisy*, pp.295–96.

image. The clothes represent the body transformed, its feminization fetishized in the soft, flowing materials ("taffetas," "velours," "satin"). If, as Naomi Schor has argued, the detail is gendered as feminine, and if, as I have tried to show, this elaborate detailing of clothing, materials, jewelry, makeup functions as a feminized fetish, creating, for the eyes of the world, the image of a woman, we must ask where, in this " body/fetish," in this economic system whose role it is to both hide and reveal castration, is the abbé's penis hiding? [83] What bodily marker signals to the world that this elaborately detailed production of the "feminine" is also and at the same time, the revelation of the "masculine"?

In all the particulars of clothing, of makeup that change according to the occasion (going to the theater, receiving guests at home, attending mass), one detail never varies. There is one, obsessive marker, that I believe, serves as the "ur-fetish" of Choisy, displacing the penis, by an economy of exchange that both hides and reveals its true value: "Mme de Noailles m'avait prêté ses grands pendants d'oreilles," "mes pendants d'oreilles brillaient d'un bout de la salle à l'autre," "me voulant toujours fort ajusté avec des pendants d'oreilles," "J'y allais habillée fort modestement, j'avais seulement mes boucles d'oreilles de diamants," "J'envoyai à Paris de mes poinçons de diamants, qu'on troqua contre de fort belles boucles d'oreilles." The same detail returns with the identical insistence in *La marquise/marquis de Banneville*:

> Elle n'avoit que des boucles d'oreille d'enfant, et peu de Pierreries; la Mère donna toutes les siennes, qui estoient mal en oeuvre, et, sans faire beaucoup de dépense, on trouva moyen de luy faire deux paires de pendans d'oreilles de Diamans.(48)

> Un jour qu'elle estoit à la Comédie dans la première loge, elle remarqua dans la loge voisine un jeune homme fort bien fait, avec un juste-au-corps d'écarlate, en broderie d'or et d'argent, mais ce qui luy donna plus d'attention, c'est qu'il avoit aux oreilles des boucles de diamans fort brillantes.(50)

If we consider that one of the primary metamophoses organized by the unconscious is the psychic phenomenon of "displacement," I think we can see in this detail a complex fetish that both represents and denies castration. On the one hand it seems rather obvious that "piercing" the ears is a displaced

[83] Naomi Schor, in her *Reading in Detail: Aesthetics and the Feminine* (New York: Methuen, 1987), remarks that the "censure of the particular is one of the enabling gestures of neo-classicism which recycled into the modern age the classical equation of the Ideal with the absence of all particularity" (3), and she then goes on to equate the detail to the "feminine" (4): "The detail does not occupy a conceptual space beyond the laws of sexual difference: the detail is gendered and doubly gendered as feminine." For a rereading of the "feminization of the fetish" in nineteenth-century literature and society, see, Emily Apter, *Feminizing the Fetish: Psychoanalysis and Narrative Obsession in Turn-of-the-Century France* (Ithaca: Cornell University Press, 1991).

act of castration. It is the symbolic inscription on the body of the psychic castration that "displaces upwards," the vagina, the "actual" site that the fetishist cannot contemplate. At the same time, the "pendants d'oreille," slipped into and dangling from the hole in the earlobe, substitute for the penis, the penis that covers the castration wound, compliments its absence, and presents to the world a symbol of perfect, heterosexual, plenitude.

Choisy tells us that on his mother's death he was most happy to receive, as his part of the shared familial inheritance, his mother's earrings. Up until then he had only paltry earrings of little worth. Now, however, his inheritance endows him for the first time with highly valuable jewelry ("je me voyais des pendants d'oreilles de dix-mille francs").[84] In a sense, therefore, it is from the mother that Choisy comes into possession of the "family jewels." His mother leaves him what she never had. Nevertheless this metaphorical inscription functions for Choisy as a validation of his own interior psychic reality. The mother's earrings double back reiterating the originary importance of this "ur-fetish." The earrings inherited from the mother represent the origin of all fetishism, the jewels that represent (stand in for) what was never there, and yet what leaves such an indelible mark on the child's psyche, the desired and feared maternal phallus. In this sense, Choisy's earrings are a constant reinscription on the body of an originary fantasy. They serve as a displaced reminder of a scenario in which Choisy as desiring subject is inscribed: they represent, ab origine, the ur-fetish—the mark of the mother's (imagined) phallus, as it is reinscribed on and in the body of the son. The abbé (but also all of his cross-dressed characters, male and female) is recognizable by this complex symbol, the fetish, of their own psychic indeterminacy that remains the most highly charged, visible and "precious" ("je me voyais des pendants d'oreilles de dix mille francs") part of their masquerade. It is what the text constantly calls attention to, what, across a crowded room or theater, everyone notices: it is the shining beacon that calls attention to Choisy, and it calls attention to him by symbolizing the tangled interweave of desire and anxiety, castration and pleasure that he both hides and so luxuriously reveals to the world at large:

> On me fit la guerre que j'avais été un peu coquette, sur ce qu'en passant sur les chaises je m'arrêtais quelquefois pendant que le bedeau me faisait faire place, et m'amusais à me mirer pour rajuster quelque chose à mes pendants d'oreilles ou à ma stinquerque . . . mais j'avais eu tant de plaisir de me voir applaudir de tout le monde . . .[85]

Although Choisy produces his body to figure as exteriority what is both an affirmation and denial of the internal consequences of castration he, nevertheless, seeks in his sexual pleasures to inscribe this chiasmatic reversal on

[84] *Mémoires de l'abbé de Choisy*, 324.
[85] *Mémoires de l'abbé de Choisy*, 295–96.

his partners. It has been remarked by most studies of transvestism that the majority of (male) cross-dressers are heterosexual.[86] Choisy seems to confirm this observation, although he certainly does not appear to be exclusively heterosexual, in the sense that he is not indifferent to "small" flirtations with men.[87] His extended sexual relations are, however, with young women whom he seduces by circumventing, through his cross-dressing, and thus through the social inscription of himself as female, the traditional safeguards early modern European society erected for policing illicit encounters between the sexes. It is because he is "seen" as a woman that neither the young objects of his seduction, nor their caretakers, are able to muster the conventional social defenses against his sexual aggression:

> "Je ne me suis point défendue," me disait-elle un jour, "comme j'aurais fait contre un homme: je ne voyais qu'une belle dame, et pourquoi se défendre de l'aimer? Quels avantages vous donnent les habits de femme! Le coeur de l'homme y est qui fait ses impressions sur nous, et d'un autre côté, les charmes du beau sexe nous enlèvent tout d'un coup et nous empêchent de prendre nos sûretés."[88]

Charlotte, one of his young conquests, "loves" Choisy for his androgyny, the combination in/on one person of feminine beauty and masculine "courage." This is just like the little girls who played with the young Choisy and Philippe d'Orléans. She intuits that underneath the "habits de femme" there is something else ("le coeur de l'homme"). Even with making rather large allowances for the too self-consciously naive tone of Charlotte's ingenuous explication of her rather promiscuous attraction to Choisy, even when we consider that his bourgeois neighbors, her guardians, are not above being tempted by the financial gain that might come their way by humoring this high-class personage who has moved into their neighborhood, we cannot but be struck by the tone of sexual ambivalence that Choisy's gender masquerade induces. We should also pay attention to the spiraling gender displacement that (and this is at least the first level of Choisy's attack on the sexual complacency that underlies Classicist France's notion of self-evident identity), leads us back to the conundrum of gender/sexuality that cross-dressing as fetishism both hides and reveals. Fetishism does not negate

[86] Ackroyd, *Dressing Up*, 14: "most transvestites are firmly heterosexual and cross-dressing often increases their heterosexual activity; their obsession fuels their sexuality."

[87] Several ambiguous phrases reinforce our belief that with Choisy any distinct separation of gender *or* sexuality is highly problematic. Cf. *Mémoires de l'abbé de Choisy*, 290: "j'ai joué la comédie cinq mois durant sur le théâtre d'une grande ville, comme une fille; tout le monde y était trompé; j'avais des amants à qui j'accordais de petites faveurs, fort réservé sur les grandes"; and, "Il s'en alla brusquement; j'eusse bien voulu l'adoucir par quelques petites paroles, je ne le voulais pas perdre, et mon coeur se gouvernait à son ordinaire, il balançait entre elle et lui."

[88] Ibid., 298.

heterosexuality.[89] It is, as Freud was the first to remind us, a way of preserving heterosexuality, a way of warding off homosexuality.[90] In Choisy's case his fetishism both reaffirms and contests heterosexuality in that it seeks a complementarity, at the very same time that the way in which this complimentarity is sought also decenters biological sex from its normalizing position within a heterosexist ideology.[91] What is radical, it seems to me, is that Choisy, by his mise-en-scène of the sex/gender conundrum within the parameters defined by Classicism's dominant (sexual) fiction opens up spaces of confusion, contradiction, and displacement that allows for a glimpse of "seeing/being" otherwise. It is this glimpse that uncovers, through his parade/masquerade that all gendered sexuality is a production not a given. As Rose has put it, "A confusion at the level of sexuality brings with it a disturbance of the visual field."[92] I wonder if Choisy, or cross-dressers in general who are precisely engaged in a form of exaggerated sex/gender trompe l'oeil, could not be said to turn this proposition around so that what disturbs the field of vision (that is, a socially preconceived and naturalized image of a male or a female) carries with it a disturbance in (the perceiver's) sexuality?[93] In this way, Choisy's parodying of Classicism's production of sexuality serves as a movement out of the tyranny of the dominant fiction.

Choisy seeks out young women to be his playmates in his cross-dressing scenarios, to help him primp and preen before his mirrors and his audience. They help to validate his femininity, by incorporating him/her in their own

[89] Judith Butler, in her chapter on drag ("Gender Is Burning") in *Bodies That Matter: On the Discursive Limits of Sex*, (New York: Routledge, 1993), is of the same opinion when she writes, 125: "There is no necessary relation between drag and subversion, and that drag may well be used in the service of both the denaturalizaiton and reidealization of hyperbolic heterosexul norms." I am mindful however of the consensus among students of transvestism, that it and drag although related are not identical phenomena, cf. Ackroyd, *Dressing Up* 14: "It is also necessary to distinguish transvestism from drag because, although there are connections to be traced between the two phenomena, they remain fundamentally separate. Drag is primarily a homosexual performance; most transvestites are heterosexual."

[90] Freud, "Fetishism" (Standard Edition, 21:154): "We can now see what the fetish achieves and how it maintains it. It remains a token of triumph over the threat of castration and a protection against it; it also saves the fetishist from becoming a homosexual by endowing women with characteristic trait which makes them tolerable as sexual objects."

[91] Madeleine Kahn, in her *Narrative Transvestism: Rhetoric and Gender in the Eighteenth-Century English Novel,* (Ithaca: Cornell University Press, 1991), states a similar point, in a more negative vein (27): "The acting out of transvestism is a continual play between the extremes of gender stereotypes. That is, the process of dressing up as the most womanly woman to reinforce one's essential manhood actually reasserts the socially constructed extremes of gender difference, even though it temporarily clouds them."

[92] Rose, *Sexuality in the Field of Vision,* 226.

[93] The preconceptions we have of what a "man" or a "woman" looks like are so ingrained as to enable Freud to use these preconceptions as the starting point of his discussion of sexual development in his (in)famous essay "Femininity" (lecture 33 of *New Introductory Lectures on Psychoanalysis*, (Standard Edition, 22:113): "When you meet a human being, the first distinction you make is 'male or female?' and you are accustomed to make the distinction with unhesitating certainty."

social (sexed) sphere. Concurrently, however, Choisy uses these young woman sexually in exhibitionist scenarios whose effects range far beyond the interpersonal dynamics between two individuals to become a radical putting into question of Absolutism's self-authorizing institutions.

Garbed as Mme de Sancy or as the comtesse des Barres, Choisy enjoys caressing, fondling, kissing, and having sex with his young women, most specifically in the presence and usually under the unsuspecting eyes of their parents (usually mothers) or (female) guardians. While living as the countess in the château de Crespon near Bourges, Choisy dazzles his neighbors by his outfits, his table, his talents as a musician and as an actress (and ultimately his readers by this self-indulgent display of narrative narcissism). Seduced by his refined Parisian manners two local society women vie for the honor of having him educate their daughters, instructing them into the ways of a Parisian "femme du monde." Choisy schemes to cooperate with their own vanity. His desire has been piqued by one of the young girls, and under the pretext of teaching her the latest Parisian hair-styling techniques s/he convinces her mother to leave her daughter with her(him) for several weeks. The young girl is quickly seduced by the "beautiful countess" and initiated into the delights of sex with Choisy. S/he however is not content to let things remain there, in an intimate tête-à-tête, but needing the reflection, even the uncomprehending reflection, of her/his neighbors, s/he often invites them into the bedchamber and proceeds to make love to her/his newly conquered mistress in front of them:

> Monsieur et madame étaient dans la grande ruelle, et commençaient à me conter une histoire arrivée depuis peu à Bourges, lorsque je dis à mademoiselle de La Grise qui faisait la sérieuse:
>
> "Approchez-vous mon enfant; venez me donner le bonsoir, et puis vous dormirez; nous ne voulons pas vous contraindre."
>
> Elle s'approcha, et je la pris entre mes bras, et la fis passer du côté de la grande ruelle; elle était sur le dos, et moi j'étais sur le côté gauche, la main droite sur sa gorge, nos jambes entrelacées l'une dans l'autre; je me penchai tout à fait sur elle pour la baiser.
>
> "Voyez," dis-je à madame Gaillot, "la petite insensible! elle me fait faire tout le chemin, et ne répond point aux amitiés que je lui fais."
>
> Cependant j'avançais, je baisias sa bouche plus vermeille que le corail, et lui donnais en même temps de plus solides plaisirs; elle n'eut pas la force de se retenir et dit à demi-haut, avec un grand soupir:
>
> "Ah! que j'ai de plaisir!"
>
> "Vous voilà donc réveillée, ma belle demoiselle?" lui dit M. Gaillot.[94]

What this scene (and the others that repeat it) tells us about seventeenth-century society (and perhaps about our own) is that people believe not what

[94] *Mémoires de l'abbé de Choisy*, 345.

they see but what they think they see.[95] For the onlookers to this scene Choisy is a woman. So is Mlle de La Grise. The spectators are thrown into sensory confusion precisely because what is going on right in front of their eyes does not correspond to their view of sex. Two women, especially an older and younger one, are not, for all sorts of defensive reasons, seen as potential sexual partners. Rather, what is substituted is a vision of "female" social bonding that excludes sexuality and remains, most felicitously for the invisible psychic but also social and economic dynamics that inform the parameters of the "sexually possible," in the realm of benign friendship.

Is there no possibility of impropriety, therefore, no possibility of sex between two females in the world of seventeenth-century France? The obvious titillation that the seventeenth century took in all those equivocal narrative and theatrical plots where women, cross-dressed as men, found themselves in uncomfortable situations, where they, their virtue, and social propriety were saved only in extremis by the intervention of a coup-de-théâtre, should at least allow us to suspect that there existed unconsciously the desire for sexual (lesbian) transgression. It is this desire for transgression that Choisy both realizes and at the same time undermines; despite a first level of sexual violation that is scandalous in its own right (the perverse seduction of a young virgin), the more pernicious, inarticulable threat of lesbianism, although suggested, is held off, by heterosexual recuperation: "she" is really a "he." [96]

But, his seduction of these women is only a part, a lesser part, of Choisy's shocking delight. The greater part of his pleasure is the exhibitionist relish Choisy takes. His sexual life is theatrical. It is performed for an audience, an audience that gazes on the spectacle produced by Choisy for the confusion of their eyes and the delectation of his own. How are we to understand Choisy's trompe l'oeil exhibitionism? His need for uncomprehending spectators, for "seeing himself being seen" and being seen in woman's dress having sex as a "man," is inextricably tied to the intensity of his pleasure:

[95] This is perhaps the point to bring in Thomas Laqueur's *Making Sex: Body and Gender from the Greeks to Freud*, (Cambridge, Mass.: Harvard University Press, 1990), where in his discussion of the Galenic "one sex-model" he shows that despite the "objective-proof," offered by dissection of sexual bimorphism, despite, that is, the "visual signs of difference," dissectors, physicians, theologians continued to "see the sexes not as anatomically different but in terms of the reigning medico/theological ideology which said female organs were the same as male organs only inverted." Cf. 54–68.

[96] Rudolf M. Dekker, Lotte van de Pol, *The Tradition of Female Transvestism in Early Modern Europe* (New York: St. Martin's Press, 1989), 54: "Before 1800, when men dressing as women were seldom found, there did exist a tradition of cross-dressing among women, . . . male transvestism certainly occurred far less frequently in the seventeenth and eighteenth centuries than it does today." Van de Pol and Dekker remind us that although in the seventeenth century there was both a literary and historical tradition of cross-dressed women, commonly cross-dressing was a way of protecting one's virginity, of escaping sex (at least heterosexual sex) therefore. Male cross-dressing, especially à la Choisy was infinitely less common. In a patriarchal society it seems almost normal for women to cross-dress as men, for by this they both recognized and showed they aspired to the " nobler," more prestigious social role.

> En disant cela, je la fis remettre à sa place, et repris, sous prétexte de la baiser, l'attitude convenable à nos véritables plaisirs. Les personnes qui les regardaieant les augmentaient encore; il est bien doux de tromper les yeux du public.[97]

We have seen the extreme importance actual mirrors play in his daily life: Choisy and mirrors form a visual and psychic tropism, where there is one, we find the other.[98] In some simple sense, we could understand this exhibitionism as just one more component of his castration anxiety: the narcissist libido originally invested in the penis is displaced onto, eroticizes, the entire body which becomes a substitute for the threatened genital. In traditional analyses of exhibitionism, the exhibitionist needs the horrified, amused, scandalized reflection in the eyes of his victims to confirm his own "uncastrated" state. The reaction of the other proves that his penis is there. But what of Choisy? To whom is his exhibitionism directed, in whose eyes does he want, need the reflection of his own virility? I think it would not be too great a leap of analytic casuistry to propose a double (that is, "fetishized") response. On the one hand, cross-dressed and the object (in his own narcissistic narrative) of desire of both men and women, Choisy regresses to an early infantile stage, where he is able to bask in the returned glow of his mother's eyes. This internalized maternal gaze becomes, in the adult Choisy, disseminated out and onto the world. He remains the object of universal admiration, "the most beautiful," the "most talented," the "most elegant." He captures and remains the object of his mother's desire, ambition, intrigues. At the same time however, this extreme pleasure ("je jouissais du plus grand plaisir qu'on puisse goûter en cette vie")[99] remains tributary to, endangered by the looming presence of the king, the uncastratable father, who, as the true object of the mother's desire and therefore of Choisy's, remains the threatening presence always ready to descend from his Olympian heights and sunder the child (Choisy) from the mother. So, as long as Choisy can produce himself as castrated (i.e. in female garb, identified with the mother in an attempt to seduce the king and to hide from him too) he safeguards his penis. But, as soon as he "is" the castrated woman, he obsessively must deny this castration by manifesting the presence of the hidden penis: he seduces young women. It is this oscillation, which is really a game of hide-and-seek, that engages Choisy in a constant attempt to be the object of the father's desire (the mother, in which case he is castrated), or to rebel against

[97] Cf., for example, the ditty sung about him in his "quartier" (*Mémoires de l'abbé de Choisy*, 346):

Qu'on a de plaisir à le voir
Dans un ajustement extrême
A la main son petit miroir
Dont il s'idolâtre lui-même.

[98] *Mémoires de l'abbé de Choisy*, 306.

[99] Ibid., 290.

the father (in which case he is also threatened with punishment/castration).[100] It is, I believe, ultimately to the androgynous gaze of the mother/father that Choisy both exhibits and exposes himself. This double movement allows us to see in Choisy's masquerade his inscription in Absolutist patriarchy and, by the particular form this inscription takes (cross-dressing), his subversive relation to Absolutism's main state apparatuses, marriage, the Church, and the government (i.e. the king).

Although we cannot doubt the pleasure these sexual encounters procure him, in one further twist of fetishistic narcissism Choisy's greatest joy comes from dressing these women up as young men and parading them in front of the eyes of his neighbors and the world at large as the masculine counterparts to his feminine persona:

> J'achetai dès le lendemain l'habit que j'avais loué pour elle et qui semblait fait exprès; je le fis mettre dans une armoire avec la perruque, les gants, la cravate et le chapeau, et lorsque mes voisines me vinrent voir, le hasard fit qu'on ouvrit cette armoire et qu'on vit cet habit; aussitôt on se jeta dessus, et c'est ce que je demandais: on le mit à la petite fille, et la voilà redevenue un beau garçon.
>
> Après la visite, elle voulut se déshabiller; je ne voulus jamais le souffrir, et lui dis que je lui en faisais présent, qu'aussi bien je ne le mettrais jamais, et que, pour me le payer, je lui demandais seulement qu'elle le mît toutes les fois que mes voisines me feraient l'honneur de venir souper chez moi.[101]

Restructuring the social/gender predicates for the heterosexual couple, Choisy and his/her mates point to the widening gap between sex and gender and at the same time, in dizzying reversal (a reversal that reinscribes the "fetish," the missing phallus in an entire sociosexual economy), create a normalizing parody of all the social institutions that are founded on an unproblematic coalescence of, as Butler would say, "sex, gender and desire."[102] Once Choisy and his "mate(s)" are successfully accommodated by

[100] The analysis of this form of castration anxiety (which takes as its point of departure the positive and negative Oedipus complex) is discussed by Freud, most notably in "From the History of an Infantile Neurosis" ("The Wolfman") Standard Edition, vol. 17 and again in "Dostoevsky and Parricide" (Standard Edition, vol. 21).

[101] *Mémoires de l'abbé de Choisy*, 300.

[102] There has been much recent work on the social construction of both "sex" and "gender." Judith Butler has written (*Gender Trouble*, 6): "When the constructed status of gender is theorized as radically independent of sex, gender itself becomes a free-floating artifice with the consequence that 'man and masculine' might just as easily signify a female body as a male one, and 'woman' and 'feminine' a male body as easily as female." In a more strictly psychoanalytic sense, Jean Laplanche *(Castration, symbolisations*, 33 n.1) has defined the difference as follows: "The distinction between 'sex' and 'gender' is indispensable in psychoanalysis. . . . It is especially indefensible to align one of these terms on the side of anatomy and the other on the side of psychology. By 'sex' it is fitting to designate the ensemble of psychic or physical determinations, behaviors, phantasms directly related to sexual function and pleasure. By 'gender' the ensemble of psychic or physical determinations, behaviors, phantasm, relation to the dis-

the social sphere in which they live (a sphere that varies in the *Mémoires* between the bourgeoisie and the aristocrarcy, but which remains resolutely aristocratic in the "fairy tale") he can proceed to stage for those hungry eyes that form his audience, the parodic mise-en-scène of the institutions of absolutist France.

The first and most highly invested of those institutions, the institution that forms the sexual, political, and economic base of society is, of course, marriage. In each of the different episodes of Choisy's life, a mock marriage ceremony between Choisy in his feminine persona and the young woman with whom s/he is living in her masculine persona forms the central conundrum of the episode. In the Sancy/ Maulny episode the entire family participates in this parody of a marriage ceremony, performed with the consent of the parish priest:

> Nous fîmes la cérémonie avant souper, afin de nous mieux réjouir toute la soirée; j'avais une robe de moire d'argent et un petit bouquet de fleurs d'oranger derrière la tête comme la mariée; je dis tout haut, devant tous les parents, que je prenais M. de Maulny ci-présent pour mon mari, et il dit qu'il prenait madame de Sancy pour sa femme; nous nous touchâmes dans la main, il me mit au doigt une petite bague d'argent, et nous nous baisâmes; j'appelai aussitôt les corroyeurs mes cousins et les corroyeuses mes cousines. . . . Il était près de minuit; chacun dit qu'il fallait coucher les mariés; le lit était tout prêt et la chambre fort éclairée; je me mis à ma toilette on me coiffa de nuit avec de belles cornettes et force rubans sur la tête; on me mit au lit. . . . Tous les parents vinrent nous baiser, la bonne tante nous tira le rideau, et chacun s'en alla chez soi. C'est alors que nous nous abandonnâmes à la joie . . .[103]

Many elements are striking in this scene but perhaps the most disturbing is the underlying theatricality—that is, how the "suspension of disbelief" so important to the illusory world of the theater—one is reminded of all the scenes of complicitous disguise in Molière—seems to operate in this world of cross-dressing and the willful confusion of genders, so that the very foundations of social institutions, institutions supposedly grounded in reality, are shown to be, in their parody, equally illusory. If, as Butler has argued, gender is a performance, a performance that reveals the inherent "production" of all gendered sexuality, then Choisy's enormous talent for theatricality, for producing his own persona and then having that persona orchestrate, around its illusoriness, all the most highly invested of social/sexual rituals becomes what can only be seen as a mise-en-scène of those rituals which is by the very same token a "mise-en-question" of them. His entire

---

tinction: masculine-feminine. The distinction of genders envelops secondary somatic differences and extends to the notion of grammatical 'gender,' including the diverse 'habitus,' dress, and social roles."

[103] *Mémoires de l'abbé de Choisy*, 302.

society is shown to be founded on a theatricality that is no more real or solid than its whirling displacement. [104] Choisy brings the spectacle—so important for seventeenth-century Europe's political and social elaborations of divine-right monarchies, where the creation and manipulation of images of the king are inextricably intertwined with the projection of a paternal (phallically empowered) sexuality—down to the level of quotidian life, and by producing that life as spectacle, a world of illusion (*theatrum mundi*) in the bedroom he effectively uncovers the secrets of the imperium: finally, it is the "costume" that does make the man (emperor) and woman.

The spectacular mock marriages, although narrated in the tone of amusing *badinerie*, draw into their playfulness the collusion of both church and state. Although fetishism according to Freud's genial remark represents a psychic defense to a threat he compares with a dire menace to the "throne and the altar" in exterior sociopolitical reality, Choisy's fetishistic exhibitionism seems, under its playful aspect, to aspirate into its very center these two pillars of absolutist society.[105] In this way we can understand better, perhaps, Stallybrass and White's description of neurosis as "the psychic irruption of social practices which have been suppressed," that is, the way an individual idiosyncrasy condenses and displaces social pressures that prove too onerous for that subject's seamless insertion into his/her culture's dominant fiction.[106] At each of these marriage ceremonies the *curé*, that fixture of seventeenth-century French social life who assures the suture of the spiritual (which represents at the same time the vast, economically empowered institution that is the Church) to the social and assures the social's imbrication in the spiritual, is a member of the wedding party. His presence in the parody is taken for granted and being a bon vivant he gamely acquiesces to Choisy's constant demands that the "marriage" be acceptable to him (to the Church):

[104] See Butler, *Gender Trouble*, 136 "In other words, acts, gestures and dress produce the effect of an internal core or substance, but produce this on the surface of the body, through a play of signifying absences that suggest, but never reveal, the organizing principle of identity as a cause. Such acts, gestures, enactments, generally construed are perfomative in the sense that this essence or identity that they otherwise purport to express are fabrications manufactured and sustained through corporeal signs and other discursive means. That the gendered body is performative suggest that it has no ontological status apart from the various acts which constitute its reality. This also suggests that if that reality is fabricated as an interior essence, that very interiority is an effect and function of a decidedly public and social discourse." Butler has come back to modify her ideas of the gendered body as "performative," limiting the excessive use of the term she originated in *Bodies That Matter*, particularly in the introduction.

[105] Freud, "Fetishism" 21:153: "What had happened, therefore, was that the boy had refused to take cognizance of the fact perceived by him that a woman has no penis. No, that cannot be true, for if a woman can be castrated then his own penis is in danger; and against that there rebels a part of his narcissism which Nature has providentially attached to this particular organ. In later life grown men may experience a similar panic, perhaps when the cry goes up that throne and altar are in danger."

[106] Stallybrass and White, *The Politics and Poetics of Transgression*, 176.

"C'est ma petite femme, disais-je à M. le curé."

"Vous êtes donc aussi mon petit mari !" s'écria la petite fille en ouvrant les yeux qu'elle avait tenus longtemps fermés.

"J'y consens," lui dis-je, "je serai ton petit mari, et tu seras ma petite femme; voilà M. le curé qui y consentira aussi."

"De tout mon coeur," dit-il en riant.[107]

The "altar" gets drawn unwittingly into all of these exhibitionistic scenarios that repeat, while inverting, the central ritual of social life. The Church and the entire Judaeo-Christian tradition that originates with the rather blood-thirsty judgment of Deuteronomy against the "abomination" of cross-dressing are aspirated into and collude with Choisy's perversion of traditional gender roles. Although it may seem gratuitous to attribute a conscious aggression against this tradition to what is presented as a harmless divertissement, the insistence with which the text returns to the active participation of the clergy in the "innocent play" ("qu'y a-t-il de plus innocent?") indicates Choisy's less than pure intentions:

Les jours suivants se passèrent aussi agréablement, ce fut une plaisanterie perpétuelle sur notre petit mariage; M. et madame Gaillot retournèrent à Bourges, et en parlèrent à tout le monde, et lorsque madame de La Grise me vint voir:

"Comment, mon beau monsieur," me dit-elle en riant, "vous épousez ma fille sans me le dire."

"Au moins, madame," lui dis-je, "ç'a été en bonne compagnie et en présence de mon curé."[108]

As for the throne, it would be unthinkable in absolutist France for us to expect a direct attack on the monarch. The king was too revered a figure to receive directly the aggressivity and hostility of his subjects in any but extreme cases. In general, despite the myriad remonstrances and the protests against injustice, the sacred person of the king was spared direct attacks.[109] His surrogates, however, were not. When we wish to see the wrath and anger that form the other side of the desire for Absolutism, we need only look at the venomous attacks on the kings' ministers. It was they, the Concinis, the Richelieus, the Mazarins who stood in for, represented the "bad" father. On their person was the negative side of the populace's yearning for its father acted out.

[107] *Mémoires de l'abbé de Choisy*, 347.

[108] Ibid. In order to avoid the reader's confusion, it must be noted that in this episode, it is Choisy, as the countess, who is here assigned the male role—the bridegroom. In his marriage with "M. de Maulny" s/he is the bride.

[109] I am aware of the long tradition, exacerbated by the religious controversies of the sixteenth century, of antimonarchical writings (*Vindicae contra tyrannos, ou Le reveille-matin des gaulois; Discours de la servitude volontaire*, etc.) as well as this tradition's renewed vigor in the seventeenth-century Cf. Christian Jouhaud, *Les mazarinades: La fronde des mots*, (Paris: Aubier, 1985). Nevertheless, even in these writings the sacred person of the just monarch was affirmed at the same time that the evil king was effaced under the figure of the tyrant.

Choisy, although never attacking the king directly, ends up seducing him. The tranquillity of life in Bourges and the surrounding countryside is thrown into turmoil by the arrival of the intendant, the king's political and economic representative. In order to properly impress this little "king" ("les intendants sont les rois des provinces, on ne saurait leur faire trop d'honneur") who wields fiscal power over Choisy and whom s/he needs to sway in her/his favor, the countess decides to employ the entire panoply of her charms. Nothing is too good for the intendant; delicious dinners, walks in the château's park, small intimate concerts where, it goes without saying, the countess plays, "divinely," to the delight of the royal representative. The pièce de résistance, however, is the little "comedy" that Choisy and his young charge perform for him. Choisy, who we remember, told us that s/he had acted on the stage at Bordeaux for over five months, is so good in her/his role that the intendant is obliged, amid continual squeals of theatrical pleasure, to admit: "J'ai ouï," disait-it, "la Duparc, elle n'approche pas de madame la comtesse." Better than the reigning actress of the day, Choisy's triumph is complete. Although we are accustomed by now to the abbé's narcissistic descriptions of his own arts and triumphs, what I find particularly striking is not so much the constant attempt to reenforce the subject's narcissism as the revelation of what roles exactly Choisy chooses to perform in the seduction of the intendant. Choisy and his ward perform several scenes from Corneille's *Polyeucte*. This play was chosen because, s/he tells us, it is "une comédie sainte," where one sees only "de bons sentiments."[110] But, besides the play's obvious uplifting morality I find it intriguing that the only dramas Choisy mentions are by Corneille (*Polyeucte, Cinna, Le Cid)*. In other words, Choisy, chooses to act out, cross-dressed, in front of the king's envoy, those plays most representative of the neo-Classical theatrical revolution introduced onto the French stage by Corneille, a revolution that, as we know, can be seen in its ethics and esthetics to reflect the coming into being of the absolutist state in all its sexual predicates. This revolutionary theatrical esthetic, becomes "embodied" precisely in Corneille's passionate protagonists, who line up and face off in their dramatic predicaments across the abyss of a politicized, naturalized sexual division. Corneille's theatrical universe is a world divided into the symmetrical (but unequal) camps of men and women. [111] All of the dramatic, tragic tension of his drama can be seen to stem from this original, ideologically invested sexual division. I therefore find it particularly amusing to imagine the scene of Choisy dressed as the countess des Barres playing the role of Pauline to his young mistress's Sévère. It is as if in one fell swoop the entire

[110] Passages cited here are from *Mémoires de l'abbé de Choisy*, 341, 342, 339.

[111] I have talked about Corneille's theatrical revolution and its ideological predicates and importance for the emerging absolutist state in *Corneille, Classicism and the Ruses of Symmetry* (Cambridge: Cambridge University Press, 1986). Each of the plays Choisy mentions is discussed in detail in that work.

world of absolutist France is parodied in its most profoundly invested esthetic, political and sexual underpinnings by this one fe/male. S/he succeeds in seducing the king by blurring all the distinctions of sex and gender in a dazzling dance of veils in which gender is sundered from its supposed grounding in sexuality which, in turn, is thrown out of any stable relation to all the sublimated rhetoric of noble but doomed heterosexual love—the dominant fiction in which absolutist France saw itself. It was a vision that informed enormous political, social, and cultural changes in seventeenth-century France, that gave "body" to those changes, ratifying them and reflecting them back to the world at large as the very underpinnings enabling the changes of the developing nation-state. All the weight of these changes, all the power of a sociosexual system finds it origin and end (the mutuality of reflection) in Corneille's theater that Choisy, by his own theatricality, throws into social disarray. The intendant, however, is simply seduced by the pleasure Choisy offers him. He and the members of the party leave "fort content de la réception." We are led to understand that Choisy, his parish, and his friends were particularly well treated in the fiscal report the intendant filed with Paris.

Lest we imagine that seventeenth-century France was a cross-dressers paradise, a universe where Choisy simply acts out his questioning the sexual/gender predicates of society at large without criticism, we are reminded in the *Mémoires*, obliquely it is true, that Choisy's "comedy" does meet with resistance. It is one thing to be the center of attention of the small provincial world of Bourges, or the equally protected bourgeois society of the St. Marceau quarter in Paris. It is quite another thing to venture out into the public space of absolutist Paris, to the theater where his reception is not always without interest or consequence:

> Je hasardai un jour d'aller à la comédie avec mon cher Maulny et sa tante, mais je fus trop regardée, trop considérée; vingt personnes par curiosité vinrent attendre à la porte lorsque nous remontâmes en carrosse. Quelques-uns furent assez insolents pour me faire des compliments sur ma beauté, à quoi je ne répondis que par une mine modeste et dédaigneuse; mais je n'y retournai pas de longtemps, pour éviter le scandale. . . . Je pris alors la résolution de demeurer souvent dans ma maison, ou du moins dans mon quartier du faubourg, où je pouvais faire tout ce qui me plaisait sans qu'on y trouvât à redire.[112]

Here we witness, if only obscurely, outside reality, the reality of curiosity and of hostility that greets the androgynous cipher in the world which is threatened by his/her ambivalence. A far more disastrous rebuff is experienced by Choisy in the more protected, more aristocratic world of the Opéra. In this instance, we see that although Choisy can seduce representatives of the law in a marginal sphere, when s/he approaches too closely

[112] *Mémoires de l'abbé de Choisy*, 305.

to the embodiment of that law itself, the dauphin, s/he is rudely reprimanded and ejected from the sphere s/he troubles. Sexual ambiguity may be allowed in society's margins, when it comes too close to the center, however, it is acutely expulsed. The traumatic scene occurs at the opera, in the box of the duchess d'Uzès who, having spotted Choisy across the room because his "pendants d'oreilles" shone from one end of the auditorium to the other, invites Choisy into her loge where she is sitting with the dauphin:

> J'avais une robe blanche à fleurs d'or dont les parements étaient de satin noir, des rubans couleur de rose, des diamants, des mouches. On me trouva assez jolie; monseigneur voulut que je demeurasse dans sa loge, et me fit part de la collation qu'on lui servit; j'étais à la joie de mon coeur.
>
> Rabatjoie arriva; M. de Montausier venait de ses visites, d'abord madame d'Uzès lui dit mon nom, et lui demanda s'il ne me trouvait pas bien à son gré. Il me considéra quelque temps et puis me dit:
>
> "J'avoue, madame, ou mademoiselle (je ne sais pas comment il faut vous appeler), j'avoue que vous êtes belle, mais en vérité n'avez-vous point honte de porter un pareil habillement et de faire la femme, puisque vous êtes assez heureux pour ne l'être pas? Allez, allez vous cacher, M. le Dauphin vous trouve fort mal comme cela."

Having come too close to the center of power, Choisy is reprimanded with the reigning Aristotelian logic of the time: since he had the good fortune to be born a man, why (says this former military leader) sacrifice this blessing for an inferior station? Ridiculed and banished by the "father," despite the protests of the dauphin who, we are told, finds him "belle comme un ange," Choisy's joy is destroyed ("la brutalité de M. de Montausier me renversa tout.")[113] It is after this public condemnation that s/he decides to leave Paris and seek refuge in the provinces from where, as we have seen, s/he takes revenge on the society that slighted her/him.

Choisy, condemned to live in a society rigidly divided into sexed differences, oscillates between an ostentatious questioning of that society's basic gender/sexual predicates through the spectacular mise-en-scène of his own body and a resigned attitude of gender conformity. The *Mémoires*, while most obviously dedicated to the former of the two poles, also mention the latter, obliquely. At the end of each episode of cross-dressing when, tired of living his life as a constant spectacle, Choisy tells us that he leaves France to travel. His journeys take him occasionally to England, but most often to Italy. There, he intriguingly is dressed as a man, and he gives himself over to his "second vice," gambling, and usually ends up in desperate financial straits. In fact, the *Mémoires* begin and end with his mentioning, as if en passant, this other aspect of his life:

[113] Ibid., 327, 326.

> Le jeu, qui m'a toujours persécuté, m'a guéri de ces bagatelles pendant plusieurs années, mais toutes les fois que je me suis ruiné et que j'ai voulu quitter le jeu, je suis retombé dans mes anciennes faiblesses et suis redevenu femme.[114]

> Une passion chasse l'autre: je me mis à jouer à Venise, je gagnai beaucoup, mais je l'ai bien rendu depuis. La rage du jeu m'a possédé et a troublé ma vie. Heureux si j'avais toujours fait la belle, quand même j'eusse été laide! Le ridicule est préférable à la pauvreté.[115]

Despite Choisy's considerable accomplishments in seventeenth-century society, by his own admission his passional life seems reduced to, and inscribed within, a circle of cross-dressing/gambling. When one passion dominates, the other is held off, when the first wanes, the other returns to the fore. How can we understand this circle, a circle that is particularly intriguing because, rather than self-enclosed, it can be seen to link the intrapsychic dimension of Choisy's personality to those greater social phenomena that dominated seventeenth-century life, spectacle and gambling, in this way suturing the individual to the social, and reinscribing the social in the psychic.

That the two passions, the sexual (cross-dressing) and the economic (gambling), are inseparable is made readily apparent to us in that most quintessential and unrealistic of fictions, the fairy tale. Choisy's *La marquise/marquis de Banneville*, a short story which admirably combines the different elements of castration, narcissism, and fetishism we have been tracing throughout this chapter, ends as most fairy tales do, with (an implied) "and they lived happily ever after." The "they," of course, refers to the story's protagonists, the beautiful marquise, a boy raised and cross-dressed as a girl, and the object of her passion, a young marquis. The spiraling chiasmus of their love comes up against the cynicism of the marquise's guardian, her uncle, whose financial greed pushes him to consent to their (quite unconventional) marriage: he knows the secret here, she is really a he, and therefore consents to the marriage because he recognizes that it will be sterile and that, therefore, his own children will inherit the marquise's fortune:

> Elle en parla à son oncle [about her desire to marry], qui d'abord luy représenta toutes les épines du mariage, et qui finit par y consentir. Il en estoit ravi dans le fond de son coeur. Il voyait par là trente mille livres de rente assurées à sa Famille, et ne craignoit pas que sa Niece eust des Enfans avec le Marquis de Bercour, au lieu que, ne se mariant pas, sa fantaisie d'estre Fille pouvoit changer avec l'age, et avec sa beauté, qui passeroit indubitablement. Ainsi le mariage fut arresté.[116]

[114] Ibid., 290.
[115] Ibid., 360.
[116] *La marquise/marquis de Banneville*, 59.

The uncle represents the not-so-honest *honnête homme*, that spokesman for seventeenth-century France's right-thinking society. He is cynically manipulative of the secret of his "niece." Once again, he believes what he sees. This marriage of his cross-dressed nephew can produce no heirs, and he decides to humor this dysfunctionally gendered person because by catering to this desire his family will be enriched. In a sense therefore, this slight fairy tale incorporates into its very center the inextricable intertwining of economy and sexuality whose interweave is most apparent in the overinvested locus of marriage.[117] But this is a fairy tale, and in fairy tales good triumphs over evil. What does the marquise discover on her wedding night but that the "marquis" is not a he, but a she:

> Qui pourroit exprimer icy la surprise et la joie de la petite Marquise? Elle ne douta plus dans ce moment qu'elle ne fust un Garçon, et se jettant entre les bras de son cher Marquis, elle lui causa la même surprise et la même joie. . . .
>
> Le lendemain des Noces, ils reçurent les complimens ordinaires et huit jours après ils partirent pour la Province où ils sont encore dans un de leurs Chateaux. L'Oncle doit les y aller voir, et sera bien surpris en voyant naistre d'un pareil mariage quelque bel Enfant, qui luy ôtera toute l'espérance d'une grande succession.[118]

In fairy tales, as we know, true love conquers all. Like myth, with which it shares many functions, the fairy tale reconciles those contradictions that appear irreconcilable in the real world: the two young lovers get to keep their (cross-)gender identity, the marquise remains a woman, thus keeping the *agréments* that are the mark of her sex; the marquis, a man, keeps the freedom of masculinity; together they get to have a fulfilling (heterosexual) sex life (each cross-dressed); their love is blessed with children; and finally, they keep the family fortune to themselves and their descendants. The only loser in the story is the rapacious uncle who believed his eyes and his greed. In this story the bad "father," the cynical, avaricious representative of the law, is defeated.[119]

In real life, however, things do not necessarily work out so felicitously.

[117] Jonathan Dollimore talks cogently about the mutual imbrications of sexuality, economy, and politics in his "Subjectivity, Sexuality, and Transgression: The Jacobean Connection," in *Renaissance Drama as Cultural History* ed. Mary B. Rose, (Evanston: Northwestern University Press, 1990), Cf. in particular, 35: "because of the complex connections between sexuality, gender, and class, between sexual and economic exploitation, economic and political anxieties can be displaced onto the domain of the sexual and conversely, the sexual comes to possess enormous signifying power."

[118] *La marquise/marquis de Banneville*, 60.

[119] "Pour moy," luy dist la petite Marquise, "je suis trop accoutumée à estre Fille, je veux estre Femme toute ma vie. Comment m'y prendrois-je à porter chapeau?" "Et moi," dit le Marquis, "j'ai mis l'épée à la main plus d'une fois sans estre embarassé, et je vous conteray quelque jour mes avantures. Tenons-nous en donc où nous en sommes. Jouissez, belle Marquise, de tous les agrémens de vostre Sexe, et je jouiray de toute la liberté du mien"(*La marquise/marquis de Banneville*, 60).

The perfect harmony between sexuality and economics is but an illusion, a myth. Choisy seems to have lived split between the two, buffeted back and forth, "happy" when he cross-dressed and could seduce those who formed his world, made "destitute" through compulsive gambling when obliged by the fear of ridicule to dress according to the dictates of the normal gender expectations of society at large. Since, as we have seen, it is impossible to separate the ways in which sexuality and economics are inextricably entangled, how can we understand this oscillation in Choisy, how, and in what way is his cross-dressing linked to his compulsive gambling?

To begin to understand how these two invested social loci are also joined in the psyche, we might look to Freud's early sexual theories to provide us with a clue. In his discussion of "The Sexual Aberrations" in *Three Essays on the Theory of Sexuality* Freud, after discussing the various perversions that are grounded in infantile sexuality, goes on to discuss the etiology of neuroses:

> But psychoanalytic teaching . . . shows us that it is by no means only at the cost of the so-called *normal* sexual instinct that these symptoms originate—at any rate such is not exclusively or mainly the case; they also give expression (by conversion) to instincts which would be described as *perverse* in the widest sense of the word if they could be expressed directly in phantasy and action without being diverted from consciousness. Thus symptoms are formed in part at the cost of *abnormal* sexuality; *neuroses are, so to say, the negative of perversions.*[120]

What Freud, is proposing is the idea that when a "perverse" sexual instinct is repressed, it returns as a "neurotic symptom." When, however, a perversion exists unrepressed, that is, it is allowed (by the psyche and society) to reach its aim more or less unimpeded by repression, the "pervert" lives what can be considered an unneurotic life. When its expression is impeded, repressed, the sexual drive will return as the symptom(s) of a psychoneurosis. The model Freud is proposing in the 1905 essay is in a sense a homeostatic one: neurosis is the negative of perversion; when (particular perverse) sexual instincts are blocked they reappear as neurosis.

What, the question still remains, is the connection between cross-dressing (as perversion) and compulsive gambling (as obsessive neurosis)? And to answer the question we return to the center of all absolutist life—to the father, to Louis XIV. In his book *Enlightenment and the Shadows of Chance*, Thomas Kavanaugh revisits the seventeenth century to discuss the origins of a social phenomenon that was to dominate French (aristocratic) life during more than a century and to have, as he demonstrates, a decisive impact on the literary production of the Enlightenment. Attempting to interpret why the aristocratic society of the seventeenth century was so obsessed with

[120] Freud, *Three Essays on the Theory of Sexuality*, 7:165.

high-stakes gambling Kavanaugh reminds us that it was Saint-Simon who first proposed as an answer to this question a "political" rationalization:

> Other historians, following the interpretation most eloquently defended by Saint-Simon, claim that like some latter-day Machiavelli, Louis XIV single-handedly imposed the fashion of high-stakes gambling as a cunning strategy to ensure the financial ruin of the nobility and thus eliminate any reenactment of the rebellious "frondes" that had traumatized his youth.[121]

Although Kavanaugh goes on to state that most modern historians find this an inadequate account for so complex a socioeconomic phenomenon, what I find intriguing is the echo I hear between Saint-Simon's account in which Louis is accused of trying to castrate the aristocracy (financially) out of fear of their rebellious potential and Choisy's own version of the plan to emasculate Philippe d'Orléans recounted in the *Mémoires pour servir à l'histoire de Louis XIV*. In other words, across the century the figure of the father/king looms on the horizon of seventeenth-century France uniting in his person the two most invested social systems, sexuality and economy, which are joined by the anxious fear of castration that informs them both.

Although the phenomenon of compulsive gambling has been one of the most resistant to any effective treatment, its etiology has been variously studied in analytic literature. All of the works that attempt to analyze the hold of compulsive gambling return to the explanation first put forward in Freud's brief essay "Dostoevsky and Parricide." In that essay Freud links Dostoevsky's parricidal fantasies to and through his castration anxieties that, he says, are intimately connected to the "bisexual nature" of the Oedipus complex:

> A further complication arises when the constitutional factor we call bisexuality is comparatively strongly developed in the child. For then, under the threat to the boy's masculinity by castration, his inclination becomes strengthened to deflect in the direction of femininity, to put himself instead in his mother's place and take over her role as object of his father's love. But the fear of castration makes this solution impossible as well. The boy understands that he must also submit to castration if he wants to be loved by his father as a woman. . . . Castration is terrible, whether as a punishment or as the price of love.[122]

Freud goes on to make another related and startling comparison between masturbation and (one form of) the obsessive hand gestures of the dealing and manipulation of cards (or chips). The connection once again would be that the underlying masturbatory fantasies are incestuous ones—the (male)

[121] Thomas Kavanaugh, *Enlightenment and the Shadows of Chance* (Baltimore: Johns Hopkins University Press, 1993), 33.

[122] Sigmund Freud, "Dostoevsky and Parricide" (Standard Edition, 21:183).

child's desire for the mother, and the fear of retaliation by the father.[123] The importance of bisexuality, that is in Freud's account, "an undifferentiated nature prior to sexual difference" (the original psychic androgyny), underlies both of these developments.[124] Most contemporary analytic accounts of gambling take up these two insights of Freud's: on the one hand the desire of the male child to be the object of his father's love, to place himself in the position of the mother; and, on the other, the masturbatory fantasies and fears associated with the desire to possess the mother. [125] In either case, what we have is an internal struggle for and against the father's love which is interpreted in both instances as scenarios of castration. That certain cultures link the manifest with the repressed, join the spectacular mise-en-scène of the body crossed-dressed to the obsessive masochistic habits of the gambler, is suggested to us by Georges Devereux who in his study of the Mohave tells us that in their culture they consider "transvestites to be lucky gamblers."[126]

Choisy, as we know, was not so lucky. More like the modern-day depiction of gambling Choisy seems to represent the obsessive player, doomed to financial ruin, and in a sense masochistically relishing that punishment. Choisy's life oscillates between the spectacular mise-en-scène of his body, and the abjection of obsessive gambling. Both are manifestations of an inability to accept the sociosexual laws of absolutist France. The joyous mise-en-scène of the ambiguous cross-dressed body is a manifestation against its too-smooth insertion into the sexual parameters of Classical France, parameters embodied by the loved/hated father/king. This androgynous ("both/and") persona seems to bring into the very heart of Classical France the grotesque body, the motley carnivalesque body of another time, another subjectivity. It is the body that Classicism's law represses at the same time that it bears its impress as its subjugated other. On the other hand, the ob-

[123] Ibid., 193: "The 'vice' of masturbation is replaced by the mania for gambling; and the emphasis laid upon the passionate activity of the hands betrays this derivation."

[124] Rose, *Feminine Sexuality*, 49 n. 14, distinguishes two different (Freudian and Lacanian) meanings of bisexuality: "the concept of bisexuality—not an undifferentiated sexual nature prior to symbolic difference (Freud's earlier sense), but the availability to all subjects of both positions in relation to that difference itself."

[125] "Inevitably, the ontogenesis of interest in gambling in the individual derives from infantile Oedipal conflicts. In the gambler we may expect to find a repressed tendency to homosexuality, or bisexuality, arising from the fact that at some time during the development of the ambivalent relationship with the father the male gambler-to-be sought to make himself the object of his father's love. In part, he identified with his "castrated" mother, seeking to become her rather than striving for dominant possession of her. Gambling emerges as a questioning of fate, the father surrogate: it takes the form of a question, 'Does my father love me?' But either answer (win or loss) is intolerable." (Peter Fuller, Introduction, 102, in *The Psychology of Gambling*, ed. Jonathan Halliday and Peter Fuller, [London: Allen Lane, 1974]). This is a good collection of classic analytic essays on gambling by, among others, Sigmund Freud, Ernest Jones, Ralph Greenson, Sandor Ferenczi, Robert Lindner.

[126] Ibid., 29. This is Fuller's paraphrase of Georges Devereux's "Psychodynamics of Mohave Gambling."

sessive gambling seems to be a more abject attack on the father, through a masochistic dilapidation of his patrimony, the financial component of Classicism's patriarchal economy.

Choisy seems to swing between these two poles, perverse and neurotic, that represent at one and the same time a personal psychic dilemma that is inextricably rooted in the socioeconomic life of absolutist France. Is there any resolution possible to Choisy's constant *va-et-vient* between these two poles, is there any way to accept the father's love and his punishment? Finally, of course, we have no way to know how Choisy actually accommodated himself to the exigencies of a life that, after all, was rather successful. As a historian and academician, he receives the respect of his contemporaries. Perhaps Choisy found in midlife his own accommodation both to the internal and external exigencies that would confine his person in an "either/or" body. On his embassy to Siam in 1685–1686, he is on a voyage where he tells us:

> Je n'aurai gueres offensé Dieu pendant deux ans. Hélas, peut-estre que par là ce seront les deux plus belles années de ma vie! Hé, comment ferions-nous pour offenser Dieu sur ce vaisseau? On n'y parle que de bonnes choses, on n'y voit que de bons exemples, les tentations sont à trois ou quatre mille lieues d'ici. Franchement nous n'avons pas grand mérite de vivre dans l'ordre.[127]

Choisy seems to find a resolution to his constant oscillation. In his attempt to "vivre dans l'ordre," to conform to the space assigned to him by his society, he finally opts for ecclesiastical orders. He becomes a priest. In middle age Choisy chooses the priesthood as the best of all possible worlds: it allows him to wear priestly vestments, without eliciting the least social ridicule, while at the same time, the profession of the priesthood recognizes that despite the dress he is also a "man"; under those priestly garments is a penis that he can finally affirm, at the same time, of course, that this affirmation is an absolute, eternal disavowal of its symbolic potential. By taking his vows of celibacy, Choisy pays the ultimate price to the father and to castration: he asserts that he has a penis, but simultaneously that this penis is no threat to the father: voluntarily and in the spirit of Christian love, he has sacrificed it. In return, however, he receives the father's love and his permission to live in the world dressed in those elegant robes that reinscribe on his body that indeterminate space in which his "parade" of masculinity is conjoined with the masquerade of femininity in a closed circle of desire, transgression, and pleasure.

[127] François Timoléon de Choisy, *Journal du voyage de Siam (1685–1686)*, ed. Maurice Garçon (Paris: Éditions Duchartre et Van Bruggenhoudt, 1930), 74–75.

4 *Nun-Sense:* Marie de l'Incarnation, Mysticism, and the Oedipal Trap

J'eusse estimé le jour perdu pour moy lequel se fut passé sans souffrir. . . . J'estois insatiable et je ne trouvois point assez d'instruments de mortification pour satisfaire à mon désir.

Marie de l'Incarnation, *La vie de la vénérable mère Marie de l'Incarnation*

It is obvious, without the slightest doubt, that this great mystic is a real woman.

Henri Brémond, *Histoire littéraire du sentiment religieux en France*

In a sense, then, renunciation takes place *through* the very desire that is renounced, which is to say, the desire is *never* renounced, but becomes preserved and reasserted in the very structure of renunciation.

Judith Butler, *The Psychic Life of Power*

As the absolutist imperative comes to dominate the moral and intellectual universe of seventeenth-century France, its political and social agenda becomes inextricably interwoven with the ideological underpinnings of Classicism's esthetic dictates. The pressing demands of *politesse* and *bienséance* which foreclose from cultured discourse all references to the brute physicality of the body curiously gain the force of social law at the precise moment that the body reappears, resistant and troubling, in those powerfully charged scenarios of demonic possessions or mystical ecstasies that proliferate during this conflicted historical moment. Throughout the century, the scandalous eruption of the supernatural into a world that is being ever more tightly bound to the path of rational, ordered discourse cannot but strike us as a unsettling symptom, disruptive of the smooth construction of the absolutist body politic. That the stage upon which this disruption is most floridly displayed is primarily (but not exclusively, cf. Jean Joseph Surin, confessor of the mystic Jeanne des Anges) the female body allows us to suspect that behind the religious scenarios that are acting upon and that are being acted out in these bodies lie more primitive conundrums linking sexuality and gender to questions of subjective empowerment in seventeenth-century culture.

To ignore that culture's profound anchoring in religion would be to commit an egregious anachronism. No work of the century can be easily divorced from the religious fervor that, one way or the other, had a profound impact on its artistic, literary, and intellectual accomplishments. Molière, Corneille, Pascal, Racine, La Fayette, Bossuet, Fénelon, Boileau, to name only the most outstanding literary figures of the time, are each in his or her own way deeply involved in the religious controversies of Counter-Reformation France as these controversies intersect with matters of social and political theory and practice. All areas of everyday life were touched by the Church in its dominant (i.e. Roman Catholic), its heretical (Protestant), or, more rarely but also more spectacularly, its extravagant (demonic/mystic) forms. We perhaps tend to forget, or at least are inclined to let fade into the background, that this century—remarkable in so many ways—is particularly noteworthy for the flowering of an intensely experienced apostolic vocation. The desire to evangelize France, to convert Protestant heretics who were seen as forming a divisive state within the state, and thus of being a constant provocation to Absolutism's imperious desire for the order of the One, dominated domestic policy throughout the reigns of Louis XIII and XIV. At the same time Counter-Reformation zeal, in an explosion of missionary fervor that resulted in an unprecedented explosion of devotional literature and an equally unparalleled growth in religious (particularly female) orders, was equally directed at those religiously orthodox but lax members of the population.[1] From the Berullian reformation of spirituality at the century's beginning, through the Jansenist-Jesuit debates that dominate the midcentury, and on to the Quietist quarrel that pitted Fénelon and Bossuet against each other at the century's end, religious controversy was constantly at the center of public and private life. Behind the spiritual and devotional issues at the forefront of these debates lay the never easily divorced dialectic of sexuality and power. Although it would perhaps be an error to distin-

[1] The bibliography of the religious history of Counter-Reformation France is immense. Some of the more general histories that may help the reader are Henri Brémond, *Histoire littéraire du sentiment religieux en France depuis la fin des guerres de religion jusqu'à nos jours*, 12 vols. (Paris: Armand Colin,) 1967, Pierre Broutin, *La réforme pastorale en France au XVIIe siècle*, 2 vols. (Paris: Desclée, 1956); Louis Chatellier, *L'Europe des dévots* (Paris: Flammarion, 1987), Pierre Chaunu, *L'église, culture et société: Essais sur réforme et contre-réforme* (Paris: SEDES, 1984); Jean Delumeau, *La peur en Occident* (Paris: Fayard, 1978); André Latreille, Etienne Delaruelle, and Rémy Palanque, *Histoire du catholicisme en France* (Paris: Edition Spes. 1957–62); Robert Mandrou, *Introduction à la France moderne* (Paris, Albin Michel, 1974); and Elizabeth Rapley, *The Dévotes: Women and Church in Seventeenth-Century France* (Montreal: McGill-Queen's University Press, 1990).

guish an exemplary choice of religious figures based on gender (certainly the century was equally well supplied with both male and female reformers), it does strike one that the women religious of the period remain more prominently enigmatic, more disturbingly equivocal, than their male counterparts. Most probably this is the case simply because the male figures were more easily accommodated by the institutional structures of a patriarchal Church.[2] It was they who through their ordination were invested with ecclesiastical and pastoral authority. Since St. Paul, this authority to administer the sacraments, to preach, and thus to evangelize had been unequivocally denied women. By the same Pauline injunction women had been silenced by the early Church: they could not speak on matters of doctrine or practice, and this sanction was reiterated throughout the centuries.

In her studies of medieval religious women Caroline Walker-Bynum has argued that since women were precisely denied ecclesiastical authority and were thus, following the Pauline dictate, prohibited any public forum for expressing their own religious fervor, they "compensated" for the lack of official authorization through the prestige that their own ecstatic form of religious devotion—bodily manifestations, visions, ecstasies, the signs of heavenly grace—bestowed upon them.[3] Despite the enormous changes that, on one level, separate the lives of women in the late Middle Ages from the lives of those in seventeenth-century France and despite the increasing social need for women, both religious and lay, to educate and minister to the poor and ill, the Church's continued refusal to allow women any publicly sanctioned role in evangelization perpetuated traditional structural constraints on them. It might be argued that these social restraints exacerbated those psychic conflicts that became manifest in other, more marginal types of religious expression.[4] For several of these French "mystic" women, and

[2] For a discussion of those religious reformers who did not easily fit into established churches, see Leszek Kolakowski, *Chrétiens sans église: La conscience religieuse et le lien confessionel au XVIIe* siècle, trans. Ann Posner (Paris: Gallimard, 1969). Michel de Certeau, in *Heterologies: Discourse on the Other*, trans. Brian Massumi, (Minneapolis: University of Minnesota Press, 1986), deals with the more linguistic deviations of seventeenth-century (heterodox) mystic speech. Linda Timmermans, in *L'accès des femmes à la culture, 1598–1717* (Paris: Honoré Champion, 1993), discusses in great detail the debates surrounding female religious vocations in the seventeenth century.

[3] Caroline Walker-Bynum, *Holy Feast and Holy Fast: The Religious Significance of Food to Medieval Women* (Berkeley, University of California Press, 1987), 282: "Men were authoritative by office or ordination; women's religious powers derived from inspiration, from ecstatic visions." She repeats this point in her later *Fragmentation and Redemption: Essays on Gender and the Human Body in Medieval Religion* (New York: Zone Books, 1992).

[4] Elizabeth Rapley, in *The Dévotes, Women and Church in Seventeenth-Century France,* discusses the controversies surrounding the different female orders in France, and shows how, despite public indignation at the supposed new liberties women were seen as taking, their services, especially in the realm of education, became indispensable as the century progressed. Cf. chap. 3, "The Teaching Congregations," 42–73, and chap. 7, "Development of a Feminine Pedagogy," 142–66.

in many of the most illustrious and /or notorious—Mme Acarie, Jeanne de Chantal, Jeanne des Anges, Antoinette Bourignon, Mme Guyon—religious devotion was displayed as holy ecstasy. Despite the various forms this ecstasy could and did take, it nevertheless was perceived as an excess, disturbing in its eccentricity. Although centered in/on the body, religious ecstasy always pointed paradoxically away from the body. It was received as a sign of a beyond (celestial or diabolical?) coming from an ineffable other whose extraordinary spiritual love (or, in the case of Satan, malice) could only be made manifest, paradoxically, in the disconcerting ambiguity of the corporal. In a sense, therefore, the bodily manifestations of these female mystics must strike us a particularly invested example of the epistemic shift that traduces the body in its corporeality away from public discourse and into diverse forms of psychological interiority. The bodies of these women are so poignantly present on a social/religious stage from which the grotesque is being cast out. The condition of their visibility is precisely that they be seen through—they are always the sign of something else, something extrasensual. The bodies that are so spectacularly exhibited are the reflections of another world making itself manifest in and through our fallen condition. At one and the same time they are bodies and not bodies, but holy theaters on whose stages God or the devil can still be made palpably present to an absolutist world. These spectacular bodies are, we might say, the necessary condition for Absolutism. In their very obvious physicality they represent the metaphysical, the unseen primum mobile that grounds divine-right monarchy and serves as the proof of its very raison d'être: God's manifesting His presence and authority. In a sense, therefore, must we not see the ecstatic bodies of these female mystics as inextricably connected with that other ambivalent physico-metaphysical construct, the "corps glorieux" of the seventeenth-century monarch, its repressed, inverted, but strangely corroborating other?

Marie Guyart (1599–1672) is one of the most interestingly complex examples of this sorority of seventeenth-century female mystics. Her life, about which more will be said shortly, begins as Henri IV is attempting to reimpose a semblance of unity on a France still severely rent by almost thirty years of civil/religious strife. Marie reaches adulthood during that crucial era which has been described by the historian Lucien Febvre as the moment of a "great psychological revolution" in European thought. For Michel Foucault this same period of course is the pivotal moment of epistemological change that will separate the world of the Renaissance from the universe of Classical representation. That the period 1590–1630 was a highly conflicted moment embracing often greatly contradictory currents becomes obvious when we consider that during this era, alongside the elaboration of a radically new rationalist discourse in philosophy we see France overrun by a veritable "mystic invasion," product of a Counter-Reformational frenzy.[5] The effects of this invasion continue to be felt late into the century.

Finally, the last part of Marie's life corresponds to the consolidation of Absolutism as a political reality with the concomitant triumph of French arms across Europe and the imposition of French neo-Classicism as the dominant philosophical and esthetic doctrine in the West. Her autobiography, first published in 1676, four years after her death can be considered a transitional document, tracing as it does the spiritual and material existence of this extraordinary woman as her life intersects with both the great religious revival and the great colonial adventure of seventeenth-century France. At the same time the text itself, which traduces this change into print can also be read, because of its hybrid nature, as an exemplary *translatio* of the baroque body into Classical esthetic constraints. We can read this work in a strangely aporetic sense as a "martyr's" life. It is the narrative of a life that bears witness to this momentous shift in French devotional and intellectual existence where the physicality of the body is immolated on the altar of discursive logic. It does so by focusing our attention in troubling ways on the struggles of a woman, who unbeknownst to her, incorporates in her own life and body the tumultuous changes that are convulsing the body politic of France.

Hers is a life, therefore, that corresponds mutatis mutandis to the turbulent passage from the baroque to the Classical with all the obvious and all the unsuspected repercussions that such a fraught, because never truly definitive, passage entails. It is a passage that is most obviously marked, as we have come to see, on and across the body—the individual body of those subjects for whom this passage is not navigated smoothly, the body of those who resist, knowingly or unwittingly, their own subjective insertion within the new parameters of the changing symbolic order that is painfully being put in place.[6] Is it any coincidence that those embodied subjects that manifest their resistance to this enormous change in politics, in religion, in sexual and family structures, are those others whose place is being radically cir-

[5] Lucien Febvre, *Annales* 13 (1958): 639, quoted by Michel de Certeau, in *La possession de Loudun* (Paris: Gallimard, 1980), 10.

[6] Michel de Certeau as well as Catherine Clément and Hélène Cixous in their different ways insist that resistance to the enormous social changes will be most noticeably expressed through corporal signs. See also Michel de Certeau, *La fable mystique* (Paris: Gallimard, 1982), trans. Michael Smith, *The Mystic Fable* ref. 1:14: "It is the ambition of a Christian radicalism traced on a background of decadence or 'corruption,' within a universe that is falling apart and must be repaired. It reiterates at the level of biographical experience all the vocabulary of the Church Reformation: division, wounds, sickness, lying, desolation, and so on. Individual bodies tell the story of the institutions of meaning." Clément and Cixous speak more to the universal difficulty of women's bodies ever fitting adequately into masculinist schemes: *The Newly Born Woman*, trans. Betsy Wing (Minneapolis: University of Minnesota Press, 1986), 7: "Societies do not succeed in offering everyone the same way of fitting into the symbolic order; those who are, if one may say so, between symbolic systems, in the interstices, offside, are the ones who are afflicted with a dangerous mobility."

cumscribed, as Michel Foucault has argued, by the new society of emerging absolutist France, the mad, the children and, of course, the women?[7]

Because of her particular devotion to and repeated unions with the body of Christ ("Le Verbe Incarné") Marie Guyart took, upon entering the Ursuline convent of her native city of Tours, the name Marie de l'Incarnation, thus forever branding onto her public and religious persona the mark of her own ambivalent subjugation to the flesh that both obsessed and repelled her.[8] Despite the severe mortification that must certainly strike modern readers as an indication of a floridly masochistic relation to the world and to her God, by any account Marie de l'Incarnation led an extraordinarily active and (in spite of what now strikes us as a hopelessly colonialist attitude) productive life. To orient the reader, who in the discussion that follows may not be immediately familiar with her, I offer a thumbnail sketch of this life.

Marie Guyart was born in 1599 in the provincial city of Tours into a modest family of shopkeepers (bakers). Like its surrounding province, Tours was situated in a rather religiously ambivalent region where Protestantism and Catholicism had vied for supremacy during the turbulent wars of religion (not unlike the town of Loudun, relatively close by, site of the infamous possession of Ursuline nuns). At the beginning of the seventeenth century, during Marie's childhood, Tours was being invested with the new devotional fervor of the Catholic Counter-Reformation; many religious orders were establishing or reestablishing monasteries in the city (the Carmelites, the Ursulines, the Benedictines). On the maternal side of the family, Marie may have heard talk of some (tenuous) nobiliary affiliations. Through her mother, Marie could believe herself connected with the noble

[7] I am here following Foucault's schema of equating the imposition of the absolutist regime with what he calls "the period of the great enclosure." Cf. Michel Foucault, *Histoire de la folie à l'âge classique* (Paris: Gallimard, 1972), chap. 2. For works that deal more specifically with the reinforced exclusion of women from the public sphere, cf. Joan DeJean, *Tender Geographies: Women and the Origins of the Novel in France* (New York: Columbia University Press, 1991), and Faith Beasely, *Revising Memory* (New Brunswick: Rutgers University Press, 1990).

[8] Her son and editor Claude Martin writes: "A cause de l'union étroite qu'elle avoit contractée et si souvent réiterée avec le Verbe Incarné, elle pria qu'on joignît à son nom de Marie celuy de l'Incarnation, afin de porter comme une légitime Epouse le nom de son Epoux. Cela luy fut accordé et depuis on l'appella Marie de l'Incarnation" (*Vie*, 201). For my reading of Marie de l'Incarnation I will be using the edition published by Claude Martin and reissued in 1981 by the monks of Solesmes—*La vie de la vénérable mère Marie de l'Incarnation*, edited and presented by Dom Claude Martin (reproduction de l'édition originale de 1677 préparée par les moines de Solesmes, introduction par Dom Jean Lonsagne, tables par Dom Guy Oury [Solesmes, 1981]). For a general discussion of the life and career of Marie de l'Incarnation, who, since the pioneering work of Brémond, has been the object of ever-increasing critical attention, the reader should consult: Brémond, *Histoire littéraire du sentiment religieux* vol. 6; Marie-Florinne Bruneau, *Women Mystics Confront the Modern World: Marie de l'Incarnation and Madame Guyon* (Albany: SUNY Press, 1998); Françoise Deroy-Pineau, *Marie de l'Incarnation: Marie Guyart femme d'affaires, mystique, mère de la Nouvelle France* (Paris: Robert Laffont, 1989); Natalie Zemon Davis *Women on the Margins: Three Seventeenth-Century Lives* (Cambridge, Mass.: Harvard University Press, 1995).

Babou clan, one of the region's more substantial families.[9] These rumors strike us more as familial fantasies, as the family romance of the Guyarts rather than as accurate genealogy.

After a childhood unremarkable except for her early pious visions and vocation (I will discuss the religious episodes in more detail later), she is married at nineteen, gives birth to a son, and is widowed a scant two years after her marriage. Following the death of her husband, her early widowhood is a period marked by financial insolvency, by intense religious visions and ecstasies, and by an equally intense mortification of the body. Against the wishes of her family—her father, but more particularly her sister and brother-in-law whose successful fluvial transportation business she had helped manage—Marie decides to leave her young son, to abandon the "world," and to join the Ursuline order recently established in Tours. No sooner does she take the veil than she begins to be obsessed, following another vision, with the desire to go to Canada to join the recently established French colony there and to found an Ursuline convent in Quebec. True to the Ursuline calling this convent would instruct the young female children of both the French settlers and the native peoples in the verities of the Catholic faith. In June 1639 she and three companions (two nuns and her lay patron, Mme de la Peltrie) set sail from Dieppe for Quebec. After a perilous Atlantic crossing where her ship is miraculously saved in extremis from certain destruction by an iceberg and she and her companions from a watery grave, the convoy arrives three months later in Canada.[10] In the newly established colony, Marie lives an exceptionally active existence as Superior of her convent during its first, traumatic years. Throughout her life in Quebec, whether as Superior of the convent or in less-exalted positions, she manages both the incessant material business of the convent and its school. She effectively deals with the representatives of both the French religious (Jesuits) and administrative authorities (obviously all male), ministers to the large and varying contingent of native wards in the convent's charge, main-

[9] *Vie*, 4: "Sa mère, qui s'appelloit Jeanne Michelet, avoit quelque chose de plus: elle estoit issue de la noble et ancienne Famille des Babou, qui s'étant rendue recommandable du temps de François I par les grands hommes qu'elle a donnez à l'Eglise et à l'Etat, est encore devenue plus illustre par ses alliances aux plus nobles Maisons du Royaume.

[10] "Ce fut une glace grosse jusqu'au prodige, à ce que disoient ceux du Vaisseau, laquelle paroissant dans une brume et venant fondre sur nous d'une furie, et impetuosité incroyable, ne nous menaçoit de rien moins qu'un assuré naufrage. Tout le monde crioit: misericorde, nous sommes perdus; de sorte que dans cet empressement de mort, qui selon toutes les apparences humaines nous étoit inévitable. Je disposois mes habits en sorte que quand le fracas se feroit, je ne pûsse être veue qu'avec decence. Dans cette extremité le Reverend Pere Virmond, qui ne voyoit plus de remede naturel à un si grand mal, fit un voeu à la sainte Vierge au nom de tous; la Mere Marie de Saint Joseph ma compagne commença les litanies de cette divine Mere ausquelles tout le monde répondoit. En un instant le Pilote qui gouvernoit ayant été commandé de mettre le gouvernail d'un côté sans y penser le tourna d'un autre, ce qui fit faire un tour au vaisseau, en sorte que la monstrueuse glace qui alors n'étoit pas à la longueur d'une pique, vis à vis de la fleche se trouva au côté : nous l'entendîmes bruire tant elle étoit proche, et ce fut un miracle évident" (*Vie*, 393–94).

tains a voluminous correspondence with friends, patrons, and religious authorities back in France, and writes articles for the Jesuit *Relations* that are published more or less annually. In her efforts to deal with the indigenous populations more effectively, Marie learns at least three Amerindian languages—Huron, Algonquin, and Montagnais. She authors bilingual dictionaries to aid her fellow nuns acquire these languages in order to communicate with and teach their students better. Marie lives through the waves of panic that repeatedly sweep over the colony, threatened by impending attacks (real or imagined) by the various hostile native tribes and the rival English. She also survives a blaze that destroys the convent (1650) and an earthquake that almost demolishes Quebec (1663). In 1672, at the age of nearly seventy-three, she dies and is mourned, we are told, by all of Canada, as "a second Saint Teresa, or rather, Canada's own Teresa."[11]

This final, lapidary comparison of Marie de l'Incarnation to St. Teresa of Avila—reformer of the Carmelite order, indefatigable founder of monasteries, famous mystic whose spiritual treatises were translated and disseminated throughout France and Europe in the early seventeenth century—is telling. This rhetorically overdetermined analogy will afford us an entry into an understanding of Marie's own existence in its convoluted spiritual, political, and sexual dimensions. These various dimensions are all interwoven and compounded in her spiritual autobiography, as this autobiography is made available to contemporary readers of absolutist France and to us, through the careful, perhaps too careful, editing and emendations of the son whom she twice abandoned (as she entered the convent and as she left France), and whose own life continued to be inextricably connected with hers. Despite his active leadership in his own Benedictine order, Claude Martin is remembered today because of his self-appointed mission of bearing witness to his mother's exceptional relation with God and exposing this relation to the eyes of the world.

Although clearly written under the influence of the immensely popular model of St. Teresa's *Libro de la vida* which had through its successive translations become the spiritual and rhetorical archetype of (especially female) religious writings, writings aimed as both describing the journey of the pining soul for union with its divine master and a primer for embarking on such a spiritual voyage, Marie's account follows Teresa's example yet differs radically from it. Teresa who writes with the weight of the paranoia peculiar to sixteenth-century Spain—the Inquisition with its political and religious intrigues is always lurking somewhere in the background—begins

[11] *Vie*, 748. In the discussion that follows I will not be concentrating in any detail on Marie's sojourn in Canada, perhaps, historically speaking, the richest part of her autobiography. The history of her missionary endeavors in Canada, as fascinating as it is, is more intensely focused on the daily life of her convent and the colony, on the quotidian cares and practices of the nuns. During this period her bodily manifestations are reduced to the common practices of simple mortification. The history of her life in Canada is explored in both Deroy-Pineau and Bruneau.

her autobiography by stating that she has undertaken this task at the direct request of her confessors. She has committed her life's journey to writing so that her religious superiors may judge whether her visions, ecstasies, and supernatural gifts are indeed divinely inspired as she claims, or rather diabolical illusions as her enemies assert.[12] At a time when the relation between the divine and the diabolical was unclear at best, and deeply complicitous in the eyes of many, the primary aim of these female narrations was first and foremost to distinguish the godly from the satanic and to establish that the writing subject, although female, did indeed conform to the Church's view of religious orthodoxy.[13] In order for this verification and "absolution" to take place, a strangely complicitous, seductive dialogue between the writer and her confessor (and behind him the entire corpus of ecclesiastical authorities) is inscribed within these spiritual autobiographies, as a constant subtext. While speaking of God, this "conversation" is always couched within a rhetoric of humility that is, at the same time, an alluringly seductive performance whose object is the male world of theological and political power which has both excluded the female writing subject from its institution and which nevertheless looks on with wary fascination at this "weaker vessel" upon whom God may or may not be bestowing his special gifts.[14] Throughout the long and vexed history of female mystics (Catherine of Siena, Catherine of Genoa, Angela of Foligno, Teresa of Avila) and their male confessors we see these strange *dialogi d'amore*, where the extraordinary relation with God that the women claim to have is mediated by and through the dependence of the woman on her male confessor, a relation more often than not marked by a certain power struggle that without too much exaggeration one could define as both voyeuristic and sadomaochistic.[15]

[12] Cf. for example, *Libro de la vida* (in *Obras completas*, transcription, notes, and introduction by Efrén de la Madre de Dios and Otger Steggink [Madrid; Biblioteca de Autores Cristianos, 1967]), "Prologo," 28: "Eternal praise to God who, for so long, waited for me, and to whom my whole heart pleads that he bestow his grace so that I might, with all truth and clarity, compose this narration that my confesors have asked of me."

[13] Michel de Certeau whose writings have been influential in forming my own understanding of the complex interweave among the political, the sexual, and the religious has pointed out the extreme difficulty of clearly separating out the manifestations of the divine and the diabolical in seventeenth-century France: "On the map of France, in the middle of the seventeenth century, we find, often in the same places, both cases of possession and centers of "devotion" . . . Nancy, Evreux, etc. During its years of madness Loudun is also a center of spirituality. . . . The devil's stages are at the same time centers of mysticism" (*La possession de Loudun*, 12).

[14] Alison Weber, in a recent book that analyses the rhetorical strategies of Teresa of Avila, mentions the particular use of the "captatio benevolentiae" trope in her writings, as a sign of the necessity, both religious and political, to seduce the reader by appealing through humility to his or her goodwill, see *Teresa of Avila and the Rhetoric of Femininity* (Princeton: Princeton University Press, 1990), 48–50.

[15] For a discussion of the vexed relation between the female mystic and her confessor, cf. Walker-Bynum, *Holy Feast*, esp. chap. 5, and also *Fragmentation and Redemption*; and Jean-Noel Vuarnet, *Extases féminines* (Paris: Arthaud, 1980), especially his chapter on Angela da Foligno. Also Michel de Certeau's interesting analysis of the intense and tense relation uniting

The *Vie de la vénérable mère Marie de l'Incarnation* published in 1676 is, as most commentators of the work have noticed, firmly situated in this chain of female spiritual narratives. In some sense, the text like the life itself is predictably imitative in its paradigmatic structure and rhetoric. The visions, the ecstasies, the mortifications, the self-doubts and self-hatreds, for as fascinating as they are as manifestations of a troubled individual conscience, are to be found, mutatis mutandis, in all the preceding autobiographical accounts of female spirituality.[16] They obey rhetorically and spiritually what has since the late Middle Ages become the more or less required autobiographical cursus of ecstatic female spirituality. Marie's text, however, is noteworthy for two outstanding reasons. On the one hand, it is a fascinating historical document, affording us a particularly vivid view of the life of the French colonist in Quebec seen through the eyes of a woman who endured and forced upon herself enormous physical and mental suffering. On the other hand, it is striking that this particular spiritual narrative is psychically and rhetorically a hybrid text: Marie's life is written by two hands, her own and her son's. This is the only major confessional autobiography since St. Augustine that purports to recount the extraordinary journey of a singular soul where the primary interlocutor is not simply an "adopted spiritual son/follower" but, in a strangely perverse fashion, the author's biological child.[17]

The *Vie* starts out with the traditional rhetorical disclaimer stating that the author has undertaken the task of writing about the "extraordinary" grace she has received from God at the express request of her confessor. The conventional importance of this relation (between Marie and her confessor) has already been undermined by the preceding epistles however, which establish the real interlocutor of her spiritual autobiography to be not her confessor but her son.[18] Claude Martin, whom she abandoned when she left the secular world for the Ursuline order, eventually becomes a Benedictine

Jeanne des Anges and her confessor Jean-Joseph Surin, in *La possession de Loudun* and *La fable mystique*, vol. 1.

[16] For a recent study of the French spiritual autobiographies of the seventeenth century see Nicholas Paige, *Being Interior: Autobiography and the Contradiction of Modernity in Seventeenth-Century France* (Philadelphia: University of Pennsylvania Press, 2000).

[17] Vuarnet in *Extases féminines* emphasizes as paradigmatic the intensely (sublimated) intimate relation that seems always to exist between the mystic and a confessor/ scribe/ interlocutor. He points out how often this relation takes on, rhetorically, the form of a "mother/son" dialogue—where the "spiritual" filiation takes the place of any biological relation, p. 88: "Mysticism, in effect, does not only depend on experience but also and no less on the transmission of (the) experience. In women mystics this transmission which comes to them from the father gets carried out by being directed at a filial witness who understands and authorizes the experiences by becoming its guarantor. This witness cannot be either a son or a stranger. Close but also distant, he belongs to a spiritual family, a family without any direct filiation—an adopted son, or nephew."

[18] The body of the text begins: " Celuy qui me tient la place de Dieu sur la terre pour me diriger dans ses voyes, m'ayant commandé de mettre par écrit, autant qu'il me sera possible, les graces et les faveurs, qu'il a plû de me communiquer: je commenceray mon obéissance pour son honneur" (*Vie*, 1).

priest himself, and it is to his desire to understand and to know this remarkable mother that we owe the publication of her life.[19] Marie's decision to become a nun and then to leave France for Canada represents an intense oedipal drama the effects of which continue to reverberate proleptically and retrospectively in these two lives. It is the impossibility of separating the oedipal dynamic from the spiritual narrative that accounts in large part for the text's fascination. Its interest is most specifically that of a transitional document in which are traced the contentious social, sexual, and religious conflicts taking place in seventeenth-century French society as they reappear in this four-handed exercise, transformed, disguised in the highly charged physical and spiritual descriptions of the mother and the fascinated and enthusiastic commentaries of the son.

It is in response to the repeated and insistent requests from her son back in France ("il y a quelques années par une sainte franchise vous me pressiez de vous faire le récit et la conduite qu'il a plu à la divine Majesté de tenir sur moy et de vous faire part des graces et des faveurs qu'elle m'a faites") that Marie finally agrees to put down in writing the story of her exceptional relation to God.[20] She agrees to this, however, only on the stipulation (purely rhetorical?) that this narration be kept private. It is not intended for public consumption, but, as she writes, is for her son's eyes only:

> Je les ay fait, avec repugnance, et les envoye avec peine. Mais puisque la grace et la nature ont surmonté toutes mes inclination, j'ay à vous dire mes intentions là-dessus, qui est que je ne desire pas que qui que ce soit en ait la communication et la connoissance que vous. Je me confie que vous me garderez la fidelité que je vous demande, et qu'après ce que vous avez demandé de moy, vous ne me refuserez pas ce que je desire de vous. Et parce que l'on fait des visites dans les Maisons Religieuses, je vous prie d'écrire sur la couverture, "Papiers de conscience," afin que personne n'y touche, et n'y jette les yeux sans scrupules.[21]

Already we are at the very inception of this narration in murky waters, waters where the pure source of divine love mix with and become inseparable from and contaminated with the decidedly more human streams of desire and guilt. Right from the beginning we have to be constantly aware of this contamination of the religious by the familial that is always operative in this text. Marie is addressing her son, the living proof of her inextricable ties to the body, at the same time that she addresses a fellow religious, another soul who has renounced the body, and with whom she communes, at times as an equal, but more frequently as a spiritual guide in the life that he, too, aspires to lead. While Claude Martin is acutely aware that the project

[19] For an introduction to the life of Claude Martin, written in the same breathlessly enthusiastic style as his work on Marie de l'Incarnation, cf. Brémond, *Histoire littéraire du sentiment religieux*, vol. 6, chap. 6.

[20] *Vie*, Premiere lettre à son fils, xxiii–xxiv.

[21] *Vie*, Seconde lettre à son fils, xxxi–xxxii.

of making public the intimate workings of his mother's body and soul may be seen as highly suspect by many and for many different reasons, he nevertheless persists in his endeavor by appealing to several examples from Church history that appear to justify this seemingly suspect project.[22] This convoluted relation is constantly present at all levels of the text. It continuously interweaves the life of the body that has been abandoned with the price for this abandonment, persistent guilt. This guilt, too, is multilayered. It resurfaces in the mother's text as the tenacious need, we might think, of punishing the sinful body. In the son's commentaries it resurfaces as the necessity to understand and even to forgive this mother whose abandonment of him inheres in him as an unsutured wound and reappears as the double compulsion to peer into the inner workings of his mother and to expose this intimate space to eyes of the world.

On the very first level of contradiction, therefore, we can understand this narration as a gift, offered by a mother to a son, in order to compensate for the maternal presence she herself has denied him:

> Si faisant la lecture des écrits que je vous envoye il vous vient en la pensée, ce qui a pu flechir la bonté divine à me faire de si grandes misericordes, et à me prevenir de la sorte des benedictions de sa douceur: Je vous diray que j'y ay souvent fait reflexion, et qu'après y avoir bien pensé, je n'ay rien veu en moy que miseres et indignitez, ou si du côté de la creature il peut y avoir quelque cause, je n'en puis donner d'autre que vous, que j'ay abandonné pour son amour dans un temps, où selon toutes les raisons humaines vous aviez le plus de besoin de moy, et sur tout de ce que j'en avois eu le dessein et pris la resoluton avant même que vous fussiez au monde. . . . Car si je vous ay abandonné dès votre enfance par le mouvement de sa grace, sans vous laisser d'autre appuy que sa providence toute pure, il vous a pris dans sa protection paternelle, et vous a richement pourveu. . . . Vous avez donc beaucoup gagné en me perdant et mon abandonnement vous a été utile.[23]

Ostensibly, therefore, these memoirs are written in great part as an explanation in guise of a disculpation of the *felix culpa* of her desertion of him. There is a strangely ambiguous dialectic at work here, which can operate only if the text is kept in a constantly poised rhetorical equilibrium between two registers, one divine—the purely spiritual display of the extraordinary holy gifts given Marie; the other corporal—the aborted maternal relation that continues to inflect the spirituality of both mother and son. The desire of the son to know the mother is met, in the text, by the mother's desire to

[22] *Vie*, preface, viii: Ce n'est pas non plus une chose inouie et sans exemple qu'un fils écrive la vie de sa Mere: si Saint Augustin ne l'eût fait, nous n'eussions pas connu l'éminente vertu de sainte Monique. Ce seul exemple suffiroit pour justifier mon dessein, mais j'en puis encore produire deux autres . . . S. Pierre, Abbé de Cluny, qui a fait l'éloge de la bienheureuse Raingarde sa mere . . . et le second du Venerable Guibert, Abbé de Nogent, qui écrivant sa propre vie a aussi écrit celle de sa mere.

[23] *Vie*, Premiere lettre à son fils, xxvi–xxvii.

show herself to the son. And yet, the narration is not only a private peep show into the strangely fascinating inner world of Marie de l'Incarnation, but becomes, in 1676, a public spectacle. Dom Claude, obviously ignoring the explicit request of his mother, publishes her story and exposes her life to the world, but in a version supplemented and censored by his own extensive emendations.

The *Vie* before us may have one central protagonist but, as I've said, it is a life that through the son's persistent intervention has not one author, but two: "Il y a plus d'un autheur; il y en a deux, et l'un et l'autre étoient necessaires pour achever l'ouvrage. Cette grande servante de Dieu y a travaillé elle même et son fils y a mis la derniere main, en sorte neanmoins qu'il n'y parle que comme un écho."[24] Claude fights his way back into the life from which he was ejected, but, strangely it is as an echo that he inscribes himself in this text and in Marie's life. With the disappearance, literal and figurative, of Marie from his existence, the text appears, we might say, as a doubly evocative maternal substitute, or rather as a substitute in writing of the aborted maternal/filial relation. It can be read from a double perspective, either the constant pursuit by the child of the mother or, in reverse fashion, the mother's persistent flight before the rapacious grasp of the child.

Could we not see this complex rhetorical exercise, with the discordant inversion of both generational and gender roles, as a new avatar of the Narcissus myth—the mother as the fleeing Narcissus, the child in the role of the pursuing nymph—at the same time that this myth is given a particularly Christian inflexion: the flesh (of the mother) is transformed into the constantly replenished and constantly evanescent logos of the text? Marie offers this auto/biography thus transforming her narcissism into a highly invested example of what we might call a typical feminine *imitatio Christi* where the mothers's body, having become text ("hoc est corpus meum") is offered to nourish and sustain, spiritually, a bereft and melancholic child?[25] But the son, unable to accept the unmediated maternal substitute on its own terms, unable to remain in the tormenting, passive position in front of this painful absence, sets about inverting the situation, placing himself in the role of stylistic and spiritual arbitrator, thus assuring himself the control over the continued (printed) presence of the mother.

This auto/biographical rescripting of the Narcissus myth affords an un-

[24] *Vie*, preface, 2. Claude comes back a second time to the image of the echo; cf. viii, where he writes, "j'ay dit que son fils y a encore travaillé comme un Echo. L'on peut bien certes lui donner icy cette qualité puisque l'Echo est le fils de la voix, et comme un supplément qui l'étend au delà de sa propre activité, lors meme qu'elle n'est plus.'

[25] Both Marie and her son suffered from "melancholia." Brémond (*Histoire littéraire du sentiment religieux*, 6:114) quotes a letter from Marie to her son in which she tells him not to let others' opinion of him as "melancholic" affect him. She tells him that she too has been thought of as such: "et ne vous mettez pas en peine si un grand recueillement vous fait passer pour mélancolique; l'on a presque toujours dit cela de moi, et c'était lorsque mon esprit était en de très grandes jubilations avec Dieu." The relation between narcissism and melancholia since has been established, see Freud's *Mourning and Melancholia* (Standard Edition, vol. 14).

canny inversion of the traditional gender roles ascribed to the characters in the (standard version) of the tale. For here the (adult male) child is equated to the female pursuer (Echo) of the male object of desire, the mother (Narcissus/Marie). Claude chases the narcissistic mother who disappears into a doubly inaccessible "beyond"—first into the religious (breaking of any ties to the secular/familial world) and then, fleeing across the ocean, into the unimaginable otherness of Canada. All that is left to the empty arms of the beseeching child is to echo her presence, to be that echo which, as all have remarked, is not simply a repetition, but an emendation, a correction of the maternal voice. It is a corrective echoing that prepares the maternal absence for public dissemination in a way that both excuses and attempts to heal the irreparable, original breach.[26]

This flight into metaphor (I am the echo), a metaphor which itself cannot escape its own imbrication in both a cultural myth and a concomitant psychic construction exists here at the outset of this auto/biography as the trace of a trauma that the following narration both highlights and eclipses. Marie's decision to leave the secular world and to enter the convent was the result of a wish that, we are told, she had cherished since childhood.[27] Her marriage and the birth of her son are, at least from the point of view of eternity, but small detours on her spiritual journey. Despite her own projects, however, and despite the rather austere (would we now say abusive—in the sense of emotional deprivation ?) manner in which she raised her child ("Il y avoit bien dix ans que je le mortifiois, ne permettant pas qu'il me fît aucunes caresses, comme de mon côté je ne luy faisois point, afin qu'il n'eût

[26] All of the commentators of the text address the strange editorial role of Claude Martin. The general consensus is that he "polished" the text, making sure that he was on safe ground "doctrinally speaking," that he removed provincialism and archaisms from his mother's writings, that he changed some too-explicit references to the body, and in general assured that the "baroque" language of his mother, would be acceptable to the triumphantly prevailing "Classical" esthetics of the 1670s. Dom J. Lonsange, writing in his introduction to the 1981 Solesmes edition also states, 13: "Then again, Marie de l'Incarnations's style risked shocking the readers whose taste by then had become more demanding. The year 1677, date of the premiere of *Phèdre*, is precisely the year by which we can think of classical literature as having reached its greatest flowering. . . . Thus he tries his best to smooth out all those expressions which he considers too unseemly." Perhaps Natalie Zemon Davis can be seen as typical of the commentators who reduce Claude's role to that of editor without delving into the more complex psychoemotional relation this editorship both hides and reveals. Cf. Davis, *Women on the Margins*, 129–31, and in particular, 130: "In writing about her body, Marie sometimes went too far for her son's taste, or for the taste of the readers he hoped for beyond her sister religious." Timmermans comments more generally on the male role of correcting texts penned by women (*L'accès des femmes* 545): "During the seventeenth century respect for the original was not a widely shared concern; all those texts not initially destined for publication are revised, be their author a man or a woman. But through the correcting, masculine and learned values are introduced into feminine literature: either through a desire to conform to stylistic norms, or through a care for universality, exhaustivity, coherence and linearity, . . . or doctrinal precision."

[27] *Vie*, 9: "Elle n'avoit jamais eu le coeur au mariage, mais que son inclination la portoit à être Religieuse de l'Ordre de saint Benoist dans Beaumont . . . qu'elle en avoit fait même l'ouverture à sa mère, qui luy témoigna bien de la joye."

aucune attache à moy")[28] these plans are met with strong resistance on her son's part. Learning surreptitiously of her plans to abandon him and join the convent, he runs away from home because of "une melancolie profonde où il tomba" just before her planned entry into religion. This three-day escapade plunges his mother into anxious self-doubt. To make matters worse, once she has joined the convent Claude continues to pursue her from outside the walls, crying for the nuns to return his mother to him:

> Dieu permit que j'eusse d'abord une bonne épreuve: une troupe de petits écoliers compagnons de mon fils s'assembla au tour de luy et commença à le huer et à crier de ce qu'il avoit été si fol et si simple que de me laisser entrer en Religion, disant que maintenant il étoit sans pere et sans mere . . . cela émût si fort cet enfant, qu'il pleuroit lamentablement. Ils vinrent donc un grand nombre à la porte du Monastere, où avec une grande confusion ils faisoient des bruits et des cris si étranges afin qu'on me rendit, qu'ils se faisoient entendre de toutes parts. D'abord je ne sçavois ce que c'étoit, mais parmy ces voix confuses j'entendis celle de mon fils qui à haut cris disoit: rendez-moy ma mere, rendez-moy ma mere. . . . Il venoit à l'Eglise lors qu'on disoit la Messe et passant la tête par la fenêtre de la grille de la Communion: Hé, disoit-il, rendez-moy ma mere.[29]

It is the echoing crescendos of this cry that reverberate throughout the *Vie* as Claude's attempt both to understand this incomprehensible abandonment and to reinscribe it anew through his own insistent presence in the text. In a sense, therefore, the position of echo that defines Claude's role in his mother's *Vie* can be seen to collapse the trauma of the son and the ecstasies of the mother into a strange dialogue of loss and reunion. In a compelling fashion, this extraordinary familial tug-of-war between a mother and her son over the very complex and contradictory desires of the one to pursue what she sees as a personal and spiritual vocation over and against societal expectations and filial desires can be seen to echo in this one exceptional document the more general, convoluted transformations of sexual/familial subjugation in emerging absolutist France.[30] The echo of Claude's loss and Marie's abandonment of her maternal function (at least in relation to her son) continually condenses the more complex dynamics of the public roles allowed and refused to seventeenth century women in a highly

[28] *Vie*, 175. Another revelatory instance is disclosed by Claude—just before taking the veil and therefore leaving him forever, she is described (178): " C'étoit le lieu et le temps de luy donner un baiser, pour derniere marque de son affection mais elle ne le fit pas, comme elle n'avoit jamais fait auparavant, ce qui me semble rare dans une mere."

[29] *Vie*, 181. The phrase quoted previously is on page 174.

[30] I am not, of course, claiming that Marie's abandonment of her son to follow her religious vocation was in and of itself exceptional. This appears as a rather common occurrence in the spritual itinerary of several seventeenth-century religious women, Jeanne de Chantal and Mme Guyon, as well as in the history and legends of the early Church (cf. St. Thecla). What is exceptional is how this scene, this act, is represented as the textual/spiritual pivot of Marie de l'Incarnation's *Vie*.

charged scenario of guilt and obsession, of spiritual emptiness and bodily excess, finally into an insoluble conflict that can only attempt to resolve itself (in language) through a rhetorical appeal to inadequate binarisms. The appeal to these binary oppositions—body/soul, mother/child, life in the world/religious clausura—to explain this process of change merely exacerbates the already enchafed societal contradictions that they repeat but cannot overcome.

Recent work by feminist scholars has done much to demonstrate how changes in seventeenth century society had a direct impact on the role and place of women in the evolving sphere of cultural politics. Scholars such as Joan DeJean, Faith Beasely, Erica Harth in the United States, and Linda Timmermans in France have shown both the important but too often occluded role women played in the development of Classical culture, in the areas of memoirs, fiction, and philosophical and psychological treatises.[31] In the more properly religious domain, Elizabeth Rapley has traced the emergence during the Counter-Reformation of new forms of female spirituality that tried to resist the traditional roles assigned women by the Church. Instead of the choice of marriage and life in the world or a religious vocation and thus *clausura*, the Counter-Reformation saw, first in Italy then in France, a new desire emerge on the part of women to practice what they considered a Christian life, ministering to the poor, the sick, the outcasts of society, without submitting to the law of *clausura*.[32] A new type of female religious order was trying to emerge that would be situated in that in between space, in between the two poles (confinement in the family, confinement in the convent) that the male-dominated Church had definitively assigned to women. What is striking in Rapley's account of these different attempts at reform are the examples of almost unanimous outrage with which these endeavors were met on the part of the population at large. Women who had not taken the veil, but who nevertheless attempted to live in female communities and to practice a (new) form of Christian piety, were deeply suspect and often the objects of hostility especially when they transgressed the conventual limits placed on them and ventured out into the public sphere.[33]

[31] J. DeJean, *Tender Geographies*; Beasely, *Revising Memory*; Erica Harth, *Ideology and Culture in Seventeenth-century France* (Ithaca: Cornell University Press, 1983); and *Cartesian Women: Version and Subversion of Rational Discourse in the Old Regime* (Ithaca: Cornell University Press, 1992); Timmermans *L'accès des femmes*.

[32] See Rapley, *The Dévotes*, esp. chaps. 1 ("Women and the Counter-Reformation in France") and 2 ("The Defense of the Status Quo"), from which I borrow much of the information in the following paragraphs. The Ursuline order which Marie was eventually to join originated in Italy as precisely this in-between attempt to avoid *clausura* and to serve in the world, cf. 48–60.

[33] Ibid., 56: "Respectable society was not yet ready for these uncloistered nuns; their appearance on the streets gave rise to much scandal and derision. In Grenoble, 'when they came out of their house, they were abused both by words and by actions.' In Lyon, their walk to

Neither religious nor secular society was ready to accept this new type of female circulation. Women on the streets were considered public women, streetwalkers. These "new religious" aroused anxiety in a populace unable to situate them within the terms previously available to them in their culture. The ambiguity (were they prostitutes or chaste religious?) was too fraught. Their attempt to live outside of the frame defined for women in a society still rigidly committed to a firm rearticulation of patriarchal prerogative must have precipitated enormously threatening fantasies of female sexuality unfettered from the bonds that previously held it in check. Although the rededication to a Christian life and works preached by the Council of Trent had a profound resonance in many Catholic women, the structures available to them to live this life seemed restrictive and outdated. Nevertheless any attempt at radically altering the existing parameters was met with institutional opposition. The role that these different groups of uncloistered religious assigned themselves, especially that of teaching the children of the poor, could be seen as an usurpation, as it was, of the tightly guarded male privilege to preach and evangelize. Women were no more welcomed uncloistered into the world than they were to be allowed to assume such traditional male functions. Eventually, in order to preserve both the institutional support and the public approbation needed for their survival these newly founded female orders were obliged to accept *clausura*, to organize themselves along existing conventual models and to take themselves off the public stage.[34] As Absolutism advances during the course of the century one can see that, in the religious sphere as in the sociopolitical, women's activity, which had enjoyed a relatively freer reign of expression in the chaos of the religious wars and during the nobiliary rebellions of the first third of the century, was gradually but firmly relegated to the confined spaces of the salons and the convents, there to turn inward what had been an active political, even military role. Confined to those enclosed spaces women were to develop those more feminine pursuits of conversation, seduction, and ecstatic mysticism.[35]

---

church gave rise to jeering, by passers-by who took them for women of ill-repute. In Dijon, 'Whenever they passed on the streets, they were looked upon with scorn; the little children shouted after them and threw mud at them.' "

[34] Ibid., 22: "This sudden invasion by female volunteers of an area that women had not trodden before forced Catholic reformers to define and clarify the place of women in the Church. The clarification was mostly negative. The very strength of Catholic Reform lay in its respect for tradition. Tradition had always allowed for feminine religious life, and indeed piety had encouraged it. But before the sheer weight of numbers of women who were now seeking admission some people in the Church took fright. . . . According to tradition, the female sex was weak and flawed, and unfit to enter religion's inner courts. A powerful antifeminism, raised through time almost to the level of Christian doctrine, awaited women at the Church door."

[35] DeJean argues in *Tender Geographies* for precisely such a coerced turning inward of feminine activity as she traces the forced retreat from the stage of public political existence of those "amazones" who, in their memoirs, will replace public activity by "private" conversation, conversation that will, she argues, eventuate in the "birth of the modern novel."

Two early and apparently antithetical experiences are reported by Marie as defining moments of her young life: her first rapturous vision of her future "husband/lover" and her childhood infatuation with the "preaching" clergy. Marie reports that at the age of seven she had her first vision, a dream really, where she sees Jesus descend from heaven toward her:

> Je n'avois qu'environ sept ans, qu'une nuit pendant mon sommeil il me sembla que j'estois dans la cour d'une école champêtre, où avec une de mes compagnes je faisois quelque action innocente: ayant les yeux levez vers le Ciel, je le vis ouvert, et nôtre seigneur Jesus-Christ en forme humaine, qui en sortoit, et qui par l'air s'en venoit droit à moy, le voyant, je m'écriai à ma compagne: Ah! Voila notre Seigneur, c'est à moy qu'il vient; et il me sembloit que cette fille ayant commis une imperfection, il m'avoit choisie plûtot qu'elle.[36]

There is, as many have noticed, enormous (contradictory?) pride at work in mystic discourse. From the very beginning Marie's first memory is not only of being visited by Christ, but of being chosen, preferred, because she is more perfect than her playmate. Furthermore, this dream scene functions, in the narrative of her life she is elaborating, as the decisive moment of interpellation, where she is "hailed" into her subjective positioning as a libidinal object, always the object of divine love. This interpellation, establishes from the outset the powerful erotic charge (it is after all a scene of seduction, but the question remains, who is seducing whom?)[37] that is inseparable from the religious experience and yet that the conscious aspect of that experience, encoded by an entire history of both rhetorical techniques and ecclesiastical boundaries, will not be able to tolerate. I am suggesting that a very subtle play is at work here whereby the intensity of the rapture is never containable by the representations that would enfold it (the images, the stock figures—Jesus, the Holy Ghost—as they are given in a culturally coded symbolic system), but that the intensity coming from within, from, we might say, the instinctual impulses, always threaten to overwhelm the representations, to escape the cultural structures designed to contain it, and engulf the self.[38] It is this inability to accept the libidinal impetus to her own

[36] *Vie*, 2.

[37] Jean Laplanche, in *Vie et mort en psychanalyse* (Paris: Flammarion, 1970), points out (24) that "the object of the drive can be, absolutely, a phantasmatic object and it may actually be this, first and foremost," that it can be a individual or communal fantasy, that is, God, Jesus. Laplanche goes on to state that in the case of hysteria the father is the object rather than the subject of seduction (60): "Hysterics lie. . . . They have taken their imagination for (a) reality; and, then they have translated . . . their desire into a reality: here, in what we call the 'primal fantasy' of seduction, it is their own desire to seduce the father that they have transformed, in reverse fashion, into a scene of being seduced by the father."

[38] Antoine Vergote (*Guilt and Desire: Religious Attitudes and Their Pathological Derivatives* [New Haven: Yale University Press, 1988], 80) talks about the role of the "instincts" as the source for the desequilibrium between affect and representation which feeds directly into an unquenchable feeling of guilt; "it is precisely the instincts that are responsible for constantly reawakening the sense of lack in the subject in so far as they the inextinguishable source of all

religiosity that will turn, as an attempted catharsis, the body against itself in those equally heady scenes of masochistic mortifications (to which we will come in a moment). The erotic inflection of her vision becomes clearer, in her dream, as Christ draws closer:

> Cette surabdorable Majesté s'approchant de moy, mon coeur se sentit tout embrazé de son amour, et je commençay à étendre les bras pour l'embrasser: alors ce plus beau de tous les enfans des hommes, avec un visage plein d'une douceur et d'un attrait indicible, m'embrassa, et me baisant amoureusement, me dit, Voulez-vous estre à moy? Je luy repondis: Ouy, et ayant eu mon consentement, nous le vîmes remonter au Ciel. A mon réveil mon coeur se sentit si ravi de cette insigne faveur.[39]

This dream serves as the prototype for all the later ecstatic visions Marie experiences as she progresses on her spiritual journey. All are repetitions of this initial scene, all contain, in that particularly troubling way that Bataille describes, the inextricably bound strands of an intensely felt sexuality, expressed in and through an equally intense rhetoric of loss of self in union with the divine other.[40] Although Marie's interpellation by God is represented as a seduction, what strikes us as important is not so much the sexuality of the vision, that is, the images themselves, but the intensity of the expression, an intensity that reveals the inexpressible affect that exists behind or beyond the vision. Affect, inherently mobile, is thus able to attach itself to rhetoric, to vision, to objects in the real world and to infuse them with an aura and force that they themselves do not possess.[41]

Finally, and perhaps most important, we cannot forget that these scenes function theatrically. They are spectacular mises-en-scène of the visionary subject who is situated both as object not only of Marie's supernatural husband/lover but of the readerly gaze. Nor should we forget that the first and most intensely focused of these readers is her son, Claude.[42] Can we not

---

desire and insofar as they are, paradoxically, forces both alien to and internally active within the individual's will. The ideal of perfection conceals an imaginary representation of a man completely free of this internal feeling that he is foreign to himself, a feeling that inhabits him as a result of the fact that he is an instinctual and affective being."

[39] *Vie*, 3.

[40] Georges Bataille, *L'érotisme* (Paris: Minuit, 1957), states (273) that "at a most basic level, the systems of sensuality and of mysticism are not different."

[41] "Affect" is perhaps the most difficultly circumscribable psychic dimension. The most interesting, extended treatment of "affect" is presented in André Green's *Le discours vivant: La conception psychanalytique de l'affect* (Paris: P.U.F., 1973).

[42] Talking in a similar context about Angela da Foligno, and more specifically, about the ambiguous relation that exists between "mystic" women and their confessors/ scribes/acolytes, Vuarnet remarks (*Extases féminines*, 79): "It is as a woman that she gives herself to God, but as a spectacle that she offers herself to the young man." He also pinpoints the necessity in mystic discourse, as we see here in Marie, for the ambivalent relation between the subject of the mystic experience and her interlocutor (89): "What matters is that all these extatic women speak in a special way to a person of the opposite sex and encourage, in an equally privileged way, the fascination of men."

propose then, at the outset, ready to expand our hypothesis as we proceed, that these projected visions, visions given to us as text which, on one level at least, are highly erotic snapshots of Marie's union with God (unions that progress in intensity to culminate in a mystic marriage), have the concentrated, phantasmatic, appeal of the primal scene, that they can in fact be considered to be the primal fantasy of this composite *Vie*? In these visions, which are projected for Claude's eyes alone, as we've seen, he is in the anxious position of all children who fantasize the forbidden scene of parental union, precisely from the position of being a priori excluded from it. This originary and necessary exclusion only exacerbates a sense of always having been abandoned, but immediately excuses and explains this abandonment as not really a repudiation but more important a necessary sacrifice to and for God. He is thus both excluded and included in a more perfect, spiritual reality. Since, however, the reader's eyes are conflated with Claude's what we have is a very baroque *mise-en-abîme* of textual reality and pretextual fantasy that carries right into the heart of the Classical moment a conflicted and perhaps unassimilable charge of erotic and familial phantasm. In these visionary fantasies (which are structurally identical to the role of the erotic tableaux in our pornographic novels,[43] and to those intercalated scenes of sexuality and destruction in Racine) the multiple readers of the text participate in the voyeuristic delectation and anxiety of the split authors, whose projected fantasies seduce the readers' own versions of the family romance into a spiraling of individual and collective "ex-stasis."

The second moment to which I want to call our attention is another scene which rather than presented as an inner vision is contributed as firmly rooted in daily life in the real world. The contrast between the two scenes is not the opposition of just interiority and exteriority but also (a certain) passivity to (a certain) activity: in the dream/vision we have just examined, Marie remains in a passive (traditionally perceived as feminine) receptive relation to an active (masculine) subject. Here the situation appears reversed:

> Dès mon enfance ayant appris que Dieu parloit par la bouche des Predicateurs, cela me sembloit admirable, et j'avois une grande inclination à les aller entendre. . . . J'avois les Predicataeurs en si grande veneration, que quand j'en voyois quelqu'un par les rues, je me sentois portée d'inclination à courir apres luy et à baiser les vestiges de ses pieds, une petite prudence me retenoit: mais je le conduisois de l'oeil jusqu'à ce que je l'eusse entierement perdu de veue. Je ne trouvois rien de plus grand que la parole de Dieu, et c'étoit ce qui produisoit en mon coeur l'estime de ceux ausquels nôtre Seigneur en avoit commis le ministere. Lors que je l'entendois, il me sembloit que mon coeur étoit comme un

[43] The same metaphor appears in Marie's fantasies of mystical union and in the pornographic texts. In both, the union is expressed in "liquid" terms, a melting away. After a new "mystical union," Marie writes (*Vie*, 195): "J'eus assez de liberté pour dire Complies au Choeur, nonobstant les restes des écoulements et des embrassemens divins, dont mon ame avoit été remplie, et dont elle étoit encore toute liquefiée . . ."

vase, dans lequel cette divine parole découloit comme une liqueur . . . mon ame . . . ayant receu cette plenitude abondante, ne la pouvoit contenir . . . il me faloit parler par paroles exterieures . . . ce que je faisois aux personnes de notre maison avec un grand zele et leur disant ce que le Prédicateur avoit préché, y ajoutant mes propres pensées qui me rendoient éloquente.[44]

What is intriguing in this second early memory is the youthful Marie's already strong identification (admiration and imitation) with a seductive masculine presence and role in the world. [45] In the commentary that follows immediately after this reported scene and which functions, as do all of Claude's explanations, rather as a secondary elaboration, Claude interprets the true import of the scene.[46] For him, Marie's youthful infatuation with mendicant preachers was a sign that God had predestined her "for all eternity" for the "Apostolic role" she was fated to fulfill.[47] Neither Claude nor Marie could ignore, in the religious and social context that was theirs, that his use of the word "Apostolic" was freighted with sexual and political taboo. For the Church it was precisely this "Apostolic" vocation that was safeguarded as an exclusively masculine prerogative.[48] Women were not allowed to preach, nor were they permitted to overstep those claustral limits placed on female religious to remain modestly out of the eyes of the world.

Marie's obsession with preachers could be seen as an early masculine identification that will soon come to be defined by her world as unacceptable both sexually and politically. I am suggesting that from the beginning there is an issue of conflicted "gender" (the enfolding of the political onto the sexual) identification that is transgressive of the socially normative values of her society. Marie, as a very young girl, wants to be a preacher (that

[44] *Vie*, 17–18.

[45] Would it be an exaggeration to suggest that behind her first identification with the preacher lies a more intense identification with God, that is, with the primitive, prehistoric Father? Cf. Julia Kristeva, *Histoires d' amour* (Paris: Denoel, 1983), trans. Leon Roudiez, *Tales of Love* (New York: Columbia University Press, 1987), 26: " When the object that I incorporate is the speech of the other . . . I bind myself to him in a primary fusion, communion, unification. An identification . . . Freud has described the One with whom I fulfill the identification . . . as a Father; . . . he made it clear that this father is a 'father in individual prehistory.' "

[46] A "secondary elaboration," according to Jean Laplanche and Jean Bertrand Pontalis, *The Language of Psychoanalysis*, trans. Donald Nicholson-Smith (New York; Norton, and Co., 1973), is in the most general sense a "rearrangement of a dream so as to present it in the form of a relatively consistent and comprehensible scenario" (412). They also point out the role of "censorship" secondary elaboration represents, making the dream material palatable to the ego and superego; it is to the analogy of this psychic role that I attribute Claude's interpretations of Marie's material, bringing it to the "Classical" theological authorities of his day in an palatable, that is, orthodox, form.

[47] "Dieu luy avoit donné cette haute estime des Prédicateurs dès son enfance et par ce sentiment si extraordinaire, il la disposoit deslors aux emplois Apostoliques ausquels il l'avoit destinée de toute éternité" (*Vie*, 19).

[48] Claude writes (304): "Aussi ne trouve-t-on point que l'Eglise ait jamais donné à aucune la qualité d'Apôtre, ce titre glorieux n'étant accordé qu'à ces grands hommes que Dieu a donnez à son Eglise pour en être le fondement et les principales colonnes."

is, assume a male role) and she is clearly made to understand that this is not acceptable.[49] The conflict between the intense pleasure she associates with the apostolic mission and the impossibility of assuming that active role (and probably a sentiment of guilt for desiring such a transgressive activity), fuses with the anxiety of the too intensely libidinal (bodily?) sensations of her spiritual fantasies and plays an important, if unconscious, role in determining her later vocation as a masochist and a missionary. At first these transgressive desires appear as fantasies of escape:

> Dès mon enfance, il me semble que Dieu me disposoit à la grace que je possede maintenant, car j'avois plus l'esprit dans les païs éloignés, pour y considerer les genereuses actions de ceux qui y travailloient et enduroient pour Jesus-Christ, que dans le lieu où j'habitois. Mon coeur se sentoit uni aux ames Apostoliques, d'une maniere toute extraordinaire. [50]

Within the terms available to Marie in the world that was hers, these fantasies fix themselves on the colonial possibilities that she read about in the Jesuit *Relations*, and that she dealt with in the everyday affairs of her brother-in-law's business. To be united with those new Apostles, to be like them ("il m'étoit avis que j'étois une meme chose avec eux") Marie must leave behind the world she knows.[51] Her flight out of France and toward the unknown in a sense represents, therefore, an unsexing, an attempt to be "une meme chose avec eux," to free herself even further from the confines of her sexed body. This escape from France is also, and perhaps even more so, a withdrawal from the ubiquitous reminder of that female body and its sexuality, from, that is, her own imbrication in the oedipal trap. Her voyage to Canada will be a definitive abandonment of Claude. He exists in her

[49] L. Timmermans commenting on just this aspect writes (*L'accès des femmes*, 533): "But she [i.e Marie] doesn't considers herself to be an apostle, and from the beginning, does not allow herself an apostolic mission. Marie therefore distinguishes between legal theory and an actual practice." Claude, in order to recognize both the reality of the situation and its religious impossibility writes, 304, that "si l'on ne peut pas lui donner le nom d'Apôtre, on peut au moins luy donner celuy de femme apostolique."

[50] *Vie*, 19. Once again there is a strange play at work between in Timmermans's words "un état de droit et un état de fait" that allows for an ambiguous interpretation of Marie's conventual transgressions. It can be argued, as she does, that although she and her sister nuns leave the convent, travel across France to Paris and from there to Dieppe and across the ocean, they nevertheless retain their rule: "Car dans toute la traverse nous gardâmes exactement nos regles" (*Vie*, 394). But we should not forget that there is throughout the autobiography the desire to demonstrate, precisely, that she was not transgressive, but that she, unlike other unruly women, was not only saintly but obedient to all the rules of her order and the Church.

[51] Further on in the *Vie*, (300–301) we see the intensity of this desire/identification: "C'étoit un esprit Apostolique que s'empara du mien. . . . Cet esprit Apostolique me portoit en esprit dans les Indes, dans le Japon, dans l'Amerique, dans l'Orient, dans l'Occident dans les parties Septentrionales les plus inaccessibles et dans toute la terre habitable où il y avoit des ames raisonnables, . . . je me promenois en esprit dans ces grandes et vastes étendues des Indes, du Japon et de la Chine et j'y accompagnois les ouvriers de l'Evangile, ausquels je me sentois étroitement unie parce qu'ils se consumoient pour les interests de mon celeste et divin Epoux; il m'étoit avis que j'étois une meme chose avec eux."

world and in her mind as a constant souvenir of a sexual past and a familial imperative to which she had been subjected, something continually standing as an obstacle to her spiritual perfection either as the spouse of God or as a missionary carrying his word to the "savages," particularly the young female Amerindians, of the New World.[52] In a sense, therefore, we must understand Marie's imperious desire to journey to Canada, a desire that took years of pleading, plotting, and manipulating to realize, as a doubly convoluted attempt on her part to refashion herself according to her own transgressive desires. On the one hand the flight to Canada is an attempt on her part to go back to the heroic moment of the very early Church, when many things, including the active role of women, were still possible.[53] On the other (without there being an opposition, of course, but an inextricable interweave) it is a flight into denial, a denial of the demands of filiation, of sexuality and of her own situation in an oedipal scenario that constantly haunts her as a sign of her own fallen nature, that is, she was both "sexual" and an "unnatural" mother.

These two early scenarios, I believe, can help us understand, or at least begin to understand, Marie's extremely complex life as it is described and revised by her and her son. In them we see expressed, in apposite form, the braid of both passive and active drives. These drives are inextricably bound

[52] Marie, but even more so Claude, stress her natural repugnance to marriage and her particular devotion to virginity. Addressing Claude directly (in the *Vie* . . . there is a constant oscillation between a mother/son dialogue, heightened often by the intercalation of letters Claude received from his mother and more objective third-person narration) she writes (11): "si vous en sçaviez les particularitez que vous sçaurez dans l'éternité, et comme il falloit que je fusse engagée dans les croix du mariage. Il faut neanmoins que je vous avouë, que si j'eussse eu une conduite et direction spirituelle, je n'y aurois jamais consenti, mais j'en étois entierement dépourveu." Claude for his part appears much more intent on effacing this marriage (and thus his origin) as much as he can, by emphasizing his mother's particular modesty and devotion to the virginal state (and thus in a sense, rhetorically, restoring her virginity to her): "Elle a eu dès son enfance un amour tout particulier pour cette vertu angelique, et elle l'a toujours conservée depuis avec un zele merveilleux. C'est ce qui lui avoit fait prendre la resolution de consacrer à Dieu sa virginité dans un monastere dès l'âge de quatorze ans, qu'elle en eut reconnu plus particulierement le prix et la valeur: et si elle s'engagea dans le mariage, ce ne fut que par la seule obeissance qu'elle devoit à ses parens. Mais quelque engagement qu'elle eût, elle ne perdit jamais l'amour de la continence: car elle avoit une extreme aversion des lois de cet état, d'où vient qu'encore quelle fut fidele à en rendre les devoirs, puisque Dieu le vouloit, neanmoins de sa part elle ne les exigeoit jamais. Aussi . . . comme elle le témoigna un jour à une religieuse de Quebec, avec laquelle s'entretenant familierement, et l'entretien étant insensiblement tombé sur son état de mariage, elle lui dit, confidemment qu'elle n'en avoit pas retenu la moindre idée, et que depuis elle n'y avoit pas plus pensé que si elle n'y eut jamais été engagée" (397).

[53] Peter Brown, in *The Body and Society: Men, Women, and Sexual Renunciation in Early Christianity* (New York: Columbia University Press, 1988), demonstrates how the role of women in the early church was perceived differently by the various Christian communities that proliferated around the Mediterranean. Although he underscores the importance of the Pauline injunction against women's active role in the Church, he also reminds us that in many different sects of early Christianity women often played an active role both as martyrs and evangelists. Cf. esp. chap. 7, "A Promiscuous Brotherhood and Sisterhood: Men and Women in the Early Churches," and chap. 13, "Daughters of Jerusalem: The Ascetic Life of Women in the Fourth Century."

to gendered representations, themselves inseparable from societally informed expectations. The libidinal charge in both types of scenarios is intense, alternating between ecstatic visions of spiritual and corporal union with a divine Other in which the distinction between subject and object is undone, and moments of equally fierce physical mortification, where it would seem that the distinction is intensified by the same (libidinal) force of trying to subdue the body in its physical quiddity.

To hear Marie tell it, the period of both her most intense visions of holy union and most extreme physical mortification begins during the early part of her widowhood, almost immediately after she rejects any idea of a new marriage (an idea that her family encourages). Marie's first descriptions of her intensified longings for, and the satisfaction she receives from, Christ are couched in terms that would seem to corroborate the hypothesis of several psychoanalytic theorists who have suggested that at the heart of the mystic longing for union, for the dissolution of the self in the other, lies a primitive, unsatiated oral avidity:

> Vous êtes enfin ma vie, qui me remplissez. Ouy: *j'ay ouvert ma bouche et vous l'avez remplie de vôtre vie et de vôtre divin Esprit.* J'avois une experience de tout cela dans ce benit Sauveur, qui de la sorte m'était une vie et un aliment divin, et qui me faisoit encore experimenter ce qu'il dit ailleurs. . . . J'entrois en luy et par luy. En lui, dis-je, où je découvrois des divins Mysteres, qui m'étoient comme des pâturages feconds dont mon ame étoit repue.[54]

There is an appetitive longing in these initial images, a feeling of the body (here equatable to the "self") as empty, with the concomitant image of God

[54] *Vie*, 37. Walker-Bynum develops a sociohistorical explanation in *Holy Feast and Holy Fast* which accounts for the overwhelming emphasis on food, nourishment, and bodily intimacy in the spiritual images and discourse of late medieval women. Cf. for instance 193–194: "Food related behavior was central to women socially and religiously, not only because food was a resource women controlled but also because by means of food women controlled themselves and their world. Bodily functions, fertility and sexuality, husband, mother, father and children, religious superiors and confessor, God in his majesty and the boundaries of one's own self—all could be manipulated by abstaining from and bestowing food." Women's relation to food, to God as food, and to themselves as nourishment are transformed into the main rhetorical images of women's relation to God in this period, a period, as Walker-Bynum points out, in the increasingly popular "eucharistic" practices and images that invade medieval culture. On another theoretical front, psychoanalysis has offered the hypothesis that the basis of the desire for "mystical union" is to be sought in a very primitive, and problematic, relation between the nurturing breast (the mother) and the child. Guy Rosolato, for instance, in "Présente Mystique" points out (14): "Defective maternal relations have been noticed in women mystics such as Mme Guyon, Antoinette Bourignon," while Michel Ledoux writes in "La relation d'absence," (236): "it has become more and more clear to us that everything that had been expressed could be listed in the archaic register of the fusional relation whose prototype is the one that from the beginning is found between the mother and the child." Both articles are in *Résurgences et dérivés de la mystique, Nouvelle Revue de Psychanalyse*, 22 (autumn 1980). Vergote, in *Guilt and Desire*, also talks about the importance of the "oral position" (140): "a passion for the absolute is a sign of the oral position, . . . it is the avid search for the mythical object of attachment that would abolish any interior sense of emptiness."

as either a being who replenishes, or upon whom the body, vampirelike, seeks satiation.[55] As Marie's spirituality evolves, and as she ages, this presence of the body will become more and more ephemeral until, at the end of her life, she achieves an asceticism that, after all the other senses have been mortified, attacks the still present originary emptiness/avidity through a constant taste of bile that impedes any oral gratification. For the time being, however, still in her youth, Marie tackles more aggressively the body as the obstacle that stands in her way to perfection.

There seems to be a convoluted dialectic at work between the denial of the body and the florid exuberance of her visions. Is there just a casual relation between the fact that in the narration, despite familial pressure for her to do so, Marie's decision not to remarry, that is no longer to be a sexual being, is immediately followed by her first great (and for her terrifying) vision? The vision is presented as a ravishing of the body—the body projected outside the self in a horrifying scene of drowning in blood, Christ's blood that is flowing because of her iniquity:

> Un matin que j'allois vacquer à mes affaires, que je recommandais instamment à Dieu avec mon aspiration ordinaire. *(In te Domine speravi, non confundat in aeternum)* que j'avois gravée en mon esprit avec une grande certitude de foy qu'il m'assisteroit infailliblement, en cheminant je fus subitement arretée interieurement et exterieurement, et par cet arrest si subit toutes les pensées de mes affaires me furent ôtées de la memoire. Alors les yeux de mon esprit furent ouverts en un moment, et toutes les fautes, pechez et imperfections que j'avois commises depuis que j'etois au monde me furent representez en gros et et détail, avec distinction et clarté plus certaine que toute certitude que l'industrie humaine pourroit exprimer. Au meme moment, je me vis toute plongée dans du sang, et mon esprit fut convaincu que ce sang étoit celui du Fils de Dieu, de l'effusion duquel j'étois coupable par les pechez qui m'étoient representez et qui avoit été répandu pour mon salut. Si la bonté de Dieu ne m'eût soutenue en cette rencontre, je croy que je fusse morte de frayeur . . . [56]

What is striking in this image is not so much the "blood" which as Walker-Bynum reminds us had, by the late medieval period, become a commonplace image, but the intense and abject sense of guilt that the image ex-

[55] May one suggest, following Vergote and psychonalytic theory, that this oral avidity that is particularly insistent in mystic discourse is related in some primary and profoundly troubled connection to the mother? Cf. 62: "If primary attachment to the mother is particularly intense it may give rise to the mystical quest for God as the absolute object of desire. This transference onto God occurs because the bond with the primordial object [the mother] is always experienced as something that has been cut off from the subject and because the intensity of the bond is dangerous to him." (But this does not explain how in the personal history of each mystic this essentially universal broken bond is fixated in a particularly specific way to distinguish the mystic's psychic development from more "normal" individuals.)

[56] *Vie*, 26.

presses.[57] What we have is a fantasy (a vision) that reveals a horrible sense of culpability while no particular reason for the guilt, other than a general sense of unworthiness ("all my sins, my unworthiness"), is offered. In Marie's narration is a constant oscillation between these images of an profoundly abjected sense of her own unworthiness and images of ecstatic union where she is the admirable object of divine love mediated by the extraordinary punishments she inflicts on her guilty body.[58]

After reading François de Sales's *Introduction à la vie dévote,* Marie announces to her confessor her wish to take a vow of "eternal chastity." Since this is not a pledge to be taken lightly, the confessor ponders his answer for more than three months, testing her resolve (or we might say, engaging in a subtle form of sadomasochistic casuistry with his more-than-willing penitent), before allowing her to take so great a step.[59] At the same time that she rejects any further sexual relations, thus consciously denying the body, she exacerbates her recently instituted acts of penance (also approved by the same confessor). The feelings of abject unworthiness that we must assume are in some unconscious relation to a fear of (and as desire for) sexuality, turn Marie against her body, as she institutes a series of ever more intense ritual mortifications:

> Si auparavant j'avois commencé à me mortifier, tout cela ne me sembloit rien. Coucher sur les ais m'étoit trop sensuel; je mettois tout le long un cilice sur lequel je couchois. Les disciplines d'orties dont je me servois l'esté, étoient si sensibles apres en avoir employé trois ou quatre poignées à chaque fois, qu'il me sembloit être dans une chaudiere bouillant et pour l'ordinaire je m'en sentois trois jours durant, puis je recommençois. La douleur en étoit si grande, que

[57] Walker-Bynum, *Holy Feast and Holy Fast*, 56, asserts that "late medieval spiritual texts were awash in reference to the blood of the lamb."

[58] Freud in *The Economic Problem of Masochism* (Standard Edition, 19:157–73) brings out the unconscious sense of guilt that the image conveys: "A sense of guilt, too, finds expression in the manifest content of masochistic phantasies: the subject assumes that he has committed some crime (the nature of which is left indefinite) which is to be expiated by all these painful and tormenting procedures." Julia Kristeva, in her elaboration on masochistic "abjection" in *Pouvoirs de l'horreur* (Paris: Seuil, 1980) and *Histoires d'amour* has of course developed the link following Melanie Klein and early object-relations theory, between what she will define as the "abject" and the primitive infant/mother (food) relation. In both types of images—abjection and ecstasy—the dominant metaphors employed by Marie are "liquid" and "liquefaction".

[59] Further on Marie offers us another view of her relation with her confessor. " Mon confesseur qui prenoit grand soin de me mortifier n'en laissoit passer aucune occasion. Il me faisoit mourir toute vive et plus il me mortifioit, plus j'étois portée à luy dire toutes mes pensées . . . il m'étoit impossible de vivre à ma liberté ayant desir d'être toujours assujettie" (489). At times, and this might be my own sadism at work, we have the impression that very little separates Marie de l'Incarnation from "O." Louise J. Kaplan (*Female Perversions: The Temptations of Emma Bovary* [New York: Doubleday, 1991], 337–38) offers a description of "O's" dependent relation to her master that is eerily evocative of Marie de l'Incarnation: "In O's progressive dehumanization, as there is progressively less of O's self, she transforms her master, creating in him the omnipotent, omniscient, coherent other in whose arms she can take refuge."

> je ne sentois pas les chardons, voulant m'en servir après. Je ne laissois pas de me servir d'une discipline de chaînes, mais ce n'étoit rien en comparaison de la douleur des orties. Je mangeois de l'absinthe avec la viande, et hors le repas j'en tenois long temps dans la bouche et apres en avoir bien goûté je la mangeois.[60]

Marie herself allows as to how her mortifications must be kept secret because if they were known by her entourage she would surely be judged mad ("folle"): "Ceux que je frequentois ordinairement n'eussent jamais jugé que je me fusse arrestée à tous ces exercises de mortification, c'eût été assez pour leur faire croire que j'étois une folle, aussi me donnois-je garde qu'on ne s'en apperceut."[61] She is thus aware of the excessive nature of her acts, acts that rather than identify her as spiritually significant to her family and acquaintances would signal her as deranged. Her mortifications must remain clandestine: they must be performed on a secret stage, beyond the prying eyes of her entourage, for God alone. Nevertheless, we must always be aware of the double spectator of these of mortifications. The narration discloses this private stage for her son's eyes (and thus by relay to the reader's) as she elaborates in almost excruciating detail the lengths to which she went to punish her sinful body and the descriptions of that body:

> La longueur du temps à coucher sur le bois avec le cilice me macera si fort la chair du côté où je me couchois qu'il devint insensible, en sorte qu'en me touchant je ne me sentois pas. . . . Car la dureté du bois et la pesanteur du corps faisoit entrer le crin dans la peau, en sorte que je ne pouvois dormir qu'à demi, ressentant toujours la douleur des picqueurs. Je prenois plaisir de dénier à la nature tout ce qu'elle aimoit, et il ne m'étoit pas possible de me faire du bien en quoy que ce fût. . . . Après avoir passé le jour en toutes ces peines j'allois la nuit dans une caverne, où il y avoit des bêtes venimeuses. . . . Je passois là longtemps à prier Dieu, et à faire de longues et fortes disciplines, après lesquelles je m'allois coucher sur mon ais, ou sur une balle de marchandises.[62]

We can see that within the limits of a narrative tradition, Marie's secret masochistic stage is not all that far removed from those Sadeian monasteries with their own sadomasochistic rituals which were to appear a hundred years later. These examples of Marie's desperate attempt to reduce the body to a "senseless" state are of course doomed to failure by the extremely labile nature of that same sexuality she attempts to evacuate. As Freud pointed out in the *The Economic Problem of Masochism*, "even the subject's destruction of himself cannot take place without libidinal satisfaction."[63]

[60] *Vie*, 63. Vergote (*Guilt and Desire*, 102), writes of the relation among guilt, desire, and self-punishment: "In guilt neuroses, ritualized acts become forms of defense against the subject's aggressive representations, as well as against the retaliation he fears because of the law of retaliation."

[61] *Vie*, 64.

[62] Ibid.

[63] *The Economic Problem of Masochism*, 19:170.

What Freud was cannily alluding to was the reflexive, libidinal nature of the masochistic gesture which because of its erotic charge reinscribes, as it heightens, the very transgressive pleasure that the gesture was, on one level, intended to suppress.[64]

These scenes of mortification (and there are many more), for however powerfully intriguing, eliciting as they cannot help but do the corresponding sadism of the reader/son, are only one-half of the picture of Marie's eroticized relation to her body and to her God. While her descriptions of her self-imposed austerities are striking for their richly textured realism, her versions of mystic union are singularly bland in their hyperbolic generalizations. True to the traditional rhetoric of mystics, Marie claims that words fail her, that there is no discursive way to describe what she feels, and that all description is inadequate to the experience. Nonetheless, as Leszek Kolakowski and Michel de Certeau have pointed out, this admission of the "impossibility of expression" is followed by prodigally abundant attempts at expressing the inexpressible.[65] To cite just one example, Marie's description of her "mystic marriage" to the Incarnate Word, which is the highest mystical experience, the goal to which all the penance and all the prayer leads and which is described precisely in the words of her son as "l'état . . . dans lequel l'ame ne change plus, où il n'y a plus d'efforts ny de désirs et où l'on jouït d'une paix profonde et inalterable,"[66] can stand as a phantasmatic counterpoint to her scenes of penance:

> Etant donc comme abîmée en la presence de cette suradorable Majesté, Pere, Fils, et Saint-Esprit en reconnoissance et confession de ma bassesse, et luy rendant mes adorations et mes hommages, la personne sacré du Verbe divin me donna à entendre qu'il étoit vrayement l'Epoux de l'ame qui luy est fidelle: j'entendois cette verité avec certitude, et la confiance qui m'en étoit donnée m'étoit une preparation prochaine de la voir effectuée en moy. En ce moment cette adorable Personne s'empara de mon ame et l'embrassant avec un amour inex-

[64] Judith Butler, in *The Psychic Life of Power* (Stanford: Stanford University Press, 1997), writes on precisely this point (101): "Disciplinary apparatus fails to repress sexuality precisely because the apparatus is itself eroticized, becoming the occasion for the incitement of sexuality and, therefore, undoing its own repressiveness."

[65] Kolakoswski (*Chrétiens sans église*, 46) refutes the claim of the mystics that their experience is indescribable and thus incomprehensible and uninterpretable to those who have not had the same experience in the following terms: "Pretending that one cannot understand mystic texts without having oneself experienced mystic states presupposes that mystic texts are not adequate to the mystic states of their authors and that this state includes certain elements that are not communicable. I am entirely ready to recognize this restriction because it is an absolute and banal fact that it is impossible adequately to express in language the qualitative content of any experience whatsoever, for however elementary it may be. But our study deals with what is intersubjective, therefore expressible. All the mystics claim that it is absolutely impossible to describe their experiences, while nevertheless abundantly describing them, which leads us to conclude that they do think that description is, despite everything, possible to a certain degree. . . . All scientific analysis deals not with these experiences, but with their (verbal) expression."

[66] *Vie*, 706.

plicable l'unit à soy, et la prit pour son Epouse. Quand je dis qu'il l'embrassa, ce ne fut pas à la façon des embrassemens humains, rien de ce qui peut tomber sous les sens, n'approche de cette divine operation, mais il faut s'exprimer selon notre façon grossiere de parler puisque nous sommes composez de matiere. Ce fut par des touches divines, et par des penetrations de luy en moy, et d'une façon admirable, par un retour reciproque de moy en lui, de sorte que n'étant plus à moi, je demeurois tout à lui par intimité d'amour et d'union et étant en quelque sorte perdue à moy-même je ne me voiois plus, étant devenue luy meme par ma perte. Neanmoins par de petits moments je me connoissois et avois la veue du Père éternel et du S. Esprit, et ensuite de l'unité des trois divines personnnes.[67]

In this ultimate phantasmatic projection desire reaches its ultimate goal which is its own self-enclosed stasis in union with the other/lover/God. In this stasis desire would appear to attain its own paradoxical objective which is the end of desire itself. What is particularly striking about the narrative descriptions of Marie's agonies and ecstasies is their extraordinary visual detail. Despite Marie's assertion, as we've seen, that she had to make sure not to reveal her mortifications to the people around her, her writings serve as a dramatic mise-en-scène of her most intimate relations to her body and to her God. The visionary aspect of her prose illuminates the performative dimension of her attempts at creating an uncircumscribed persona for herself, at the same time that it teases the scopic impulse of the spectator/reader summoned to bear witness to this compelling spectacle of abjection and exaltation.

How are we to understand this extraordinary relation between Marie and her body, her God and her reader/son? What is the relation between spiritual exaltation and both the physical and moral masochism that is so pervasive in this text as to be its dominant trope? Even when we consider the exceptional differences that separate our understanding of spirituality from the dominant modes of such an understanding in post-Tridentine France, Marie's exorbitant descriptions strike us, as she feared they would her contemporaries, as something that situates her (as she wished of course, but not exactly as she wished), beyond the limits of the normal.

Ever since the triumph of rationalist science in the nineteenth century it has become commonplace to dismiss the excesses of female mystics as symptoms of hysteria.[68] Certainly the study of Jeanne des Anges, the pos-

[67] *Vie*, 106.

[68] Cf. Cristina Mazzoni's *Saint Hysteria: Neurosis, Mysticism, and Gender in European Culture* (Ithaca: Cornell University Press, 1996), is an interesting treatment of the interrelation of scientific discourse, literature, and mysticism in nineteenth-century culture. The reader could also consult Janet Beizer, *Ventriloquized Bodies: Narratives of Hysteria in Nineteenth-Century France* (Ithaca: Cornell University Press, 1994), and Monique David-Ménard, *Hysteria from Freud to Lacan: Body and Language in Psychoanalysis*, trans. Catherine Porter (Ithaca: Cornell University Press, 1989).

sessed abbess of the Ursuline convent in Loudun, by two of Jean-Martin Charcot's pupils, Gabriel Legué and Gilles de la Tourette, was influential, not only in applying Charcot's principles to historical figures, but of institutionalizing a diagnosis that, with its later Freudian accretions, has persisted to the present.[69] Recent work of leading feminist theoreticians in both France and the United States has done much to reveal the maculinist ideology at work in these attempts to "hytericize" woman who do not seem to fit within the normative parameters allowed them in patriarchal culture.[70] At the same time contemporary theoreticians of politics and gender as well as several women analysts have given us other interpretive strategies that I believe do not condemn all analytic attempts to describe such exalted behavior merely as ideological repetitions of the same symbolic prison from which these women were trying desperately to escape. I propose that one way we could interpret this extraordinary life is by reading it as a strangely performative scenario of (to borrow Louise Kaplan's resonant term), a specifically "female perversion."[71]

Joan Riviere's 1929 essay "Womanliness as Masquerade" has proven to be particularly influential for recent theorists attempting to redefine issues of sexual and gender identity.[72] There she described the case of a highly competent, successful woman who nevertheless was constantly self-deprecatory and childishly seductive of older men whose approval she desperately needed to ward off invasive feelings of anxiety. Riviere offered the hypothesis that her patient was suffering from enormous anxiety resulting from her own phallic aggression and castration desires: she fantasized that her professional success was in some sense due to having "stolen the father's penis/phallus," and she lived in fear of his retaliation. In order to ward off this retribution she felt obliged to "cloak" herself in the mantle of an exces-

[69] Their study which has a preface by Charcot has been reedited, see Gabriel Legué and Gilles de la Tourette, *Soeur Jeanne des Anges, supérieure du couvent des Ursulines de Loudun (XVIIe)*: Autobiographie d'une hystérique possédée (Montbonnet-St. Martin: J. Millon, 1985). Interestingly these two women met for a brief time when Jeanne des Anges, on her journey to Annecy to expiate a vow she had made, stopped off at Marie's convent in Tours, just as Marie herself was being troubled by visions of the Devil: "La mere prieure des Ursulines de Loudun passant par nôtre monastere pour aller à Annecy visiter le tombeau du bien-heureux François de Sales, je luy communiquai ce qui m'étoit arrivé; elle me dit que souvent le Diable faisoit la meme chose à leurs exorcistes" *Vie*, 206.

[70] The two best-known examples of French theory are Hélène Cixous and Catherine Clément, *La jeune née*, trans. Betsy Wing (*The Newly Born Woman*, Minneapolis: University of Minnesota Press, 1986), esp. chap. 1, "The Guilty One"; and Luce Irigaray, *Speculum de l'autre femme* (Paris: Minuit, 1974) trans. Gillian Gill, *Speculum of the Other Woman* (Ithaca: Cornell University Press, 1985).

[71] In the discussion that follows I am indebted to Kaplan's *Female Perversions* as well as to Judith Butler, *Gender Trouble: Feminism and the Subversion of Identity* (New York: Routledge, 1990), and *Bodies That Matter: On the Discursive Limits of Sex* (New York: Routledge, 1993).

[72] The essay was republished in *Formations of Fantasy*, ed. Victor Burgin, James Donald and Cora Kaplan (London: Methuen, 1986), 35–44.

sive, stereotypically acceptable form of "femininity." In other words, Riviere was suggesting that "womanliness" was not an inherent sexual feature of females, but a psychically acquired characteristic, a masquerade that women are forced to perform in order to conform to certain normative gender roles and thus to ward off masculine wrath.[73]

In her book *Female Perversions: The Temptations of Emma Bovary*, the American analyst Louise Kaplan, influenced by Riviere's seminal essay as well as by her own therapeutic work and recent discussions about ideologies of gender, has proposed a novel interpretation of a "psychic strategy" that she suggests is helpful for understanding how the unconscious (as it is understood in analytic literature) and "gender" (as it is understood in social/political psychology) come together in certain defensive "perverse scenarios." The aim or these scenarios is essentially to safeguard very early, primitive conceptions of sexuality in the face of enormous, contradictory social pressures toward gender conformity.[74] The book is extremely rich and her examples so nuanced and numerous as to make any attempt at paraphrase reductive. I shall nevertheless present what I believe to be the points most salient for our attempted understanding of Marie de l'Incarnation. This understanding (at least my understanding) cannot properly be concerned with her as a bearer of some religious truth, but as an example of a highly complex woman, positioned within the contradictions of the social, sexual, and spiritual aporia of seventeenth-century French society, a society itself in tumultuous transition.

According to Kaplan, what is essential for understanding her definition of a "perversion" is that it is a "mental strategy that uses one or another social stereotype of masculinity or femininity in a way that deceives the onlooker about the unconscious meaning of the behavior she or he is observing."[75] In other words, for Kaplan, perversion always takes the form of an elaborate scenario in which the subject of the perversion acts out a rather rigidly fixed unconscious "script." In its outward manifestation the scenario, or script, would seem to conform to normative gender stereotypes, but in fact masks unconscious conflicts about sexuality/gender that are residues of very primitive sexual trauma. Furthermore, what distinguishes a perversion in Ka-

[73] Riviere pointedly concludes (38) that there is no essential difference between the masquerade and womanliness: "My suggestion is not, however, that there is any such difference; whether radical or superficial, they are the same thing." In *Gender Trouble*, Judith Butler in her discussion of Lacan's and Riviere's notion of masquerade, poses the problem in the following terms (47–48): "Does masquerade, as Riviere suggests, transform aggression and fear of reprisal into seduction and flirtation? Does it serve primarily to conceal or repress a pregiven femininity, a feminine desire which would establish an insubordinate alterity to the masculine subject and expose the necessary failure of masculinity? Or is masquerade the means by which femininity itself is first established, the exclusionary practice of identity formation in which the masculine is effectively excluded and instates as outside the boundaries of a feminine gendered postion?"

[74] Kaplan, *Female Perversions*, 9–12.

[75] Kaplan, *Female Perversions*, 9.

plan's definition from other psychic defensive strategies is its performative nature.[76] What we have, therefore, is a defensive mental strategy, whose meaning is obviously unavailable to the protagonist of the scenarios of exaggerated virility or femininity. What is known, or rather compulsively felt, is the need to "act out" the scenario, according to immovably structured rituals. These rituals repeat very primitive conflicted conceptions of infantile sexual identity that bear the wounds of the trauma of the primal scene.[77] And as we will see in our discussions of the primal scene in Racine, these wounds will resurface in sadomasochistic fantasies of dismemberment, fragmentation and destruction.[78] According to Kaplan, the sadomaochistic impulse that is present to a greater or lesser extent in all perverse scenarios has as its desperate goal the destruction of all distinction between the sexes and the generations.[79] This distinction, or rather the acceptance of it, is the essential crux of the Oedipus complex and its resolution. Reduced to its most salient distinguishing feature the Oedipus complex implies that the human child comes to terms with ineradicable difference, the difference between the sexes and the difference between the generations. The perverse scenario, on the other hand, which is fueled by the trauma of the primal scene (a scene which although situated on one level at the opposite pole from the oedipal complex and on another is inextricably connected to it), therefore would have as its hidden, compulsive goal, the obliteration of the oedipal structure, as well as the moral and ethical universe that is dependent on the resolution of the oedipal complex.[80] It would be no less than a massive, disguised attack on the entire sociopolitical structure inside of which the subject feels both trapped and betrayed.

The above synopsis focuses on perversions in general, without being gender specific. Kaplan, however, is particularly concerned with "female perversions," which differ from perversions typically found in male patients in

[76] Ibid., 10: "A perversion is a psychological strategy. It differs from other mental strategies in that it demands a performance. . . . The enactment or performance is designed to help the person to survive, moreover to survive with a sense of triumph over the traumas of her or his childhood."

[77] Kaplan, *Female Perversions*, 127, states that "the trauma of the primal scene puts the earlier infantile traumas into a new perspective by transporting them into a situation where they are given erotic and genital interpretations. . . . The primal scene trauma consists not only of the sadomasochistic, submission-dominance fantasies that the child attributes to the parents' sexual behavior, but of his exclusion from this exciting, imagined scene."

[78] Ibid., 125: "The more adept we become at reading perverse scripts, the more we come to realize that every perversion is an effort to give some expression to, while yet controlling, the full strength of potentially murderous impulses to chew up, tear apart, explode, hack to pieces, burn to ashes, rip through to create one hole out of mouth, belly, anus, and vagina. By violating every boundary between one body part and another, the pervert totally eliminates the distinction between the sexes and with it all distinctions between child and adult generations."

[79] Kaplan, *Female Perversions*, 235, affirms that "it is the central aim of the perverse scenario to disavow the differences between the sexes or generations."

[80] For a more elaborate discussion of the complex role of the primal fantasies (of which the primal scene is one), see below chap. 5 "Racine's Oedipus."

several intriguing ways. An important difference that Kaplan finds between male and female perverse scripts is that in the latter the explicit sexual dimension (in the acting out of the perverse scenario) is not necessarily present.[81] Furthermore, and this is where Riviere's influence becomes more explicit, Kaplan suggests that although both male and female perversions exaggerate one form of gender stereotyping (i.e. hyper "virility" for men in order to disguise unacceptable feminine gender identifications), female perversions more generally display an exaggeratedly conventional (i.e. socially normative) femininity in order to mask the woman's more violent, "castrating," and competitive drives, drives that are deemed more "virile" thus socially unacceptable.[82] In other words, female perversions are perversions insofar as the female protagonist of the perverse scenario presents herself to the world as a woman but in female drag.

All the characteristics that a given society attributes to the feminine, and in the case of the seventeenth century, these would surely include humility, passivity, obedience, (sexual) innocence and ignorance, will appear in hypertrophied form in a "perverse strategy." The most perverse woman, according to Kaplan, would be one who appears as the "model citizen," and, I would add, for Classicism the model citizen of the "Heavenly City," a perfectly self-abnegating, cloistered, obedient, controlled, nun.[83] She would need the very thick walls of the convent to reassure her anxieties about the extremely powerful drives—of lust and aggression—that she fears will overwhelm her in the world.[84]

Marie's moments of most florid exaltation and most desperate bodily

[81] "The current list of paraphilias still assumes that the essential element in a perversion is that there is an obligatory precondition for sexual excitement and orgasm. It does not explain why the perverse precondition has the power to enable erections. Nor can it account for the female perversions, in which sexual excitement and sexual performance are rarely what first meet the eye and never the crucial decisive element" (*Female Perversions*, 20).

[82] "Many a brilliant and successful woman unconsciously interprets her genuine power as stolen phallic trophies. She exhibits her talents and achieves her ambitions but is always devising some appeasement for having won. She is always edgy that something terrible will happen to her unless she goes through a placation to the Gods. She survives the winning and the keeping of her hard earned power by presenting herself to her male colleagues as a saint, a self-deprecating, self-sacrificing masochistic woman." (*Female Perversions*, 272).

[83] "Or she could have become a model citizen of a utopian community—a nunnery, a commune, a collective farm. There she would have enthusiastically accepted the drab uniform and number assigned her. She would have flourished in the regimentation. Her excessive ambition to be a perfect little girl could have been satisfied by obeying the rules better than anyone else. Her bodily mortification, saintly asceticism or puritanical self-sacrifice would have been a perfect disguise for her forbidden sexual lust" (*Female Perversions*, 461–62).

[84] Of course, what must be understood in this discussion is that we are talking here not of normal individuals whose gender identity can correspond to socially expectable norms of "masculinity" or "femininity," but of individuals whose gender masquerade is compulsively necessary to quell troubling anxiety: "It is never the behavior itself that determines whether an act is a perversion but the mental energy that empowers the act and the unconscious fantasies that accompany it. We are justified only in suspecting that a behavior might be perverse if it is designed to assuage anxiety and shame" (Kaplan, *Female Perversions*, 367).

mortification come, as I've said, during the time of her early widowhood, during a period when she was unfettered from the normal constraints imposed upon women by seventeenth-century patriarchy. Widowhood had set her loose in the world. No longer bound (and protected?) by the structures within which a rigidly patriarchal society had contained her, Marie seems ill at ease in a situation that, with the obvious class and financial differences, a century and a half later the marquise de Merteuil of *Les liaisons dangereuses* was to celebrate. Rather than savor the only relative freedom allowed a woman in early modern society, the "independent" state of widowhood—the ward of neither a father nor a husband—Marie seems to come undone by the liberty this situation offers. She flees back to her father's house, choosing to isolate herself in the attic. There she gives herself over to a rigidly constructed, obsessive set of religious practices. In a sense these rituals (of ecstasy and mortification) only increase when she ventures forth, as one might say a free agent, into the rather rowdy milieu of her brother-in-law's business. It would seem that the greater the freedom that is forced upon her, the greater her sense of anxiety, and the more she needs to protect herself from what she claims is the "ungodliness" of the world. We might venture to interpret this "ungodliness" as her own sexual and/or aggressive feelings that threaten her sense of security in the world and that must be kept at bay by ever more exaggerated penitential practices. As her sense of frenzied anxiety grows, the convent with its cloistered life offers itself as the only institutional structure available to her that can reimpose, from the exterior, those limits that protect her from herself. The conventual life affords her, or so it seems at first, an institutionally established, socially validated haven where the rituals that she has elaborated to defend herself in the world can mesh with a preexisting ordered system already in place and sanctified by tradition and by the reigning sociopolitical structures.

If, however, life in the cloister has its pleasures, chief among which is the security that comes from the rigidly hierarchized organization of the convent, the minutely orchestrated routines of the body's material and spiritual obligations throughout the days, the weeks, the months, and the years, the intense satisfaction of being sequestered in an entirely female community, it also has it drawbacks: the Ursulines did not look favorably on excessive acts of mortification which struck them as perhaps a bit too "prideful," a bit too showy. What the Ursuline rule required was a docile conformity that showed, more effectively and more usefully, one's passive submission to and disappearance into the anonymity of the spiritual community. Marie, therefore, in order to conform to the rule of her order must sacrifice to this rule her penitential practices and the pleasure produced by those acts of self-mortification:

> Une des premieres choses qu'on me fit observer fut de me faire suivre la vie commune et de quitter mes tuniques de serge, mes instrumens de mortification,

> ma façon de couche, etc. et de tout cela l'on ne me laissa que ce qui s'accommodoit à la Regle. Quoyque j'aimasse la mortification, et que je me portasse d'affection à tous ces petits exercices de penitence dans le monde, je ne ressentis pas neanmoins en cette occasion une pensée n'y un mouvement contraire à l'obeissance.[85]

Marie and her censor/son are in a difficult spiritual bind here. On the one hand, the passage demonstrates (as she will continue to do throughout the remainder of the narrative) her apparently unequivocal conformity to the ecclesiastical rule of obedience. Throughout the narrative Marie insists on her blind, unquestioning submission to the rules of her order and to the religious hierarchy in general. She is careful to repeat time and again how she eschews any act of willfulness, or pride, that would make her stand out from her sister religious. In order to fit into the rule, to conform to the Law, Marie forfeits her sacrifice of the body. She abandons the pleasure of her suffering and the temporary quelling of her anxiety, of her guilt that such pleasure/suffering affords her. If, however, on the other hand, we accept that a perverse scenario always stages the conflicted dynamics of a split psyche turned against itself (there is, one has learned since Freud a phantasmatic identification with both an active and passive pole which can be identified with different psychic instances—the "ego" or the "superego," for instance—Marie's conforming to the rule of her order, while eliminating the active pleasure she tells us she had in inflicting pain on the body (or rather, on what the body represented), exacerbates the passive pleasure she receives by conforming to her society's fetishization of femininity, as docility, as meek subservience.[86] Marie's sacrifice of her secret pleasure to the law allows her the more pervasive satisfaction of appearing a perfectly dutiful daughter in the eyes of that law. In other words, we return here to the image of herself as the faultless virgin, the "chosen" object of Christ's love that we saw in her first dream/vision. In order to deserve Christ's embrace, Marie must strive for consummate humility, total submission. She must be the most perfect, that is, the most passively submissive of all her sister religious. In order to receive the passion of her divine lover, in order to keep Christ's love coming, in order in a sense to keep the paternal/godly phallus constantly desirous of her, constantly erect, Marie feels compelled to be the most abjectly passive, receptive vessel. Marie's sacrifice of her own peni-

[85] *Vie*, 180–81.

[86] Jean Laplanche in *Vie et mort en psychanalyse*, 176–77, offers the most satisfactory discussion of the sadomasochistic dialectic: "If in the sadistic scenario, pleasure is in the subject and unpleasure in the object, the introjection of the latter and its integration into a structure of the personality (the Ego) will end on the interiorization of the scene in its entirety, thereby explaining quite easily the paradox of masochism: the masochist would pleasure only through his phantasmatic identification with the active pole of the scene. . . . The fact remains that the subject is masochistic only in so far as he suffers in order to have pleasure, and not only to be able to have pleasure."

tence is a sign of what we might call her sexual enslavement to Christ. In order to keep him coming to her, she must garb herself in the holy vestments of humility and abjection, in the masquerade of a perfect "femininity."[87]

How else can we understand what Marie tells us of her experiences of convent life, of its joys and its disappointments? Despite her having abandoned her son, defied her family, and braved society's hostile judgment in order to enter the convent, once inside what she herself describes as an "earthly paradise," and once having given up her sadomaochistic enactments, she has the last of her ecstatic visions and then is overcome by melancholia. Having conformed to the law by abandoning the mistreatment of her body, this body begins to mistreat her. She begins to experience terrible migraines that will remain with her for the rest of her (cloistered) life. At the same time, she is troubled, she tells us, by visitations from the devil who inspires evil, blasphemous thoughts in her. Finally, in desperation she even entertains thoughts of suicide.[88] With the end of her ecstatic visions, what she sacrifices in the form of active bodily pain/pleasure, returns to haunt her body and mind:

> Me voilà replongée dans l'abîme de mes croix; il ne me sembloit pas qu'il dût jamais y avoir de consolation pour moy; parceque mon ame étant entierement dans la tristesse et tous mes sentimens crucifiez de toutes parts, je ne croyois pas qu'il y eût esperance d'en sortir. Je pensois s'il n'y avoit point quelque creature qui me pût aider, mais il me sembloit qu'elles avoient toutes du mépris pour moy et quoyque je visse clairement qu'à cause de mes malices elles avoient raison de m'avoir en horreur, cela ne laissoit pas de me mettre dans une angoisse interieure qui estoit extreme. Me voyant si imparfaite, j'eusse voulu que l'on m'eût mise dans le dernier avilissement, car comme je voyois mes

[87] Kaplan talks about the female perverts "sexual" thralldom to her lover: (211). She borrows the term *Hörigkeit* from Richard Von Krafft-Ebing who used it to describe "sexual bondage or extreme sexual submissiveness" which he attributed more generally to women than to men. Kaplan writes (*Female Perversions*, 215): "*Hörigkeit*, like all perversions, is a full-time occupation. The woman afflicted with *Hörigkeit* lives only for her moments of ecstatic *unio mystico* the sexual union in which the man's mighty phallus confirms the outlines of her feminine self. Without this she is relentlessly self-critical. . . . She is quick to acknowledge that she is nothing without her lover. She speaks of her lover's erect penis the way the fetishist speaks. . . . With it inside her or potentially inside her, she feels complete and whole and good and electrifyingly alive. . . . As the slave of love knows all too well, love can always be taken away, but power is eternal. She is bound to her lover because only an eternally erect penis can confirm her femininity."

[88] Cf., for example, 204: "Quelque tems apres que je fus revétue du saint habit de la Religion, . . . les tentations commencerent à m'attaquer de toutes parts . . . c'étoient des tentations de blaspheme, de deshonnesteté, d'orgueil . . . il me sembloit que j'étois trompée du Diable." The devil twice visits her, at night, in her cell; she describes (205) that "je ne fus pas plutôt sur ma couche, qu'il se presenta à mon imagination un spectre horrible en forme humaine, que je voyois aussi clairement qu'en plain jour quoy que j'eusse les yeux fermez et que je fusse sans lumiere; il avoit un visage long, tout plombé et bleuâtre, les yeux plus gros que ceux d'un boeuf, et pour se moquer de moy il me tira sa langue longue et épouvantable avec une grimace et un hurlement effroyable que je crû avoir été entendu de tous les dortoirs."

fautes je croyois que toutes mes soeurs les vissent aussi clairement que moy, et dans cette pensée je ne paroissois en leur presence qu'avec honte et confusion.[89]

It would seem that once Marie is forced to abandon the actual physical mistreatment of her body, an abuse that contained its own charge of erotic release, what Freud termed "moral masochism," an underlying sense of abjection, guilt, and self-punishment, returns in fantasies of unworthiness, where she is pursued by self-recriminations, moral castigations, and paranoid doubts.

In *The Economic Problem of Masochism*, Freud, while distinguishing between three types of masochistic behavior, nevertheless emphasizes that all types of masochism are interconnected and that they are fueled by a sadistic and labile libido that is inextricably connected to the anxieties of the oedipal drama.[90] His intricate explanation of "moral masochism" seems particularly suggestive for understanding the complex dynamic involved in Marie's self-deprecations, her intense sense of abjection, and what strikes us as an irrational need for chastisement.

According to Freud, "moral masochism" would represent a struggle between the ego and forces in the "superego." The latter, he has told us, is the product of "the introjection into the ego of the first objects of the id's libidinal impulses—namely the two parents."[91] However, through the resolution of the "Oepidus complex," the ego's relation to these two primitive imagoes becomes delibinalized, sublimated and through this sublimation, the "superego," an abstract sense of conscience, emerges. In other words, according to Freud's schema, the "superego" comes to stand in for the primitive ego's libidinal rapport to an introjected, fantasized parental couple.[92] Depending on the social context in which the child develops, this "abstract" sense of conscience will become, in certain people, attached to a sense of the "dark powers of destiny," and embodied in such notions as "Providence, . . . God, or . . . God and Nature."[93] In "moral masochism," Freud argues, this desexualized relation to the forces that supposedly rule our destiny becomes resexualized. Borrowing from his discussion in a previous essay, "A Child Is Being Beaten," where he had established in that sadomasochistic scenario the analogy between being beaten by the father and the desire to "have a passive (feminine) sexual relation to him," he now

[89] *Vie*, 220–21.

[90] Freud, *The Economic Problem of Masochism* (Standard Edition, 19:161): "Masochism comes under our observation in three forms: as a condition imposed on sexual excitation, as an expression of the feminine nature, and as a norm of behavior. We may, accordingly, distinguish, an *erotogenic*, a *feminine*, and a *moral* masochism. The first, the erotogenic, masochism—pleasure in pain—lies at the bottom of the other two forms as well."

[91] Freud, *The Economic Problem of Masochism*, 19:167.

[92] "In this process the relation to those objects was desexualized; it was diverted from its direct sexual aims. Only in this way was it possible for the Oedipus complex to be surmounted. The super-ego retained essential features of the introjected persons—their strength, their severity, their inclination to supervise and punish" (*Ibid.*).

[93] Ibid., 168.

speculates that at work in that fantasy is a regressive return, through masochism, to the unavowable oedipal desire for a "sexual" relation with the punishing/ loving parent. For Freud the perverse force of "moral masochism" would be this regressive potential. It is the "discovery" that what appears to be the product of a purely abstract morality in fact enables the forces of the libido to break away from their sublimated cathexes, and to reestablish, albeit unconsciously, their primitive erotic attachment to their first objects of love and hate. The Oedipus complex continues to exert its libidinal pull in and through "moral masochism," constantly exciting the subject to ever more abject self-recriminations because these recriminations, are, in essence, sexually stimulating. "Conscience and morality," Freud concludes, "have arisen through the overcoming, the desexualization, of the Oedipus complex: but through moral masochism morality becomes sexualized once more, the Oedipus complex is revived and the way is opened for a regression from morality to the Oedipus complex."[94]

In Marie's case, therefore, we can see, if we apply Freud's insights to her own intensely expressed sense of guilt and abjection, another side of a complex, perversely libidinalized scenario that functions across her erotico-mystic experience. Despite her attempts to flee the constraints of patriarchal filiation, despite her rupture with a "world," which in the first third of the seventeenth century is being brought more firmly into line by the redeployment of the imperatives of a expanding patriarchal/absolutist society, Marie appears caught in an oedipal structure that is reaffirmed by the very "abstract," metaphysical structures to which she turns in her flight away from the body and its unruly drives. In the course of the century, even as Christianity becomes (in its institutional forms) more "intellectual," more abstract, and in line with the political imperatives of Absolutism, it remains for Marie and her sister religious, anachronistically trapped in its essential contradictions—primarily the doctrinal paradox of the flesh made word, and in the ritual of the Holy Eucharist, of this word being transformed into flesh. Marie's piety, as her new religious name never ceases to remind us, is based on the wonder of the Incarnation, the divine made flesh, and with this flesh, itself inscribed within the parameters of the "oedipal family" (father, mother, child) as a site of adoration and reconciliation, Marie's attempts at flight into the life of the spirit through her religious practices in the language, images, and rituals that are available to her constantly reinscribe the world she would disavow and its desires in her mind and body. These devotional rituals attempt to go through or beyond the body, but, by the very libidinal force that impels them forward, they can only return again and again, in ever more exacerbated and agonizing forms to rekindle the fires they are supposed to drown.[95]

[94] Ibid., 169.

[95] This perverse phenomenon of the libidinal force of "renunciation" that undermines renunciation is discussed by Butler, in another context, in *The Psychic Life of Power*, 56: "Pro-

Marie seems trapped in a roundelay in which these various types of masochistic behavior continually feed upon each other while finding their ultimate social/religious justification in that pillar of Christian and mystic life, the *imitatio Christi*. While Marie, on one level, can exteriorize her masochism, through an identification with, and "impersonation" of, the suffering of Christ, thus fantasizing seeing herself as Christ, that is, as masculine, on another level, she projects to herself and to the world the image of herself as the "bride of Christ," the perfect, abjected "feminine" subject.[96] We return here to some primitive androgynous, or perhaps more properly bisexual indeterminacy where Marie oscillates between active and passive identifications that her world and her own inscription of herself as a (conflicted) subject in that world coded as "masculine" and "feminine."[97] We must not forget that at the bottom of the different perverse scenarios always lurks some dimly lit but powerful scene of parental coupling in which the two fantasized partners are indistinguishable from each other (that is, they are not as yet opposed as clearly defined "sexed" subjects), and it is this very indistinctness that is freighted with a heavy dose of oedipal anxiety and, of course, sadomasochism. In a certain sense, we can interpret Marie's passive and active masochism as the perverse acting out of the confused sexual identifications of her personal primal scene in which she plays out on her own inner stage the indeterminate, not yet differentiated, roles of the active, "sadistic" father and the passive, masochistic mother, in scenarios of "marriage," of "union," and in fantasies of abjection and guilt, that are at one and the same time ecstatic and terrifying. In a more profound sense, we might even speculate that in her own private phantasmatic scenarios, Marie is acting out her society's particularly patriarchal prejudices, by having the "active," masculinely identified part of her psyche attack and punish the "body," that feminine-identified codification of the material that is inseparable from the sexual, the corrupt, and, of course, the corrupting.

Riviere's essay "Womanliness as Masquerade," so important for Kaplan's theorization of the perverse scenario has also proved essential for Ju-

---

hibition seems to reproduce prohibited desire and becomes intensified through the renunciation of its effects. . . . In a sense, then renunciation takes place through the very desire that is renounced, which is to say, that desire is never renounced, but becomes preserved and reasserted in the very structure of renunciation."

[96] C. Walker-Bynum has argued convincingly for our understanding of how a certain conception of the "femininity of Christ" was important for medieval spirituality, while affirming the traditional and conventional attributes of virility and patriarchal presence. Cf. esp. *Fragmentation and Redemption*, chap. 3, "The Body of Christ in the Later Middle Ages: A Reply to Leo Steinberg," 79–119.

[97] Both Marie and Claude on several occasions comment on her strength, even her virility. Cf. *Vie*, 183: "Je vous assure qu'il me faut un courage plus que viril pour porter toutes les croix qui naissent à monceau, tant dans les affaires particulieres que dans les generales du pais." Kaplan writes (*Female Perversions*, 509): "The feminine and masculine roles that are enacted in a perversion, male or female, epitomize in dramatic forms the very social gender stereotypes and social role conventions that a perversion pretends to be subverting and undermining."

dith Butler's recent discussions of the convoluted sociosexual dynamic at work in gender strategies. In *Gender Trouble,* after rehearsing the many permutations of Riviere's own reading of female aggression, Butler offers her own interpretation of the autobiographical aspect of the paper. It is an interpretation that has resonance for Marie de l'Incarnation despite the centuries-wide gap separating this seventeenth-century nun from us. Butler writes:

> Riviere explains the fear of retribution as the consequence of a woman's fantasy to take the place of men, more precisely, of the father. In the case that she herself examines, which some consider to be autobiographical, the rivalry with the father is not over the desire of the mother, as one might expect, but over the place of the father in public discourse as speaker, lecturer, writer—that is, as the user of signs rather than a sign-object, an item of exchange. This castrating desire might be understood as the desire to relinquish the status of woman-as-sign in order to appear as a subject within language.[98]

What was Marie's early identification with the preaching orders except, precisely, the desire to take the word, to become quite properly a "speaking subject" in the world, a role that as we've seen was absolutely denied her because of her sex. We cannot tell what Marie's father's reaction to her childish imitation of preachers was. There is very little mention of him in the *Vie*. We do know, however, that after the death of her husband Marie returned to live in her father's house, a situation that seemed to be mutually beneficial. We also know that her father was opposed to her taking religious vows, claiming he would never survive her leaving him. And he didn't. Besides abandoning her son, therefore, we might be led to speculate that Marie's taking the veil had other more dire, one might even think, sadistic consequences for her guilty conscience: she "killed" her father.[99] Her desire to find a place for herself as a subject outside of the social and sexual limits imposed on her by her world was we might suppose subtended not only by an "active" masochism but, as we have learned since Freud, by an equally present, if covert, sadism.

That the sadistic side of Marie's religious devotion should surface most directly in her convoluted relation to her son, in the relation that continually draws her back no matter how far she flees to the conflicted ties of family and sexuality, is everywhere apparent in her narrative. This sadism is both hidden and revealed in the unctuous formulaic piety with which she expresses her wish to see, to hear of, and even to help in her son's immolation in the service of God: "Il ne se passe jour que je ne vous sacrifie à son amour sur le coeur de son bien-aimé fils: plaise à sa bonté, que vous

[98] Butler, *Gender Trouble*, 51.

[99] Vie, 182: "J'eus encore un autre assaut, mon Pere qui étoit âgé lorsque je le quittay m'assura qu'il mourroit d'affliction si je me retirois. . . . En effet il mourut six mois apres."

soyez un vray holocauste, tout consommé sur ce divin Autel."[100] Claude himself, in his role of "scriptural echo," by transporting the mundane into the divine through the use of the religious allusions, repeats and underlines his mother's mortiferous wishes for him. In a telling passage he compares his mother's abandonment of him to Abraham's sacrifice of the young Isaac:

> Ce fils étoit un Isaac et un unique, que Dieu luy avoit donné pour éprouver sa foy et son amour; mais aussi il ne luy donna pas moins de force et de courage pour l'immoler qu'il en avoit donné à Abraham pour luy sacrifier le sien. Je ne doute point qu'un abanonnnement si nouveau et si contraire en apparence aux plus étroites obligations de la loy naturelle ne soit condamné de ceux qui ne se gouvernent que par les lumieres de la raison et qu'il ne soit même improuvé de quelques uns de ceux qui ont connoisssance des regles de l'Eglise puis qu'il se trouve des Conciles qui defendent aux Meres sur peine d'excommunication d'abanonner leurs enfans. Mais il faut avouer que les lumieres surnaturelles sur tout quant elles éclairent les Saints qui n'agissent que par les mouvements de la grace, font voir les choses tout d'une autre maniere que ne font celles de la seule raison. Je ne doute point que la lumiere qui fit voir au Patrirache Abraham qu'il pouvoit luy-même immoler son propre fils, apres que la voix de Dieu luy en eût fait le commandement, fût la même qui fit voir à cette ame genereuse, qu'elle pouvoit abandonner le sien, après que Dieu luy eût tant de fois declaré que c'étoit sa volonté.[101]

The violent images of "sacrifice," "immolation," and "holocaust" reverberate throughout this mother/son dialogue. In a letter to Claude that he inserts in his commentaries we read Marie's declaration of her Christian concern for him: "O, que je serois heureuse si un jour on me venoit dire que mon fils fût une victime immolée à Dieu! Jamais Sainte Simphorose ne fut plus contente que je le serois. Voila jusqu'où je vous aime, que vous fussiez digne de repandre votre sang pour Jesus-Christ." Perhaps even more pointedly she offers this confession of maternal affection: " Que je serois consolée, si on me venoit dire que vous eussiez perdu la vie pour Jesus-Christ. Et si je me trouvois dans l'occasion qu'on vous fît cette insigne faveur, nôtre divin Epoux me donne assez de courage pour vous repousser dans le feu ou sous la hache, en cas que vous voulussiez esquiver le coup par la foiblesse de la nature."[102] Although we can make rather large concessions for the rhetorical excesses of Counter-Reformation spirituality and especially to the heady evangelical zeal of Marie's own baroque style, a style in which the "concettist" topos of "life not life and death not death" that she inherited from several generations of Spanish mystics would not be unexpected, it appears nevertheless that the passion which infuses her descriptions of the tor-

[100] *Vie*, 448.
[101] *Vie*, 171.
[102] *Vie*, 455.

tures and martyrdom that she wishes for her son also offer us a more ambivalent view into her fantasy life and its underlying sadomasochism.[103]

Although Marie never had the ultimate satisfaction of seeing her son martyred for the cause, she came as close as she could. In a letter to Claude that he inserts as part of his own ongoing commentary to her *Vie,* we learn that while in Canada Marie had the satisfaction of learning that a converted Indian boy whom she called her "adopted son" had been tortured and killed for the greater glory of God.[104] The joy of feasting on the torture and death of her "son" is, we are persuaded, bound to her assurance of the eternal bliss that awaits him as one of God's chosen rather than to the delectation afforded her sadism by the grisly contemplation of the boy's demise. Nevertheless, the gruesome rhetorical scene she describes cannot but have its effect not only as a manifestation of her own perverse scenario, but of Claude's and the reader's as well:[105]

> Il y avoit à Quebec un jeune homme qu'elle aimoit selon Dieu, et qu'elle avoit comme adopté par affection, parce qui'il lui representoit celui qui étoit veritablement son fils. Ce jeune homme étant tombé entre les mains des Hiroquois, et ayant été martyrisé par ces barbares elle en fit une feste, témoignant une joye tout à fait sensible de la grace que le Ciel lui avoit faite, et desirant qu'il en fît une semblable à son fils, voicy ce qu'elle en écrit: J'avois un fils spirituel âgé de vingt deux ans nommé Joseph, lequel m'aimoit comme sa mere propre. Il a été trois jours et trois nuits dans des tourmens horribles en derision de nôtre sainte Foy, qu'il a confessée hautement jusqu'au dernier soupir de sa vie. Ce courageux serviteur de Dieu redoubloit ses prieres et ses louanges dans les tourments, car il chantoit fort bien, et cela faisoit enrager ces Barbares. N'ay-je pas

[103] The complex interweave of religious devotion, evangelism and sadism is difficult to disengage. It would appear that this desire for the "martyrdom" of the other is rather prevalent among the small, fervent group of female missionaries to Canada and their male supporters. M. de Bernières, who agrees to a bogus marriage in order to protect Mme de la Peltrie, the benefactress of the new convent, from the financial demands of her family, seems to harbor similar saintly /murderous desires for his departing friends (383): " La mère de l'Incarnation ne lui [i.e. Bernières] faisoit point de pitié, mais il souhatioit qu'elle fut sacrifiée, ou immolée ou brulée toute vive pour Jesus-Christ et il faisoit paraître de semblables desirs pour Mme de la Peltrie."

[104] Michel de Certeau, in his essays "The Institution of Rot," in *Heterologies: Discourse on the Other,* 40, talks of "the hidden alliance between mysticism and torture." Marie offers a detailed description of the torture and death of several Jesuit missionaries (*Vie*, 541): "Ces barbares se contenterent de faire mourir le simple peuple de leurs supplices ordinaires qui sont la hache et le feu. Mais au regard des peres qui étoient les Apôtres et les Fondateurs de l'Eglise, il ne se peut dire combien ils leur firent endurer de tourmens. Ils leur briserent premierement les membre de coups de bâtons, puis ils les firent brûler à petit feu leur enfonçant des tisons ardants par tout le corps, il firent ensuite rougir dans le feu le fer de leurs haches et leur en firent des coliers, et parce qu'ils avoient veu autrefois baptiser des sauvages convertis, ils firent chauffer de l'eau et quand elle fut toute bouillante, ils la leur verserent sur la teste en derision de ce saint Sacrement."

[105] Kaplan astutely remarks that the description of perverse scenarios of patients invariably "stir up" corresponding perverse scenarios of the analyst/writer/ reader (cf. *Female Perversions*, 17).

> là un bon fils: c'est plutôt mon pere et mon avocat aupres de Dieu. Je suis ravie de la haute grace qu'il a receue en perserverant jusques à la fin. Si l'on m'en venoit dire autant de vous, mon tres-cher fils, Ah, qui pourroit dire la joye que j'en recevrois?[106]

This last example will serve as a rhetorical set piece that lays out some of the most imposing psychic, spiritual, and textual conundrums that coexist in what can only be described as the baroque excess of this text. Joseph, Marie's "adopted" and martyred son, is called both her father and son by her, just as she is, by implication, both his mother and (spiritual) daughter. In the larger scope of the text this is the precise strategy that enables Claude both to assert and obfuscate the (sundered) ties that join him to Marie. By the semantic slippage allowed by the words—"mother," "sister," " father," "son," and "brother," not to mention "husband" and "wife," as they refer both to a biological family and a spiritual, religious community—the family is constantly evoked in its material, affiliated, that is, human and oedipal sense, at the precise moment when this sense is evacuated in favor of the newly installed spiritual commonwealth that supersedes it. Instead of a familial, that is bodily, bond, Marie and Claude are joined by their mutual participation in the holy community that is the body of Christ. This same rhetorical strategy that plays on the spiritual and textual communion joining mother and son also functions both to undo the familial/biological ties that connect them, and at the same time, and in a curious fashion, to reassert their imperishability.

In a typically baroque gesture the text is analogous to its subject: the body is used as the central object of our attention in so far as it is always a polymorphous and polysemic signifier, always pointing, at the same time, to the material and to the spiritual. Claude is free, therefore, to play with the religious title of "mother," as he declines his newfound relation to Marie according to both religious and secular filiations. Marie, in turn can appear as a "sister" to her son, and even, as he represents a religious superior, as his "daughter." What we are dealing with in this text, therefore, is a rhetorical strategy that, borrowing its metaphors from the vocabulary of family, attempts to destructure the familial trap while creating a new spiritual lineage, free from the ties to the body, free from genealogy. Despite all the rhetorical strategies that would liberate the subjects from familial ties, however, ties that reassert the presence of the body, and resituate them within the confines of a new spiritual family, this very rhetoric constantly reinscribes these ties at the center of this impossible community. Their disavowed origin continues to inhere in them. At the same time, and by the same token, this drive to undo what we may call the oedipal trap when it is framed, as it is here, within a narrative in which the body is ever present

[106] *Vie*, 455.

and yet forever attacked, where the subject is perpetually enmeshed in a ceaseless round of sadistic and masochistic fantasies reveals the phantasmatic presence at the heart of this and possibly all utopian constructions whose "utopianism" consists precisely in denying the body, through its displacement, fragmentation, and demise. On one level Marie's ardent wish for her son's immolation hides its sadistic drive under the generous guise of her Christian faith: the resurrection of the body is guaranteed by Christ's own triumph over death. In a sense this unshakable conviction of the triumph of life over death, of life in death which is one of mysticism's central tenets can, on another level, be also seen as one of the building blocks of narcissism.[107] Narcissism and mysticism would find their most intimate join in their relation to and their fantasy of the death and rebirth of the subject. The body remains, in life, what must be punished and abused because it is always a sign of the constant danger of not being good enough, pure enough, abject enough. Marie tells her son in a letter that even at the very end of her life when she was old and racked with pain and disease she was constantly tormented by the fear that all her years of work and penance could be effaced in an instant by a betrayal of the body: "Quand je pense neanmoins que je suis pecheresse et que par le malheur de cette condition je puis tomber en tel etat que je sois privée de l'amitié de mon Dieu . . . je suis humiliée . . . et je me sens saisie d'une crainte que ce malheur ne m'arrive." This same body in death, however, in a sense becomes the "perspectival object" of all mystic longing, the narcissistic "proof" of life's triumph over death, of the victory and incorruptibility of the divine.[108] And it is in Canada that this ultimate fascination with the body in death reveals its true hold on her and us.

In the convent at Tours Marie had a vision of a "beautiful lady with a babe in her arms," who was accompanied by a robust but older man. The woman reveals to her a distant landscape and tells Marie that she must go to this new land and build a "house" for Jesus. In a sense Marie's childhood wanderlust resurfaces as the constraints of conventual life prove too confining for her "apostolic" ambitions. At the same time the oedipal contours of this vision strike us as remarkably different from her usual "erotic" visitations. In these latter Marie sees herself alone with her father/son/lover. There is a melting of subjectivity as her heart and the sacred heart of Christ blend together or, on another occasion, the interpenetration of the one into

[107] Guy Rosolato, in his essay "Présente Mystique," 14, draws our attention to this relay—mysticism, narcissism, death: " But the fundamental paradox which is at the heart of mysticism is the same upon which narcissism is constructed: the paradox of death in life but especially of life in death, of death and resurrection, or, to sum up in one word the irrational or the mystery; resurrection, the key, the foundation, the pivot of narcissism."

[108] *Vie*, 713. See Rosolato, "Présente Mystique," 15: "The mystic path purports to live and relive death itself as the Unknown Other (the God of religion) and thus offering itself as its perspectival object the cadaver."

the other until all boundaries of the self are undone in God.[109] Here, however, her desire to leave the convent and to leave France is supported by the vision of the "human," oedipal "holy" family: mother, father, and baby. For all her own struggles with the constraints of family, Marie nevertheless insists in her spiritual dialogue with her "heavenly spouse" on the inviolability of the family: "Je le priois en outre de n'en point separer le grand saint Joseph, parceque j'avois de fortes impressions que c'étoit lui que j'avois veu être le gardien de ce grand pais . . . j'avois en l'esprit que Jesus, Marie, et Joseph ne devoient point être séparés."[110] The translation of the Ursulines from Tours and Paris to New France, this escape back to the less confining (for women) time of the "early Church," takes place paradoxically under the banner of the oedipal family and the entire sociosexual order that that order supports.[111]

Her resolve to found a convent in New France triumphs over many familial, religious, and social obstacles and finally in 1639 Marie sets sail for Quebec. Although her life in Canada provides us with fascinating details about early French colonialism in the New World, what concerns me more here is that her Canadian sojourn is marked by yet another major alteration in her mystico/bodily narrative.[112] In Canada, her ecstatic visions and visitations are "withdrawn" from her.[113] Actively engaged in the day-to-day administration of the new convent and its school, Marie seems to have finally felt that her sex and her "apostolic" vocation were no longer incompatible. Just as in Tours, however, when her special relation with God is put on hold, here in the New World her depressions, migraines, and moderate mortifications resume and continue until her death in 1672.

It would seem that this fascination with the body, its relation to both salvation and death, takes an ever more prominent place in her narrative as she ages in the harsh environment of Canada. As the life becomes increasingly focused on its end, death and the fate of the body become the narra-

[109] *Vie*, 70: "Aussi une fois je sentis que l'on avoit pris mon coeur et qu'on l'avoit enchassé dans un autre coeur; et quoi que ce fussent deux coeurs, ils étoient si bien unis que ce n'en étoit plus qu'un." Vuarnet remarks (*Extases féminines*, 19) that the image of the exchange of hearts had since St. François de Sales become stereotypical in mystic discourse.

[110] *Vie*, 317.

[111] This is a popular theme in mystic discourse. It (the oedipal familial structure) also functions in the discourse of possession and exorcism. Cf. M. Greenberg *Subjectivity and Subjugation in Seventeenth-Century Drama and Prose: The Family Romance of French Classicism* (Cambridge: Cambridge University Press, 1992), chap. 3, "Passion Play: Jeanne des Anges."

[112] Marie's life in Quebec is fascinating for its rich description of life in the new colony. That part of her story is not, however, the focus of my discussion and I must refer readers to the work of either Bruneau or Deroy-Pineau (above, n. 8) who are more concerned with the "colonial" aspect of Marie's narrative.

[113] *Vie*, 403: "Lorsqu'elle passa en Canada, Dieu lui trancha les visions, les revelations, et toutes les autres communications de cette nature, et lui commanda de mener une vie commune."

tive's perspectival focal points, both hiding and revealing the drives, fears, and unconscious motivations that the narrative keeps at bay.[114] We are kept abreast of the different deaths (natural, catastrophic, and accidental) that befall not only her sister religious but the colonists in general and the native peoples whose lives intersect with the convent on a daily basis. A morbid delectation is at work in these descriptions which would seem to indicate an endless horror/fascination with the fate of the body that remains the constant reminder of both her fallen state and her desired triumphal salvation. But, in certain circumstances this fallen state itself can be redeemed and in those cases the body is called upon to bear witness to its own *Aufhebung* to its translation from a sign of corrupt materiality to an emblem of divine love.

One of Marie's most loyal aides—Marie de St. Joseph—who had accompanied her from Tours to Canada, died in 1644. The life of this nun is recounted in great, pious detail by Claude. She was, we are assured, almost as saintly as Marie. Several "miraculous" interventions are attributed to her.[115] Twelve years after her death the sisters decide to exhume her body and rebury it in the nave of their newly rebuilt church. The body was duly disinterred, but before the new burial: "la Mere de l'Incarnation eut desir en le changeant de cercueil de voir en quel état il étoit." While at first it was decided to open the old coffin in secret lest the younger sisters be shocked by the sight, to the surprise of all, what awaits them in the coffin is not what was feared:

> Mais il arriva tout autrement; car le corps étant découvert ne rendoit aucune mauvaise odeur, et bien loin de donner de la frayeur, celles qui étoient presentes furent remplies d'une joye et d'une consolation si grande qu'elles croioient être dans le Paradis. Les costes et les autres ossemens du corps étoient entiers et placez en leur lieu naturel. Il n'y avoit rien de pourry ny de corrompu, la chair étoit seulement fondue et coulée au fond du cerceuil où elle s'étoit convertie dans une pâte toute blanche de l'épaisseur d'un doigt, en sorte que l'on eût dit qu'elle nageoit dans le lait. Il n'y avoit que la substance du cerveau et celle du coeur qui étoient demeurées entieres. Dieu n'ayant pas permis que le premier qui avoit été l'organe de tant de saintes pensées, ny que l'autre qui avoit conçu tant de bons desirs et fait tant d'actes d'amours fussent sujets aux loix du

[114] The idea of the "objet de perspective" was first put forth by the French psychoanalyst Guy Rosolato in *Éléments de l'interprétation* (Paris: Gallimard, 1985). Tom Conley, in his *Film Hieroglyphs: Ruptures in Classical Cinema* (Minneapolis: University of Minnesota Press, 1991), xxii–xxiii, has glossed the concept in the following way: "This term applies to the way subjects . . . visualize or indicate through the bias of speech nodal points in their descriptive relation to the world they see and live. . . . It figures a concentrated point of attention that captures what a subject chooses to see, simply because in it resides what cannot, because of its paradoxical evidence and accessibility, be seen."

[115] *Vie*, 602: "Depuis la precieuse mort de cette pure et innocente vierge beaucoup de personnes tant de la France que du Canada l'ont invoquée dans leurs necessitez tant spirtuelles que corporelles, et ont declaré qu'elles ont reçu de Dieu ce qu'ils avoient demandé par son intercession."

> Sepulcre. . . . Aucune ne fut effrayée de voir et de toucher ce corps, non plus que la masse blanche ou chair consommée. . . . Au contraire toutes furent penetrées d'un sentiment d'amour et de devotions envers cette precieuse defunte et c'étoit à qui baiseroit ses ossemens et luy rendoit les derniers devoirs de la pieté Chrétienne, les ossemens étoient huilleux et rendoient une odeur d'iris, tres douce et tres agreable.[116]

The body has been reduced to the fragrance of irises, to milk, with its two most important organs, the mind and the heart intact. Death has been overcome. What remains is not the horror of fleshy corruption but the symbol of divine transcendance. It is to this transcendance that Claude will bring his mother, at the end of her long life and decidedly exceptional life. Although he knows that only the Pope can officially sanctify her life, Claude makes a strong case for Marie's eventual beatification. To prove to the world and even more, we must assume, to himself that this "universal" mother was a saint whose love for God and for His creatures was so overwhelming that it raised her above common humanity, and therefore above mere human concerns, such as her abandonment of her son, and of her maternal responsibilities, Claude excuses the weakness of the flesh by tracing its elimination.[117] As the narrative reaches the end of Marie's earthly existence she will be reduced to a nonbody, a body cleansed of all its earthly imperfections, where only the quintessence, a mere whiff of an iris, sign of the body's transcendence remains.

In a ceremony of rhetorical divestment Claude describes, one sense at a time, Marie's final triumph over her body. Taste, smell, sight, and touch are transformed in a litany of abnegation and transformation:

> Elle avoit tellement mortifiée les appetits de la bouche que sa vie étoit un jeune continuel, et elle mangeoit si peu qu'à peine prenoit-elle suffisamment de la nourriture pour la soutenir. On ne la pouvoit voir manger sans être édifié.[118]

> Quand elle rencontroit des charognes puantes et des cloaques infectes ou quelque autre semblable puanteur, elle y demeuroit le plus qu'elle pouvoit avec autant de plaisir que les plus sensuels pourroient faire parmy les parfums les plus delicieux.[119]

> Que dirai-je de la mortification de la vue? C'est principalement en ce point qu'elle faisoit voir qu'elle étoit morte aux créatures. Elle avoit toujours les yeux fermés.[120]

[116] *Vie*, 603.
[117] Marie de l'Incarnation has not been sanctified by the Catholic Church. She has been elevated to the rank of "Venerable."
[118] *Vie*, 620.
[119] *Vie*, 621.
[120] *Vie*, 622.

> Mais c'est principalement sur le toucher qui est un sens universel et étendu par tout le corps qu'elle a exercé les rigueurs de sa mortification . . . à force de grandes macerations des haires et des cilices ses membres se trouverent enfin tout engourdis et comme demy-morts.[121]

Step by step Marie has beaten the body down, reduced it to the merest shadow of itself and by so doing has, or so Claude would have us believe, transformed her body, her self, into an object of veneration. Marie's baroque excess has become the perfect Classical female body. What remains is a nothing, a diaphanous absence, the body finally traduced offstage, out of sight. Rather than the spectacularly ecstatic body of Marie's spiritual marriage to Christ, a body displayed in its excess, or the abjected, mortified body, a body of blood, of suffering, of wounds, a body of smell and taste, the last images we have of her is of the body effaced. She has been reduced to nothing, to the scent of an iris, or perhaps, in her case, the headier fragrance of a narcissus. In her gradual effacement, Marie becomes "Our lady of perpetual renunciation," Claude's personal and direct channel to God. Claude has traduced this mother who left him into a symbol of the new Classical Age—"our St. Teresa," as Bossuet will call her. In order to accede to the place of St. Teresa, Marie and her writings, her ecstatic visions and bodily mortifications pass under and through the censorious gaze of her son and emerge transformed. We can only wonder, however, if Marie—who had to leave France and travel to the ends of her world, to Canada, a journey which is, as we have said, at one and the same time a voyage out (in space) and back in time (the fantasy of returning to the primitive Church) in order to escape those social contradictions that inhere in her and from which she never ceases to suffer—would be entirely content with her reinsertion into this new dialogue. In this refashioned conversation, her passionate intercourse with her lover/God is superimposed on a new mother/son dialogue in such a way as both to reiterate her flight from her earthly ties to sexuality and to the body and constantly to reaffirm them also. The publication of her life with its filial emendations condemns her to continually reinscribe this body in the familial/social system she fled through those scenarios she passionately enacts before the eyes of the world, scenarios whose religious rhetoric can only barely subsume their phantasmatic oedipal pull. This public exposure can always be read in an ambivalent manner, therefore, both as a refusal of a system of patriarchal containment which she on one level successfully challenged, fleeing into a world of empowered femininity, and which, on another, through the continuous efforts of her son, reinscribes her, phantasmatically, in the sexual/libinal structure that she cannot escape and that he would not have her renounce.[122] The only resolution to this tan-

[121] Ibid.

[122] Kaplan in *Female Perversions* makes the point that although the perverse scenario purports to undermine the social system it mimics, it only succeeds in reaffirming it. Cf. 367,

gle of familial resentment and spiritual transcendence is the narration itself, the remnant that is left after the final disappearance of the body and its ultimate translation into words. The words, however, always bear the imprint of not one but two bodies. The work of two hands, Narcissus's and Echo's, the text, that is, joins them across the physical and spiritual abyss, that forever and at the same time sunders them. It is in the reading of this denied but curiously shared life that these two wounded subjects can at last be reunited, perhaps only in print but, in that sense at least, also in history.

---

where she states that "a perversion, when it is successful, also preserves the social order, its institutions, the structures of family, the mind itself from despair and fragmentation," and again, 509: "The feminine and masculine roles that are enacted in a perversion, male or female, epitomize in dramatic forms the very social gender stereotypes and social role conventions that a perversion pretends to be subverting and undermining."

5 *Racine's Oedipus:*
Virtual Bodies, Originary Fantasies

Every myth points back to an origin. Any interrogation of origins necessarily opens onto myth.

Jean Paul Valabrega, *Phantasme, mythe, corps et sens*

Because no form of power is total . . . the body continues to exercise a disturbing influence even when it is absent.

Francis Barker, *The Tremulous Private Body*

Thus the itinerary of Freudian psychoanalysis would be a quest for . . . what of the body resides in words, is inscribed in traces, or remains engraved in memory to such an extent that it appears only as reminiscence.

Pierre Fédida, "L'anatomie dans la psychanalyse"

THERE IS A FUNDAMENTAL PARADOX at the heart of any discussion of Racinian dramaturgy. While the tragic dilemma of Racine's theater is profoundly anchored in the passionate, forbidden sexuality of its characters, passions that are inextricably tied to the desiring body, this body is absent, banished from the lexical construction of the Racinian text. How are we to understand the conundrum of a theater that, more than any other, presents sexual desire and its frustration as the enchafed crucible of tragedy, when the crucible itself has been exiled from the field of representation? Almost all contemporary commentators on Racine have argued that "incestuous" desire, that is, the body's sexual transgression of its culture's limits, is the crucial, tragic element at the heart of his drama. In its plots and peripeteia, Racine's theater ingeniously reconfigures how his protagonists are to negotiate the difference between the generations and between the sexes without referring, except in the most oblique terms, to the body. It is this body, nevertheless, that bears the burden of failing to comply with a law that always proves too restrictive of the characters' passion.[1] Tragically, death intervenes, in extremis, to remind us of the body's presence, but only, so it seems, when the body is most definitively erased from the dramatic stage.

Racinian theater appears to be a totally "disincarnated" drama.[2] There is, of course, the pervasive presence of the "eyes," a presence that has attracted the attention of Racine's exegetes in its doubly involuted function: simultaneously an organ of vision and an avenue of entrance into the psychic life of the characters. At the same time the ambivalence of the eyes, an opening both outward and inward, allows for the translation of interior emotion into exterior physicality—tears. [3] Polite verbal testimonies to the body also betray its veiled presence. Besides *voir*, verbs such as *frissoner*, *pâlir*, *rougir*, *trembler* all point to a site from which these actions issue, but which remains itself beyond discourse, or rather, wholly subsumed in a discourse of allusion.[4] At the very same time that these verbal constructions seem to point almost secretively to the body in which they are grounded, they also immediately point away: they signal the inappropriateness of any more specific allusions to what is after all the tragic center of Racinian theater. Instead of this body, what the Racinian text describes is an "aura," the effects of the body are translated into a chiasmatic rhetoric: a language that is totally decorporealized (in the sense that the writings of a Rabelais, a Montaigne, or, as we have seen, a Molière are "embodied") and yet that

[1] Both Roland Barthes (who states in *Sur Racine* [Paris: Seuil, 1963], trans. Richard Howard, *On Racine*, [New York: Hill and Wang, 1964], 9, that "incest, rivalry among the brothers, murder of the father, overthrow of the sons—these are the fundamental actions of the Racinian theatre" and Charles Mauron (who writes in *L'inconscient dans l'oeuvre et la vie de Racine* [Paris: Corti, 1969], 30, that "oedipal incest and its derivatives are found all through Racine"), the two critics most profoundly marked by psychoanalysis, have underlined the essential "incestuous" kernel at the heart of Racinian tragedy.

[2] A paradox made all the more intriguing if we follow Anne Ubersfeld, one of France's most articulate exegetes of theater, who claims that drama is in essence corporal: "The fascination of the theater . . . is due first of all because it is an object in the world, a concrete object, and then because its materiel is not an image but real objects and beings: human beings, above all the bodies and voices of the actors. . . . Theatrical praxis is materialist: what it says is that there is no thought without bodies; the theater is made up of bodies and the body comes first and asks to live" (*Lire le théâtre* [Paris: Éditions Sociales, 1978], 300).

[3] See, for instance Jean Starobinski, *L'oeil vivant*, (Paris: Gallimard, 1961) "Racine et la poétique du regard," 71–89. Barthes, *On Racine* 22, states that "in Racine there is what we might call a fetishism of the eyes." Jacques Schérer (*Racine et/ou la cérémonie* [Paris: P.U.F., 1982], 32) points out that of the 4088 words in Racine's dramatic vocabulary, the verb *voir* appears "at the top of the list" with 1156 examples. The art historian Norman Bryson, writing about seventeenth-century French art (*Word and Image: French Painting of the Ancien Régime* [Cambridge: Cambridge University Press, 1981], also discusses, in his chapter on Lebrun, the disappearance of the body with special reference to Racine: "In Racine, who was also, we remember, the Court's historian, the body is almost entirely optical, . . . the rest of the body has been erased and discarded and all that is left of it is this all-signaling zone around the orbits of the eyes; as the last trace of a natural body which remains ungovernable by the will."

[4] Cf. Barthes, *On Racine*, 15: "The Racinian body is essentially disturbance, defection, disorder."

continues to bear the impress of the absent body if only as a lingering affective resonance.

The justification most often invoked to explain the absence of any but the most veiled references to the body in its *Kreaturlichkeit* of course is the concept of *bienséance* which, when coupled with those other rules of French neo-Classical protocols, the "three unities," can be seen as doing to the theatrical body precisely what Foucault suggested the general epistemic shift of the seventeenth century did to those suddenly socially undesirable others—the mad, the heterodox, the feminine. The body is circumscribed, limits are imposed on it (limits to its visibility), it is objectified as foreign to a certain esthetic (but also sexual and political) ideal, and then it is banished.[5] The body in French Classical drama is expelled from the stage, exiled to another site, to the *coulisses* of representation because its presence proves too disruptive of the absolutist call to order.[6] If we follow Foucault's argument, we can see that the seventeenth century in its diverse discursive practices, of which *bienséance*, must figure, begins to encircle a carnality that in its excessiveness proved too threatening to the unitary order that was being elaborated. The "quiddity" of bodies on stage proves too seductive.

That the appeal of the body could always seduce the spectator, could undermine the entire moral /religious order so shakily in place[7] is shown to us in the diaries of François Hébert, curate of Versailles, who writing of his vaguely troubling discomfort upon viewing the young ladies of Saint-Cyr performing in *Esther* reveals both the enticement and danger of the body. He writes in his journal: "Croyez-vous d'ailleurs qu'il soit fort décent à des personnes de notre caractère d'assister à une tragédie représentée par des jeunes filles fort bien faites, et qu'on ne peut pour lors se défendre de regarder pendant des heures entières? N'est-ce pas s'exposer à des tentations et le peut-on en conscience?" In another passage he continues in the same vein "Quelques courtisans . . . m'ont avoué que la vue de ces jeunes demoiselles faisait de très vives impressions sur leur coeurs que, sachant qu'elles étaient sages, ils en étaient incroyablement plus touchés que de la vue des comédiennes."[8]

[5] I am referring here, as I will continue to do, to Michel Foucault's idea of the "great enclosure," the symbolic movement he describes in *Histoire de la folie à l'âge classique* (Paris: Gallimard, 1961) by which difference is imposed, through a defensive gesture of "othering." This gesture, translated into epistemic terms, is one way the early Foucault proposed to see the rupture between the world of the sixteenth century (of the Renaissance) and that of the eighteenth (Classical representation). The seventeenth century straddling this divide participates unevenly in both.

[6] For the history of the imposition of the three unities and the notion of *bienséance* see Jacques Schérer, *La dramaturgie classique en France* (Paris: Nizet, 1959).

[7] For an overview of the fear of both the body and the body's presence in/as theater see Jean Delumeau, *Le péché et la peur : La culpabilisation en Occident, XIIIe–XVIIIe siècles* (Paris: Fayard, 1983), esp. chaps. 15 "Péché et péchés," and 16, "Le modèle ascétique."

[8] *Mémoires du curé de Versailles,* quoted in Raymond Picard, *La carrière de Jean Racine* (Paris: Gallimard, 1956), 425. The inherently amoral aspect of the theater, its socially and morally disruptive potential is the subject, overt or covert, of the antitheatricalist debates

To avoid these "vives impressions," all attempts are made, when it comes to staging *Athalie* at the same place, to render the demoiselles as unappealing as possible, without removing them entirely from the stage: there are no more elaborate costumes, no throngs of courtiers admitted nightly to see the play, no dancing, no music.[9] What remains is a theater "where there is practically no physical description."[10] In its stead we have, on stage, before our eyes, bodies reduced to being but "talking heads," bodies that are there and yet curiously absent. Or rather, the presence of the body is not in the body, but of the body, the body transformed into language. And, paradoxically, this language, in order to be proffered, must be embodied, of course, must be spoken to an audience, an audience whose participation in the passion and tragedy of the Racinian hero returns the body to itself but in a different place. For, confronted with a tragic world from which the body is effaced, Racine's audiences respond corporally; they weep.

Writing to Mme de Sévigné, the marquise de Coulanges tells her, "*Mithridate* est une pièce charmante, on y pleure; on y est dans une continuelle admiration."[11] In his own preface to *Bérénice,* Racine refers to the tears of his audience, tears that he thinks reflect the pleasure his tragedy has given them: "Je ne puis croire que le public me sache mauvais gré de lui avoir donné une tragédie qui a été honorée de tant de larmes, et dont la trentième représentation a été aussi suivie que la première."[12] As for *Iphigénie*, in the *Entretien sur les tragédies de ce temps* (Mar.-Apr. 1675) we find the following dialogue : "Avez-vous vu *Iphigénie*? demande lui. C'est une pièce dont bien des gens ont été charmés. —Je l'ai trouvée fort belle, répond l'autre, et même, je n'ai pas honte de dire que je n'ai pu m'empêcher de pleurer une fois ou deux en la voyant."[13] The audience weeps thus signaling an affective resonance—the sign that the trials of these characters reduced to the status of talking heads becomes "incorporated" in those bodies that are at the margins of the represented universe, those bodies that are silently, breathlessly present at the sacrifice that the play unfolds before them.

The body, banished from the realm of dramatic representation, resists, remains present, but displaced to the margins of representation, to the audi-

---

throughout the century. See Jonas Barish, *The Antitheatrical Prejudice* (Berkeley: University of California Press, 1981), a good overview of the heated debates surrounding the role and social function of theater in the sixteenth and seventeenth centuries.

[9] See Picard's discussion of the production of *Athalie* at Saint-Cyr, *La carrière de Jean Racine*, 415–422.

[10] Leo Bersani, *A Future for Astyanax: Character and Desire in Literature* (Boston: Little, Brown, 1976), 19.

[11] Quoted in Picard, *La carrière de Jean Racine*, 176.

[12] Preface to *Bérénice*, in Jean Racine, *Théâtre complet* ed. Maurice Rat (Paris: Garnier frères, 1960), 300. All subsequent references are to this edition.

[13] Quoted in Picard, *La carrière de Jean Racine*, 221. Picard tells us, in reference to *Bérénice*, that "Racine was right to be proud of the tears that had honored his tragedy: they were a sign of his audience's communion in tender feelings" (166).

ence. Nevertheless, how are we to understand this plangent pleasure, these tears, signs of an affective state, which the psychoanalyst Joyce McDougall tells us is situated in an indeterminate locus, floating between psyche and soma: "An affect," she writes, is "never a purely psychic phenomenon nor purely a somatic one."[14] Yet the question remains, what "affect?" Why are these eyes weeping, what have they seen, what have they come to see that induces tears? Or perhaps, a more pertinent question, a better question, since we are dealing with "affect" would be, What have they heard? What have the remains of the body, traduced into the voice of the actors, told them? And how has this telling moved them to tears?

In a sense, and by way of a very preliminary answer, we can propose that these are tears of mourning, the melancholic tears of a body responding to its own effacement, its (self-) immolation on the stage of French Classicism. The Classical stage represents the ceremony by which and through which the modern, passionate ego is called into being by the sacrifice of what was its grounding in a world that no longer exists. It was vanishing in the tumultuous cauldron of change that seventeenth century France underwent in its evolution from an outmoded feudal society to the triumph of the absolutist monarchy. It was in this period of change and sacrifice that a new subjectivity emerges. And, I would suggest, it emerges precisely in that indeterminate space separating and joining the Racinian spectacle to its spectators. It is a reticent and melancholy space, the tearful space of tragedy.

The stately image of Classical France to which we have been accustomed by almost two hundred years of academic history tends to obscure a reality of almost constant social and religious turmoil. In his essays on cultural history, Guy Rosolato has remarked that it is always in periods of crises, periods that mark the end of an old order and the as-yet-unsure beginnings of a new regime that the rituals of scapegoating and of sacrifice assume an unprecedented role in the actual or imagined life of the state.[15] Certainly seventeenth-century France, oscillating on the fraught divide between the world of the Renaissance and the universe of Classical representation, proves no exception to this rule.[16] In the most obvious sense can we not see the series of spectacular executions (Marillac, Montmorency, Cinq-Mars, de Thou) where Richelieu lays the foundations of the absolutist state, as a succession of nobiliary sacrifices? In these ostentatious executions a waning feudal order is forced to recognize its own impotence in front of emergent

[14] Joyce McDougall, *The Many Faces of Eros* (New York: Norton, 1995), 157.

[15] Guy Rosolato, *Le sacrifice, repères psychanalytiques* (Paris: P.U.F., 1987), 180: "Sacrificial activity becomes exceptionally intense during periods of crisis when conflict threatens the power of the leader, when a new ideology starts to appear and is recognized only by a minority that has not as yet the means to realize its objectives."

[16] I am using here for heuristic purposes the great division of epistemic models that we find in Michel Foucault's early writings. See *Les mots et les choses: Une archéologie des sciences humaines* (Paris: Gallimard, 1966) and *Histoire de la folie*.

Absolutism and the new socioeconomic imperatives of which divine right monarchy is the most seductive metaphor. Among the different social and religious roles of the sacrificial act, one stands out. In the atmosphere of impinging chaos, the immolation helps to reaffirm limits, both temporal and spatial. Sacrifice is always seen as an originary act, an act that establishes a before and an after.[17] Spatial limits tracing a border between an inside and outside, between, in a sense, an "us" and a "them" are also constituted. In this sense the parameters that serve to define the habitus of a community are justified by this act.[18] By constituting these limits, both temporal and spatial, a community defines itself over and against its other(s).[19]

The sacrificial ceremony, furthermore is inherently theatrical: a stage is set upon which the officiating priest and his helpers confront an innocent victim. Around them, around the altar, the members of the community, the other actors in this spectacle, stand in witness. Without the testimony of these onlookers a sacrifice would prove meaningless. Thus, from its very center, in its spectacularity, the ceremony of immolation appears structurally analogous to the theater. It may even be, as many have argued, that the origins of theater are to be found in sacrificial rituals. Sacrifice and theater, particularly tragic drama, seemed conjoined at their origins and their end: both have a particularly telling role in representing to the community the laws of the sacred and the consequences of their transgressions. In order to exist as a cohesive unit society must be constantly reminded of its past, its origins, its aspirations, and its promised continuity into the future.

In ancient society, the locus of sacrifice, and in a later, more developed polities, the place of the stage represents the foundational rituals through which a nation recognizes itself. It is not simply a felicitous coincidence that the English word "scaffold" (as the French *échafaud*, from whence it derives) in its earliest meanings referred to the platform upon which either an execution was carried out or a drama performed.[20] By sundering the body of the guilty victim, sacrifice/execution uncovers, according to Foucault, the most radical dissymmetry that exists between divine (or "divine right")

[17] "Every sacrificial act . . . should be a point of departure, an origin" writes Rosolato (*Le sacrifice*, 47).

[18] Ibid., 87, Rosolato states that "the sacrificial victim marks the boundary between outside and inside. . . . The sacrifice has value only on the inside of the tribe." René Girard in his several books (*La violence et le sacré* [Paris: Grasset, 1972] and *Le bouc émissaire* [Paris: Grasset, 1982], although thoroughly informed by psychoanalysis, prefers a Christological approach to his similar discussions of the dynamics of scapegoating and sacrifice. For the importance of sacrifice in early Greek culture, one should also consult Walter Burkett, *Homo Necans: The Anthropology of Ancient Greek Sacrificial Ritual and Myth*, trans. Peter Bing (Berkeley: University of California Press, 1983).

[19] "There is, therefore, a symbolic birth or rebirth of the group the symbol of which insofar as its origin is real, historical and mythic becomes fixed on the sacrifice." (Rosolato, *Le Sacrifice*, 68).

[20] See, for an elaboration of this analogy, Mitchell Greenberg, *Corneille, Classicism and the Ruses of Symmetry* (Cambridge: Cambridge University Press, 1986), introduction.

power and mere quotidian resistance.[21] Although the violence of the scaffold was never far removed from the lived experience of most seventeenth-century urban life and, as the illustrations of the Callot brothers makes clear, quite a common sight across the length and breadth of rural Europe, there was a constant displacement at work during the period by which the violence of the sacrificial act, its bloody reality, was, for courtly society and that portion of the bourgeoisie that defined itself in the image of court life, gradually transposed from the executioner's block to the theatrical (and eventually operatic) stage. We might propose here, with the promise of greater elucidation in a moment, that the theater, especially the passionate tragedy of Racinian drama, in its plots but also, and perhaps more important, in its function as social mediator, continues to enact the ongoing fascination of the sacrificial ritual carried over and transformed in the realm of dramatic sublimation.[22] In both cases we are called upon to witness the im-

[21] Michel Foucault, in *Discipline and Punish, the Birth of the Prison* trans. Alan Sheridan (New York: Pantheon, 1977) points out that the execution of criminals, especially those accused of lèse-majesté, were designed to point out the enormous dissymmetry that existed between the king (the law) and the criminal who dared contravene his prerogatives (52): "The public execution, then, has a juridico-political function. It is a ceremonial by which a momentarily injured sovereignty is reconstituted. It restores the sovereignty by manifesting it at its most spectacular. . . . Its aim is not so much to re-establish a balance as to bring into play, as its extreme point, the dissymmetry between the subject who has dared to violate the law and the all-powerful sovereign who displays his strength." And, he continues, 130, that "in monarchical law, punishment is a ceremonial of sovereignty; it uses the ritual marks of the vengeance that it applies to the body of the condemned man; and it deploys before the eyes of the spectators an effect of terror as intense as it is discontinuous, irregular and always above its own laws, the physical presence of the sovereign and of his power." Curiously, Freud makes a similar point about why the audience of a tragedy pleasures in the afflictions that befall the hero in "Psychopathic Characters on the Stage" Standard Edition (above, introduction, n.2), 7:306: "It [i.e. drama] appeases, as it were, a rising rebellion against the divine regulation of the universe, which is responsible for the existence of suffering. Heroes are first and foremost rebels against God or against something divine; and pleasure is derived, as it seems, from the affliction of a weaker being in the face of divine might."

[22] The primordial role of theater as a social mediator by which the individual is inserted in the collective is underscored by Ubersfeld (*Lire le théâtre*, p. 39): "It is becoming clear that theatrical activity, as representation, is above all, a dialectical space." "Every theatrical text is the response to a demand on the part of the audience, and it is here that is most easily made the articulation between theatrical discourse, history and ideology" (256). For a discussion of the "translation" of the scene of sacrifice in the seventeenth century from the executioner's block to the religious practices of Catholicism, see Jean-Marie Apostolidès, *Le prince sacrifié: Théâtre et politique au temps de Louis XIV* (Paris: Minuit, 1985). Lest this association I am proposing between the sacrifice and theater appear too facilely "a-historic" let me offer the following anecdote about the "premiere" of *Britannicus* which was poorly attended because, according to Jeanne Roche-Mazon in her *Autour des contes de fées* (Paris: Didier, 1968), 140–41, it took place at the same time as the execution of the marquis de Courboyer, guilty of the crime of lèse-majesté, who was executed, after being tortured, at three o'clock in the afternoon, place de Grève: "At the same time that day, the *comédiens français* of the Hotel de Bourgogne, were sounding the three bells announcing the beginning of their play. They were to perform for the first time a new tragedy, called *Britannicus*. Boursault, the poet, was at that instant entering the theater, fearing that he would be 'crushed in the crowd,' and that he would find the theater full of the enthusiastic fans of this M. Racine whom he did not like. But, to his happy surprise, the theater was almost empty: the marquis de Courboyer, who that very day was demonstrating

position of the law that for many psychoanalytically informed anthropologists and sociologists would ultimately be the "incest-taboo," the moral imperative by which a particular society defines the place of the subject in relation to the difference between the generations, and the difference between the sexes. It is this law that is universally present in all commonwealths and that precisely establishes the difference between human and nonhuman societies.[23] Understanding that sacrifice is a punishment of and retribution for the transgression of these limits helps us to see how the Oedipus legend (as myth and drama) can be viewed as the particularly invested link among the incest taboo, the ritual of sacrifice, and the origins of tragic theater.[24]

There is, obviously, a difference between the actual sacrificial ritual and its translation into/as representation. For, as Nicole Loraux, reminds us, even in those more "primitive" times of ancient Greece, while the polis, in its tragedies, offered itself the ambivalent pleasures of those many scenes where young virgins are offered up in sacrifice, it was representing in tragedy what the state would never have dreamt of enacting in reality: "Of course, in real life the city did not sacrifice its young girls, but during a performance it gave its inhabitants the double satisfaction of transgressing in imagination the taboo of *phonos* and about dreaming about virgins' blood."[25] Loraux is underlining here the duplicitous sadomasochistic dynamic of tragic representation which, as Freud had already implied, is an essential part of the compelling fascination the theater exerts on its audience.[26] And as she does, so must we underline the importance of this transgressive satisfaction as imaginary, that is, as a highly convoluted psy-

---

his nobility to the public, had attracted to his show [i.e., his execution] all the merchants of the rue St. Denis who normally go to the Hôtel de Bourgogne to see the premieres of all the plays that are performed there. . . . *Britannicus* had no success, and without a doubt Mme d'Aulnoy is, at least in part, responsible. At the same time that her clever novel was reaching its conclusion on the scaffold, the few spectators present in the Hôtel de Bourgogne were not clear-headed enough to listen to Agrippine and Néron. They were all thinking of what, at the same moment, was happening in the place de Grève."

23 "The law is first and foremost a moral law, the law of family and the prohibition of incest." (Guy Rosolato, "Du père," in *Essais sur le symbolique* [Paris: Gallimard, 1966], 53).

24 For an elaboration of the "oedipal" undercurrent of seventeenth-century tragedy, see Mitchell Greenberg, *Canoncial States, Canonical Stages: Oedipus, Othering and Seventeenth-Century Drama*, (Minneapolis: University of Minnesota Press, 1994), introduction. See also for its particular importance for Racine, Philip Lewis, "Sacrifice and Suicide: Some Afterthoughts on the Career of Jean Racine," in *Biblio 17, Actes de Baton Rouge* 1986, 53–75.

25 Nicole Loraux, *Façons tragiques de tuer une femme* (Paris: Hachette, 1985), trans. Anthony Forster, *Tragic Ways of Killing a Woman* (Cambridge: Harvard University Press, 1987), 33.

26 Freud, "Psychopathic Characters on the Stage," 7:307: "Suffering of every kind is thus the subject-matter of drama, and from this suffering it promises to give the audience pleasure. Thus we arrive at a first precondition of this form of art: that it should not cause suffering to the audience, that it should know how to compensate, by means of the possible satisfactions involved, for the sympathetic suffering which is aroused." For a further elaboration of the inherently masochistic nature of theatrical pleasure, see Jean-François Lyotard, "Oedipe juif," in *Dérive à partir de Freud et Marx* (Paris: 10/18, 1973), and Phillipe Lacoue-Labarthe, "Theatrum Analyticum," *Glyph*, 2 (Baltimore: Johns Hopkins Press, 1977). See also Michel Gribinski, "A l'italienne," in *Nouvelle Revue de Psychanalyse*, 46 (1992): 69: "It could be said that

chic act in which individual fantasies and collective myths are, for a moment, allowed to coalesce and to produce theatrical pleasure. In the sacrificial function of theater is an extremely rich area of overlap, where the external social, political, and sexual ideologies that legislate the public life of the citizen (with their corresponding myths) in the polis, come inverted into the intrapsychic life of the spectator and, for the time of the spectacle, they cohabit, reflecting each other in the affective response of the spectator to the theatrical illusion.

Perhaps no dramatist of the Classical age better understood and manipulated this ambivalent space where outer reality and inner fantasy intermixed than Racine. In all his tragedies the protagonists waver between the demands of the state and the demands of passion, demands that are, in fact, inseparable. The impossibility of divorcing the one from the other, along with their irremediable confusion, a confusion that is at the very heart of the tragic dilemma, finds its most compelling metaphor, as countless commentators have suggested, in the ambivalent image of the Racinian altar.[27]

The presence of the altar in all the tragedies becomes an even more compelling image because, in Racinian tragedy, as compared (an unavoidable comparison) to his predecessor Corneille, the altar, among its other dramatic functions, is that overdetermined metaphor that represents the impossible separation of the public and the private spheres. Whereas in Corneille the family mirrored the state, there was still a separation possible between the two. In Racine, we have moved to the far side of the "great enclosure," that divide that marks the rupture of the two conflicting epistemic systems which, Foucault suggests, presides over seventeenth-century thought. Here in Racine where from the beginning, in *La Thébaïde*, the family is the state, there is no longer any division possible between the political dimensions of the tragic and the private world of the protagonists. The origin of the tragedy and the origin of the family are confounded: they are one and the same.[28] Sex and politics are shown, *ab origine*, to be conjoined. The founding moment of the state is a sexual/ political moment, the coupling of the throne and the bed:

> Malgré tout son orgueil, ce monarque si fier,
> A son trône, à son lit daigna l'associer . . .
> (*Bajazet*, II, i)

we have a sacrificial practice of pleasure and fantasy and that we thus rediscover through that practice the genesis of theatrical drama: drama comes from sacrificial rites."

[27] "In Racine's tragedies we find an enigmatic and mute character—the altar—which is the symbol of ambivalence because we never know, until the last second, if the priest who approaches the altar is there to celebrate a marriage or to perform a sacrifice," Charles Mauron, *L'inconscient dans l'oeuvre et la vie de Racine* (Paris: José Corti, 1969), 37.

[28] For an elaboration of this discussion see Mitchell Greenberg in *Subjectivity and Subjugation in Seventeenth-Century Drama and Prose: The Family Romance of French Classicism* (Cambridge: Cambridge University Press, 1992), chap. 6, "Racine's Children."

Before, however, we are able to enter this extremely rich space of overlap, the space where private phantasy and public myth intermingle in Racinian tragedy, we must confront one of the most ideologically glaring battles of seventeenth-century French society. For, as we move across the century the ongoing evolution of sensibility in the continuing struggle between carnival and Lent, the epistemic legacy of a subjectivity incarnated in what we have been calling the carnivalesque body is abandoned, immolated in a chain of significant, punctual gestures. Throughout the century, in different venues, the body in its *Kreaturlichkeit* is sacrificed to a discursive order in which its vanishing into invisibility becomes the mark of Classicism's gradual but eventual victory as a representational imperative.[29] That Racine is the heir to this century-long battle and in a perverse sense one of its greatest technicians compels us, before confronting the dynamics of fantasy and myth in Racine's sovereign tragedies, fantasies which all find their affective anchor in the body, to uncover the dynamics of the immolation of that body that served to define the epistemological parameters of Classical representation inside of which Racine moved with such grace and passion.

In the ongoing dialectic between the grotesque and the Classical the body is dealt its most devastating blow not from the center of absolutist France, but from the forlorn periphery of a ravaged Teutonic province. Alone, in war-torn Germany, warmly ensconced beside his *poêle*, Descartes, an itinerant French soldier/philosopher describes for us the method with which he wishes to sweep away the structures of scholastic philosophy and magisterially to impose the foundations of (what will become known as) the unitary ego. What is particularly intriguing in this celebrated anecdote is that the modern ego is brought into being by and through its own narration: the Cartesian "moi" emerges on the stage of Western philosophy in and as its own originary fable. And this fable, like all fabular origins is predicated on a sacrifice, the sacrifice of what the Cartesian ego casts as its other, the body:

> Puis, examinant avec attention ce que j'étais, et voyant que je pouvais feindre que je n'avais aucun corps, et qu'il n'y avait aucun monde, ni aucun lieu où je fusse; mais que je ne pouvais feindre, pour cela, que je n'étais point; et qu'au contraire, de cela même que je pensais à douter de la vérité des autres choses, il suivait très évidemment et très certainement que j'étais; au lieu que, si j'eusse seulement cessé de penser, encore que tout le reste de ce que j'avais jamais imaginé eût été vrai, je n'avais aucune raison de croire que j'eusse été: je connus de là que j'étais une substance dont toute l'essence ou la nature n'est que de penser, et qui, pour être, n'a besoin d'aucun lieu, ni ne dépend d'aucune chose

[29] The body's erasure, as a sociological phenomenon, is traced by Norbert Elias in *The Court Society* (New York: Knopf, 1980), and *The History of Manners*, trans. Edmund Jephcott (New York: Pantheon Books, 1978).

> matérielle. En sorte que ce moi, c'est-à-dire l'âme par laquelle je suis ce que je suis, est entièrement distincte du corps, et même qu'elle est plus aisée à connaître que lui, et qu'encore qu'il ne fût point, elle ne laisserait pas d'être tout ce qu'elle est.[30]

With this sacrifical gesture, Descartes inaugurates the reign of a unitary ego capable of self-reflection and self-knowledge, able to cast a cool glance at the ambient universe, judge it, measure it, and ultimately colonize it. This ego that situates itself at the center of the world of unreliable appearances seizes itself, first and foremost, in its abstraction. Descartes's first gesture of separation begins by radically sundering the mind from the body. The body denied is banished to the world of appearances. It becomes for the Cartesian universe an object, an object of representation, an object of discourse. In this investiture the body in Descartes is reduced to the cadaver, both an object of empirical science and of horror.

Although Descartes's "Method" is the most famously innovative of seventeenth-century theories, his discursive gesture of bodily abandonment, if we follow Francis Barker whose book *The Tremulous Private Body* has influenced my own thinking, participates in a general ideological revolution by which the emergent bourgeois subject situates itself in the world. In a complex and rich argument Barker traces the emergence of "bourgeois subjectivity" though readings of several idiosyncratically chosen seventeenth-century writers (Pepys, Shakespeare, Descartes, Milton, Marvell) and through an analysis of Rembrandt's painting "The Anatomy Lesson." Barker follows the early Foucault, extending the latter's hypothesis of the "great enclosure" to include precisely the subjective positioning and affective resonances of the "body." It is, Barker believes, the epistemic shift by which the body becomes exiled from itself, split off, as we have seen in Descartes's text, from its grounding in/as the subject, and then exiled into representation, that marks the beginning of the interiorized, "guilty" subjectivity that characterizes the emergence of what will become known as the bourgeois subject. The body, marginalized, placed just beyond the borders of discourse, nevertheless, continues, from its exile, to exert pressure on the representational imperatives that have banished it:

> The carnality of the body has been dissolved and dissipated until it can be reconstituted in writing at a distance from itself. As the subject, in a private condition writes, from that blind place within which it is necessarily blind in order to see, of necessity censored in order to write, it unfolds itself now within a mode of representation which is no longer of a substance with the materiality of the old body. As the flesh is de-realized, representation, which becomes at last representational, is separated from it. . . . Neither wholly present, nor

[30] René Descartes, *Discours de la méthode*, ed. Geneviève Rodis-Lewis (Paris: Garnier Flammarion, 1966), 60.

wholly absent, the body is confined, ignored, excribed from discourse, and yet remains at the edge of visibility, troubling the space from which it has been banished.[31]

Descartes's text forcefully participates in the seventeenth century's turn toward the modern principally by this excising of the body from the realm of intimate cerebration. Even when the body is allowed to return (as in his discussion of the heart and the circulatory system in part 6), it comes back into the text as an object (a corpse), a dissected exemplum offered up to the anatomical gaze of emerging empiricism.[32] Descartes removes himself from the "great theater of the world," to think and to write the birth of the integral ego. This new ego, at first, turns away from chaotic existence, turns away from the body, the Boschian carnivalesque body's insertion in its world, represses that body. Yet we might speculate that by this forcing of that body (and its world) into the realm of representation, into the realm of the invisible, and thus into what will become known as the "unconscious," it reinforces philosophically a certain "oedipalization" of the unconscious, the unconscious as an oedipal scenario. Jean-Joseph Goux has gone so far as to suggest that in this philosophic turn away from body, in the institution of a philosophic method based on this repression, Descartes can be described as a truly oedipal philosopher:

> No philosopher allows us to appreciate the Oedipean strategy better than Descartes. In this sense, it is appropriate that Descartes's thought should be viewed as the starting point for the philosophy of the modern era. With Descartes, the very order of his method . . . rigorously repeats the sequence of signifcant moments in Oedipus's story. . . . It is quite clear that beneath the intellectual precision of Descartes's philosophemes we rediscover with astonishing precision the no less rigorous sequence of mythologemes that constitute the Oedipean posture. Of course, what is involved is not a simple transposition, but the persistence of a configuration, a decisively deepened understanding of a certain regime of subjectivity that was prefigured whether Descartes knew it or not, by Oedipus's. Murder of the father, response to the Sphinx, possession of the mother: Descartes gives a perfected ontological dimension to the protophilosophical mechanism typified by the Oedipus myth. Each of these three great moments in the heroic Oedipean drama can be recognized in the three great moments of Descartes's undertaking.[33]

[31] Francis Barker, *The Tremulous Private Body: Essays in Subjection* (London: Methuen, 1984), 62–63.

[32] For the return of the body in Descartes, cf. Barker, *The Tremulous Private Body*, 100–103. See also Luce Irigaray's discussion of the Cartesian body (in relation to "admiration") in *Éthique de la différence sexuelle* (Paris: Minuit, 1984), 75–84. See also Dalia Judovitz, *Subjectivity and Representation in Descartes: The Origins of Modernity* (Cambridge: Cambridge University Press, 1988).

[33] Jean-Joseph Goux, *Oedipe philosophe* (Paris, Aubier, 1990), trans. Catherine Porter, *Oedipus, Philosopher* (Stanford: Stanford University Press, 1993), 159–60.

The new ego, the product of a method that is a sacrifice, surely re-creates simultaneously with its own emergence, if only for its pleasures, new stages on which to recount, and by the recounting, naturalize its own autochthonous birth. For the interiorized, psychological subject of modernity, heir to Descartes's fable, effectively mirrors the seventeenth century's representational turn. This twist away from the body, the body's reposition as a discursive object, and the way this object nevertheless continues to exercise pressure from those same margins of discourse that would exclude it coalesce in the passion(s) of the newly born interiority. This subject and his passions will reappear, in turn, at the center of that society's greatest tragic creations. New "theaters of the mind," which also must be "theaters of the (repressed) body" stage for that ego (and for us) the ritual acts of sacrifice and redemption that allow it, in the turbulent life of seventeenth-century Europe, to establish its own foundations, to stage for itself its own originary narratives.[34]

While Descartes sat alone in his wartime retreat mapping the body's demise, at the same time the creators of the myth of absolute monarchy from Richelieu to Louis XIV, with their cohort of economic, esthetic, and religious propagandists, invested immense amounts of psychic, political, and, economic energy (and Racine, as we know in his role of court historian, participated actively in propagating this myth) in creating the stage upon which the person and the persona of the king, in his "corps glorieux," were able to represent themselves as a transcendental essence of the French nation. So while, philosophically, the body is sacrificed on the altar of the (emergent) unitary ego, politically, the body of the king, the idealized masculine body of Louis XIV, came to embody the transhistorical quintessence of the French nation at a time when that nation vigorously and pointedly attempted to impose both its culture and its politics across Europe.[35]

It has been argued that the entire thrust of French Absolutism's hegemonic policies coalesce in and as the representation, the heavily invested narcissistic representation, of the king's body.[36] In the countless portraits (pictorial, sculpted, and rhetorical) disseminated during his long reign, but also in the panegyric descriptions of his prowess in war, in love, and as a patron of the arts and sciences, Louis XIV was transformed into a transcendental image of the glorious nation whose essence he embodied. The image of the king, the king as image—the resplendent portrait(s) of Rigaud, for in-

[34] I am borrowing the terms "theater of the mind" and "theater of the body" from the psychoanalyst Joyce McDougall. See her *Théâtres du je* (Paris: Gallimard, 1982) and *Théâtres du corps* (Paris: Gallimard, 1985).

[35] See Louis Marin, *Portrait of the King,* and *Food for Thought*. See also, J. M. Apostolidès, *Le roi machine*. For detailed references on these works, see above, introduction, n.7.

[36] Ernst Kantorowicz's book, *The King's Two Bodies: A study in Medieval Political Theory* (Princeton: Princeton University Press, 1957), has been at the origin of the spate of studies on the ideological manipulation of the iconographic representations of the king in early modern Europe.

stance—purported to present a vision of royal majesty that always appeared as an asymptotic ideal held out to astonish the king's national and international audience. For what the image that Louis's "corps glorieux" reflects, in a time of enormous social change, is a pervasive desire for unity, for a nonvulnerable integrity. The king's luminous "body royal" functions as an apotropaic talisman warding off the fears of chaos, of social anarchy, of the fragmentation of the body politic.[37] It is a reassuring reflection that offered security and protection to a nation whose recent tumultuous history had ill prepared it (and the monarch) for the difficult tasks of facing the newly competitive economic and political conjuncture of a rapidly developing mercantilist Europe.

Let us remember not only the real political and social turmoil that marks French (and European) life throughout the seventeenth century but also the psychoemotional impact this turbulence had on Louis' own sense of his position in the world. Writing to his son in his *Mémoires*, the monarch seems haunted by the social unrest that marked his youth and that continued to characterize the early years of his reign:

> Mais il faut se représenter l'état des choses: des agitations terribles par tout le royaume avant et après ma majorité; une guerre étrangère, où ces troubles domestiques avaient fait perdre à la France mille et mille avantages; un prince de mon sang et d'un très grand nom à la tête des ennemis; beaucoup de cabales dans l'état; les parlements encore en possession et en goût d'une autorité usurpée; dans ma cour, très peu de fidélité sans intérêt, et par là mes sujets en apparence les plus soumis, autant à charge et autant à redouter pour moi que les plus rebelles.[38]

We might speculate that there was a particularly felicitous conjunction in and on the person of Louis XIV of an individual's psychic receptivity with the general ideological shifts of seventeenth century French society. One might even venture the hypothesis that it was by Louis' spectacular self-

[37] Louis XIV in a sense was the first modern manipulator of his own image. His theatricalization of his persona disseminated this image across France and Europe. In this he seemed to have already understood the psychological role played by all charismatic leaders in focusing on themselves the desires (and fears) of their people. As Eugène Enriquez states: "At the same time it is absolutely necessary that this party have at its head a leader with enough charisma and able at the same time to incarnate and to symbolise the state and the nation in their permanence so that the majority of the people can have the feeling that the social body finds its unity in a physical body whose beauty, grace, force and wealth it can admire" (*De la horde à l'état: Essai de psychanalyse du lien social* [Paris: Gallimard, 1986], 334). In Louis's case it seems clear that he came to embody a sexualized figure of bodily integrity, that was a needed antidote to the fear of social fragmentation (the result of the French wars of religion, and more recently of the *Frondes*. Eugénie Lemoine-Luccioni offers a psychoanalytical explanation of why this idealized body is the male body: "Man is one, thanks to the signifier of his lack, the 'phallus,' which happens to be the symbol of his sexual organ, the penis. . . . Man is and remains, as a man, and supposing that he exists as a man who would not also be a woman—one" (*Partage des femmes* [Paris: Seuil, 1976], 9).

[38] Louis XIV, *Mémoires*, ed. Jean Longnon (Paris: Tallandier, 1978), 33.

fashioning of himself as the "Sun King," that narcissistic and highly patriarchal, if not to say phallic, representation of his being as the nodal point of the universe, a point that held the universe together and prevented it from fragmenting anew into disarray, that he was both controlling his own personal demons and more importantly establishing himself as representation, as the image embodying all that to which France aspired.[39]

The appeal of absolute monarchy, the appeal to the charismatic leader, would be impossible without an underlying metaphorical structure that equated the king, the political/metaphysical father of the nation, to the biological father of individual family units. Almost all the theologo-political writers of the sixteenth and seventeenth centuries were unanimous in their appeal to the patriarchal biblical tradition in order to legitimate the origin of the state in the patriarchal family.[40] Louis was acutely aware of the importance his status as "patriarch" played in the creation of his own image. In several instances in his *Mémoires*, he returns to the theme of paternity to tell the dauphin how seriously he took his role as *père du peuple*:

> Je parus enfin à tous mes sujets comme un véritable père de famille qui fait la provision de sa maison, et partage avec équité les aliments à ses enfants et à ses domestiques.
>
> Il est beau de mériter d'eux le nom de père avec celui de maître, et si l'un nous appartient par le droit de notre naissance, l'autre doit être le plus doux de notre ambition.[41]

[39] Here is Louis's own description of why and how he chose the sun for his emblem: "Ce fut là que je commençais à prendre [cette devise] que j'ai toujours gardée depuis, et que vous voyez en tant de lieux. Je crus que, sans s'arrêter à quelque chose de particulier et de moindre, elle devait représenter en quelque sorte les devoirs d'un prince, et m'exciter éternellement moi-même à les remplir. On choisit pour corps le soleil, qui, dans les règles de cet art, est le plus noble de tous, et qui, par la qualité d'unique, par l'eclat qui l'environne, par la lumière qu'il communique aux astres qui lui composent comme une espèce de cour, par le partage égal et juste qu'il fait de cette même lumière en tous lieux, produisant sans cesse de tous côtés la vie, la joie et l'action, par son mouvement sans relâche, où il paraît néanmoins toujours tranquille, par cette course constante et invariable, dont il ne s'écarte et ne se détourne jamais, est assurément la plus vive et la plus belle image d'un grand monarque" (*Mémoires*, 135–36). Nannerl Keohane, in her *Philosophy and the State in France* (Princeton: Princeton University Press, 1980), describes the almost visceral feeling of security the king inspired in his subjects (59): "It would be hard to exaggerate the importance of the concept of the French King as the representative of the common interest, the source and embodiment of the good of all. . . . There was a sense of security when the monarch was personally in charge of things, a trust in the benevolence of his will, which can only be explained by the belief that he apprehended and spoke for the good of the entire society in a way no other human being could approach."

[40] In his introduction to Sir Robert Filmer's *Patriarcha* (Oxford: Basil Blackwell, 1949), perhaps the most famous treatise linking kingship and paternity, Peter Laslett writes that "the analogy between the family and the state is, of course, so obvious . . . it appears so frequently in the writings of the sixteenth and seventeenth centuries, and it occupies such an important place in so many of them, that it can be justifiably supposed that its use during this period was one of the reflections of patriarchal institutions" (27).

[41] Louis XIV, *Mémoires*, 111, 90.

In its flight away from heterogeneity toward the order of the One, the seventeenth century reinforced its need for security by investing in the symbol of integrity, the image of the noneffluent masculine body, which reaches its apogee in the figure of the father/king. The kingly body combines fertility with sovereign power which, as Georges Dumézil remarks, "are interdependent powers, actually two faces of power."[42] And yet, the appeal to the king as *Urvater*, evokes coterminously the uncomfortable associations with the desire to eliminate the father, and thus, of the father as he exists conflictually in the oedipal dynamic. In patriarchal societies, such as evolving absolutist France, the blind spot of ideology is a direct attack upon the father in any of his legal, theological, or merely familial avatars.[43] This does not mean that the intense feelings these social organizations carry with them simply do not exist. Rather, we must assume that the more intense the attachments, the more intense the love that is demanded, the more profound the feelings of aggressivity and of guilt that must be repressed or sublimated into acceptable outlets.[44] I suggest, therefore, that the father, the king, although an object of intense longing, also stimulated, as Freud suggested in his political musings in *Totem and Taboo*, the other side of the love that the father inspires, an aggressive hatred, a desire to sacrifice the father and take his place.[45] The king in his paternal body thus exists in that very tendentious position as a new Oedipus, both the object of devotion and the object of sacrifice of his people.[46]

Images, however, can never be reduced to a univocal meaning. Rather they condense in themselves multiple, often contradictory vectors. Can we not see, therefore, superimposed on/as the solar image—on the glorious shining body royal of the *Urvater*—still another, mythic reflection? This re-

[42] Georges Dumézil, *Ouranos-Varuna,* quoted in Didier Anzieu, "Oedipe avant le complexe," in *Les Temps Modernes*, 245 (Oct. 1966): 705.

[43] Writing about the intense ambivalence toward the father, Rosolato states: "As for the murder of the father . . . in the myths of monotheism it never appears directly. The entire endeavor has as its aim to avoid it. One must thus admit that this murder constitutes the secret, fundamental crux in relation to which all the sacrificial substitutions are organized and thanks to which the alliance is achieved." (*Le Sacrifice*, 74).

[44] Although in several spectacular instances the negative, aggressive desires toward the father are acted out, that is, the assassinations of Henri III and Henri IV in France and the beheading of Charles I in England, we more commonly witness the displacement of these aggressive drives onto the father's surrogates—those ministers Concini, Richelieu, Mazarin, Olivares, Buckingham, who are and are not the father and who receive the wrath of the populace.

[45] Enriquez elaborates on Freud's insights about the reciprocal relation of love/hate between fathers and sons and the necessity, in order to form stable social structures, for this rivalry to be mediated by rituals of sacrifice and initiation. See *De la horde à l'état*, particularly "L'ordre des générations: Le rapport aînés/jeunes," 241–53. The ritual sacrifice of kings in African tribal societies is discussed by Luc de Heusch in "The Sacrificial Body of the King," in *Fragments for a History of the Human Body*, ed. Michel Feher (New York: Zone, 1989), vol 3:386–96.

[46] Jean-Pierre Vernant reminds us that Oedipus "without the complex" was from the beginning a double figure, a sacred figure, both a political leader (a "divine king") and a victim the *pharmakos* of Thebes. See, "Ambiguïté et renversement: Sur la structure énigmatique d'Oedipe Roi," in Jean Pierre Vernant and Pierre Vidal-Naquet, *Oedipe et ses mythes* (Brussels: Éditions Complexe, 1988).

flection would protect the image from its own oedipal vulnerability, close it off from the violence that simultaneously it consistently evokes. The reflection of Louis that beams from royal portraits, as well as in the king's translation into all the solar iconography radiating from his bedchamber at Versailles, the center of the absolute universe, transforms the king into a perfectly contained, self-enclosed being, invulnerable to the ravages of time, to the corruption of the (merely physical) body.[47] The sun served as a triumphant and yet tantalizingly unattainable model for the rest of France (and Europe) mired in the quotidian indignities of the physical (grotesque) body. Yet, the sun closes in on itself, blinded by its own radiance in which the subject of representation and the object of representation are one. Narcissism, as a psychic phenomenon and absolutism as a state system seem felicitously conjoined in the image Louis projects of himself, as king and as "France."

Absolutism is perhaps the first modern avatar of totalitarian government. Georges Balandier offers us a definition of totalitarianism that I find particularly telling for my purpose. It is, he says, a government that desires "the submission of all and everything to the State," where "the unifying function of power is carried to its highest degree. [48] If the desire of Absolutism is "the desire for the One," it must constantly interweave politics and passion, the individual and the collective.[49] In this, his narcissistic creation of himself as the transcendental sun/"corps glorieux." Louis, in his splendid isolation, becomes an impossible ideal that mirrors to his subjects what they should be

[47] We know with what obsessive attention Louis took his role (that is, his self-representation) of king seriously, turning himself into an automaton of kingly functions (cf. Apostolidès, *Le roi machine*). The abbé de Choisy, in his *Mémoires pour servir à l'histoire de Lous XIV*, ed. Georges Mongrédien (Paris: Mercure de France, 1963) recounts (in yet another panegyric stroke added to the king's portrait) with what fortitude, valor, and bravery the king denies the indignities of his physical body, in order not to ruin the image of his "corps glorieux." After recounting the famous surgical procedure on the king's "fistula," the abbé presents Louis's royal acceptance of his operation and his insistence on resuming his regal functions: "Le Roi avait dit quelque chose à M. de La Rochefoucauld de l'opération qu'on lui devait faire. Félix [the surgeon] donna deux coups de bistouri et huit coups de ciseaux: il avait essayé sur des corps morts; et il prétend que cela épargna quelques coups de ciseaux. Le Roi ne souffla pas pendant l'opération; et dès qu'elle fut faite, il envoya dire à Monseigneur qui était à la chasse et à Madame. . . . Après l'opération il [Félix] recommanda surtout au Roi de demeurer en paix au moins jusqu'à suppuration; mis il n'en fit rien: les devoirs de la royauté le pressaient. Il fit appeler ses ministres et voulut tenir le conseil. . . . Il donna le lendemain audience aux ambassadeurs et aux ministres des princes étrangers, et leur parla avec une présence d'esprit et une gaieté qui les força d'écrire à leurs maîtres ce qu'ils venaient de voir et d'admirer. On voyait pourtant la douleur peinte sur son visage; son front était presque toujours en sueur de pure faiblesse; et cependant il donnait ses ordres, et se faisait rendre compte de tout. Il mangeait en public dans son lit, et se laissait voir deux fois par jour aux moindres de ses courtisans. Il ne témoigna aucune impatience à tous les coups de ciseaux qu'on lui donna; il disait seulement: 'Est-ce fait, messieurs? Achevez, et ne me traitez pas en roi; je veux guérir comme si j'étais un paysan' "(166–68).

[48] Georges Balandier, *Pouvoirs sur scène* (Paris: Balland, 1980), 19.

[49] This is André Green's succinct definition of narcissism. See *Narcissisme de vie, narcissisme de mort* (Paris: Minuit, 1983), 55.

but also what they can never be: Louis as Narcissus becomes the subject of universal interpolation.[50]

Ironically, Louis's narcissistic creation of himself, on the one hand presents in royal display a "body" that in its creation shines like the sun upon the court, its rays extending from there to the most remote provinces of the realm. On the other, it perversely signals yet another sacrifice or denial of the body. As we know Narcissus in his oblivious self-sufficiency repudiates allotropic sexuality. In the most common version of the myth, Narcissus, lost as he is in the mortiferous contemplation of his own beauty, rejects the amorous advances of the nymph Echo. Narcissus's rejection of Echo can be seen as a denial of the body, of the body as woman, and thus rejoins the foundation of phallocracy that many have also seen represented in Oedipus's "victory" over the Sphinx.[51] In both ancient myths, we see a common theme therefore, man can be "man" only by objectifying and then rejecting the woman-body-other. Yet, at the same time that this rejection leads to the institution of (a particular kind of) government, politics, and "culture," it also inevitably leads, on another level, to self-blindness and death.

When he comes to describe the political role of the monarch whose decisions command the fate of the nation, Louis, too, tells the dauphin to take a narcissistic stand, to deny the body, to allow passion (that is, women) no place in politics:

> Dès lors que vous donnez la liberté à une femme de vous parler des choses importantes, il est impossible qu'elles ne nous fassent faillir. La tendresse que nous avons pour elles, nous faisant goûter leurs plus mauvaises raisons, nous fait tomber insensiblement du côté où elles penchent; et la faiblesse qu'elles ont naturellement, leur faisant souvent préférer des intérêts de bagatelles aux plus solides considérations, leur fait presque toujours prendre le mauvais parti. Elles sont éloquentes dans leurs expressions, pressantes dans leurs prières, opiniâtres dans leurs sentiments.[52]

[50] I am refering here to the Althusserian notion of interpellation by which the subject is called (by ideology) into his/her place by the "transcendent" subject who in turn is ratified by the response of the object to this interpellation. As Louis Althusser points out, this is inherently a "specular" relation. See his *Positions* (Paris: Éditions Sociales, 1970), 118–19.

[51] Stephen Heath underscores this point in his discussion of the oedipal myth reread by Hegel in "The Ethics of Sexual Difference," in *Discourse*, spring-summer 1990, 128: "For Hegel, the Sphinx stands at the beginning of the history of consciousness. Or rather, that beginning comes with its defeat: Oedipus solves the riddle, flings the Sphinx over the rock, gets rid of the monstrous; philosophy, consciousness in its movement to attain true knowledge, starts from there, from that solution, the passage to the Greek world. Which means that what is put aside as Oedipus answers "man" and Hegel repeats him is the otherness—as it then becomes—to that Western term: the cultural difference of the Sphinx-Orient immobile to history, before the stirring of consciousness . . . the sexual difference of the Sphinx-Woman troubling identity in her representation, as riddling presence at the city gates, the hybrid to which man's "man" replies, ending the trouble by erasure." For further commentary on Oedipus as the originary "philosopher," see Goux, *Oedipus, Philosopher*.

[52] Louis XIV, *Mémoires*, 259.

On the one hand, therefore, the "corps glorieux" of Louis reflects both the oedipal king, symbol of paternal virility (but also object of filial aggression), and, in one and the same image, Narcissus, the emblem of sexuality's denial (but also of invulnerability to external aggression/desire). The body, the woman, is repudiated: Echo gradually withers away. All that remains of her desire is her plangent, disembodied voice. She cries to Narcissus from the rocks and reeds that surround the mirror in which he contemplates his own beauty. Echo, reduced to a disincarnated cry, calls out from beyond the frame inside of which Narcissus is lost in his own mimetic self-representation.

I suggest that this effacement of the (textual) body that we have been tracing as being integral to the elaboration of French seventeenth-century ideology and aesthetics reflects the textual/sexual ideology of Classical patriarchy. For, once again, the body that is repressed is coded as grotesque, as feminine, insofar as femininity in the vocabulary of the political leaders is what is dangerous—because open, effluent—to the social order. To claim that this attitude toward women, but even more pointedly toward their own desire, should be integrated into the ethics and aesthetics of Classical doctrine as a manifestation of patriarchal monarchy is not particularly novel.[53] The way Racine took up this ideological imperative and succeeded in using it by creating some of the most passionately moving heroines on the French stage is not only novel but perversely seductive.

When we come to Racine, therefore, to his tragic universe, we would do well to remember how this bourgeois subject never ceased, in the words of Mauron, "wanting to identify with the king. This assimilation [of himself and the king] had been, for such a long time, the symbol of salvation for him. Any participation in the majesty of royalty goes to his head."[54] But when we say that Racine identifies with the king, what exactly do we mean? With which king does he identify? Obviously not with Louis, condemned to suffer and die in his body, but rather with the King, the dazzling, paternal image of the absolute. In both his role as dramatist, and later, having abandoned the theater, in his function as royal historiographer whose job it is to record for posterity the heroic deeds, military and civic, of his king, Racine

[53] For a more detailed discussion of this question, see Greenberg, *Corneille, Classicism and the Ruses of Symmetry*, esp. the introduction.

[54] Mauron, *L'inconscient dans l'oeuvre*, 285. Picard, in *La carrière de Jean Racine*, also underlines the familial/economic situation of Racine (he describes Racine as "a prudent bourgeois, who saves his money and looks after his investments," 294), trying to make a place for himself in the court. It is especially interesting to note how Racine's social status as bourgeois caused so many aristocratic tongues to wag when he and Boileau received the position of royal historiographer (cf. Picard, 313–29). Barthes, *On Racine*, also speaks to Racine's "class jealousy" of the aristocracy, of his desire to write for them and thus to receive their approving look (35): "Racine himself seems to have experienced the world . . . as opinion: he made his way only through the attention of the Great ("sous le regard des Grands"), and explicitly wrote only to receive that attention ("et n'a explicitement écrit que pour recueillir ce regard").

was called upon to participate in the creation of the mythic dimension of the absolutist enterprise. Tragedy and history are the two sides of Racine's identification with the image of majesty. We cannot, however, understand narcissistic identification unambivalently. We know since Freud that "identification" is not merely a positive phenomenon but contains within the same affirmative gesture of admiration the aggressive desire to incorporate the object with which one identifies and thus to destroy it.[55] In a sense, therefore, must we not see in Racine the inherently ambivalent filial relation to the (image of the) king? The son who, in his oedipal relation to the father, wants to be (like) the king but to do so must also kill him and thus bear the burden of intolerable guilt? Racine in his tragedies plays out, over and over again, the conflicted response of the emerging subject of absolutist France to the social and sexual imperatives that presided over this subject's conflicted origins in desire and guilt—origins that remain all the more mysterious because the body in which they once might have found a grounding and thus an explanation has been banished. Like Echo it has vanished into thin air, leaving (but of course, this is essential, perhaps the most essential) a constant reminder of its presence/absence, its alluring voice.

There is something compelling about voice in general, but the voice that carries the affect of Racinian tragedy is particularly seductive. What does the young Marcel, the precociously overstimulated theatergoer, desire of a rendition of *Phèdre* by "la Berma" but to be transported out of his straitened bodily reality, moved and changed by the way the famous actress will give voice to Racine's verses?:

> Berma in *Andromaque*, . . . in *Phèdre*, was one of those famous spectacles which my imagination had long desired. I should enjoy the same rapture as on the day when a gondola would deposit me at the foot of the Titian of the Frari or the Carpaccios of San Giorgio dei Schiavoni, were I ever to hear Berma recite the lines beginning,
>
> On dit qu'un prompt départ vous éloigne de nous,Seigneur, etc.
>
> I was familiar with them from the simple reproduction in black and white which was given of them upon the printed page; but my heart beat furiously at the thought—as of the realisation of a long-planned voyage—that I should see them at length bathed and brought to life in the atmosphere and sunshine of the golden voice.[56]

It is the "golden voice" of the actress incarnating the sensuality of Racine's poetry that carries the audience out of its own body, back to place it re-

[55] Rosolato writes that "narcissistic identification comes ladened with aggressivity" (*Le sacrifice*, 29).

[56] Marcel Proust *A l'ombre des jeunes filles en fleurs*, (Paris: Gallimard, Bibliothèque de la Pléiade, 1954), 1:440–41; trans. W. C. K. Scott-Moncrieff, *Remembrance of Things Past*, vol 2: *Within a Budding Grove*, (New York: Random House, 1957), 14–15.

members but where it has never been. It is this sensuousness that interpellates the audience, seducing them, drawing them out of their daily existence, and, like a pied piper, leads them down roads that although ignored by them they have traveled before: the voice's extremely primal affect directs the audience out of the present and back to a more primitive, less contingent fantasy of the body.[57] The enticing music of Racine's poetry sings a siren's song that lures the audience into the meanders of the Racinian tragic labyrinth in a quest that although inarticulable by the audience is the very crux of Racinian dramaturgy. This quest begins with Echo's sad query, a query that as we've said reverberates throughout the tragic universe of Racine, the "who am I?" of the anguished protagonist. This question takes us to the heart of each character's tragic dilemma at the same time that it reflects the larger sociohistoric situation of the nascent absolutist subject, formed at the conjunction of the oedipal king/father and the absent mother (Echo). The Racinian question "Who am I?" proffered by the tragic voice is the most poignant of questions because no satisfactory answer is ever forthcoming. In its very demand, which is ultimately a cry for a grounding, an "origin," it always contains within itself the illusory fantasy of the "perfection of an original unity" that would establish once and for all an absolute identity and that would, at the same time, by the very presuppositions of the question, preclude any satisfactory response.[58] Instead of an answer, culture on the one hand, the human psyche on the other respond with myths, with fantasies.[59] These fantasies, these myths, always return to the body, to the most basic questions of the body, the difference between the sexes, their conjunction in producing new bodies, and the concomitant and conflicted desires that constantly exceed the limits that any particular society with its laws and traditions would impose on it. [60] In this sense we must understand Racinian tragedy as in essence a tragedy of origins, a tragedy that reflects the impossible quest of a subject, subjugated to the imperatives of the absolute. These imperatives demand that he or she be "one," integral, a "unified" subject at the same time that the contrasting claims of the material

[57] Joyce McDougall, talking about the affective resonance of the voice, particularly the "maternal voice," suggests: "The mother's voice rekindles fantasies of the wish for fusion, with the consequent loss of both subjective—and sexual—identity" (*The Many Faces of Eros*, 82).

[58] Rosolato, "La voix," in *Essais sur le symbolique*, 290, writes about "the myth of origins from which there can be but a falling off. An origin, that is also to say, the perfection of an original unity that can only be broken."

[59] Rosolato states that "any quest for an origin, on the condition that it is pushed far enough, comes up against the unknown. We will see [therefore] that for the subject it is the phantasm, just like for the community it is the myth, which is brought in to serve as a supplement, through an imaginary scenario steeped in the illusion of knowing, for the inaccessibility of the unknown" ("Les phantasmes originaires et leurs mythes correspondants," in *La scène primitive et quelques autres, Nouvelle Revue de Psychanalyse*, 46 (autumn, 1992): 226.

[60] Didier Anzieu, *The Skin-Ego*, trans. Chris Turner (New Haven: Yale University Press, 1989) gives a succinct formulation of the interrelation between psychic structures and physical reality (96): "every psychical function develops by supporting itself on a bodily function whose workings it transposes onto the mental plane."

body, claims that tell him/her that he or she is not one but two, not two, but many. In the impossible desire to resolve their dilemma the Racinian heroes, and their audience, are drawn on a labyrinthine journey to the origin: an origin that always entices because it holds out the prospect of recouping an initial (lost) unity, but that also in its elusiveness proves to be chaotic, fragmentary, unseizable.

And what is the story that is carried by the Racinian voice? What does its melodious, seductive song recount? In essence, I propose that the narrative ("le dit") this voice recounts is the conflicted coming into being of the absolutist subject, its genealogy, its sacrifices, and it does so by a constant rescripting of the Oedipus legend. Recent psychoanalytically informed studies of Racine tend to describe his tragedy as "pre-oedipal," especially when compared to a "post-oedipal" Cornelian drama.[61] This distinction seems to me to be both justifiable and yet too unequivocal. Racine's tragedies function on several psychic, social, and dramatic levels, simultaneously and dynamically, each continually interweaving with the others. On the level of dramatic narrative, as Philip Lewis has exhaustively demonstrated, Racinian tragedy squarely confines us within the compass of the oedipal legend.[62] From the beginning of Racinian dramaturgy *La Thébaïde* plunges us into the trauma created by Oedipus's transgressions, murder and incest:

> Mais ces monstres, hélas! ne t'épouvantent guères;
> La race de Laïus les a rendus vulgaires;
> Tu peux voir sans frayeur les crimes de mes fils,
> Après ceux que le père et la mère ont commis,
> Tu ne t'étonnes pas si mes fils sont perfides
> S'ils sont tous deux méchants, et s'ils sont parricides?
> Tu sais qu'ils sont sortis d'un sang incestueux,
> Et tu t'étonnerais s'ils étaient vertueux. (I.i)

Racinian tragedy is born of incestuous oedipal blood. What Jocasta's speech does is to situate, by its reference to the "race de Laïus," the archaeology of the Racinian universe in a genealogy that is marked by sexual, that is, bodily, excess—the body gone wild. Yet the origin of Oedipus is not in Oedipus but, as Jocasta puts it, in his blood. Oedipus's misdeeds are but the punishment for prior dereliction: before Oedipus was his father and his (sexual)

[61] I am thinking here particularly of Mauron, who is heavily influenced by the British Kleinian school's approach to pre-oedipal fantasies. See *L'inconscient dans l'oeuvre*, 122: "Racinian tragedy is pre-oedipal; the forces of life and death fight it out there. Cornelian tragedy is post-oedipal: the conflict here is between passion and duty." Both Barthes and Leo Bersani see strong "pre-oedipal" patterns at work in the plays. Cf. the latter, *A Future for Astyanax*, 38: "The Oedipal stage provides a reinforcement for archaic pre-Oedipal passions."

[62] Lewis, "Sacrifice and Suicide," 57: " So the point of departure of Racinian theater is a chilling evocation of the descendancy of Laius." But see his entire discussion of the oedipal legend, and "oedipal effects" in all eleven tragedies.

crime—the homosexual rape of Chryssipus, his host's son. This act earns Laius the dubious distinction of introducing homosexuality—as transgression—into the Greek world. From the beginning, the Oedipus legend returns us to the body, the body's desires that wreak havoc on civil life.[63] Homosexuality and incest, by refusing the limits of sexual difference and generational difference, blur the primary distinctions making political life impossible. Instead of order, incest produces chaos, metaphorized by those monsters both real and metaphoric that haunt the Racinian universe. It will fall to Theseus, heir to Oedipus's expiation, to attempt to eliminate the monstrous from the far reaches of the Greek world, only to have it spring up anew within his own court, at the center of his own family.[64]

Trying to decide on whether the Racinian world is "pre-" or "post-" oedipal seems to confuse several different layers of the tragic spectacle's impact, the layer of a persistent, preexisting cultural narrative, "un lieu de mémoire" (i.e., the Oedipus legend), with the particular affective resonance this narrative has on the spectating public (the "Oedipus complex"). The theater functions here as a mediating site between cultural myths and individual fantasy.[65] The place of the stage in all its ideological ambivalence always represents a transitional space, a space in which are mediated the sexual, political, and economic contradictions in whose intermeshing human subjectivity is constantly being repositioned. Once again we are situated in that indeterminate space between ideology and biology, between cultural narrative and sexual affect. To try to articulate their powerful hold on us I suggest we begin by returning to that other indeterminate "corporal aura" that floats between body and mind, between body and bodies, the "voice,"

[63] Anzieu reminds us in his exploration of the construction and ramifications of the oedipal legend, "Oedipe avant le complexe ou de l'interprétation psychanalytique des mythes," in *Les Temps Modernes*, 245 (Oct. 1966): 675–715, that even before the legend reaches his father, Oedipus's genealogy begins with sexuality and violence: "Oedipus, king of Thebes, is a descendant of Harmony, the only daughter of the illicit loves of Ares and Aphrodite: in Oedipus incest and parricide will find their most unadorned expression, just as Ares and Aphrodite are the chief representatives of aggressivity and sexuality" (682).

[64] For the links connecting Oedipus to Theseus, besides the Lewis article cited above, see Anzieu, esp. 685–87, "Thésée ou le complexe d'Oedipe en demi-teinte."

[65] Many critics have pointed to the theater as a privileged dialectical site mediating between the public and the private. See, for instance, Ubersfeld, *Lire le théâtre*, 39: "It has become clear that theatrical activity, as performance, is a dialectical space par excellence." And she continues (265): "Every theatrical text is the response to a demand on the part of the audience, and it is here that the articulation of theatrical discourse, history and ideology is most easily made." For his part the psychoanalyst and critic André Green writes in *Un oeil en trop: Le complexe d'Oedipe et la tragédie*, (Paris: Minuit, 1969), trans. by Alan Sheridan, *The Tragic Effect* (Cambridge: Cambridge University Press, 1979), 23: "Between the two, at the meeting-point of the individual and society, between the personal resonance of the work's content and its social function, art occupies a transitional position which qualifies the domain of illusion, which permits an inhibited and restrained jouissance obtained by means of objects that both are and are not what they represent."

which with its bivalent nature can serve as a shuttle weaving the one to the other.[66]

Freud tells us we are particularly sensitive to Sophocles's *Oedipus Rex*, because it reverberates within us with the echoes of a scenario we have heard before:

> If *Oedipus Rex* moves a modern audience no less than it did the contemporary Greek one, the explanation can only be that its effect does not lie in the contrast between destiny and human will, but is to be looked for in the particular nature of the material on which that contrast is exemplified. There must be something which makes a voice within us ready to recognize the compelling force of destiny.[67]

There is, Freud is saying, an affective resonance between the dramatic narration of Sophocles's tragedy and the effective lived experience of audiences (regardless of historic differences). For the moment I would like to to return to Freud's initial clue and to concentrate on the importance of the medium that embodies the question, the "voice" in its role as an "intermediary object," mediating between the body and the world, between inner psychic life and external sociopolitical reality. Considerations of the role of "voice," will offer us a bivalent entrance into the particular fantasies that connect the oedipal narrative (which is a narrative of cohesion and thus intimately connected to the absolutist quest) to the pre-oedipal fantasies (fantasies that because they are of violent fragmentation, of chaos, prove to be inimical to absolute desire) in Racinian tragedy.

In their study of originary fantasies, Laplanche and Pontalis tell us that from his very first, tentative theorizations, Freud recognized the importance of the "entendu" (the heard, the overheard, the sound, the noise) in these fantasies.[68] For Freud, "sound," the overheard, could be interpreted as pertaining to a double register: on the one hand, as "noise" (" le bruit") to the register of the percept, the "sensorium"; on the other, as the "articulation"

[66] I take the term "corporal aura" to describe the voice from Rosolato, "La voix," who gives this definition (302): "In this way the Voice, which in a first discussion appeared as an emanation, a 'corporal aura' can be considered as an intermediary object."

[67] S. Freud, *The Interpretation of Dreams* (Standard Edition, 4: 262). Ned Lukacher takes up this passage and comments on it to argue the importance of voice for the primal scene: "There is a 'voice within us' that enables us to recognize the 'the compelling force' of *Oedipus Rex* because this voice has already told us all of this before. Because this voice has already called upon us and because we have already forgotten it, the repetition of the entire process gives *Oedipus Rex* the appearance of the 'compelling force' of destiny. Our aesthetic and intellectual response to the tragedy of Oedipus is in effect the unconscious repetition of the primal scene of the call to conscience" (*Primal Scenes: Literature, Philosophy, Psychoanalysis*, [Ithaca: Cornell Un. Press, 1986], 81).

[68] Jean Laplanche, Jean-Bertrand Pontalis, *Fantasme originaire: fantasmes des origines, origines du fantasme* (Paris: Hachette, 1985), 50: "In the first theoretical drafts suggested by the question of phantasms, Freud gives pride of place to the role of the heard/sound." I will be following their argument on the importance of sound in the following paragraphs.

("le dit") of familial history, of legend. In other words, Laplanche and Pontalis split the "heard" into physical and metaphysical dimensions, both the literal explosion of sound into or onto the infant's perception of its environment and the ideological notion of the articulated "story," a political structure that gives meaning to the infant by placing him/her in a line of descent.

These two aspects of "voice" will be differently exploited by Freud's followers. Laplanche and Pontalis, for instance, underline the idea of the voice's eruption into the uniform world of the infant, creating a tear, a rip in that undifferentiated perceptive field between the infant and the world. This sound can be the call of the mother, or another percept that effectively situates the infant in the position of interpellated subject. So, in the first instance voice, as the overheard, situates the child in his earliest subjective position as the object of another's (the "Other's" in Lacanian terms) demand.[69] The voice of the other calls the infant into being: it functions as the origin of his subjectivity in that it acts as a division between the infant and the mother, and thus leads the infant out of that monad and into a relation to the law orchestrating his world's symbolic systems. The second vector of the overheard, would be its role of (familial) legend, that is, the call to the child to situate him/herself within a narrative in which he or she must assume his or her proper role: "the rumor or familial legend, this spoken or secret speech, that preceeds the subject and into which he must come in order to find himself."[70]

This distinction is taken up and expanded upon by Guy Rosolato who divides the "heard" into the linguistic categories of Voice and Speech ("Voix," "Parole"). For Rosolato (who is influenced by Theodor Reik's earlier writings about the "cry") the Voice (as undifferentiated sound), by preceding "speech" is a vector of abstraction, emanating from and constantly reminiscent of, he says, an "origin," a "primal unity" (of child and mother?) and thus of leading us beyond or through myth to the primordial question of origins.[71] Rosolato offers a complicated and enriching discussion of Voice as it intertwines with cultural myths (the voice of the shofar in Abraham's aborted sacrifice of Isaac, for instance, representing the voice of God/father) and personal fantasies (paranoiac auditory hallucinations). At the same time his insistence on the function of the voice as leading back to myths of

[69] The importance of the concept of "interpellation" for understanding the subjective positioning of "individuals" is used by Louis Althusser (following Lacan) in *Positions* (Paris: Éditions Sociales, 1970), 118–19.

[70] Laplanche and Pontalis, *Fantasme originaire*, 51.

[71] Rosolato, "La voix" 291: "Speech yields to Voice which detaches itself from it becoming a vector, an abstraction emanating from an origin, from a primal unity in which there is a primitive adhesion of meaning to meaning. We will designate the Voice thus: as harking back through myth to the origin, and more generally as a question implicity asked about this origin, and therefore being able to capture the relevant phantasms." Here Rosolato expands upon many of the suggestions put forth by Theodor Reik in his *Ritual: Psychoanalytical Studies* (London: Hogarth Press, 1931). See in particular the sections "Kol Nidre," 167–220; and "The Shofar," 221–362.

origins also connects the importance of the voice to the fantasy of the "primal scene," that violent fantasy where the child situates himself in the (impossible) position of being present at the scene of his own conception. For Rosolato, the voice leads through the myth of an initial unity back to the primal scene:

> The myth would exist at the level of an idealized nostalgia for an original unity that the infantile fantasy of the Primal Scene keeps alive. The movement upstream of the various tributaries toward a source requires here a return to a precise fount where are "fused" the generations, the difference between the sexes, love and hate, and especially the three oedipal poles—the child depicted as present not only at the union of his parents but also at his own conception.[72]

Rosolato concludes his discussion of "Voice" by indicating where the two vectors he has adumbrated lead in the psychic construction of the individual. On the one hand, the vector of myth, he suggests, leads back to the primal scene and thence to the "phantasmatic metamorphoses" of the father, as "Phallus," the (Lacanian) arbiter of the law, and from that association to the "ego-ideal" and to the "Superego." On the other, the voice, in its return to the "origin" (in and through myth) carries us back to the "Id" ("this zone of abolition that exists when all illusions are returned to prehistory"). Finally, Rosolato proposes that the "voice" as "corporal aura" can be considered an "intermediary object," insofar as its appeal to an origin leads us "through myth and fantasy to the Superego, with the judgments of 'inner' voices, and through the Superego to the Id, and its drives."[73] The voice therefore, for Rosolato, would be intermediate, situated at the confluence of Id and Superego and capable of resonating from the one to the other.

Still another Anglo-French analyst, Joyce McDougall, also takes up the importance of the Voice in its division between sound (which is, we remember, never "merely sound," that is, never affectless, meaningless) and Speech. For McDougall, verbal communication which, although she insists, is "transmitted by the mother," comes to represent an external or "third" power that will protect the child from being enveloped ("devoured") by the "siren-mother." "The mother's voice," she writes, "rekindles fantasies of the wish for fusion, with the consequent loss of both subjective—and sexual—identity, whereas the words learned from her compel separation and autonomy."[74] McDougall thus underlines both the attraction and danger of the "originary" voice. It is a siren's song that draws the child back into the desire for fusion, that is, nonindividuation, with the fantasy of an all-embracing, and thus devouring mother. In order to protect the child from these tempting fantasies, McDougall translates the Lacanian "voice of the father"

[72] Rosolato, "La voix," 291.
[73] Ibid., 302.
[74] J. McDougall, *The Many Faces of Eros*, 82.

back into the linguistic register (from whence Lacan took it) of speech. Although she does not explicitly say so, this speech (as a structured symbolic system) would represent the intervention of the father (the "law") in the "Edenic," but also "hellish" mother-child monad. The "speech" of the father prevents the child's reabsorption into the "voice" of the mother, thus allowing it access to politico-cultural existence.[75]

Finally, in her study of the role of women and of women's death in Greek tragedy, Loraux informs us that since in "tragedy, everything happens ["passe"] by and through words," she will situate her study of tragedy under the sign of a sympathetic "listening."[76] By emphasizing the importance of the aural over the spectacular aspect of tragedy, Loraux would seem to be positioning herself against the typical critical gesture, and certainly the gesture of the seventeenth century's most celebrated theoretician of the theater, the abbé d'Aubignac, for whom the theater was preponderantly a visual spectacle:

> Ce poème est nommé Drama, c'est à dire, Action, et non pas Récit; ceux qui le représentent se nomment Acteurs, et non pas Orateurs; ceux-là même qui s'y trouvent presens s'appellent Spectateurs ou Regardans, et non pas Auditeurs; Enfin le lieu qui sert à ses Représentations, est dit Théâtre, et non pas Auditoire, c'est à dire, un lieu où on regarde ce qui s'y fait, et non pas où l'on Ecoute ce qui s'y dit.[77]

Loraux's use of the word "listening" for her study of Greek tragedy resonates with all the associations the word carries with it of the analytic session. The word "écoute" in French bears the echoes of the protocols of that session where the patient's free associations engage with the analyst's empathic, active, listening. Loraux thus encourages us to lend an attentive, analytic ear to "tragedy," and to listen to the voices, the varied, nuanced echoes that resonating from the suppressed body continue to tell us what a purely visual interpretation would miss. Loraux's call for "listening" to the shouts and murmurs of the tragic protagonists tempts us beyond the specta-

[75] Although this is a very idiosyncratic survey, I shall point out what strikes me as the resonances in the preceding psychoanalytic theories of voice with the early, preanalytic theories of Julia Kristeva. Kristeva's notion of the "pre-oedipal Chora"—the preverbal, presymbolic language that soothes the child in its rhythmic, modulated rocking tones and thus establishes a primary maternal linguistic stratum that is reawakened in the melodies and rimes of poetry and music—is an important theoretical formulation for Racine tragedies in that it provides one more way of thinking the affective power of the tragedies, in yet another declension of the way "sexual difference" comes to the subject. See Julia Kristeva, *Polylogue* (Paris: Seuil, 1977).

[76] Loraux, *Tragic Ways of Killing a Woman*, vii: "So words are read to replace, if not to recover words that were heard, words to which the Athenian public listened closely in the tragic performance. Those words could be heard in more than one way, in many different ways. . . . Just as a reminder, and for general interst, I will mention some of the reasons for making tragedy mainly a matter of listening."

[77] François Hédelin, abbé d'Aubignac, *La pratique du théâtre*, quoted in Timothy Murray, *Theatrical Legitimation* (New York: Oxford University Press, 1987), 282.

cle and situates us on that "other scene," where the tragedy plays out scenarios unknown to the characters themselves and, perhaps, even unknown to the playwright. They are not ignored by the audience, however, who react, as we've seen, with tears, the cathartic response of the body to the tragic voices it has heard before reverberating anew on its own inner stage.

Racinian tragedy is carried by the voice, a voice that, as we have just seen for psychoanalysis (at least), is always double. It reminds us of the body which has been banished, functioning as it does as its stand-in. There exists in that voice both a seductive appeal to some originary unity that escapes the subject (both the subject of tragedy and the tragic spectator) and the vector of the law that recites the history of the subject, his/her place in a genealogy, a family, which is always a political (that is, socially symbolic) construct. We must be sensitive in our "listening" to the ambivalence of this voice. On the one hand, it actively participates (by its superegoic function) in the construction of the absolutist desire for a coherent subject, by substituting a cerebral construct (the plot) for the body. On the other, it constantly demonstrates the impossible grounding of this subject and, therefore, its impossibility, *tout court*, in the disruptive primal fantasies, where the body returns but as violence, as fragmentation. An attentive listening constantly oscillates between plot and affect and results in sympathetic tears, thus reuniting in an cathartic gesture the most salient bodily features of Racinian tragedy—the voice that speaks, the ear that hears, and the eyes that weep.

The theater's dominance in periods of historical transition, in those periods of enormous social conflict and change, seems particularly acute perhaps because, more than any other form of representation, the theater most actively engages individual myths—those narratives individuals construct and are constructed by to explain and thus situate themselves within social and economic forces that preexist them—with collective narratives.[78] In a sense, therefore, if we agree with André Green, who defines the theater as "situated between dreams and phantasy," we can see that the experience of the theater, on one level at least, is always the experience of a constant reprocessing and reproduction (through a representation) of subjectivity—always an ongoing process of renegotiating the conflicting demands of individual desire and societal law.[79] For his greatest creations—*Andromaque, Iphigénie, Phèdre*—Racine, in opposition to his elder rival Corneille, retreats from the stage of history and returns to the more archaic cosmology of myth. Each of these different scenarios is affiliated in their genealogy to the overriding myth of Oedipus, his family, his descendants, and with the consequences of his fate. Even those historically based tragedies, *Britanni-*

[78] A. Ubersfeld, *Lire le théâtre*, 15: "Theater strikes us as a privileged art, of capital importance, because it shows, better than the other arts, how the individual psyche is invested in a collective relation."

[79] Cf. Green, *The Tragic Effect*, 2.

cus and *Mithridate*, or the biblical tragedy of *Athalie* can be seen, conjuring up as they do forces of an unconscious familial-sexual terror, to supersede the merely picturesque qualities of the historical and to plunge back into the mysterious, sacred world of oedipal fantasies.

All the tragedies in the Racinian canon are linked to a common grounding in a mythic vision that is at once familial and terrifying. Could I offer as an hypothesis that the entire Racinian endeavor is merely to rescript, in absolutist garb, the story of Oedipus as it intersects with Racine's own "personal myth(ology)?" It would, it seems to me, be more fruitful to acknowledge the obvious hold on Racine of this conflict of subjectivity that the Oedipus myth represents—especially as it acts out the imbrication of desire and the law in and through the subject formed at its interstice—but even more important, to ask why and to what effect does this rewriting of Oedipus as the drama/tragedy of familial sexuality appear at this historic juncture? What is the importance of the representation of Oedipus on the stage of seventeenth-century Absolutism?

Without wishing to be too reductive of the enormous complexity of Racinian dramaturgy, nor to ignore the equally intricate involution of Racine's personal history in the social problems of his period, I think that we can, for hypothetical reasons, reduce the conflict of Racinian tragedy to the battle for integrity in a subject whose very existence is not integral, that is, not one, but two. At the same time, and by the very same token, this duality, this duplicity that must be removed, repressed, or extirpated, that forms the impediment propelling tragic action and informing the very being of the tragic hero, is at the very heart of the Oedipus myth as it constantly attempts to refashion the journey of Oedipus away from forces of duality and contradiction toward an attempted (but always unsuccessful) compromise with societal laws. We should not forget that the story of Oedipus, first and foremost, is as Marie Delcourt reminds us "the most complete of all political myths," in that it presents, she says, "the most detailed amalgamation in one narrative of the mythic preparations for kingship."[80] At the same time, as Delcourt goes on to demonstrate, Oedipus's political role, his position of king, is inextricably tied to his erotic life, which is from the beginning predestined to the horrors of uncontrolled, incestuous sexuality. Oedipus, therefore, as king, the hero who saves the city, cleanses it, but also is the defiler who introduces impurity into the polis. From its genesis the myth of Oedipus represents the impossibility of separating out politics from sexual desire: the hero as civil liberator but also as contaminator, "Oedipus tyrannos," the ambivalence that resides in a single character who is at one and the same time father, king, and victim, an ambivalence that can be resolved only through death.

[80] Marie Delcourt, *Oedipe ou la légende du conquérant* (Paris: Faculté de philosophie et lettres, 1944), 108.

Despite all its subtle nuances, its different tonal variations, Racinian tragedy in its different guises repeats this singular absolute obsession of Oedipus—to know the truth, which he believes is self-evident, and thus to assert his unsullied right to the Theban throne, to be sovereign.[81] In the world of absolutist France, the question of political sovereignty—the role and status of the monarch—is inseparable from the metaphysical, that is, psychosexual, aspirations of the absolutist subject inserted in the conflicted intermeshing of the emerging bourgeois family. Racinian drama inhabits a tragic locus novel in its intensity and its narrowness of focus. For however grandiose its exterior trappings (imperial Rome, majestic early Greece, ancient biblical royalty, or the princely seraglio of Istanbul), the tightly organized, tragic arena in Racine always points away from the stately decor of majesty and returns us to the restricted confines of the family. André Green suggests that this constrained familial space most adequately represents the earliest and deepest ties—ties of love and of hate, binding children to parents—and thus also has the greatest potential for engendering tragic emotions.[82] Michel Foucault, in a decidedly less psychoanalytic vein, has also pointed out that it was precisely during the course of the seventeenth century that the family, as the nexus in which the private (the sexual) and the public (the social) are inextricably intermeshed, came to assume an even more enchafed role as the mediator between societal (juridical) injunctions and (subjective) sexuality. The family becomes, according to Foucault, "the interchange of sexuality and alliance: it conveys the law and the juridical dimension in the deployment of sexuality; and it conveys the economy of pleasure and the intensity of sensations in the regime of alliance."[83] Racine's tragedy, as the tragedy of conflicted familial origins, reflects the intensity of this mediation.

The problem of political sovereignty so crucial for seventeenth-century French society was rescripted by Racine as the essential (but unrealizable) task of his protagonists. Inversely their desire for sovereignty, for the absolute, is inseparably connected in its plots and peripeteia to the "family romance" of Classical French subjectivity.[84] We can understand how a monarchical scenario, on one level at least, reflects the very primitive fantasies of

[81] Lucien Goldmann speaks of the tragic dilemma in Racine as the desire for the "absolute": see his *Racine* (Paris: L'Arche, 1956), and *Le dieu caché* (Paris: Gallimard, 1955), 47.

[82] "The family, then, is the tragic space *par excellence*, no doubt because in the family the knots of love—and therefore of hate—are not only the earliest, but also the most important ones" (Green, *The Tragic Effect*, 7).

[83] Michel Foucault, *The History of Sexuality*, trans. Robert Hurley, vol. 1 (New York: Pantheon, 1978), 108.

[84] Green, *The Tragic Effect*, 37: "To ask oneself whether kinship relations constitute the tragic or whether the tragic elucidates these kinship relations may be meaningless, formulated in that way. Let us say rather that they reveal something essential about the subjectivity that is inseparable from the tragic, by uncovering the relation of the subject to his progenitors, that the study of these relations may be fully conceived only in the context of the tragic, so revealing its role as constituent of subjectivity."

all children who, at a very early age and on the interior stage of their own private theater, cannot but see their own families as absolutist "courts." Their parents, cast in the roles of king and queen are seen as having frighteningly total power over their affective (that is, erotic) existence.[85]

While Racine's dramatic plots focus on the tragic predicament of his protagonist, this predicament is always brought to the foreground by a political crisis. All the tragedies are situated on the fault line separating the death of an old political regime and the birth of another, as yet unfocused, order. This crisis, internalized in the Racinian hero as a passionate, guilt-ridden rift in his/her own emotional world, is exacerbated by being presented against a background of impending political chaos. What we hear echoing across the Racinian world, at the beginning of each play, is that something in the order of that world has been irrevocably changed: "Cet heureux temps n'est plus. Tout a changé de face," declares Hippolyte at the beginning of *Phèdre*; in *Athalie* Abner tells Joad, "L'audace d'une femme, arrêtant ce concours/En des jours ténébreux a changé ces beaux jours"; and in *Britannicus* the play opens with Agrippine's declaration, "Tout ce que j'ai prédit n'est que trop assuré;/ Contre Britannicus Néron s'est déclaré." In a sense, following the model of Sophocles's *Oedipus Rex*, Racine constructs his tragedies so that we are plunged from the very beginning into a familial crisis that is also a political turning point threatening the entire world order of the play.[86]

Quickly, however, Racine moves from the political instability of the outer world into the psychological turmoil of the play's protagonist. In an extremely subtle play of inversions, the tragic plot will work itself out, resolving the political crisis by and through the sacrifice of the tragic hero. In a sense therefore, Racine moves from the larger political stage of an empire in crisis to the narrower, but analogous, ferment of the tragic hero who, becoming the victim of that world's crisis, is immolated to expiate the sins of society, and, by so doing, restore order to it. The entire play, which has whirled around the passions of the "absent" body, will at the last minute return the body to the play in order to sacrifice it, reduce it finally and utterly to cinders.

If we were to follow Roland Barthes's lead, and pare down the entire corpus of Racinian tragedy to one "primordial tragedy," rather than see the

[85] For a detailed study of the role of childhood (unconscious) fantasy in tragedy, see the exhaustive study of Otto Rank, *The Incest Theme in Literature and Legend: Fundamentals of a Psychology of Literary Creation*, trans. by Gregory Richter (Baltimore: Johns Hopkins University Press, 1992), esp. pt. 1, The Relationship between Parents and Children. For an elaboration on the particular aspect of Freud's "family romance" for seventeenth-century French culture, see Greenberg, *Subjectivity and Subjugation*, introduction.

[86] As Mauron has pointed out in his reading of Racine, in the tragedies leading up to *Mithridate* the political crisis is precipitated because the place of the father is vacant, creating turmoil in the universe of the drama. From *Mithridate* on, the father returns, only to find his place usurped, or in danger of being usurped (*L'inconscient dans l'oeuvre*, 26–31).

Racinian universe repeat, as Barthes does, the Freudian myth of the primal horde (a repetition with which I fully concur), we could also see it trace, in its great schemata parabola, the oedipal narrative of the coming into being of the king—as that figure came to represent the impossible "corps glorieux" of transcendental sovereignty.[87] If we were to trace an arc from *La Thébaïde* to *Athalie* we would, as Mauron has suggested, be able to see the gradual emergence and affirmation of the father first as monarch, then as God, and at the same time see the defeat of the mother/witch. In other words, what the essential Racinian tragedy would trace is the contested, conflicted battle for sovereignty, waged between forces of masculinity and femininity, forces that have, as we've seen been coded as "baroque" (grotesque) and "Classical."[88] On this level at least the political battle reveals its intense investments in establishing the reign of the masculine as the model for political (and thus sexual) life. In our own terms, we have already seen that in the emerging hegemonic drive of Classical esthetics, the masculine, the sovereign, is precisely coded as the "anticarnivalesque." What the sovereign cannot tolerate is division, be it the division of the physical or political body, because that would render that body open, effluent, female, and thus vulnerable. Once more the anxieties of the physical body reflect the anxieties of the *corpus politicum*, and vice versa.

This anxiety is concretely represented in the text by another character that is, in a sense, the partner of the ambivalent, omnipresent altar, the royal throne. For as capacious as the throne may be, it cannot, as we are told from the beginning of Racinian dramaturgy, be shared. The throne is indivisible:

> Jamais dessus le trône on ne vit plus d'un maître;
> Il n'en peut tenir deux, quelque grand qu'il puisse être!
> (*La Thébaïde*, IV. iii)

Despite all of their efforts, Jocasta and Antigone cannot impose a "partage des femmes" on the warring brothers Eteocles and Polynices. Born of an incestuous coupling, the twins are monstrous. The sign of their monstrosity is their implacable hatred, which is precisely intransigent in that it is a sign of their own attempts at defining themselves as masculine, that is, integral, over and against the "feminine" solution preached by their mother and sister. This unacceptable feminine political solution is so aggressively rejected because, in a more profound sense, it merely reproduces in the external political world the anguish caused by their biological twinness. The very fact

[87] Barthes, *On Racine*, 8: "If we make one essential tragedy out of eleven, if we arrange in a kind of exemplary constellation this tribe of some fifty tragic characters who inhabit Racinian tragedy, we shall discover the figures and the actions of the primeval horde."
[88] Here I am greatly simplifying Mauron's schema.

of their existence is physically repulsive for them, a "corps à corps," as Barthes calls it, of not being one, but two. Theirs is quite literally a visceral hatred, grounded in their origin as a forced cohabitation in the maternal body the trace of which has been inscribed indelibly in them as their twinship:

> Ce n'est pas son orgueil, c'est lui seul que je hais.
> Nous avons l'un et l'autre une haine obstinée
> . . . .
> Elle est née avec nous; et sa noire fureur,
> Aussitôt que la vie, entra dans notre coeur.
> Nous étions ennemis dès la plus tendre enfance;
> Que dis-je! nous l'étions avant notre naissance.
> Triste et fatal effet d'un sang incestueux!
> Pendant qu'un même sein nous renfermait tous deux,
> Dans les flancs de ma mère une guerre intestine
> De nos divisions lui marqua l'origine.
> (*La Thébaïde*, IV. i)

This heatedly visceral introduction into the psychopolitical dynamics of the Racinian world is revelatory of the extremely complex dialectic that the succeeding plays (like the unfolding of an analysis) will develop and work through. Racinian tragedy's imbrication of politics and sexuality, of course, is acutely foregrounded by the play's focusing the origin of the tragic dilemma in the body of the mother, by repeatedly emphasizing the incestuous sexuality of this body that lies at the origin of the problem. This incestuous coupling has produced twins, which for many (primitive) societies is in and of itself the sign of the monstrous. Monsters bear the mark of, give witness to, the parental fault.[89] But the fault of the parents, the sexual fault, instantly creates political havoc: twinship effaces (for the tragedy) any primogeniture, any way for a society based on the devolution of power from father to son (from king to king) to establish a precedence that would ensure political stability. Instead of orderly devolution from generation to generation, incest (the body) produces a mortiferous oscillation. Furthermore, and this is even more speculatively pernicious, although the monstrosity that wreaks havoc on Theban society is the result of transgressive parental sexuality, this excessive, unnatural sexuality is—because of the text's insistent focus on the pathetic expiatory rhetoric of the mother, Jocasta, and by

[89] In her study, *Monstrous Imagination* (Cambridge, Mass.: Harvard University Press, 1994) Marie-Hélène Huet points out how monstrosity in early modern Europe was often thought to be an effect of the mother's aberrant sexual desires, stating that "a persistent line of thought argued that monstrous progeny resulted from the disorder of the maternal imagination, . . . the monstrous child bore witness to the violent desires that moved the mother at the time of conception or during pregnancy" (1).

echoing the hollow silence, the absence of the father—coded as feminine. In a sense Oedipus whose presence pervades the enitre tragedy is also evacuated from it. Oedipus is dead; he is not represented on stage. The guilt that is his is transferred onto the only surviving member of the incestuous couple, Jocasta, who is thus situated by the play, as the "ur-model" of the dangerous, politically anarchic threat of female sexuality. It is a threat that will continue to haunt the entire Racinian world.

In Racine, Jocasta remains on stage (and this is all the more revelatory, for in the classical Sophoclean rendition of the myth, she kills herself, leaving Oedipus alone and alive) as the constant reminder of the reality of the flesh, of its dangerous potential constantly to exceed any of the bounds with which society would constrain it. Oedipus, on the other hand, has vanished from the world. The father is gone, he has become an immaterial abstraction. At Colonus he undergoes an "assumption," being freed of his sins, of his body. This ultimate absolution has transformed Oedipus into a metaphysical imperative:

> *Oedipus at Colonus* is imbued from beginning to end with an intensely sacral atmosphere. . . . The man who is most degraded, and for that reason untouchable, enters the Eumenides' wood, a place that is pure, and therefore holy and inviolable—a solemn redoubling of the sacred that reactivates its originary power and prepares the ultimate reversal, the uplifting of Oedipus. The most rejected, the most excluded of men—this aged and polluted body of a criminal—becomes the miraculous source of blessings for Athens. Oedipus is transformed from an untouchable human wreck into a perpetual and inexhaustible treasure.[90]

Oedipus, the *pharmakos*, is expelled from Thebes, leaving his wife/mother and their monstrous progeny behind. Wandering blind and aimless across the deserts that separate the space of nature from the limits of the polis, Oedipus is doomed to the fate of his body. Only at the end of his wanderings, at the moment of his death, a moment that predates the tragic conflict of *La Thébaïde* does his wandering end at the gates of Athens. There and only there can his sacrifice be fully valorized, as an acceptance of a divine knowledge that is simultaneously the "terror," the horror of a self-knowledge that blinds. Welcomed by Theseus, Oedipus becomes Athens's "holy terror." At his death Oedipus regains a semblance of majesty. At the very moment that he is divested of his sacred suffering, the sovereignty of this fate is transferred to Theseus, that slayer of monsters and seducer of women, the hero who most forcefully represents by these dual feats the civilizing, masculine virtues of Greek society.[91] In return for

[90] Goux, *Oedipus, Philosopher*, 185–86.

[91] Anzieu underlines the many resemblances between Oedipus and Theseus, their inherent mutuality: "Like Oedipus, Theseus goes looking for his father and kills him, but from the beginning he knows who his father is, and it is indirectly that he provokes his death. In the same

Athens's hospitality, for Athens's accepting to provide him with a sepulcher, Oedipus hallowed secret remains with the kings of that city. It is a secret that is passed from king to king, forming a chain, an oedipal legacy of sovereignty. The oedipal desire for the rule of the One, the masculine imperative of/for sovereignty, passes from Thebes to Athens, and from Athens it goes on to colonize the West.[92]

Metaphysically, that is, "politically" speaking, the entire movement of Racinian tragedy will be to flee the sinful flesh of the mother and come into the place of Oedipus the king. Racine's task will be to concretize, through the tragic narration, precisely the Absence the father has become, the father no longer condemned to the passions of the body but, freed from that physicality, become pure "essence," finally the law (the God of *Athalie*). But, of course, the only way tragedy can move us toward this absolute moment of the law is by embodying this movement as a turn away from the material, from the flesh. In other words, Racinian "absolute tragedy" can work its ideological sleight-of-hand by which the body is denied and the spirit made triumphant only by two mutually interrelated moves: (1) equating, as we've seen with Jocasta, all the sins of the corporal with the body coded as "feminine" (most notably, but not exclusively, in the female protagonists); and (2) showing the temptations of the flesh, incarnated in the feminine, to be inherently a threat to any form of stable, political life.

Using the recent studies of the phantasmatic aspects of female sexuality by several French women analysts, Eugène Enriquez offers an explanation of why the place and status of female sexuality seems to pose a threat to masculine notions of political stability. Emphasizing the specter of the "archaic mother" as destabilizing for both men and women, Enriquez's (classically Freudian) point seems particularly congenial to our understanding of the dynamics of Racine's tragic world:

> The social order is founded on symbolization and repression. There can be no order without words that prohibit and words that represent, no order without taboos and safe havens. But woman (either mother or daughter) threatens the social when she enunciates the primacy of pleasure, of bodily relations, of the double relation, of reality over words, representations and mediated relations.
>
> Man can only be fascinated and terrorized by the threat that a precocious femininity poses to the realm of law and order. All the more so because it is never simply a question of 'women left to themselves' the young man also . . .

---

way Theseus's incest is displaced from his mother to his sister-in-law while Phèdre's is displaced from her son to her stepson. In Theseus's fate the Oedipus complex will be expressed by approximations" ("Oedipe avant le complexe," 686).

[92] Gilles Deleuze and Félix Guattari, in *L'anti-Oedipe* (Paris: Minuit, 1975), trans. Robert Hurley, Mark Seem, Helen Lane, *Anti-Oedipus* (New York: Viking Press, 1977), talk of the colonizing potential of the oedipal: "Oedipus is always colonization pursued by other means . . . where we Eurpoeans are concerned, it is our intimate colonial education" (170).

can fall victim to this impossibility of freeing himself from the archaic mother.[93]

The throne (and therefore political order), which as we've already seen in *La Thébaïde* is by its exclusivity defined as a masculine (in that no *partage* is possible), has been usurped in *Britannicus*, as it will also be in *Athalie* ("une impie étrangère / Du sceptre de David usurpe tous les droits" (I.i)—the image of the scepter underscores even more, if need be, the sexual perversion that this political act also represents). In a less radical form the feminization of the throne will also be the threat to political stability in *Bajazet* and in *Bérénice*. Néron's desperate struggle to become emperor, that is, sovereign, manifests itself by a double gesture: he literally dethrones Agrippine, and ravishes Junie, bringing her from her dwelling into the imperial palace and thus into the orbit of his lust. Both of these actions of course are but two sides of the same coin; Néron's double attempts to assert his sovereignty. These aborted acts of political and sexual independence are inextricably connected to his visceral attraction/repulsion to his mother Agrippine. It is only by striking out against her, in a perversely pleasurable act of ingratitude, the first step toward the eventual (unrepresented, but always known) matricide, that Néron can, as Agrippine, adroitly perceives, be free:

> Ce jour, ce triste jour frappe encor ma mémoire,
> Où Néron fut lui-même ébloui de sa gloire,
> Quand les ambassadeurs de tant de rois divers
> Vinrent le reconnaître au nom de l'univers.
> Sur son trône avec lui j'allais prendre ma place:
> J'ignore quel conseil prépara ma disgrâce;
> Quoi qu'il en soit, Néron, d'aussi loin qu'il me vit,
> Laissa sur son visage éclater son dépit.
> Mon coeur même en conçut un malheureux augure.
> L'ingrat, d'un faux respect colorant son injure,
> S'éleva par avance; et courant m'embrasser,
> Il m'écarta du trône où je m'allais placer.
> Depuis ce coup fatal le pouvoir d'Agrippine
> Vers sa chute à grands pas chaque jour s'achemine.
> (I. i)

Agrippine is, of course, prescient. While both the origin and the bloody denouement of her political downfall are situated beyond the representational parameters of the tragedy, the political/sexual imbroglio that forms the central tragic axis of the play clearly establishes the incestuous battle between these two "monsters" as leading to only one issue: Agrippine's elimination by her son. Neron is politically and sexually in Agrippine's thrall: she

[93] Enriquez, *De la horde à l'état*, 214. See the whole section "La femme, jouissance et la mort," 212–33.

has organized his sexual life (his marriage to Octavie), thereby subordinating his desire to hers. Néron can only desire within the confines outlined by his mother, within her desire, and the enormous frustration this produces precipitates the aggressive necessity to eliminate her. He cannot exist as a free agent as long as his mother, literally her physical presence, remains between him and the world:

> Eloigné de ses yeux, j'ordonne, je menace,
> J'écoute vos conseils, j'ose les approuver;
> Je m'excite contre elle, et tâche à la braver:
> Mais, je t'expose ici mon âme toute nue,
> Sitôt que mon malheur me ramène à sa vue,
> Soit que je n'ose encor démentir le pourvoir
> De ces yeux où j'ai lu si longtemps mon devoir;
> Soit qu'à tant de bienfaits ma mémoire fidèle
> Lui soumette en secret tout ce que je tiens d'elle.
> Mais enfin mes efforts ne me servent de rien:
> Mon génie étonné tremble devant le sien.
> Et c'est pour m'affranchir de cette dépendance,
> Que je la fuis partout, que même je l'offense.
> (II. ii)

Néron's lust for Junie is, as Agrippine perceives, but the other (sexual) side of his attempt to eradicate her politically. The battle in *Britannicus* therefore is a double-pronged effort to eliminate the devouring, incestuous mother. But it is infinitely more than that, too. It is an imbroglio where politics and sexuality (and sexuality as inherently incestuous, that is, apolitical) constantly reshuffle the fate of the Roman Empire, as they redefine the very biological predicates of gender roles.

Roland Barthes, in his essay on Racine, has astutely remarked that in Racinian tragedy sexuality (the perceived notions of masculinity and femininity as attached to some biological, natural essence) is shown to be a "myth," a social construction. Barthes tells us that in Racine sexuality is "de-essentialized": it is no longer attached to some presupposed "biological" reality but rather is a production of political forces: " The division of the Racinian world into strong and weak, into tyrants and captives, covers in a sense the division of the sexes: it is their situation in the relation of force that orchestrates some of the characters as virile and others as feminine, without concern for their biological sex."[94] It is this political production of sexuality that enables Barthes (and us, through his reading) to see how certain of Racine's female protagonists—Agrippine, Roxane, Athalie—can be perceived as "masculine" in that they are active, aggressive, dominating (and essentially castrating), while several of his male characters—Britanni-

[94] Barthes, *On Racine*, 13.

cus, Néron, Bajazet, Hippolyte—are all viewed in their passivity as "feminine."[95]

Although I believe that Barthes has given us an extremely perceptive insight into how sexuality functions in the Racinian world, I would like to place a small addendum to what allows us to understand this "de-essentialized" sexuality as part and parcel of the coming into being of the oedipal subject whose trajectory the "ur-Racinian" tragedy adumbrates. While it is true that, as Barthes claims, sexuality in the Racininan universe is divorced from biology, by this very same gesture that sexuality is defined as "monstrous" by the text. This negative projection represents, on yet another level, the ideological imperative, the societal desire, for an adequate, that is, "normative" equation between biology and (psycho-)sexuality. What I mean by this is that all the characters mentioned above are tragic because they are associated with the "monstrous," with what is seen as an aberration in the "natural order" of the world. So, although, as Barthes says, sexuality in Racine is not (self-evidently) "natural," it is precisely because it is not natural, viz. monstrous, that this scenario of Racinian sexuality is perfectly consistent with the oedipal legend that on another level the plays reproduce.

For what do we see when we look carefully at all these "monstrous" (because sexually "inverted") couples? Of course, speaking in classical analytic terms, the confrontation of the young male with the aggressive, threatening, castrating figure of an older, sexually experienced female refigures the resurgence of, as Mauron would have it, the terrifying image of the devouring "archaic mother." But, when we translate these same structural givens into the terms of the mythical representation of the oedipal legend, we see emerging from the shadows the grizzly images of the destroyed, mauled, partly eaten remains of those young men who, in their attempts to achieve kingly status, confronted the Sphinx and failed to satisfy her. The "monstrousness" of Racine's aggressively active female protagonists replicates the monstrous hybrid nature of the Sphinx who lingers at the gates of Thebes, wreaking havoc on the polis. Marie Delcourt reminds us that the Sphinx can be seen as just another in a line of "mortiferous" female beings (the Erinyes, Keres, the Harpies, being other related creatures) who, in their "hunger for food and erotic pleasure," all prey on nubile young men."[96] The Sphinx is a vampirish sexual predator and before her meeting with Oedipus, all of the young men who confront her fall prey to her passionate riddle. When Oedipus enters upon the scene, therefore, he appears not only as the savior of the city but, also and concomitantly, of masculinity. His solving of the riddle imposes the reign of (masculine) abstract reasoning: the

[95] Serge Doubrovsky, in his Lacanian reading of *Britannicus*, "L'arrivée de Junie dans *Britannicus*: La tragédie d'une scène à l'autre," in *Littérature*, 32 (Dec. 1978): 27–54, picks up on Barthes's statement and offers a complex analysis of the "feminine" position of Néron.

[96] Delcourt, *Oedipe ou la légende*, 110.

confrontation represents the triumph of masculine ideality over female materiality.

The politics that the Oedipus myth represents, the politics that is condensed in and on the figure of the riddle-solving perpetrator of parricide and incest, is also an originary moment of Western masculine hegemony. It is an absolutist politics that, in the very answer "man" (which sends the Sphinx—oriental, female monster—to her suicide), is the verbal gesture of inclusion/exclusion that will mark the coming into being of Western consciousness as both consciousness of self and therefore the idea of a self that necessarily excludes its other. It is the *heimliche* from which the *unheimliche* (the Sphinx, and all that her monstrousness represents—the body, as female, as chaotic, as death) is cast beyond the pale. This gesture that incorporates thought as self-evidence introduces this thought in and as a masculine prerogative, as male, thus arrogating to itself the light of intelligence and casting out into the darkness all that is not "I." All that is other, all that is nonintegral, is eliminated, ushering in the reign of masculine, oedipal hegemony.[97]

It would seem that the Racinian tragic world, on the level that it reflects for Absolutism the coming into being of the desire for the king ("Oedipus tyrannos"), obsessively repeats how that absolutist political construction must be coterminous with the *mise-en-place* of the oedipal sexual configuration. This configuration always already inscribes the fate of human infants as having necessarily to resist the siren pull of the mother. They must, in order to be, in order for society to exist and survive, break free of her hold and align themselves (both male *and* female children) with the symbolic law of the father. In the narration of the oedipal sexual trajectory both the boy child and the girl child, in order to assume a position of independent sexual and political subjectivity, in order to become absolutist subjects, must separate from the mother. This separation is accomplished by their (different) identifications with the father, who splits the child from the mother in a symbolic double gesture. First, the child is made to recognize that it is the father and not him/herself who is the object of the mother's desire. Consequently, that desire is henceforth both "illegal" (i.e. incestuous) and destined to remain forever frustrated. It is this realization that leads the child out of the too-suffocating embrace of the mother and onto the path of social development.[98]

[97] See Heath, "The Ethics of Sexual Difference," and Goux, *Oedipus, Philosopher*, for a detailed analysis of the sexual/philosophical implications of this portion of the Oedipus legend.

[98] Enriquez pithily summarizes this complex problematic in the following way (*De la horde à l'état*): "All love is, by definition, endogamous and incestuous. How can we not love those bodies with which every human being has a spontaneous sensual and sensory relation, because of biological reasons and because of the prematurity of the individual. . . . The degenitalization of love becomes, therefore, indispensable for the creation of social ties. The prohibition of incest is indeed the founding prohibition of civilization. If we admit that mother-son incest is older and more violently protested than father-daughter incest, another role of the prohibition

Certainly the harrowing tragic duels that pit these young "feminized" men against the Sphinx-like devouring older woman and end in death and social disorder seem to sketch out for us the terrors (political and sexual) that would await civilization in general at their defeat—chaos, fragmentation, and eventual extinction. Agrippine is incestuous ("Mais ce lien du sang qui nous joignait tous deux /Écartait Claudius d'un lit incestueux"), homicidal ("Il mourut. Mille bruits en courent à ma honte"), and sexually manipulative ("Je vois de votre coeur Octavie effacée/Prête à sortir du lit où je l'avais placée," IV. ii). Roxane appears insatiable in her sadistic cruelty. But, perhaps, as we might expect, the most frightening avatar of the Sphinx in Racine is Athalie, the last, the most powerful, and the most horrifyingly unnatural ("injuste marâtre") woman in Classical tragedy, whose sanguinary image Racine has engraved on our imagination:

> Qui sait si cet enfant, par leur crime entraîné,
> Avec eux en naissant ne fut pas condamné?
> Si Dieu, le séparant d'une odieuse race,
> En faveur de David voudra lui faire grâce.
> Hélas! l'état horrible où le ciel me l'offrit
> Revient à tout moment effrayer mon esprit.
> De princes égorgés la chambre était remplie;
> Un poignard à la main, l'implacable Athalie
> Au carnage animait ses barbares soldats,
> Et pousuivait le cours de ses assassinats.
> (I,ii)

None of the young men confronting these devouringly possessive woman can hope to escape unscathed from their embrace, which as Mauron reminds us recasts as tragedy that most horrifyingly primitive of human fantasies: "the greatest human anxiety is to reach out one's arms to a being who turns out to be murderous."[99] Finally, it falls once again to a young prince, a victim of his parents homicidal aggression, ignorant of his royal origins, to successfully confront the Sphinx, correctly answer her questions, and precipitate her (eventual) downfall:

> ATHALIE: Comment vous nommez-vous?
> JOAS: J'ai nom Eliacin.

---

appears in all its scope: the prohibition aims at distancing, at definitively separating, sons from their mothers. . . . The son must always struggle with the phantasm of maternal plenitude. Even if the mother be devouring, possessive, castrating or simply loving, she performs, by this very love, violence on the body of the child-phallus from which he must succeed in freeing himself" (191), and again (193) he states that "the only essential incest is incest with the mother, be that for men or for women. The rule of human life, the possibility of civilization is: 'Don't go back to your mother.' "

[99] Mauron, *L'inconscient dans l'oeuvre*, 37.

ATHALIE: Votre père?
JOAS: Je suis, dit-on, un orphelin
Entre les bras de Dieu jeté dès ma naissance,
Et qui de mes parents n'eus jamais connaissance.
ATHALIE: Vous êtes sans parents?
JOAS: Ils m'ont abandonné.
ATHALIE: Comment? et depuis quand?
JOAS: Depuis que je suis né.
ATHALIE: Ne sait-on pas au moins quel pays est le vôtre?
JOAS: Ce temple est mon pays; je n'en connais point d'autre.
ATHALIE: Où dit-on que le sort vous a fait rencontrer?
JOAS: Parmi les loups cruels prêts à me dévorer.
. . . .
ATHALIE: Mais de vos premiers ans quelles mains ont pris soin?
JOAS: Dieu laissa-t-il jamais ses enfants au besoin? (II. vii)

With the correct answer, "Dieu," that is to say the father, Eliacin/Joas has reaffirmed the paternal principle that triumphs in this battle for the restitution of oedipal, political devolution. Not only does he thus prepare the way for the vindication of the entire ascending line of his divinely ordained genealogy but he also affirms the legality of his successors, ending as we know with Christ. He thus establishes the triumphant reign of the eternal King.[100]

The triumph of Joas over the Sphinx-like Athalie intervenes in the last tragedy of Racine. We should not forget that the final word Racine wrote for the theater was "père," thus reasserting, if need be, where his theater, at least on the level of its narrative unfolding, stood in relation to the entire ideological thrust of seventeenth-century French absolutist culture.[101] In the intervening plays, before this conclusive resolution, the disruptive forces of female sexuality are held at bay by those equally terrifying fathers of the Racinan mythic world. Mithridate, Agammenon, Titus (perversely, melancholically), and finally Joad in *Athalie* by representing a culturally sanctioned ideal of virility defend absolutist culture against the lure and terror of the feminine, asserting over the devouring demands of maternity, the separating, individuating, but no less terrible exigencies of patriarchy.

But, for the time being I would like to concentrate on the most exemplary (for the Oedipus legend) of those Racinian fathers—Theseus, as he is in-

[100] It is the triumph of the father/king that ensures, or at least attempts to ensure, the fixity of the oedipal sexual scenario, which, as Bersani tells us, "is the basis not of a psychic ascension, but rather of a legalization of emotional rigidities and moral tyrannies" (*A Future for Astyanax*, 38).

[101] Franco Moretti reminds us that while the actual day-to-day institutions of absolutist culture were varied, fraught with contradictions, and hesitant about their own potential, the theater represented a world freed of those contingencies. The theater represented the "desire" for absolutism; see "A Huge Eclipse," *Genre*, 15 (1982): 29: "If the general culture of absolutism qualified the sovereign power it conferred upon the king with countless hesitations and uncertainties . . . tragedy surrenders such power to him wholly and without the slightest reserve. In the world of tragedy, the monarch is truly absolute. . . . Tragedy then stages not the institutions of absolutism, but its culture, its values, its ideology."

scribed within the meanders of Racine's most brilliantly seductive tragedy *Phèdre*. The trajectory of royal habilitation we have been pursuing, and its concomitant valency of an oedipalized sexuality reaches its narrative culmination in *Phèdre*, and it does so by concentrating in one powerfully evocative drama all the diverse aspects, political and sexual, of the oedipal problematic.

Beneath the dilemma of the heroine condemned to the passion of her body, a lust she claims not to be able to master despite all her efforts and that thus makes her prey, Sphinx-like, on the body of her husband's son, the young, "superbe Hippolyte," can we not see in *Phèdre* a displacement of the archaic conflict between the generations of men for political and sexual dominance? In his complex reconstruction of the different mythological intermeshings of the themes of incest and kingship in ancient Greece, Didier Anzieu presents Theseus as an Oedipus in "demi-teinte":

> Theseus, king of Athens, is a distant descendant of Erichtonios, that is to say, he owes his primal origin to a half-consummated coitus between a half-brother and a half-sister: in Theseus the oedipal fate will be developed in halftones, the incest theme will concern a sister-in-law, then a stepson, the parricide will be both indirect and only halfhearted.[102]

But, it is precisely this "demi-teinte," this blurring and thus mythic softening of the too-direct horrors of the Oedipus legend itself that allows us a more "normative" solution to the turbulent, chaotic, asocial demands of the body that Phèdre's lust for Hippolyte represents. By the time Racine came to write *Phèdre*, the oedipal conflict had become so internalized that politics and sexuality seamlessly coalesce in this drama. All the characters are entrapped in a reciprocity of desire in which each, by mirroring the desire of the others, becomes for those others a monster.

In the tragedy that bears her name alone only since the 1687 edition of the play, Phèdre is the center of the drama because it is in her, in the visceral, insatiable needs of a body cursed by its own "blood," that the oedipal crime of transgressive incest surfaces as both desire and terror. Unlike the grotesque Sphinx at Thebes, however, Phèdre's hybrid, monstrous nature is not represented on the body, but in the body: Phèdre's monstrousness is internalized as her conflicted passion and guilt. Phèdre appears as the interstice of "biology" and "ideology" in that in her, in her mythically conflicted origins (daughter of the sun and of chtonian deities), nature and culture are already at war, and in this war, her body, her accursed passions are what fall to her lot, as female, in a genealogy of women:

> PHÈDRE: O haine de Vénus! O fatale colère!
> Dans quels égarements l'amour jeta ma mère!

[102] Anzieu, "Oedipe avant le complexe," 682.

OENONE: Oublions-les madame; et qu'à tout l'avenir
Un silence éternel cache ce souvenir.
PHÈDRE: Ariane, ma soeur, de quel amour blessée
Vous mourûtes aux bords où vous fûtes laissée!
OENONE: Que faites-vous, madame? et quel mortel ennui
Contre tout votre sang vous anime aujourd'hui?
PHÈDRE: Puisque Vénus le veut, de ce sang déplorable
Je péris la dernière et la plus misérable. (I. iii)

In this most intensely constricted of Racinian tragedies, the echoes of the body return, first in Phèdre, later in Hippolyte, and in both cases they return as politically and sexually unacceptable:

Je le vis, je rougis, je pâlis à sa vue;
Un trouble s'éleva dans mon âme éperdue
Mes yeux ne voyaient plus, je ne pouvais parler;
Je sentis tout mon corps et transir et brûler;
Je reconnus Vénus et ses feux redoutables,
D'un sang qu'elle poursuit, tourments inévitables.
(I. vii)

It is this irreducible presence of the body, and Phèdre's impossibility to master its imperious desires that paradigmatically situates her as one of those monsters that Greek masculinity, represented most notably by Theseus, must contain and eliminate.[103]

Although Theseus is also marked by his body (his sexual exploits are legendary and intimately defining of his heroic essence), the play in an ambivalent gesture constantly reminds us of his sexuality but also points away from it. Theseus's unbridled sexuality is presented (especially, and significantly, by his son) as a thing of the past, "Cher Théramène, arrête; et respecte Thésée/ De ses jeunes erreurs désormais revenu." This might just seem a dutiful vow on the part of the son as an attempt to idolize the father. But we could just as well see it as a denial by the son. Despite the over-

[103] Joan DeJean reads Phèdre's famous monologue as a Racinian riff on Sappho, and Sapphic passion. See *Fictions of Sappho* (Chicago: University of Chicago Press, 1989). Perhaps this is the place for small excursus into the importance and multiple meanings of *sang* (blood) in the Racinian corpus. Obviously, *sang* is an important signifier not only for a nobiliary culture but also for a culture where Galenic medical theories dominate. The single word functions always on several levels at once, metaphorically and metonymically, synchronically and diachronically. While on the one hand *sang* is used to refer to the physical substance that flows through the circulatory system, the loss of which causes death, it is also used as a synonym for "genealogy," "family," "race," for past history and future descent. Galenic theory lends *sang* its sexual valencies: it is the concoction of the blood that produces, in its most "refined" form, sperm, and in its less-than-perfect form, milk, thus reinscribing a preexisting sexual hierarchy depending on whether its associations are to males or to females. Finally, of course, *sang* becomes both a metaphor and a metonymy for "passion," "desire," "love," in that it represents what affects all the bodily humors.

whelming evidence to the contrary that fills the entire Greek world, Hippolyte wants to believe the father is not sexual, not a potent force to be recognized and reckoned with. In this Hippolyte can be seen as acceding, as he does in the rest of his behavior, to the virginal, asexual side of his nature inherited from his amazon mother, Antiope. In the son's fantasy, Theseus's body has been eliminated. Yet this fantasized castration of the father returns to haunt and eventually destroy the son. Theseus has gone through (castration) death ("il m'enferma dans des cavernes sombres/ Lieux profonds et voisins de l'empire des ombres") and reemerges on its far side, more threateningly potent as the incarnation of the law. He thus enters the universe of the play, a doubly guilty world, ready to punish, blindly, arbitrarily, any who are suspected of sinning against the father, of encroaching upon his prerogatives, of breaching his law. And Hippolyte is the most notable victim of course, the sacrificial victim who, despite all his protests to the contrary, is guilty. He is guilty of lusting after the (always prohibited) woman, be that woman Phèdre or Aricie. Hippolyte's fate in the masculine dynamics of kingship and sexuality is to be the "sacred" (guilty/innocent) victim. There is no other possible position available to him in the world of mythic devolution. The son, by acceding to the woman (the taboo object of paternal prerogative), threatens the role of the father and must therefore either (as both Oedipus and Theseus have done before him) remove the father and take his place or die.

Hippolyte dies, condemned by his father and his world. His death is a sacrifice of the child to the order of oedipal patriarchy, and it is predestined from the very beginning by the law that presides over the world of Absolutism. In a world that wants the rule of the integral, Hippolyte, like Phèdre, is an anomaly, a dual being, a cross between "nature and culture," between the world of the father, the world of politics, and the savage universe of Antiope, his amazon mother. From Antiope comes his aversion to sexuality. But with such an antecedent this aversion can only be interpreted as the refusal of the sexuality of the father, the refusal to assume a sexuality that is already inscribed in a patriarchal political network. Hippolyte always remains on the far side of the sexuality that defines Thésée's dominion over the world, always also with a sexuality that is other. When Hippolyte falls in love with Aricie this love only relays his double nature; that is, he falls in love *outside* of paternal sexuality. His passion is "transgressive" because the only object it can find is out of bounds, is outside (as it must be) the father's law. By this same token, and in ways that relate him ever more closely to Phèdre in a mirrorlike gendered reversal, Hippolyte is "monstrous," and must therefore be eliminated from the world of the law.

Hippolyte's death is the most lushly extended evocation of the body in all of Racine's theater. But true to the Classicism's ambivalence toward the body, the evocation in Théramène's monologue is double, split between the body monstrous and the body punished. The speech begins languorously, melancholically, with the evocation of Hippolyte's long announced but forever delayed departure from Trézène: "A peine nous sortions des portes de Trézène . . ." This languid tone reflects both the internal psychological state of Hippolyte and his followers as well as the external landscape of the route they are taking, a road that meanders between land and sea. In this fashion a connection between inner and outer worlds is established, forming an intermeshing of the human and the "natural" (the cultural and the biological) that corroborates the universal significance of the sacrifice to come. This first heavy, slow pace is broken off suddenly ("un effroyable cri") by the eruption from the sea of the monstrous:

> Cepandant, sur le dos de la plaine liquide,
> S'élève à gros bouillons une montagne humide;
> L'onde approche, se brise, et vomit à nos yeux,
> Parmi des flots d'écume, un monstre furieux.
> Son front large est armé de cornes menaçantes;
> Tout son corps est couvert d'écailles jaunissantes;
> Indomptable taureau, dragon impétueux;
> Ses longs mugissements font trembler le rivage.
> (V. vi)

What most characterizes the monsters that populate the Racinian universe, be they "real" monsters (the Minotaur, or the "bull from the sea") or metaphorical monsters (Néron) is their essential heterogeneity. They are all double. The Minotaur, of course, is half human, half animal, the product of the lustful, unnatural coupling of Pasiphaë and a bull. The bull that Neptune sends from the sea is a monster most noticeably because it is a heterogeneous being, a being composed of parts from different origins—mammal, reptile, actual animals, and imaginary bestiaries. At the same time, of course, its entire being is infused, doubled by and with the idea of an excessive sexuality that cannot be properly contained, that in its essence represents transgression—the metaphorical echoes of both "cornes" and "jaunissantes" recalling the traditional symbols of cuckoldry, adultery, and (by extension, in this play) incest. In this way, the monstrousness of the bull from the sea sent to punish Hippolyte, but also to punish Thésée, is but an allegory of those crimes, those destructive, sexual impulses that threaten the absolute world of oedipal patriarchy.[104] They are (it is, the monster that is) simply the repressed desires of that order returned with an exemplary vengeance.

After the detailed image of the monstrous body of the bull from the sea, we are given the pathetic image of the human body, the shining "corps glo-

[104] Leo Spitzer, in "The 'Récit de Théramène' in Racine's *Phèdre*," in *Essays in Seventeenth-Century French Literature*, ed. David Bellos (Cambridge: Cambridge University Press, 1981), 218, insists that Hippolyte has "inherited his father's double nature."

rieux" that inspired Phèdre's lust. It is returned to the Racinian text, flayed, broken, bloodied: "tout son corps n'est bientôt qu'une plaie." Caught up in the maenadic fury of the text, whose rhythm has speeded up to imitate the murderous rapidity with which his stampeding horses have dragged Hippolyte's body across the rocky field, so that: "De son généreux sang . . . /Les rochers en sont teints; les ronces égouttantes/Portent de ses cheveux les dépouilles sanglantes," we return to the image of those broken, partly devoured bodies of all those other young men undone by the Sphinx.

How are we to understand (or is understanding possible in front of the "tragic") this sacrifice of the innocent? At the height of Racine's career, politics and sexuality only reiterate, in ever more tightly constructed scenarios, the essential violence inherent in the oedipal structure. Sexuality, as Leo Bersani has written, in its most fundamental aspect is always incestuous, and thus inimical to society at large, to the family as produced by that society and finally to the very subject formed at their conjuncture.[105] This sexuality, which reflects the father's own desire as the return of precisely what he has had to suppress to become the father, can only be branded as "monstrous": it is the return of what in one's self annihilates this self. The sexuality of the child, which we might say is always the reflection of the desire of the parents, of law, reflects back to the father the necessity of its sacrifice as that which founds the community. This community is united precisely because individual desire has been channeled into collective enterprise, into societal living. This means that the sacrifice of individual desire is relayed into a communality of mutually held ideals of which the father is the vehicle. Sexuality is corralled into law and politics. At the same time this containment is never totally successful; the repressed returns in those figures of otherness that patriarchy cannot entirely subdue—the haunting fear of female sexuality, the woman as passion, and the equally mistrusted image of the child who has not yet been brought into line.

The sacrifice that is central to Racine's entire opus turns on ridding the community of the monstrous within itself. Concomitantly this monstrous is centered on the woman and on the child—because they are always double and inimical to the world of sovereignty. When in Racine the tragic takes the form of child sacrifice as it does here as an attempt to shore up the ideology of the One, it is also, and at the same time a perverse attack on patriarchy by its own ideological predicates. The duality of being inheres in all of us, secretly undermining any ideology of the One. It therefore is a particularly aggressive counterattack by patriarchy on its descendants that Racine's theater plays out. At the same time, however, his acting out reveals the hidden ambivalence of all sacrifice, for by attacking the son, patriarchy in a very obvious sense is shown to be obliged to always turn in and to attack itself. Destroying one's progeny whose recognition the Father needs in

[105] Bersani, *A Future for Astyanax*, 42.

order precisely to be the father (without a child that recognizes and thus instantiates the role of the father, there is no father possible) destroys at one and the same time any link between a past and future.[106] This is, perhaps, the greatest tragedy that Racine's theater stages: the imperious desire to be absolute at the same time that that desire is shown to be (by the very predicates of Absolutism) impossible.

The "recit de Théramène," although a tour de force of Racinian dramaturgy, nevertheless strikes many critics, Leo Spitzer first among them, almost as a rhetorical anomaly within the canon of Classical rhetoric. Spitzer points out that this speech reveals the continued presence of the baroque within the canon of French Classicism.[107] I would like to enlarge the already notoriously capacious semantic field of the word baroque which retains all the echoes of Classicism's prejudices of what is "excessive," "indistinct," "heterogeneous," of what has had to be repressed in order to be "Classical," to make it ring synonymously with the term "grotesque" I have been using in this study to describe the presence of the body in its uncensored (by the predicates of absolutist ideology) presentability. In a sense the baroque textual/ body represented in the "récit de Théramène," in its bloodied disruption, acts as a pivot careening the Racininan text out of the political equipoise to which oedipal Absolutism tends and plunges it back into a scenario of fanatasmatic chaos.

The baroque/grotesque body repeats on the level of originary fantasies the impossibility of achieving a normative, representational stasis that would provide an unshakable foundation for the hegemonic impetus of Absolutism's political and social self-construction. I am suggesting that the intrusive reappearance of the excessive body, the body banned by the epistemic turn of Classicism, reappears (fragmented, broken) in those pivotal textual anomalies that always address, in a highly charged concentration, elements of sexuality, as seduction, castration (i.e. sacrifice), and dissolution. These reappearances are carried by the textual "voice," but here the voice is not part of the integral narrative. Rather it is the voice of the phantasmatic, interrupting that narrative proposing another, hidden corpus of dramatic verities. These originary fantasies of the Racinian universe include, along with the scene of Hippolyte's death, those famous, almost hallucinatory, nocturnal scenes wherein sexuality and violence intermingle in a nightmarelike vision: the destruction of Troy in *Andromaque*, the sack of

[106] Enriquez remarks, *De la horde à l'état*, 243: "If without a father there cannot be any children (in the social sense of the term) without children, that is, without individuals able to recognize the law of the father and to identify with the ideals for which he is the vehicle, there cannot be a father, either."

[107] Spitzer, "The 'Récit de Théramène' in Racine's *Phèdre*," 218. Barthes also uses, but for other, socioeconomic reasons, the word baroque to describe Racine; see *On Racine*, 149: "Racine is certainly a very impure, even baroque author, one might say, in whom elements of genuine tragedy mingle discordantly with the already vigorous germs of the future bourgeois theatre."

Lesbos in *Iphigénie*, the murder of the innocents in *Athalie*, the massacre of the Jews in *Esther*, the apotheosis of Titus in *Bérénice*, Néron's fantasy of Junie arriving in his palace in *Britannicus*, Mithridate's rhetorical fantasy of his destruction of Rome. What is particularly striking in all of these scenes is that here the textual voice paints visionary tableaux into which the protagonists gaze at their own projection as a vision, but an unfocusable vision. The voice and the vision become indistinguishable, the one relaying the other, instantaneously transcoding voice into vision, and vision into voice just as the quotation from Proust quoted above does—there the voice of the actress metamorphoses into a painted vision of Titian, only to morph back at the end of the quote into poetry without any discernible stop or point of demarcation. Voice, rhythm, poetry are immediately translated into/as a fleeting vision, a glance at another reality. This reality in turn is carried into our own perceptive field as the ethereally seductive voice in which poetry and painting continually oscillate between two perceptual poles, fused into one.

Although they are always present in these spectacular scenarios, Racine's protagonists gaze at their own interior vision with an intensity that reveals its at once alienating and fascinating hold on them and on us. The scenes function as moments of fixation, arresting the hero in a reverie that combines the intense visual depiction with purely fictitious invention. Their vision(s) is (are) both a beginning and an end that they regard with endless fascination. They are captivated by what they see and in that captivation they are undone. By its intense libidinal affect their fantasy arrests the protagonists gaze forever preventing any adequate understanding and resolution. Borrowing from Christine Buci-Glucksmann we might say that Racine's protagonists stare at their own inner scenes, repeat them in their incantation, with such intense fascination "with the sole aim, finally, of no longer seeing, but of being" to find, there in their unfathomable visions, the answer to their original question "Who am I?"—the question of their origins—but by the very force of their gaze no answer, except death, is ever forthcoming.[108]

In his well-known essay "Racine et la poétique du regard," Jean Starobinski was one of the first to call our attention to the profound and impenetrable depths this inner vision opened before the mesmerized gaze of Racine's heroes:

> In Racine, behind what one sees is what one dimly perceives, and farther still the presence of a reality that one can intuit without seeing any of it at all. . . . Their depth is due to an absence of an established and entirely visible nature; it is the product of what we can call at one and the same time an excess and a lack.[109]

[108] C. Buci-Glucksmann, *La folie du voir: De l'esthétique baroque* (Paris: Galilée, 1986), 74.
[109] J. Starobinski, *L'oeil vivant*, (Paris: Gallimard, 1961), 73.

Starobinski goes on to tell us that each of these famous "nighttime" scenes has the particular merit of referring to "a primary event, situated before the beginning of the represented action," of being, in other words, located on another scene, a scene that is absent from the tragedy but never ceases to exert an influence over the entire represented drama.[110]

It is the originary aspect of these scenes that I find felicitously congenial with what psychoanalysis has termed "originary fantasies." These fantasies, most specifically, the fantasy of the "primal scene," are inextricably related to the oedipal scenario, and yet, entirely "opposed" to it.[111] Tragedy results when the reminiscence of the originary fantasy erupts in construction of the oedipal plot. In a very perverse sense the primary "tragic flaw" returns in the drama to destabilize both the reliability of the tragic diegesis and the protagonist who is the product of that narrative.

Let us not forget that the oedipal narrative that these scenes interrupt is, as we have said, borne along on the "voice" of tragedy. It is "le dit" which is overheard by the audience. In his discussion of the importance of "sound" (the "noise"), Freud makes particular reference to its importance in the originary fantasies. What Freud is describing, in the above quotation when he refers to the "voice" we have all heard before, will later be fleshed out in his theory of those "originary (or primal) fantasies," the *Urszcenen*, that we all enact for ourselves on the stage of our own private theater.[112] These originary fantasies, of which the "primal scene" is perhaps the most overdetermined, are, according to the masterful analysis of Jean Laplanche and Jean-Bertrand Pontalis, all attempts, each in its own way, of supplying a response to the unanswerable puzzle of subjective "origins."

> In their very content, in their theme (primal scene, castration, seduction) originary phantasms thus point to this retroactive postulate: they relate back to origins. Like myths . . . they give dramatic form to those moments of emergence

[110] Ibid., 80. Barthes, *On Racine*, 18, refers to these same scenes as "erotic; they are, in effect, veritable hallucinations [de véritables fantasmes]. . . . The striking thing about Racininan hallucination is its plastic aspect, [they are] tableaux, they are deliberately classified under the norms of painting."

[111] See, for instance, Jean-Claude Lavie "Excellence paradigmatique de la scène primitive," in *Nouvelle Revue de Psychanalyse*, 46(1992): 14: "Oedipal rivalry and the primal scene are fatally tied together." Later he states, 21: "The primal scene, insofar as it is an element in the oedipal conflict, represents the hard kernel of the conflict. For any man, the way he has integrated the scene of his own conception will become a paradigm for his relation to the world." See also Guy Rosolato, "Paranoia et scène primitive," in *Essais sur le symbolique*, 204: "The primal scene has the advantage of being centered on the Oedipus complex. . . . It is the . . . matrix for the [subsequent] triangulation."

[112] In their classic work on the originary fantasies, Laplanche and Pontalis, *Fantasme originaire*, remind us (40) that originally Freud used the term *Urszene* as a general term, its more precisely limited sense came later: "These scenes of the originary moments, these real "scenes," are at that time called by Freud *Urszenen* ('originary' or 'primal'). Later on, as we know, this term will be reserved for the observation of parental coitus during which the child would have been present."

> where the origin of a (hi)story appears to the subject as a reality the nature of which calls out for an explanation, a 'theory.' . . . phantasms of origins: in the primal scene it is the origin of the subject which is represented, in the phantasms of seduction, the origin, the upswelling of sexuality, in the phantasms of castration, it is the origin of the difference between the sexes.[113]

These "scenes" are important for many reasons. They help in any attempt at understanding the way a particular individual subjugates him/herself to laws governing the sexual/political position he or she is to assume in order to find an adequate place in the social network. The question of origins that these fantasies answer is also "embodied," that is, it is always a question of families, of bloodlines, and genealogies, of, in other words, the particular fit of the subject (where does he or she come from?) in a line of descent and ascent that can only be inscribed in/as the body. Although the primal fantasies can be considered on the one hand at the "antipodes" of the Oedipus complex, on the other they are inextricably connected to it.[114] They help us to see how the body is made an object of ideology as it incorporates, as "fantasy," an inscription of a semiotic network of power/knowledge that preexists that particular body's entrance onto society's stage and, at the same time, they help us see how fantasies of the body become inscribed in lived sociopolitical experience.[115] In this sense the individual fantasies, in their attempt to answer the unanswerable questions of the subject, are analogous to the role that myth and mythology play in the construction of a cultural identity.[116]

[113] Ibid., 51.

[114] Rosolato offers the most succinct (and contradictory) readings of the relation of the originary fantasies (particularly the "primal scene" and the Oedipus complex): "The primal scene has the advantage of being centered on the Oedipus complex . . . it serves . . . as the matrix for the (subsequent) triangulation" ("Paranoia et scène primitive," in *Essais sur le symbolique*, 204). Then in the essay "La voix" in the same book, he writes that "the phantasm is thus at the extreme opposite pole from the resolution of the oedipal situation, of the acquired difference between the sexes and its correlative castration" (291). Lavie ("Excellence paradigmatique de la scène primitive," 14) also reaffirms the connection between the primal scene and the Oedipus complex: "Oedipal rivalry and the primal scene are fatally tied together."

[115] Norman Bryson, in *Vision and Painting* (New Haven: Yale University Press, 1983) remarks (152): "The Body is certainly that which is inserted into the given institutions of ideology, of economy and crucially of sexual identity, yet also it is that which forms those institutions, subjects them to endless revision, and if need be, overturns them."

[116] In his book *Primal Scenes* Lukacher concentrates his analysis of the interrelation of literature, philosophy and psychoanalysis on the "primal scene." The primal scene is just one of the four "originary scenarios" (castration, seduction, and for some analysts "return to the womb" are the others). What Lukacher underlines for the "primal scene" however, and what, I believe, can be extended to the other scenarios is their constructed (that is, their "poietic" rather than "mimetic") essence: "The primal scene is the figure of an interpretive dilemma; it is a constellation of forgotten intertextual events offered in lieu of a demonstrable, unquestionable origin" (24), or again (330): "The primal scene is a circumstantial construction that is predicated when there is a need to interpret but at the same time a fundamental concealment or absence of the sort of evidence that could definitively substantiate a particular interpretation." That is to say that the primal scene, like all originary phantasms, is an "après-coup" reading of a never actually "real" event/trauma. It is an interpretation, a creation, a fantasy that, as Lukacher says, "lies beyond the history of the subject but nevertheless in history" (105).

In general, psychoanalytic theory considers three (sometimes four) fantasies as "originary"; the "primal scene," that is, the view of parental intercourse by the subject, which would figure the origin of the subject himself/herself; "castration," the origin of sexual difference; "seduction," the eruption of sexuality in the history of the subject; and, less frequently, "the return to the maternal womb."[117] In a sense, therefore, it is not surprising that in Racine's plays where so much of the dramatic tension turns around the unanswerable question—Eriphile/Iphigénie's "Who am I," Bajazet's "What am I," or Phèdre's "Why me?"—her constant oscillation between a desire that shames her and a familial curse that condemns her without her ever understanding why. All of Racine's characters are condemned to a history that has inexorably shaped their own destiny but that forever escapes their understanding. It is, therefore, these originary scenarios that are the phantasmatic answer to the question of "origins"—of who they are, of what they are, and of why they are the way they are. But it is an answer that, instead of providing them with a firm definition of their being, sends them instead reeling into the inchoate.

It is also important to understand, of course, that these phantasmes are illusory reconstructions and as such we must see them as attempts, localized "theoretical attempts," to answer the profoundly enigmatic questions of subjective origins. As attempts they can only answer these questions, sibyl-like, with new conundrums. They are in the most profound sense of the term "fictions," but necessary fictions. In their very constructedness they are "historically" impossible (i.e. in the "primal scene" the subject would be present at the scene of his/her own conception) but psychically "true." The "theoretical" answer that they furnish to the subject's inquiries correspond to that subject's psychosexual self-positioning in the symbolic constructions of the world, as that positioning is shown to be forever beyond the grasp of the subject.[118]

[117] For a general overview of the problematic of originary fantasies see the classic work of Laplanche and Pontalis, *Fantasme originaire*, already mentioned, as well as the special issue of *Nouvelle Revue de Psychanalyse*, 46 (1992), "La scène primitive et quelques autres." Of particular import to my use of the term is the essay of Rosolato, "Les phantasmes originaires et leurs mythes correspondants," in the same issue, 223–45, which synthesizes his many contributions to this discussion.

[118] See Lukacher, *Primal Scenes*, 57, where he states that "recollection does not represent what is, for the simple reason that the scene itself, including the subject's role in it, was never perceived by the subject . . . in place of the original impression, one has access only to its nonoriginary revision." A more detailed explanation is furnished by Guy Fihman, in "Sur les scènes animées des ciné-rêves de Grandville," in *Nouvelle Revue de Psychanalyse*, 46 (1992): 121–39, at 121: " 'In the primal scene it is the origin of the subject that is represented.' This famous definition, which we owe to Jean Laplanche and J.-B. Pontalis, says more than Freud. The originary scene (*Urszene* or "proto-scene") is not only the real or fantasized observation of parental coitus, but the scene of the subject's own conception. Out of space, out of time, this scene has to be a construction. The primal scene owes it status to the meeting, in a nonassignable time, of two enigmas, the enigma of sexuality and the enigma of the origin of the subject. Insofar as it is a represented scene, the primal scene is born of the conjunction of the subject's questions concerning his origin with the tumultuous agitation of parental coitus or of one of its substitutes." Finally Rosolato, "Les phantasmes originaires," 229: "I will insist, therefore, on

Ned Lukacher, who has concentrated his own thinking on one of the originary phantasmes, the "primal scene," as a heuristic device linking literature, philosophy, and psychoanalysis, reminds us that for Freud, in his initial exploration of these phantasmes, they were never "found objects," that is, never "real" past traumata that analysis uncovered. Rather, Freud defined these scenes as "constructions." "Primal scenes," writes Freud, "are as a rule not reproduced as recollections but have to be divined—constructed—gradually and laboriously from an aggregate of indications."[119] From Freud's initial definition of these originary fantasies, Lukacher goes on to define the importance of this phantasmatic construction in the following way: "The primal scene is a circumstantial construction that is predicated when there is a need to interpret but at the same time a fundamental concealment or absence of the sort of evidence that could definitively substantiate a particular interpretation."[120]

What is particularly telling for the connection of this analytic concept of originary fantasies with Racinian tragedy is that they seem to function for the individual psyche depicted inside the tragedy in the same the way "myth" functions in the constitution of collective self-identity. We remember that from the beginning of his thinking about the originary fantasies Freud likened them to "a complicated process of remodeling analogous in every way to the process by which a nation constructs legends about its early history," while Laplanche and Pontalis tell us that "like myths . . . they give dramatic form those emerging moments of a (hi)story that appear to the subject as a reality." Finally, Guy Rosolato has pursued most forcefully the relation between originary fantasies and myth in "Les phantasmes originaires et leurs mythes correspondants," where for each major category of originary fantasies he apposes a corresponding myth: for the "primal scene" the creation myths, chief among them the myth of Adam and Eve; for "castration," the different "sacrificial myths of the Western monotheisms, which have at their heart," he tells us, "the desire for the death, the murder of the father"; for the fantasy of "seduction," the myth of "revelation" in Western religions, and for the fantasy of the "return to the womb," he proposes the myth of "Paradise" (in the "after-Life").[121]

For Racine, what we can call these imaginary scenarios have an overdetermined meaning for the tragedy in particular and for the role of the theater in communal life. On the one hand what do these scenarios have in common? On the first and most general level, they are rhetorical tableaux,

the *impossibility* of the observation of the primal scene, especially when we recognize its anteriority to the life of the subject, a life that is the product of this sexual causality that seeks its own origin in the different lineages themselves."

[119] Freud, Standard Edition, 17:51, quoted in Lukacher, *Primal Scenes*, 138.

[120] Lukacher, *Primal Scenes*, 330.

[121] This is a very cursory synopsis of Rosolato's complex argument. See "Les phantasmes originaires" (223–47) for the sophisticated working through of the relation between fantasy and myth.

staged scenes that exist as what Barthes has called "a theater within the theater."[122] If we follow a common analogy of seeing the theater as functioning like a dream, the "theater in a theater" would take on the significance of the dream within the dream, which presents the "true reality" of the dream. Like a dream, the play articulates in the individual and collective unconscious of the spectators, the dialectics of law and desire. Playacting, like dreaming, figures the dangerous intrusion of the passions into the universe of the law. It also, however, figures the reappropriation of these passions by the law. In this way, Anne Ubersfeld suggests, the stage allows the transgression of the ideology it represents and also the concomitant recuperation of that ideology's strictures.[123]

The relation, therefore, between these scenes and the general oedipal narrative in which they are embedded is what intrigues us as they serve each as the origin and end of the other. It is, I believe, by the fascination and pull of these erotic scenarios that Racine's theater opens up and away from the too tightly restrictive, political (oedipal) myth that the tragedy also and simultaneously enacts. Although Racine's nighttime scenes are highly constructed rhetorical artifacts meant to elucidate a character's tragic plight, their power and intensity breaks free of their anchoring in a particular character and, borne by the seductive voice, that other echo of Racinian tragedy, they carry us back, away, from "history," to the pulsations at the libidinal center of his tragic universe.

All of the scenes combine either overtly or covertly images of sexuality and violence, of sexuality as violence, and may thus be seen as variations on the themes of the primal scene, seduction, and castration. Andromaque's vision of her first encounter with Pyrrhus is perhaps the most poignantly moving and yet perversely erotic of these scenes:

> Songe, songe, Céphise, à cette nuit cruelle
> Qui fut pour tout un peuple une nuit éternelle;
> Figure-toi Pyrrhus, les yeux étincelants,
> Entrant à la lueur de nos palais brûlants,
> Sur tous mes frères morts se faisant un passage,
> Et, de sang tout couvert, échauffant le carnage;
> Songe aux cris des vainqueurs, songe aux cris des mourants
> Dans la flamme étouffés, sous le fer expirants;
> Peins-toi dans ces horreurs Andromaque éperdue:
> Voilà comme Pyrrhus vint s'offrir à ma vue.
> (III. viii)

[122] Barthes, *On Racine*, 21, writes that "the erotic scene is a theatre within the theatre, it seeks to enact the most vital but also the most fragile moment of the conflict, the one when the shadow is about to be penetrated by a burst of light."

[123] Ubersfeld, *Lire le théâtre*, 47: "The theater has the status of the dream: it is an imaginary construction which the spectator knows to be radically separated from the sphere of ordinary existence. . . . [The spectator] can allow himself to watch the laws that govern him function without being subjected to them because they are directly attacked in their constraining reality."

These are scenes of ravishment, if not rape. What is figured in them, in chiasmatic reversal, is the cataclysmic end of an entire civilization and the birth of a new order. In this sense, although always fixated on the individual's psychic trauma, they also, for Racinan tragedy, represent the "primal scene," the sexualized scene wherein a new world order, and the subject of that order are conceived. Empires collapse, dynasties are eradicated from the stage of history, and the beginning of a new regime is figured in and through the (implied) violent coupling of the bloodied male and the ravished princess.

These are scenes in chiaroscuro, backlit by flames, where the distinction of integral subjects vanish in the flash of arms, in the tumultuous, we might say, incestuous mixture of living and dead bodies, of bodies themselves arrested in the vision of their writhing violence as they pass from life to death. Finally all this indeterminacy is seized in the horrified, ambivalent glance of the resisting, fainting, and finally vanquished victim. The very structure of the scenes effaces, in the swooning abandonment of the narrator, the possibility of a stable subjective grounding. These are fantasies, "with multiple entry points," as Laplanche and Pontalis write, where subjectivity is disseminated across the fantasy: the subject can be the ravished object, the ravishing conqueror, or, even more radically, not actually present in the scenario at all, as an object, but as the "semantic structure" of its narration.[124]

The sexuality in these scenes bears the impress of an inherently sadomasochistic pulsation, returning us, as Freud would have it, to a state of primary, presubjective impulses. It is the erotic charge of this sadomasochistic chiasmus that fuels the guilty pleasure of the tragic victim and of the tragedy itself:

> Rappellerai-je encore le souvenir affreux
> Du jour qui dans les fers nous jeta toutes deux?
> Dans les cruelles mains par qui je fus ravie
> Je demeurai longtemps sans lumière et sans vie:
> Enfin, mes tristes yeux cherchèrent la clarté;
> Et, me voyant presser d'un bras ensanglanté
> Je frémissais, Doris, et d'un vainqueur sauvage
> Craignais de rencontrer l'effroyable visage.
> J'entrai dans son vaisseau, détestant sa fureur
> Et toujours détournant ma vue avec horreur.

[124] Speaking of the fantasy "A father seduces a daughter," Laplanche and Pontalis say: "The pole of the primal phantasm, on the contrary, would be characterized by the absence of subjectivity which goes along with the presence of the subject in the scene: the child, for example, is one character among others in the phantasm 'a child is being beaten'. . . . 'A father seduces a daughter,' such a formula would sum up the phantasm of seduction. The sign of the primary process here is not the absence of organization, as is sometimes said, but this particular characterisic of the structure: it is a scenario with multiple points of entry, and nothing says that in this structure the subject will a priori find its place in the word 'daughter,' one can imagine it being fixed just as well on 'father,' or even 'seduced' " (*Fantasme*, 62–63).

Je le vis: son aspect n'avait rien de farouche;
Je sentis le reproche expirer dans ma bouche;
Je sentis contre moi mon coeur se déclarer . . .
(*Iphigénie*, II. i)

Beyond the narrative expediency of informing the audience of the predicates of the present dramatic conflict, these scenes have an evocatory power that transcends their diegetic function. Their powerful erotic charge takes us out of the realm of linear dramatic narrative and plunges us back into a universe of chaotic violence, the violence of body parts, of blood, of death. It is in this dispersion of the integral body, into part-objects, objects of desire and terror, that corresponds to the violence of the "primal scene." For however elegantly his language protects the *bienséances*, in these scenes Racine's text nevertheless reveals the fantasies of traumatic ferocity which inform the inchoate sexuality below the surface of the oedipal, of what the subject had to traverse before arriving at the scene of the oedipal.[125] At the same time, this sexuality, its erotic charge re-created in and through the very evocative power of Racine's verse, returns the body that has been banished to the center of his characters' "private theater." What these scenes reveal is the presence of the body, of the passion of that body, as that which the character (the oedipalized character) would not allow. In a sense, we might say, that these scenes function as the unconscious equivalent to the grotesque (Bahktinian) body whose repression forms the inarticulable parameters of the integral oedipal, that is, Classical subject. The Classically constructed body, which finds one of its greatest technicians in Racine, is a construction that includes, occulted within itself, what it cannot admit, what must be hidden from sight, as Stallybrass and White remind us:

> The classical body splits precisely along the rigid edge which is its defense against heterogeneity: Its closure and purity are quite illusory and it will perpetually rediscover in itself, often with a sense of shock or inner revulsion, the grotesque, the protean and the motley, the neither/nor, the double negation of high and low which was the very precondition for its social identity.[126]

The intrusion of these phantasmatic scenes function to connect the violence inherent in Classicism's ideology to the body, which in turn is made to represent, in its closed, integrity, an entire weltanschauung based on a masculinist politics of order, of "reason." Concomitantly this body exists only

[125] See ibid., 22: "It is in the very nature of sexuality to have a traumatic effect, and conversely, we can finally only talk about trauma and discover in trauma the origin of neurosis in so far as sexual seduction has intervened." And, they continue, 28: "The phantasm of the primal scene with its characteristic of violence bears witness to the real introjection of adult eroticism by the child."

[126] Peter Stallybrass and Allon White, *The Politics and Poetics of Transgression* (Ithaca: Cornell University Press, 1986), 113.

by exercising a constant imperious drive to exclude that which stands in the way of its metaphysical self-centeredness. The violence of the fantasies mark the eruption of sexuality as that which is most desired and yet most unacceptable, because most freighted with the threat of the utter destruction of this body, and therefore the world, of which it has become the symbol.

For the audience of both *Andromaque* and *Iphigénie* the fantasies of violent seduction (rape) are allied, I believe, on an even more primitive level to the "primal scene," that scene that would situate the infant on the stage of its own origin. In a sense the fantasies, by situating that origin in the crucible of war, reflect the apprehension of adult sexuality as inherently violent, and this fantasized violence joins the origin of the subject with the coterminous, war-spawned beginnings of the (new) state. For *Andromaque* the scene figures the end of the dissensions left in the wake of the Trojan War, and the beginnings of a new imperium in Epirus. For *Iphigénie* it is, in a sense, the same move out of difference, from both the conflict Troy-Greece and the internecine struggles among the Greeks themselves, and into the "unified" politico-military endeavor that will mark the beginnings of Greek dominance in the West.

In the same sense, can we not see the fantasy of the young (female) Israelites in *Esther* as reproducing, on yet another, metaphysico-theological level, the destruction of the old "body politic" of Israel, already dispersed in the first diaspora, and the eventual (predicted) return to a new Jerusalem? The destruction of the body politic is projected in the fantasized massacre of the Jews trapped in their Babylonian exile:

Quel carnage de toutes parts!
On égorge à la fois les enfants, les vieillards,
Et la soeur, et le frère,
Et la fille, et la mère,
Le fils dans les bras de son père!
Que de corps entassés! Que de membres épars!
Privés de sépultures!
Grand Dieu! tes saints sont la pâture
Des tigres et des léopards.
(I. v)[127]

[127] Although it is my belief that these scenes of carnage are the phantasmatic projection of Racine's (and his period's) unconscious life, we must not forget their correspondence to scenes of real war-induced violence. Writing in his (aborted) history of Louis XIV, Racine describes the siege of Valenciennes in the following way (Jean Racine, *Oeuvres complètes*, ed. Raymond Picard [Paris: Gallimard, 1966] 2:223): The French "se rendent maîtres de la contrescarpe, ils entrent dans un ouvrage couronné qui faisait la plus forte défense de la place, et passent au fil de l'épée huit cents hommes, de deux mille qui étaient dans cet ouvrage, le reste des ennemis, se voyant attaqué par le front et par les flancs, ne songe plus qu'à se sauver: ils se pressent, ils se poussent; une partie tombe dans le fossé, l'autre se retire de fortification en fortification. . . . Une des portes se trouve extremement basse et à demi bouchée de corps morts des ennemis: les français marchent sur ces corps sanglants, et passent pêle-mêle avec les fuyants."

While in *Bérénice,* the nighttime apotheosis of Titus ("De cette nuit, Phénice, as-tu vu la splendeur"), reflected in his Jewish mistress's dazzled reconstruction, proleptically depicts the phallic triumph of a new Roman hegemony that can come into existence only through Bérénice's exclusion. The scene of Titus's ceremonial projection out of this world, and into the pantheon of Roman gods, is also (although she does not know this) the scenario of her own immolation. Bérénice, who so appetitively relives the scene of Titus's triumph amid " Ces flambeaux, ce bûcher, cette nuit enflammée" is the ravished victim of her own sacrifice and of Rome's exultation.

In *Athalie*, on the other hand the originary scenario is double. It is both a "primal scene"—a scene of fantasized coupling, but this coupling is also seen as the castration of the father by the phallic mother—and, of course, the retaliation—the bloody retribution exacted on the mother's body.[128] To the horrific scene of Athalie's massacre of the innocents, which I have already quoted, corresponds the nightmare of her mother Jezabel's murder which prefigures her own immolation. In this case the originary fantasy and the dream are one:

C'était pendant l'horreur d'une profonde nuit;
Ma mère Jézabel devant moi s'est montrée,
Comme au jour de sa mort pompeusement parée,
Ses malheurs n'avaient point abattu sa fierté;
Même elle avait encor cet éclat emprunté
Dont elle eut soin de peindre et d'orner son visage,
Pour réparer des ans l'irréparable outrage:
"Tremble, m'a-t-elle dit, fille digne de moi;
"Le cruel Dieu des Juifs l'emporte aussi sur toi.
"Je te plains de tomber dans ses mains redoutables,
"Ma fille." En achevant ces mots épouvantables,
Son ombre vers mon lit a paru se baisser;
Et moi je lui tendais les mains pour l'embrasser;
Mais je n'ai plus trouvé qu'un horrible mélange
D'os et de chairs meurtris, et traînés dans la fange,
Des lambeaux pleins de sang, et des membres affreux
Que des chiens dévorants se disputaient entre eux.
(II. v)

Although on the narrative level *Athalie* represents the (temporary) triumph of David's ancestry (that is, the entire order of masculine devolution necessary for grounding the origin of Christ in an historically accessible, divinely ordained genealogy, a genealogy which in turn will ground the divine-right monarchy of Absolutism), the fantasies oscillate between a struggle between very primitive images of the "phallic mother" and the *Urvater*,

[128] The relation of the "primal scene" to castration was first adumbrated by Freud in his discussion of the "Wolfman" (*From the History of an Infantile Neurosis*, Standard Edition, 7:29).

the punishing, tyrannical, primal (horde) father. The sexualized violence of these fantasies is so intense that the line separating the human from the animal is breached: Jezebel is torn apart and fed to the dogs. Human flesh becomes the fare of animals, and through its absorption the human is metabolized into the bestial. Here, again, can we not see the return of an extremely powerful, scandalous fantasy—the fantasy of the body as ultimately monstrous, in that it as dog meat, transgresses those lines separating the cultural from the natural, the human from the animal, thus demonstrating the inherent cataclysmic violence, a violence tinged with deep erotic fantasies, that we have already witnessed in Hippolyte's immolation, in/as his own confused, mortiferous merger with his galloping stallions?

It would be repetitive to analyze all these scenes in the specificity of their context within each tragedy. We nevertheless might speculate that the originary fantasy present in all the tragedies serves as the phantasmatic fount from which the tragic springs and to which it will return in and through the "actual" sacrifice that fulfills the protagonist's tragic fate on the narrative level of the drama. Rather than seeing a split in Racinian tragedy between a "pre-" and "post-" oedipal pattern therefore, I believe we would do better to see how the inchoate scenes of primary fantasies and the oedipal political/sexual narrative form a continuing relay, each connected to the other, each figuring the beginning and end of the other. Each would represent an "origin" with all the impossible ambiguity of that word, the impossibility of ever fixing the beginning, of the subject, of the state, in a static, given moment or event. Rather, the origin is constantly displaceable, mythically, back to a more ancient fault, psychosexually, back to a undecidable intersection between individual ("biological") desire and societal law.

If these scenes of originary fantasies can be seen as figuring the "dream within a dream," the fantasy within the fantasy that is the tragedy, can we not see them disappear, finally, unseizable, into the "navel of the tragedy?" They would represent that part of the tragedy, at once the answer to the question of origins, and its continual deferral, where no answer is possible, no origin except in a more primitive, more horrific disintegration? If, as Lacan has declared, "It is my question that constitutes me as a subject," and if the founding question of Racinian tragedy is "Who am I?" the subject of this question, the tragic subject is caught in a never ending relay, a *mise-en abîme* of swirling phantasmatic positions, that make any grounding of subjectivity, any absolute grounding impossible.[129] The question posed most plangently by the Racinian subject echoes obsessively across Racine's tragic universe. It is, of course, the tragedies themselves that both ask the question and are its answer. Recast on the seventeenth-century stage, these questions and their answers will continue to inform those discursive strategies, up to and including Freud's that circumscribe the site and destiny of the modern

[129] Jacques Lacan, "Fonction et champ de la parole," in *Écrits*, (Paris: Seuil, 1966), 294.

subject.[130] It is they, in turn, that explain the inexplicable, the story of origins, but they do so by garbing themselves in the veils of myth and fantasy, that make the narration of origins, always an originary fantasy. These "originary scenarios" disappear, like the dreams' mycelium described by Freud into the seductive echo of Racine's poetic voice, a voice that reemerges, must reemerge to ground itself in the protagonist of his tragedies, whose fate, on the narrative level, is to be sacrificed to the imperatives of tragic coherence, of oedipal sexual/social politics. Like a Möbius strip the fantasies (internal to the tragic character) return as the tragedy, that is, the sacrifice of that character, forming a never-ending involution of fantasy and tragedy.

The fantasized sexuality and violence of the originary scenarios are acted out in the tragic narrative, at the same time that this narrative only returns us to the body in order to eliminate it. The sacrifice with which we begun our discussion of Racine's theater, thus returns us once again to its compelling enigma. The theater as sacrifice mediates, as I have said, the individual and the communal, sutures the individual into the communal by the constant relaying of private fantasies and cultural myths. There are certain myths, however, the Oedipus legend for instance, that seem to have a more compelling fascination for the psychosexual and political subjects that we, in the West, are—perhaps because our political (in the broadest sense) structures find their origin in this myth that in turn returns these structures to a corresponding psychosexual grounding—the roundelay of our subjective ideology. In the confusion of those turbulent changes taking place in France and generally in Europe in the period 1630–1680, Racine's dramatic production represents a particularly enchafed locus of cultural mediation. By its very situation "at the crorssroads of the individual and the collective," Racine's tragedy, confined to the heated locus of the oedipal family, seems to double and relay in an uncanny fashion the mediating role between law and desire that Foucault attributes to that familial structure.[131] Just as the latter becomes the internalized interchange between the political and the personal, the theater, functioning at the junction of the public and private sphere, can be seen to relay, in a spectacularly seductive fashion, the dynamics of the law and desire as incorporated in plots of tragic familial strife. The theater mirrors back to the spectators the law of the father/king, and through its pleasures elaborates this law as their sacrifice.

What is sacrificed on the altar of Racinian tragedy is the motley, the grotesque, the body in its *Kreaturlichkeit*, that the tragedies exclude as the

[130] See Francis Barker, *The Tremulous Private Body: Essays in Subjection* (London: Methuen, 1984), 57: "If Freudian narration differs from Descartes in a number of its philosophical assumptions, it is nevertheless inconceivable outside the field of the Cartesian inauguration."

[131] Besides the work of André Green on the mediating aspect of the theater (*The Tragic Effect*), see Ubersfeld, *Lire le théâtre*, 39.

troubling other—the body as nonintegral, the opposite of the classical "corps glorieux," the bounded integral "One" of the father/king. In essence what Racine's theater both proposes and then denies is the production of the oedipal political /sexual subject as coeval with the elaboration of the absolutist (Classical) edifice. Sacrifice obliges this subject to assume its "proper" sexual position as masculine or feminine, in relation to absolutist desires—that is, in relation to the father/king. At the same time however, the originary fantasies upon which this "resolution" is based, continue to "work" the text (scenes of murder, mayhem, sacrifice) and constantly undermine, by returning the body as fragmentation, to the unconscious scene that denies the stable fixation of culturally imposed models. There is thus a constant oscillation between oedipal sexuality (as resolution) and originary fantasies which is responsible for the tension, the dramatic tension of the tragedy. This oscillation prevents the tragedy, and its subject(s), from ever settling comfortably, that is untragically, into hegemonic ideology. It is this space created by the oscillation between poles of fragmentation and stability, between the "pre-" and "post-" oedipal that constitutes the locus of resistance, the tragic locus of Racinian drama.

What is defined as Absolutism's "other"—the "feminine," the female body, the unstable bodies of the children in Racine—must be excluded from the evolving political structures of oedipal patriarchy. It is to the spectacle of this sacrifice that all of Racine's tragedies summon us. And we go, we attend the theater transfixed by the horror of Racine's plots and carried away by the seductive song of his verse. We are moved by his tragedies to tears, that cathartic cleansing of our guilty souls. These tears are, however, ambivalent in their very nature. They are, at one and the same time the bitter tears of loss, a sign of what we, the audience, has had to sacrifice of ourselves in order to become the father's subjects, and perversely, the sign of what still resists that ultimate sacrifice, the continued presence of the body and its affects that we carry with us on the private theater of our own originary fantasies.

By Way of Concluding

Louis XIV a revolutionary? Certainly not in life, but in death, or at least in a death represented in literature, the question especially as it pertains to the royal body appears less perverse. At the end of a long reign, the longest in European history, a reign that as historians never tire of repeating finishes on a note of melancholic lassitude, the identification of the king's body to his realm seems to have reached the perfect adequation of the physical person of the monarch to its metaphysical, transcendent symbolism in Louis's final, fatal condition. Gangrene slowly and relentlessly consumes his body, starting with the royal leg of which, when we remember the Rigaud portrait, he was so haughtily proud. Creeping inexorably up the regal limb, the disease infects the entire body, corrupting and eventually destroying it. At the very end of his long life it would seem that finally inner and outer reality are made perfectly consonant—the realm is exhausted, bled dry, political and economic corruption is rampant—just as the royal body is being undone by its own internal dissolution. Finally the state and its embodiment never seem more united than in their own undoing, in death.

In his *Mémoires* Saint-Simon gives us perhaps the most memorably rich description of the last days of the king. Due to the frustrations of his own political ambitions, Saint-Simon's narration of Louis' demise constantly transposes our gaze from its fixation on the dying body of the king to the political machinations that surround the death of this man and the contradictory forces at play in the preservation of the body politic.[1] Curiously for so ardent a "traditionalist" as Saint-Simon, the description of the scenes surrounding the death of the king and the various Machiavellian plots devised by the contentious and rivalrous political factions (principally the sup-

[1] Saint-Simon, Louis de Rouvroy, duc de, *Mémoires* vol. 5, *1714–1716*, ed. Yves Coirault (Paris: Gallimard, 1983).

porters of the regent, Philippe d'Orléans whom Saint-Simon favors and the faction around the "Bastards"—the legitimated "illegal" offspring of Louis XIV, the duc du Maine and his followers) to control the state betrays, unbeknownst to the narrator himself, the irreversible fractiousness that has crept into the very juridical and regal traditions that Saint-Simon so passionately espouses.

At the very center of Saint-Simon's apoplectic denunciation of the usurpation of the rights of the hereditary nobility is the question, the unavoidable question of the body, the royal body, in its reproductive legitimacy. Despite the complex and vexed interrogations into the political and financial stability of the realm and despite his own perspicacious vision of the multilayered and complicated interweave of personal ambition and overriding concerns for the "public welfare," Saint-Simon must, in order to defend his own threatened interests, return his gaze and reduce ours to the sight of the decaying body royal. It nevertheless is the necessity of his own political investments in the entire tradition of exclusionary prerogatives that inextricably tied the nobility to the king that brings him back, as if in an inescapable double bind, to the very body that he will claim has betrayed itself and has corrupted the French body politic. According to Saint-Simon the royal body lost in sexuality has, by exposing what for a thousand years had been kept hidden—the split between the physical body of the king and his "corps glorieux"—revealed the venality of its own illusoriness.

Saint-Simon cannot forgive Louis for instituting a governing regime from which he and the members of his class have been, he feels, unjustly and illegally excluded. His entire diatribe against the king and against the members of the lesser nobility and the bourgeoisie who have been elevated to lofty positions in the government and in society and the concomitant degradation of his cohorts—the dukes and peers of the realm—is lived by Saint-Simon as an intolerable infringement on the millenary traditions of the French state. When at end of his life and reign Louis XIV, having outlived his legitimate offspring and their children, amends his will to "legitimize" his bastards, to treat them as the "legal equals" of his dead, legitimate sons, and declare them capable of inheriting the throne of France, Saint-Simon's frustration and rage explode in a charged passage whose rhetoric is inflamed by the narcissistic wound that fuels the duke's rage:

> C'est un malheur dans la vie du Roi, et une plaie à la France qui a continuellement été en augmentant, que la grandeur de ses bâtards, qu'il a enfin porté[e] au comble inoui à la fin de sa vie, dont les derniers temps n'ont été principalement occupés qu'à les consolider, en les rendant puissants et redoutables. . . . Leur rang égalé à celui des princes du sang avait coûté au Roi le renversement de toutes les règles et les droits, et celui des lois du Royaume les plus anciennes, les plus saintes, les plus fondamentales, les plus intactes.[2]

[2] Ibid., 591–92.

The corruption of the body politic, from which, according to Saint-Simon all the ills afflicting French society stem, is due in the last analysis to a split in the royal body, a division which Saint-Simon clearly and absolutely posits as stemming from this body gone wild. Sexuality, the body possessed by precisely those forces that it cannot subdue, has undone the state. According to Saint-Simon, Louis's inordinate lust was followed by an equally extravagant, that is "unnatural" love for his illegitimate offspring. It is this love *contre nature* that betrayed the traditional laws of France and made of this king a tyrant, but a tyrant tyrannized by the capriciousness of his own body. This body becomes in Saint-Simon's description no longer a double body, but rather an irremediably split body—the royal body sundered into two irreconcilable and antagonistic halves:

> Tels furent les fruits d'un orgueil sans bornes, qui fit toujours regarder au Roi avec des yeux si différents ses bâtards et les princes de son sang, les enfants issus du trône par des générations légitimes, et qui les y rappelaient à leur tour, et les enfants sortis de ses amours. Il considéra les premiers comme les enfants de l'État et de la couronne, grands par là et par eux-mêmes sans lui, tandis qu'il chérit les autres comme les enfants de sa personne, qui ne pouvaient devenir, faute d'être par eux-mêmes, par toutes les lois, que les ouvrages de sa puissance et de ses mains.[3]

On the one hand, we have the official offspring of the state, the legitimate descendants of a millenary tradition that gives legitimacy to the entire hereditary order that, for Saint-Simon at least, justifies theologically, socially, and economically his and his caste's place in absolutist France. On the other, stands the corrupt and corrupting brood of a private body incapable of moderation. Would it be too farfetched to suggest here that we see, in the description of Saint-Simon, a description that intervenes in the millenary tradition of the "king's two bodies" the first sundering blow, the first rhetorical "castration" that operates on the royal body, the "cut" that, three-quarters of a century later, will be ritualistically enacted, by the swiftly precipitous fall of the guillotine's blade? The image of the king's two bodies, as we saw at the beginning of this study, was the vehicle for a primitive fantasy—the fantasy/desire for the charismatic leader, the uncastratable father of the nation. At the end of his long, momentous reign, a reign in which, more than any of his predecessors, Louis had worked at projecting the image of his own divinity, this image is at last undone by the very excess, the spectacular display and dissemination of his body across and throughout his realm, that underpinned his own vision of himself.[4]

[3] Ibid., 593.

[4] For a rather complete study of the sundry texts recounting the death of Louis XIV, see Francis Assaf, *La mort du roi: Une thanatographie de Louis XIV* (Tubingen : Gunter Narr Verlag, 1999).

In the end the body betrayed itself, as all bodies do, but by so doing it also betrayed the entire culture of absolutist France. At the termination of this reign, as Saint-Simon so acutely but misguidedly intuited, a new order was being fitfully put into place—shall we call it the revolutionary order of "castrated desire"—that is, desire, as sexuality, sundered the body of the monarch, and thus destabilized the ideological predicates of France's ancient monarchy? Absolutism is already undone in the decaying body of Louis on his deathbed. Saint-Simon's description undoes the illusion of the "corpus mysticum" of France, incarnated in its monarch and shows us finally that, to mix metaphors, the "emperor has no clothes," that that image, the image of the all-powerful, all-knowing father, is an empty image: the father is now dead, reduced to a body that is by this time irrevocably divided.[5] The "body royal" and the "private body" no longer coexist in the spectacular person of the king. Could Louis XIV have known or have even dimly perceived, as he looked around him at the swarm of plotting courtiers waiting for him to breath his last, that perhaps the most memorable bequest he would leave France was a new model of the body politic? It was a model that was grounded in the undoing of his own body's spectacular descent into death. Could it be that the royal body unbound becomes the harbinger signaling both the demise of the society over which Louis presided with such splendor and cruelty and, at the same time, that society's imminent rebirth in the republican fires of revolution?

[5] The gradual and inexorable degeneration of the "royal body," especially as the fantasy of the phallically powerful reproductive body, will continue throughout the eighteenth century, to conclude with the scandalous pamphlets that multiply during the reign of Louis XVI. The king's body is portrayed in these pamphlets as an object of ridicule both because of his supposedly inferior physical endowments and his sexual impotence. See Antoine DeBaeque, *Le corps de l'histoire: Métaphores et politique, 1770–1800* (Paris: Calmann-Lévy, 1993). Jay Caplan *In the King's Wake: Post Absolutist Culture in France* (Chicago: University of Chicago Press, 1999) centers his study of eighteenth-centure culture around the figure of the king's demise.

Index